Gramley Library
Salem Academy and College
Winston-Salem, N.C. 27108

SLOW VIOLENCE AND THE
ENVIRONMENTALISM OF THE POOR

SLOW VIOLENCE AND THE
ENVIRONMENTALISM OF THE POOR

ROB NIXON

Gramley Library
Salem Academy and College
Winston-Salem, N.C. 27108

HARVARD UNIVERSITY PRESS
Cambridge, Massachusetts, and London, England 2011

Copyright © 2011 by the President and Fellows of Harvard College

ALL RIGHTS RESERVED

Printed in the United States of America

Library of Congress Cataloging-in-Publication Data
Nixon, Rob, 1954–
Slow violence and the environmentalism of the poor / Rob Nixon.
p. cm.
Includes bibliographical references and index.
ISBN 978-0-674-04930-7 (alk. paper)
1. Commonwealth literature (English)—History and criticism.
2. American literature—History and criticism.   3. Ecology in literature.
4. Environmentalism in literature.   5. Human ecology in literature.
6. Postcolonialism in literature.   7. Colonies in literature.   8. Ecocriticism.
9. Human security.   10. Poor—Developing countries.   11. Imperialism—
Environmental aspects.   12. Globalization—Environmental aspects.   I. Title.
PR9080.5.N59 2011
820.9'36—dc22   2010049797

FOR ANNE

Contents

Preface

In writing this book, I have returned repeatedly for inspiration to three towering figures. Edward Said, Rachel Carson, and Ramachandra Guha are a diverse and unlikely triumvirate, by training a professor of literature, a science writer, and a sociologist respectively. Yet all three exemplify an ideal of the public intellectual as someone unafraid to open up channels of inquiry at an angle to mainstream thought; unafraid moreover to face down the hostility that their unorthodoxy often prompted. In ranging from archive-driven scholarship to the public essay to op-ed polemics, Said, Carson, and Guha all have demonstrated a communicative passion responsive to diverse audiences, indeed a passion that has helped shape such audiences by refusing to adhere to conventional disciplinary or professional expectations.

The beauty of the teaching life is this: the possibility of setting a life on course with nothing more complex than the right reverberation struck at the right time. Said had that kind of impact on me in the mid-1980s when I was a graduate student at Columbia. There I had found myself confronted with two unappetizing options: to follow either the fusty old formalists, with their patched-tweed Ivy League belle-lettrism, or the hipper new formalists, whose lemming run toward the palisades of deconstruction was then in full spate. To a young man, an unsettled greenhorn in America with a twinned passion for literature and world politics, Said offered a third way, encouraging me to reconcile those passions and find a voice in which both could be articulated. I felt emboldened by Said's determined search for a style—or rather, a whole repertoire of styles—equal to his wide-ranging commitments. He thrived on intellectual complexity while aspiring to clarity; he taught and wrote as if—and I know this should sound unremarkable for a literature professor—he yearned to be widely understood. His approach felt fervent, luminous when measured against the alternatives: close readings sealed against the world or deconstructionist seminars in which the stakes were as obscure as the language, as we poked at dead-on-delivery prose in the hopes of rousing enough life from it for our exertions to qualify as "play." Said, by contrast, was alive to the high-stake worlds of persuasion and coercion, alive to political doublespeak and to the worldly costs of verbal camouflage. As a reader, he believed in context—historical, political, and biographical context—all of which was material to him.

Said's vocal flexibility amplified his intellectual reach: across disciplines, continents, and all forms of the media. He scorned the cult of difficulty, the notion that leaden writing signals weighty intelligence. He understood that it is far more difficult to theorize with the cunning of lightness than it is to fob off some seething mess of day-old neologisms as an "intervention." His devotion to style became integral to his political idealism and inseparable from his belief in an insurrectionary outwardness.

As an environmentalist one must ask: what place for earthliness in Said's worldliness? In 2003, a month before his death, Said concluded an essay for *Counterpunch* with a yearning for a future informed by "alternative communities all across the world, informed by alternative information, and keenly aware of the environmental, human rights, and libertarian impulses that bind us together in this tiny planet."[1] Despite this late acknowledgment, one would be hard-pressed to call him, in any conventional sense, environmentally minded. However, it is quite possible, indeed probable, that as the energies of the transnational environmental justice movements I discuss in this book permeated the humanities more deeply, Said would have recognized their pertinence to his own work on bulldozed olive groves, land rights, and water politics, issues that come alive, most graphically, in *After the Last Sky*.

If Said was dismissive of what he called "the petty fiefdoms within the world of intellectual production," such impatience is equally evident in the writings of Rachel Carson, an even more maverick figure.[2] Carson believed that the mission of the public intellectual included exposing the euphemisms and bromides promulgated by cold-war America's military-industrial complex. As she famously insisted, herbicides and insecticides should be unmasked as biocides: those supposedly precise weapons in the "war" on pests targeted nothing more precise than life itself. Almost two decades before neoliberalism implemented breakneck deregulations, Carson forewarned that, if left unchecked, capitalism's appetite for the unregulated, specialist consumer product would leave behind a trail of nonspecialist fatalities.

Carson redirected some of the national anxiety away from the Red Peril to the aerosol can of Doom perched on the kitchen shelf. By revealing how small, domestic choices can help secure a more inhabitable world, *Silent Spring* altered the landscape of fear and, crucially, fear's time frame as well. The book, which appeared just weeks before the Cuban Missile Crisis, exhorted an America awash with paranoia to take charge of its fears by changing the way it lived in the short term to reduce long-term catastrophic risk. Carson's extended view of risk's time frame encouraged citizens to campaign for more stringent environmental legislation, in America and nations beyond. In so doing, Carson gave us pointers on how to hope and act across domains large and small.

Like Said, Carson voiced a profound suspicion of the certified expert whom she saw as implicated in the economics of professional capitulation in ways that jeopardized society's capacity to sustain uncompromised research. Carson had almost nothing to say directly about empire, class, and race, yet her work speaks powerfully to the environmentalism of the poor because she was passionately concerned with the complicity of the military-industrial complex in disguising toxicity, both physically and rhetorically. Her approach, moreover, helped hasten the shift from a conservationist ideology to the more socioenvironmental outlook that has proven so enabling for environmental justice movements. Above all, Carson was a renegade synthesizer: her gestures toward the big picture challenged institutionalized definitions of what constituted originality. In exposing the dubious funding of partitioned knowledge—and its baleful public health implications—she recast herself as an insurrectionary generalist.

It is a measure of how tentative the rapprochement between postcolonial and environmental studies is that Said never mentions Carson in his work.[3] (It is a measure too, one should add, of Said's persistent, baleful indifference

to any ascendant female voice.) Yet Carson in crucial ways anticipated
Said's skepticism toward compartmentalized expertise, toward the polluted funding structures of research, and toward obfuscatory language.
She too mistrusted academic endeavor that, cushioned by corporate funding, feigned objectivity; she also mistrusted scholars interested in talking,
undisturbed by inexpert audiences, always only to themselves. For Carson
the culture—and cult—of the specialist was, as Said would later recognize,
intellectually debilitating and ethically lamentable, entrammelled as it was
in cold-war geopolitics.

Ramachandra Guha is the third unclassifiable figure from whom I have
drawn particular inspiration. A sociologist by training, an environmental
historian by instinct, a journalist, opinion maker, and sports writer, Guha
is a man who, in his own judgment, decided to be "methodologically pro-
miscuous."[4] Like Carson, Guha chose the complex mix of freedoms and
risks that arise from working outside the tenured security, obligations, and
compromises that university positions entail. Equally discomfited by disciplinary and national chauvinisms, he has arguably done more than any
intellectual to dispel the myth that environmentalism is "a full-stomach
phenomenon" affordable only to the middle and upper classes of the world's
richest societies.[5] He has drawn on—indeed, drawn out—neglected strands
of American and European environmental thought while refusing them a
global centrality.[6] As far back as 1989, he dismantled the well-intentioned
but ultimately counterproductive project of deep ecology that, while posing as planetary, was at root profoundly parochial.[7] Guha underscored the
need to keep environmentalism connected to global questions of distributive justice, connected as well to the unequal burdens of consumption and
militarization imposed on our finite planet by the world's rich and poor, in
their capacity as individuals and as nation-states. While unearthing tenacious traditions of environmental thought and activism among the poor,
Guha has resisted sentimentalizing "traditional" cultures as peopled by
"natural" ecologists.

Guha has sought out collaborators who complement his expertise, notably the Indian ecologist and anthropologist Madhav Gadgil and the Catalan
economist Joan Martinez-Alier. Together they have generated an indispensable vocabulary that informs this book (and many others across an array
of disciplines). Terms like "the environmentalism of the poor," "ecosystem

people," "omnivores" (those wealthy consumers who overstrain the planet), and "socioenvironmentalism" were all brought into circulation by Guha and his collaborators.[8] Several of these terms have gone on to achieve traction in the broader worlds of the media and public policy. That success is testimony to Guha's rhetorical adaptability as he strives to be innovative yet accessible, alert to the opportunities on offer across occasions, geographies, and genres. Extrainstitutional by instinct, disciplined yet never ploddingly disciplinary, Guha is an indispensable exemplar of what used to be called the free-floating intellectual.

Writing outside the mainstreams of both Marxism and 1980s Western environmentalism, Guha had to weather, on the one hand, scorn from third-world radicals who dismissed environmentalism as reactionary, self-indulgent frippery and, on the other, from deep ecologists who charged him with being anti-ecological and anti-American.[9] Yet over the long haul his writings have decisively reshaped many debates that animate the environmental humanities and social sciences.[10]

It is from these three diverse, unclassifiable intellectuals—a Palestinian literary scholar exiled in America, a marine biologist with roots in rural Pennsylvania, and a social scientist from Dehra Dun in the Himalayan foothills—that I have drawn particular inspiration, as much from their oppositional examples as from the tenor of their thought.

Slow Violence and the
Environmentalism of the Poor

Introduction

I think of globalization like a light which shines brighter and brighter on a few people and the rest are in darkness, wiped out. They simply can't be seen. Once you get used to not seeing something, then, slowly, it's no longer possible to see it.

—Arundhati Roy

I think the economic logic behind dumping a load of toxic waste in the lowest-wage country is impeccable and we should face up to that. . . . I've always thought that countries in Africa are vastly under polluted; their air quality is probably vastly inefficiently low compared to Los Angeles. . . . Just between you and me, shouldn't the World Bank be encouraging more migration of the dirty industries to the Least Developed Countries?

—Lawrence Summers, confidential World Bank memo, December 12, 1991

When Lawrence Summers, then president of the World Bank, advocated that the bank develop a scheme to export rich nation garbage, toxic waste, and heavily polluting industries to Africa, he did so in the calm voice of global managerial reasoning.[1] Such a scheme, Summers elaborated, would help correct an inefficient global imbalance in toxicity. Underlying his plan is an overlooked but crucial subsidiary benefit that he outlined: offloading rich-nation toxins onto the world's poorest continent would help ease the growing pressure from rich-nation environmentalists who were campaigning against garbage dumps and industrial effluent that they condemned as health threats and found aesthetically offensive. Summers thus rationalized his poison-redistribution ethic as offering a double gain: it would benefit the United States and Europe economically, while helping appease the rising discontent of rich-nation environmentalists. Summers' arguments assumed a direct link between aesthetically unsightly waste and Africa as an out-of-sight continent, a place remote from green activists' terrain of concern. In Summers' win-win scenario for the global North, the African recipients of his plan were triply discounted: discounted as political agents, discounted as long-term casualties of what I call in this book "slow violence," and discounted as cultures possessing environmental practices and concerns of their own. I begin with Summers' extraordinary proposal because it captures the strategic and representational challenges posed by slow violence as it impacts the environments—and the environmentalism—of the poor.

Three primary concerns animate this book, chief among them my conviction that we urgently need to rethink—politically, imaginatively, and theoretically—what I call "slow violence." By slow violence I mean a violence that occurs gradually and out of sight, a violence of delayed destruction that is dispersed across time and space, an attritional violence that is typically not viewed as violence at all. Violence is customarily conceived as an event or action that is immediate in time, explosive and spectacular in space, and as erupting into instant sensational visibility. We need, I believe, to engage a different kind of violence, a violence that is neither spectacular nor instantaneous, but rather incremental and accretive, its calamitous repercussions playing out across a range of temporal scales. In so doing, we also need to engage the representational, narrative, and strategic challenges posed by the relative invisibility of slow violence. Climate change, the thawing cryosphere, toxic drift, biomagnification, deforestation, the radioactive aftermaths of wars, acidifying oceans, and a host of other slowly unfolding environmental catastrophes present formidable representational obstacles that can hinder our efforts to mobilize and act decisively. The long dyings—the staggered and staggeringly discounted casualties, both human and ecological that result from war's toxic aftermaths or climate change—are underrepresented in strategic planning as well as in human memory.

Had Summers advocated invading Africa with weapons of mass destruction, his proposal would have fallen under conventional definitions of violence and been perceived as a military or even an imperial invasion. Advocating invading countries with mass forms of slow-motion toxicity, however, requires rethinking our accepted assumptions of violence to include slow violence. Such a rethinking requires that we complicate conventional assumptions about violence as a highly visible act that is newsworthy because it is event focused, time bound, and body bound. We need to account for how the temporal dispersion of slow violence affects the way we perceive and respond to a variety of social afflictions—from domestic abuse to posttraumatic stress and, in particular, environmental calamities. A major challenge is representational: how to devise arresting stories, images, and symbols adequate to the pervasive but elusive violence of delayed effects. Crucially, slow violence is often not just attritional but also exponential, operating as a major threat multiplier; it can fuel long-term, proliferating conflicts in situations where the conditions for sustaining life become increasingly but gradually degraded.

Politically and emotionally, different kinds of disaster possess unequal heft. Falling bodies, burning towers, exploding heads, avalanches, volcanoes, and tsunamis have a visceral, eye-catching and page-turning power that tales of slow violence, unfolding over years, decades, even centuries, cannot match. Stories of toxic buildup, massing greenhouse gases, and accelerated species loss due to ravaged habitats are all cataclysmic, but they are scientifically convoluted cataclysms in which casualties are postponed, often for generations. In an age when the media venerate the spectacular, when public policy is shaped primarily around perceived immediate need, a central question is strategic and representational: how can we convert into image and narrative the disasters that are slow moving and long in the making, disasters that are anonymous and that star nobody, disasters that are attritional and of indifferent interest to the sensation-driven technologies of our image-world? How can we turn the long emergencies of slow violence into stories dramatic enough to rouse public sentiment and warrant political intervention, these emergencies whose repercussions have given rise to some of the most critical challenges of our time?

This book's second, related focus concerns the environmentalism of the poor, for it is those people lacking resources who are the principal casualties of slow violence. Their unseen poverty is compounded by the invisibility of the slow violence that permeates so many of their lives. Our media bias toward spectacular violence exacerbates the vulnerability of ecosystems treated as disposable by turbo-capitalism while simultaneously exacerbating the vulnerability of those whom Kevin Bale, in another context, has called "disposable people."[2] It is against such conjoined ecological and human disposability that we have witnessed a resurgent environmentalism of the poor, particularly (though not exclusively) across the so-called global South. So a central issue that emerges is strategic: if the neoliberal era has intensified assaults on resources, it has also intensified resistance, whether through isolated site-specific struggles or through activism that has reached across national boundaries in an effort to build translocal alliances.

"The poor" is a compendious category subject to almost infinite local variation as well as to fracture along fault lines of ethnicity, gender, race, class, region, religion, and generation. Confronted with the militarization of both commerce and development, impoverished communities are often assailed by coercion and bribery that test their cohesive resilience. How much control will, say, a poor hardwood forest community have over the mix of subsistence and market strategies it deploys in attempts at adaptive survival? How will that community negotiate competing definitions of its own poverty and long-term wealth when the guns, the bulldozers, and the moneymen arrive? Such communities typically have to patch together threadbare improvised alliances against vastly superior military, corporate, and media forces. As such, impoverished resource rebels can seldom afford to be single-issue activists: their green commitments are seamed through with other economic and cultural causes as they experience environmental threat not as a planetary abstraction but as a set of inhabited risks, some imminent, others obscurely long term.

The status of environmental activism among the poor in the global South has shifted significantly in recent years. Where green or environmental discourses were once frequently regarded with skepticism as neocolonial, Western impositions inimical to the resource priorities of the poor in the global South, such attitudes have been tempered by the gathering visibility and credibility of environmental justice movements that have pushed back against an antihuman environmentalism that too often sought (under the banner of universalism) to impose green agendas dominated by rich nations and Western NGOs. Among those who inhabit the frontlines of the global resource wars, suspicions that environmentalism is another guise of what Andrew Ross calls "planetary management" have not, of course, been wholly allayed.[3] But those suspicions have eased somewhat as the spectrum of what counts as environmentalism has broadened. Western activists are now more prone to recognize, engage, and learn from resource insurrections among the global poor that might previously have been discounted as not properly environmental.[4] Indeed, I believe that the fate of environmentalism—and more decisively, the character of the biosphere itself—will be shaped significantly in decades to come by the tension between what Ramachandra Guha and Joan Martinez-Alier have called "full-stomach" and "empty-belly" environmentalism.[5]

The challenge of visibility that links slow violence to the environmentalism of the poor connects directly to this book's third circulating concern—the complex, often vexed figure of the environmental writer-activist. In the chapters that follow I address not just literary but more broadly rhetorical and visual challenges posed by slow violence; however, I place particular emphasis on combative writers who have deployed their imaginative agility and worldly ardor to help amplify the media-marginalized causes of the environmentally dispossessed. I have sought to stress those places where writers and social movements, often in complicated tandem, have strategized against attritional disasters that afflict embattled communities. The writers I engage are geographically wide ranging—from various parts of the African continent, from the Middle East, India, the Caribbean, the United States, and Britain—and work across a variety of forms. Figures like Wangari Maathai, Arundhati Roy, Indra Sinha, Ken Saro-Wiwa, Abdulrahman Munif, Njabulo Ndebele, Nadine Gordimer, Jamaica Kincaid, Rachel Carson, and June Jordan are alive to the inhabited impact of corrosive transnational forces, including petro-imperialism, the megadam industry, outsourced toxicity, neocolonial tourism, antihuman conservation practices, corporate and environmental deregulation, and the militarization of commerce, forces that disproportionately jeopardize the livelihoods, prospects, and memory banks of the global poor. Among the writers I consider, some have testified in relative isolation, some have helped instigate movements for environmental justice, and yet others, in aligning themselves with pre-existing movements, have given imaginative definition to the issues at stake while enhancing the public visibility of the cause.

Relations between movements and writers are often fraught and frictional, not least because such movements themselves are susceptible to fracture from both external and internal pressures.[6] That said, the writers I consider are enraged by injustices they wish to see redressed, injustices they believe they can help expose, silences they can help dismantle through testimonial protest, rhetorical inventiveness, and counterhistories in the face of formidable odds. Most are restless, versatile writers ready to pit their energies against what Edward Said called "the normalized quiet of unseen power."[7] This normalized quiet is of particular pertinence to the hushed havoc and injurious invisibility that trail slow violence.

Slow Violence

In this book, I have sought to address our inattention to calamities that are slow and long lasting, calamities that patiently dispense their devastation while remaining outside our flickering attention spans—and outside the purview of a spectacle-driven corporate media. The insidious workings of slow violence derive largely from the unequal attention given to spectacular and unspectacular time. In an age that venerates instant spectacle, slow violence is deficient in the recognizable special effects that fill movie theaters and boost ratings on TV. Chemical and radiological violence, for example, is driven inward, somatized into cellular dramas of mutation that—particularly in the bodies of the poor—remain largely unobserved, undiagnosed, and untreated. From a narrative perspective, such invisible, mutagenic theater is slow paced and open ended, eluding the tidy closure, the containment, imposed by the visual orthodoxies of victory and defeat.

Let me ground this point by referring, in conjunction, to Rachel Carson's *Silent Spring* and Frantz Fanon's *The Wretched of the Earth*. In 1962 *Silent Spring* jolted a broad international public into an awareness of the protracted, cryptic, and indiscriminate casualties inflicted by dichlorodiphenyltrichloroethane (DDT). Yet, just one year earlier, Fanon, in the opening pages of *Wretched of the Earth*, had comfortably invoked DDT as an affirmative metaphor for anticolonial violence: he called for a DDT-filled spray gun to be wielded as a weapon against the "parasites" spread by the colonials' Christian church.[8] Fanon's drama of decolonization is, of course, studded with the overt weaponry whereby subjugation is maintained ("by dint of a great array of bayonets and cannons") or overthrown ("by the searing bullets and bloodstained knives") after "a murderous and decisive struggle between the two protagonists."[9] Yet his temporal vision of violence—and of what Aimé Césaire called "the rendezvous of victory"—was uncomplicated by the concerns that an as-yet inchoate environmental justice movement (catalyzed in part by *Silent Spring*) would raise about lopsided risks that permeate the land long term, blurring the clean lines between defeat and victory, between colonial dispossession and official national self-determination.[10] We can certainly read Fanon, in his concern with land as property and as fount of native dignity, retrospectively with an environmental eye. But our theories of violence today must be informed by a science unavailable to Fanon, a science that addresses environmentally embedded violence that is often difficult to source, oppose, and once set in motion, to reverse.

Attritional catastrophes that overspill clear boundaries in time and space are marked above all by displacements—temporal, geographical, rhetorical, and technological displacements that simplify violence and underestimate, in advance and in retrospect, the human and environmental costs. Such displacements smooth the way for amnesia, as places are rendered irretrievable to those who once inhabited them, places that ordinarily pass unmourned in the corporate media. Places like the Marshall Islands, subjected between 1948 and 1958 to sixty-seven American atmospheric nuclear "tests," the largest of them equal in force to 1,000 Hiroshima-sized bombs. In 1956 the Atomic Energy Commission declared the Marshall Islands "by far the most contaminated place in the world," a condition that would compromise independence in the long term, despite the islands' formal ascent in 1979 into the ranks of self-governing nations.[11] The island republic was still in part governed by an irradiated past: well into the 1980s its history of nuclear colonialism, long forgotten by the colonizers, was still delivering into the world "jellyfish babies"—headless, eyeless, limbless human infants who would live for just a few hours.[12]

If, as Said notes, struggles over geography are never reducible to armed struggle but have a profound symbolic and narrative component as well, and if, as Michael Watts insists, we must attend to the "violent geographies of fast capitalism," we need to supplement both these injunctions with a deeper understanding of the slow violence of delayed effects that structures so many of our most consequential forgettings.[13] Violence, above all environmental violence, needs to be seen—and deeply considered—as a contest not only over space, or bodies, or labor, or resources, but also over time. We need to bear in mind Faulkner's dictum that "the past is never dead. It's not even past." His words resonate with particular force across landscapes permeated by slow violence, landscapes of temporal overspill that elude rhetorical cleanup operations with their sanitary beginnings and endings.[14]

Kwame Anthony Appiah famously asked, "Is the 'Post-' in 'Postcolonial' the 'Post-' in 'Postmodern'?" As environmentalists we might ask similarly searching questions of the "post" in postindustrial, post–Cold War, and post-conflict.[15] For if the past of slow violence is never past, so too the post is never fully post: industrial particulates and effluents live on in the environmental elements we inhabit and in our very bodies, which epidemiologically and ecologically are never our simple contemporaries.[16] Something similar applies to so-called postconflict societies whose leaders may annually commemorate, as marked on the calendar, the official cessation of hostilities, while ongoing intergenerational slow violence (inflicted by, say, unexploded landmines or carcinogens from an arms dump) may continue hostilities by other means.

Ours is an age of onrushing turbo-capitalism, wherein the present feels more abbreviated than it used to—at least for the world's privileged classes who live surrounded by technological time-savers that often compound the sensation of not having enough time. Consequently, one of the most pressing challenges of our age is how to adjust our rapidly eroding attention spans to the slow erosions of environmental justice. If, under neoliberalism, the gulf between enclaved rich and outcast poor has become ever more pronounced, ours is also an era of enclaved time wherein for many speed has become a self-justifying, propulsive ethic that renders "uneventful" violence (to those who live remote from its attritional lethality) a weak claimant on our time. The attosecond pace of our age, with its restless technologies of infinite promise and infinite disappointment, prompts us to keep flicking and clicking distractedly in an insatiable—and often insensate—quest for quicker sensation.

The oxymoronic notion of slow violence poses a number of challenges: scientific, legal, political, and representational. In the long arc between the emergence of slow violence and its delayed effects, both the causes and the memory of catastrophe readily fade from view as the casualties incurred typically pass untallied and unremembered. Such discounting in turn makes it far more difficult to secure effective legal measures for prevention, restitution, and redress. Casualties from slow violence are, moreover, out of sync not only with our narrative and media expectations but also with the swift seasons of electoral change. Politicians routinely adopt a "last in, first out" stance toward environmental issues, admitting them when times are flush, dumping them as soon as times get tight. Because preventative or remedial environmental legislation typically targets slow violence, it cannot deliver dependable electoral cycle results, even though those results may ultimately be life saving. Relative to bankable pocketbook actions—there'll be a tax rebate check in the mail next August—environmental payouts seem to lurk on a distant horizon. Many politicians—and indeed many voters—routinely treat environmental action as critical yet not urgent. And so generation after generation of two- or four-year cycle politicians add to the pileup of deferrable actions deferred. With rare exceptions, in the domain of slow violence "yes, but not now, not yet" becomes the modus operandi.

How can leaders be goaded to avert catastrophe when the political rewards of their actions will not accrue to them but will be reaped on someone else's watch decades, even centuries, from now? How can environmental activists and storytellers work to counter the potent political, corporate, and even scientific forces invested in immediate self-interest, procrastination, and dissembling? We see such dissembling at work, for instance, in the afterword to Michael Crichton's 2004 environmental conspiracy novel, State of Fear, wherein he argued that we needed twenty more years of data gathering on climate change before any policy decisions could be ventured.[17] Although the National Academy of Sciences had assured former president George W. Bush that humans were indeed causing the earth to warm, Bush shopped around for views that accorded with his own skepticism and found them in a private meeting with Crichton, whom he described as "an expert scientist."

To address the challenges of slow violence is to confront the dilemma Rachel Carson faced almost half a century ago as she sought to dramatize what she eloquently called "death by indirection."[18] Carson's subjects were biomagnification and toxic drift, forms of oblique, slow-acting violence that, like climate change, pose formidable imaginative difficulties for writers and activists alike. In struggling to give shape to amorphous menace, both Carson and reviewers of *Silent Spring* resorted to a narrative vocabulary: one reviewer portrayed the book as exposing "the new, unplotted and mysterious dangers we insist upon creating all around us,"[19] while Carson herself wrote of "a shadow that is no less ominous because it is formless and obscure."[20] To confront slow violence requires, then, that we plot and give figurative shape to formless threats whose fatal repercussions are dispersed across space and time. The representational challenges are acute, requiring creative ways of drawing public attention to catastrophic acts that are low in instant spectacle but high in long-term effects. To intervene representationally entails devising iconic symbols that embody amorphous calamities as well as narrative forms that infuse those symbols with dramatic urgency.

Slow Violence and Structural Violence

Seven years after Rachel Carson turned our attention to the lethal mechanisms of "death by indirection," Johan Galtung, the influential Norwegian mathematician and sociologist, coined the term "indirect or structural violence."[21] Galtung's theory of structural violence is pertinent here because some of his concerns overlap with the concerns that animate this book, while others help throw into relief the rather different features I have sought to highlight by introducing the term "slow violence." Structural violence, for Galtung, stands in opposition to the more familiar personal violence that dominates our conceptions of what counts as violence per se.[22] Galtung was concerned, as I am, with widening the field of what constitutes violence. He sought to foreground the vast structures that can give rise to acts of personal violence and constitute forms of violence in and of themselves. Such structural violence may range from the unequal morbidity that results from a commodified health care system, to racism itself. What I share with Galtung's line of thought is a concern with social justice, hidden agency, and certain forms of violence that are imperceptible.

In these terms, for example, we can recognize that the structural violence embodied by a neoliberal order of austerity measures, structural adjustment, rampant deregulation, corporate megamergers, and a widening gulf between rich and poor is a form of covert violence in its own right that is often a catalyst for more recognizably overt violence. For an expressly environmental example of structural violence, one might cite Wangari Maathai's insistence that the systemic burdens of national debt to the IMF and World Bank borne by many so-called developing nations constitute a major impediment to environmental sustainability.[23] So, too, feminist earth scientist Jill Schneiderman, one of our finest thinkers about environmental time, has written about the way in which environmental degradation may "masquerade as inevitable."[24]

For all the continuing pertinence of the theory of structural violence and for all the modifications the theory has undergone, the notion bears the impress of its genesis during the high era of structuralist thinking that tended toward a static determinism. We see this, for example, in Galtung's insistence that "structural violence is silent, it does not show—its is essentially static, it *is* the tranquil waters."[25] In contrast to the static connotations of structural violence, I have sought, through the notion of slow violence, to foreground questions of time, movement, and change, however gradual. The explicitly temporal emphasis of slow violence allows us to keep front and center the representational challenges and imaginative dilemmas posed not just by imperceptible violence but by imperceptible change whereby violence is decoupled from its original causes by the workings of time. Time becomes an actor in complicated ways, not least because the temporal templates of our spectacle-driven, 24/7 media life have shifted massively since Galtung first advanced his theory of structural violence some forty years ago. To talk about slow violence, then, is to engage directly with our contemporary politics of speed.

Simply put, structural violence is a theory that entails rethinking different notions of causation and agency with respect to violent effects. Slow violence, by contrast, might well include forms of structural violence, but has a wider descriptive range in calling attention, not simply to questions of agency, but to broader, more complex descriptive categories of violence enacted slowly over time. The shift in the relationship between human agency and time is most dramatically evident in our enhanced understanding of the accelerated changes occurring at two scalar extremes—in the life-sustaining circuits of planetary biophysics and in the wired brain's neural circuitry. The idea of structural violence predated both sophisticated contemporary ice-core sampling methods and the emergence of cyber

Gramley Library
Salem Academy and College
Winston-Salem, N.C. 27108

technology. My concept of slow violence thus seeks to respond both to recent, radical changes in our geological perception and our changing technological experiences of time.

Let me address the geological aspect first. In 2000, Paul Crutzen, the Nobel Prize–winning atmospheric chemist, introduced the term "the Anthropocene Age" (which he dated to James Watt's invention of the steam engine). Through the notion of "the Anthropocene Age," Crutzen sought to theorize an unprecedented epochal effect: the massive impact by the human species, from the industrial era onward, on our planet's life systems, an impact that, as his term suggests, is geomorphic, equal in force and in long-term implications to a major geological event.[26] Crutzen's attempt to capture the epochal scale of human activity's impact on the planet was followed by Will Steffen's elaboration, in conjunction with Crutzen and John McNeill, of what they dubbed the Great Acceleration, a second stage of the Anthropocene Age that they dated to the mid-twentieth century. Writing in 2007, Steffen et al. noted how "nearly three-quarters of the anthropogenically driven rise in CO_2 concentration has occurred since 1950 (from about 310 to 380 ppm), and about half of the total rise (48 ppm) has occurred in just the last 30 years."[27] The Australian environmental historian Libby Robin has put the case succinctly: "We have recently entered a new geological epoch, the Anthropocene. There is now considerable evidence that humanity has altered the biophysical systems of Earth, not just the carbon cycle . . . but also the nitrogen cycle and ultimately the atmosphere and climate of the whole globe."[28] What, then, are the consequences for our experience of time of this newfound recognition that we have inadvertently, through our unprecedented biophysical species power, inaugurated an Anthropocene Age and are now engaged in (and subject to) the hurtling changes of the Great Acceleration?

Over the past two decades, this high-speed planetary modification has been accompanied (at least for those increasing billions who have access to the Internet) by rapid modifications to the human cortex. It is difficult, but necessary, to consider simultaneously a geologically-paced plasticity, however relatively rapid, and the plasticity of brain circuits reprogrammed by a digital world that threatens to "info-whelm" us into a state of perpetual distraction. If an awareness of the Great Acceleration is (to put it mildly) unevenly distributed, the experience of accelerated connectivity (and the paradoxical disconnects that can accompany it) is increasingly widespread.

Gramley Library
Salem Academy and College
Winston Salem, N.C. 27108

In an age of degraded attention spans it becomes doubly difficult yet increasingly urgent that we focus on the toll exacted, over time, by the slow violence of ecological degradation. We live, writes Cory Doctorow, in an era when the electronic screen has become an "ecosystem of interruption technologies."[29] Or as former Microsoft executive Linda Stone puts it, we now live in an age of "continuous partial attention."[30] Fast is faster than it used to be, and story units have become concomitantly shorter. In this cultural milieu of digitally speeded up time, and foreshortened narrative, the intergenerational aftermath becomes a harder sell. So to render slow violence visible entails, among other things, redefining speed: we see such efforts in talk of accelerated species loss, rapid climate change, and in attempts to recast "glacial"—once a dead metaphor for "slow"—as a rousing, iconic image of unacceptably fast loss.

Efforts to make forms of slow violence more urgently visible suffered a setback in the United States in the aftermath of 9/11, which reinforced a spectacular, immediately sensational, and instantly hyper-visible image of what constitutes a violent threat. The fiery spectacle of the collapsing towers was burned into the national psyche as *the* definitive image of violence, setting back by years attempts to rally public sentiment against climate change, a threat that is incremental, exponential, and far less sensationally visible. Condoleezza Rice's strategic fantasy of a mushroom cloud looming over America if the United States failed to invade Iraq gave further visual definition to cataclysmic violence as something explosive and instantaneous, a recognizably cinematic, immediately sensational, pyrotechnic event.

The representational bias against slow violence has, furthermore, a critically dangerous impact on what counts as a casualty in the first place. Casualties of slow violence—human and environmental—are the casualties most likely not to be seen, not to be counted. Casualties of slow violence become light-weight, disposable casualties, with dire consequences for the ways wars are remembered, which in turn has dire consequences for the projected casualties from future wars. We can observe this bias at work in the way wars, whose lethal repercussions spread across space and time, are tidily bookended in the historical record. Thus, for instance, a 2003 *New York Times* editorial on Vietnam declared that "during our dozen years there, the U.S. killed and helped kill at least 1.5 million people."[31] But that simple phrase "during our dozen years there" shrinks the toll, foreshortening the ongoing slow-motion slaughter: hundreds of thousands survived the official war years, only to slowly lose their lives later to Agent Orange. In a 2002 study, the environmental scientist Arnold Schecter recorded dioxin levels in the bloodstreams of Bien Hoa residents at 135 times the levels of Hanoi's inhabitants, who lived far north of the spraying.[32] The afflicted include thousands of children born decades after the war's end. More than thirty years after the last spray run, Agent Orange continues to wreak havoc as, through biomagnification, dioxins build up in the fatty tissues of pivotal foods such as duck and fish and pass from the natural world into the cooking pot and from there to ensuing human generations. An Institute of Medicine committee has by now linked seventeen medical conditions to Agent Orange; indeed, as recently as 2009 it uncovered fresh evidence that exposure to the chemical increases the likelihood of developing Parkinson's disease and ischemic heart disease.[33] Under such circumstances, wherein long-term risks continue to emerge, to bookend a war's casualties with the phrase "during our dozen years there" is misleading: that small, seemingly innocent phrase is a powerful reminder of how our rhetorical conventions for bracketing violence routinely ignore ongoing, belated casualties.

Slow Violence and Strategies of Representation: Writer-Activism

How do we bring home—and bring emotionally to life—threats that take time to wreak their havoc, threats that never materialize in one spectacular, explosive, cinematic scene? *Apprehension* is a critical word here, a crossover term that draws together the domains of perception, emotion, and action. To engage slow violence is to confront layered predicaments of apprehension: to apprehend—to arrest, or at least mitigate—often imperceptible threats requires rendering them apprehensible to the senses through the work of scientific and imaginative testimony. An influential lineage of environmental thought gives primacy to immediate sensory apprehension, to sight above all, as foundational for any environmental ethics of place. George Perkins Marsh, the mid-nineteenth-century environmental pioneer, argued in *Man and Nature* that "the power most important to cultivate, and, at the same time, hardest to acquire, is that of seeing what is before him."[34] Aldo Leopold similarly insisted that "we can be ethical only toward what we can see."[35] But what happens when we are unsighted, when what extends before us—in the space and time that we most deeply inhabit—remains invisible? How, indeed, are we to act ethically toward human and biotic communities that lie beyond our sensory ken? What then, in the fullest sense of the phrase, is the place of seeing in the world that we now inhabit? What, moreover, is the place of the other senses? How do we both make slow violence visible yet also challenge the privileging of the visible?

Such questions have profound consequences for the apprehension of slow violence, whether on a cellular or a transnational scale. Planetary consciousness (a notion that has undergone a host of theoretical formulations) becomes pertinent here, perhaps most usefully in the sense in which Mary Louise Pratt elaborates it, linking questions of power and perspective, keeping front and center the often latent, often invisible violence in the view. Who gets to see, and from where? When and how does such empowered seeing become normative? And what perspectives—not least those of the poor or women or the colonized—do hegemonic sight conventions of visuality obscure? Pratt's formulation of planetary consciousness remains invaluable because it allows us to connect forms of apprehension to forms of imperial violence.[36]

Against this backdrop, I want to introduce the third central concern of this book. Alongside slow violence and the environmentalism of the poor, the chapters that follow are critically concerned with the political, imaginative, and strategic role of environmental writer-activists. Writer-activists can help us apprehend threats imaginatively that remain imperceptible to the senses, either because they are geographically remote, too vast or too minute in scale, or are played out across a time span that exceeds the instance of observation or even the physiological life of the human observer. In a world permeated by insidious, yet unseen or imperceptible violence, imaginative writing can help make the unapparent appear, making it accessible and tangible by humanizing drawn-out threats inaccessible to the immediate senses. Writing can challenge perceptual habits that downplay the damage slow violence inflicts and bring into imaginative focus apprehensions that elude sensory corroboration. The narrative imaginings of writer-activists may thus offer us a different kind of witnessing: of sights unseen.

To allay states of apprehension—trepidations, forebodings, shadows cast by the invisible—entails facing the challenge, at once imaginative and scientific, of giving the unapparent a materiality upon which we can act. Yet poor communities, often disproportionately exposed to the force fields of slow violence—be they military residues or imported e-waste or the rising tides of climate change—are the communities least likely to attract sustained scientific inquiry into causes, effects, and potential redress. Such poor communities are abandoned to sporadic science at best and usually no science at all; they are also disproportionately subjected to involuntary pharmaceutical experiments. Indeed, when such communities raise concerns, they often become targets of well-funded antiscience by forces that have a legal or commercial interest in manufacturing and disseminating doubt.[37] Such embattled communities, beset by officially unacknowledged hazards, must find ways to broadcast their inhabited fears, their lived sense of a corroded environment, within the broader global struggles over apprehension. It is here that writers, filmmakers, and digital activists may play a mediating role in helping counter the layered invisibility that results from insidious threats, from temporal protractedness, and from the fact that the afflicted are people whose quality of life—and often whose very existence—is of indifferent interest to the corporate media.

To address violence discounted by dominant structures of apprehension is necessarily to engage the culturally variable issue of *who counts as a witness*. Contests over what counts as violence are intimately entangled with conflicts over who bears the social authority of witness, which entails much more than simply seeing or not seeing. The entangled politics of spectacle and witnessing have implications that stretch well beyond environmental slow violence. In domestic abuse, for instance, violence may be life threatening but slow, bloodless, and brutal in ways that are not always immediately fatal: a broken nose constitutes a different order of evidence from food or access to medical treatment or human company withheld over an extended period. A locked door can be a weapon. Doors for women are often longterm, nonlethal weapons that leave no telltale bloody trail; doors don't bear witness to a single, decisive blow. In many cultures, moreover, rape isn't defined as rape if it is inflicted by a husband. And in some societies, a rape isn't rape unless three adult men are present to witness it. As the journalistic chestnut has it, "if it bleeds, it leads." And as a corollary, if it's bloodless, slow-motion violence, the story is more likely to be buried, particularly if it's relayed by people whose witnessing authority is culturally discounted.

The Environmentalism of the Poor and
Displacement in Place

In the global resource wars, the environmentalism of the poor is frequently triggered when an official landscape is forcibly imposed on a vernacular one.[38] A vernacular landscape is shaped by the affective, historically textured maps that communities have devised over generations, maps replete with names and routes, maps alive to significant ecological and surface geological features. A vernacular landscape, although neither monolithic nor undisputed, is integral to the socioenvironmental dynamics of community rather than being wholly externalized—treated as out there, as a separate nonrenewable resource. By contrast, an official landscape—whether governmental, NGO, corporate, or some combination of those—is typically oblivious to such earlier maps; instead, it writes the land in a bureaucratic, externalizing, and extraction-driven manner that is often pitilessly instrumental. Lawrence Summers' scheme to export rich-nation garbage and toxicity to Africa, for example, stands as a grandiose (though hardly exceptional) instance of a highly rationalized official landscape that, whether in terms of elite capture of resources or toxic disposal, has often been projected onto ecosystems inhabited by those whom Annu Jalais, in an Indian context, calls "dispensable citizens."[39]

I would argue, then, that the exponential upsurge in indigenous resource rebellions across the globe during the high age of neoliberalism has resulted largely from a clash of temporal perspectives between the short-termers who arrive (with their official landscape maps) to extract, despoil, and depart and the long-termers who must live inside the ecological aftermath and must therefore weigh wealth differently in time's scales. In the pages that follow, I will highlight and explore resource rebellions against developer-dispossessors who descend from other time zones to impose on habitable environments unsustainable calculations about what constitutes the duration of human gain. Change is a cultural constant but the pace of change is not. Hence the temporal contests over how to sustain, regenerate, exhaust, or obliterate the landscape as resource become critical. More than material wealth is here at stake: imposed official landscapes typically discount spiritualized vernacular landscapes, severing webs of accumulated cultural meaning and treating the landscape as if it were uninhabited by the living, the unborn, and the animate deceased.

The ensuing losses are consistent with John Berger's lament over capitalism's disdain for interdependencies by foreshortening our sense of time, thereby rendering the deceased immaterial:

> The living reduce the dead to those who have lived; yet the dead already include the living in their own great collective. . . . Until the dehumanization of society by capitalism, all the living awaited the experience of the dead. It was their ultimate future. By themselves the living were incomplete. Thus living and dead were interdependent. Always. Only a uniquely modern form of egoism has broken this interdependence. With disastrous results for the living, who now think of the dead as the *eliminated*.[40]

Hence, one should add, our perspective on environmental asset stripping should include among assets stripped the mingled presence in the landscape of multiple generations, with all the hindsight and foresight that entails.

Against this backdrop, I consider in this book what can be called the temporalities of place. Place is a temporal attainment that must be constantly renegotiated in the face of changes that arrive from without and within, some benign, others potentially ruinous. To engage the temporal displacements involved in slow violence against the poor thus requires that we rethink questions of physical displacement as well. In the chapters that follow, I track the socioenvironmental fallout from developmental agendas whose primary beneficiaries live elsewhere; as when, for example, oasis dwellers in the Persian Gulf get trucked off to unknown destinations so that American petroleum engineers and their sheik collaborators can develop their "finds." Or when a megadam arises and (whether erected in the name of some dictatorial edict, the free market, structural adjustment, national development, or far-off urban or industrial need) displaces and disperses those who had developed through their vernacular landscapes their own adaptable, if always imperfect and vulnerable, relation to riverine possibility.

Paradoxically, those forcibly removed by development include conservation refugees. Too often in the global South, conservation, driven by powerful transnational nature NGOs, combines an antidevelopmental rhetoric with the development of finite resources for the touristic few, thereby depleting vital resources for long-term residents. (I explore this paradox more fully in Chapter 6: Stranger in the Eco-village: Race, Tourism, and Environmental Time.)

In much of what follows, I address the resistance mounted by impoverished communities who have been involuntarily moved out of their knowledge; I address as well the powers—transnational, national, and local—behind such forced removals. My angle of vision is largely through writers who have affiliated themselves with social movements that seek to stave off one of two ruinous prospects: either the threatened community capitulates and is scattered (across refugee camps, placeless "relocation" sites, desperate favelas, and unwelcoming foreign lands), or the community refuses to move but, as its world is undermined, effectively becomes a community of refugees in place. What I wish to stress here, then, are not just those communities that are involuntarily (and often militarily) relocated to less hospitable environs, but also those affected by what I call displacement without moving. In other words, I want to propose a more radical notion of displacement, one that, instead of referring solely to the movement of people from their places of belonging, refers rather to the loss of the land and resources beneath them, a loss that leaves communities stranded in a place stripped of the very characteristics that made it inhabitable.

For if environmental protest has frequently been incited by the threat of forced removal, it has also been incited by the threat of displacement without moving. Such a threat entails being simultaneously immobilized and moved out of one's living knowledge as one's place loses its life-sustaining features. What does it mean for people declared disposable by some "new" economy to find themselves existing out of place in place as, against the odds, they seek to slow the ecological assaults on inhabitable possibility? What does it mean for subsistence communities to discover they are goners with nowhere to go, that their once-sustaining landscapes have been gutted of their capacity to sustain by an externalizing, instrumental logic? The desperate entrapments, the claustral options that result have galvanized environmental justice insurrections, in the global South and beyond.

I would like to ground this point in Stephanie Black's superb documentary *Life and Debt.* The film can be interpreted as dramatizing the way neoliberal policies impose displacement without moving (or stationary displacement) on Jamaican communities, a process intimately connected to the long-term socioenvironmental damage inflicted on the island by slow violence. *Life and*

Debt adapts to a Jamaican context Kincaid's Antiguan polemic against tourism and against the neocolonial politics of unequal freedom of movement. This is a film about arrivals, departures, and those unable either to arrive or depart. Yet the most consequential arrival is the hardest to depict: the advent of the "free market" in the form of IMF structural adjustment, rendered visible by planes disgorging federally subsidized American milk, onions, and potatoes at prices that destroy unsubsidized Jamaican farmers whose operations were small scale but intergenerational. To compensate for the resultant agricultural collapse and the rising debt that follows from importing more subsidized American food, Jamaica must increase its dependence on tourists who, disgorged from sleek jets, are then immured in dedicated pleasure zones. Black's film sets up an implicit link between the visiting tourists' structured getaways and the structural adjustment visited upon the locals from which there is no getaway. We see guard dogs being trained to segregate mobile pleasure-seekers from trapped, angry locals forced to live their dislocated lives in place. Here, in capsule form, we witness one industry that has thrived under neoliberalism: the security industry, which has flourished on the insecurities wrought by structural adjustment, by the "opening up" of markets, and by the erosion of long-term relations to the land through the annexation—and carting off—of the very conditions of life.

Security has become one of neoliberalism's signature growth industries, exemplified by the international boom in gated communities, as walls have spread like kudzu, and the marketplace in barriers has literally soared, from Los Angeles to Sao Paolo; from Johannesburg to Jakarta; from Lagos, Lima, and Mexico City to Karachi. Ironically, as neoliberal policy makers have pushed to bring down barriers to "free trade," those same policies have resulted in the erection of ever higher barriers segregating inordinate wealth from inordinate poverty. Neoliberalism's proliferating walls concretize a short-term psychology of denial: the delusion that we can survive long term in a world whose resources are increasingly unshared. The wall, read in terms of neoliberalism and environmental slow violence, materializes temporal as well as spatial denial through a literal concretizing of out of sight out of mind.

Neoliberal assaults on inhabited environments have of course met with variable success. Whether the target is an immobile resource such as forests, a mobile resource such as water, or a fugitive resource such as wildlife, the environment itself is not a predictably quiescent victim.[41] Resistance may assume not just human forms but also arise from an unanticipated recalcitrance on the part of a targeted resource, which may prove harder to commodify and profitably remove or manage than corporate moguls foresaw. We have witnessed as much, for example, in the largely unsuccessful attempts to privatize water: if 20 percent of the world's largest cities now have privatized water systems, such efforts have sometimes experienced reversals—as in Bolivia, for instance—through a mixture of human resistance, topographical impediments, and obstacles to social engineering.

That said, we need to be cautious about romanticizing the noncompliance that may inhere in a targeted resource: relative to the accelerated plunder involved, say, in the "second scramble" for Africa—as American, Australian, Chinese, European, and South African corporations cash in on resource-rich, regulation-poor, war-fractured societies—the resistance posed by nature itself should not be overstated.[42] The recent turn within environmental studies toward celebrating the creative resilience of ecosystems can be readily hijacked by politicians, lobbyists, and corporations who oppose regulatory controls and strive to minimize pollution liability. Co-opting the "nature-and-time-will-heal" argument has become integral to attempts to privatize profits while externalizing risk and cleanup, both of which can be delegated to "nature's business."

This was dramatically illustrated by the Deepwater Horizon disaster—in the laxity that contributed to the blowout and in the aftermath. Big Oil and government agencies both invoked natural resilience as an advance strategy for minimizing oversight. Before the blowout, the Minerals Management Service of the U.S. Interior Department had concluded that "spills in deep water are not likely to affect listed birds. . . . Deepwater spills would either be transported away from coastal habitats or prevented, for the most part, from reaching coastal habitats by natural weathering processes."[43] Even after the disaster, this line of reasoning persisted. Oil industry apologist Rep. Don Young (R-AK), testifying at congressional hearings on the blowout, knew exactly how to mine this "natural agency" logic: the Deepwater Horizon spill was "not an environmental disaster," he declared. "I will say that again and again because it is a natural phenomenon. Oil has seeped into this ocean for centuries, will continue to do it. . . . We will lose some birds, we will lose some fixed sea-life, but overall it will recover."[44] BP spokesman John Curry likewise explained how industrious microbes would cleanse the oil from the gulf: "Nature," he concluded sanguinely, "has a way of helping the situation."[45] BP representatives repeatedly invoked the capacity of marine life to metabolize hydrocarbons and the dispersing powers of microbial degradation. But in conscripting nature as a volunteer clean up crew, BP and its Washington allies downplayed the way ravenous microbes, in consuming oxygen, thereby starved other organisms and exacerbated expanding oceanic dead zones.[46] What will be the long-term cascade effect of the slow violence, the mass die-offs, of phyloplankton at the food chain base? It is far too early to tell.

In short, the very environment that high-risk, deep-water drilling endangered was conscripted by industry through a kind of natural outsourcing. And so Big Oil's invocation of nature's healing powers needs to be recognized as part of a broader strategy of image management and liability limitation by greenwashing. Natural agency can indeed take unexpected, sometimes heartening forms, but we should be alert to the ways corporate colossi and governments can hijack that logic to grant themselves advance or retrospective absolution. Crucially, for my arguments about slow violence, the time frames of damage assessment and potential recovery are wildly out of sync. The deep-time thinking that celebrates natural healing is strategically disastrous if it provides political cover for reckless corporate short-termism.[47]

Writer-Activists and Representational Power

The environmentalism of the poor is frequently catalyzed by resource imperialism inflicted on the global South to maintain the unsustainable consumer appetites of rich-country citizens and, increasingly, of the urban middle classes in the global South itself. The outsourcing of environmental crisis, whether through rapid or slow violence, has a particularly profound impact on the world's ecosystem people—those hundreds of millions who depend for their livelihood on modest resource catchment areas at the opposite extreme from the planetary resource catchment areas plundered by the wealthy—the wealthy whom Gadgil and Guha have dubbed "resource omnivores."[48] The writer-activists I engage in this book share a desire to give human definition to such outsourced suffering, a desire to lay bare the dissociational dynamics whereby, for example, a rich-country conservation ethic is uncoupled from environmental devastation, externalized abroad, in which it is implicated. Correspondingly, we witness in these writers a desire to give life and dimension to the strategies—oppositional, affirmative, and yes, often desperate and fractured—that emerge from those who bear the brunt of the planet's ecological crises.

The writer-activists I discuss in these pages who engage the environmentalism of the poor are a heterogeneous cast. Some, like Wangari Maathai and Ken Saro-Wiwa, helped launch environmental movements and assumed within them the role of *porte-parole*. They also became iconic figureheads and ultimately (in a phrase that expresses a contradictory tension) autobiographers of collective movements. Others, like Arundhati Roy and Indra Sinha, affiliated themselves with well-established struggles, helping amplify causes marginalized by the corporate media. Roy also served as a transnational go-between, connecting a specific struggle against the Sardar Sarovar Dam with international campaigns against megadams and, beyond that, with the antiglobalization movement itself. For Roy, Sinha, Maathai, and Saro-Wiwa, the extra visibility they afforded the environmentalism of the poor entailed, crucially, the development of rhetorical alliances that opened up connective avenues between environmental justice and other rights discourses: women's rights, minority rights, tribal rights, property rights, the right to freedom of speech and assembly, and the right to enhanced economic self-sufficiency.

Sometimes a writer-activist's authority becomes, in their home country, a lightning rod for controversy in ways quite different from the controversies their writings stir abroad. Roy's polemical essays in support of the movement opposing the Sardar Sarovar Dam on India's Narmada River are a case in point: her testimony reached a vast international audience and enhanced the visibility of marginalized rural communities who mobilized against megadams, expressly in the Narmada Valley but more broadly across the global South. On the one hand, the *New York Times* refused to publish Roy (and other dissident public intellectuals, such as Edward Said and Noam Chomsky) presumably because her antiglobalization essays were ideologically unsettling. On the other hand, Indian opinion about her interventions split between those who lauded her for putting her celebrity in the service of the poor and those who lambasted her for behaving in a self-serving manner. An Anglophone Indian writer like Roy, whose national and international audiences are both substantial, faces particular challenges in trying to reconcile disjunctive audiences: rhetorical strategies, tonal inflections, and informational background that engage an international audience risk estranging a national one and vice versa. How different the situation is for a socioenvironmental writer like Derek Walcott from a small society that comprises an infinitesimal fraction of his audience; even after he was awarded the Nobel Prize, Walcott's books were nowhere to be found on sale in his natal St. Lucia.

But what of writer-activists operating in circumstances where no viable movement existed to challenge the imperially buttressed forces of crony capitalism, where campaigns for environmental justice took shape before the term itself existed and where such campaigns assumed the forms of at best spasmodic protest? One such activist was Abdelrahman Munif who, by shuttling across a broad spread of fictional and nonfictional forms, gave imaginative definition to the long view of the resource wars that have afflicted the Persian Gulf. His writings speak in defense of socioenvironmental memory itself—above all, the suppressed memory of the uprisings (which peaked in the 1940s and 1950s) against American petro-imperialism in partnership with an emergent petro-despotism. By the mid-1980s, when Munif's *Cities of Salt* appeared, that dissident lineage protesting the petro-state's union-busting, racist labor practices had been brutally quashed. Yet Munif was able to give imaginative and political definition to the memory of social protest while foreshadowing, with uncanny prescience, how the crushed campaigns for dignity and rights would become dangerously diverted into an anti-imperial religious fundamentalism.

In turning to the Caribbean and South Africa, I revisit the question of the writer-activist's role in fortifying embattled socioenvironmental memory. Jamaica Kincaid, June Jordan, Njabulo Ndebele, and Nadine Gordimer found themselves writing into the headwinds of an international nature industry propelled by a romanticized colonial history and by neocolonial fantasy. All four writers draw to the surface inconvenient questions about long-term ecologies of social injustice that cannot be colorfully blended into touristic boilerplate. In writing against a violent and violating invisibility they engage the contradictions that permeate the marketplace in idealized natural retreats—a marketplace premised on a retreat from socioenvironmental memory itself. At stake is the way suppressed histories of land theft, forced removal, slavery, and coercive labor achieve their most concentrated form in the figure of the spectral servant, whose obligatory self-effacement smoothes the tourist's path toward immersion in an unsullied nature rich in pure moment, in serendipitous immediacy.

The anticolonial energies that inform the essays I discuss by Kincaid, Ndebele, and Jordan are complicated by painfully riven reflections on representational authority. When you have ascended economically as a black woman or man into the middle classes, where do you stand in relation to those whose plight you depict and whose service, as a tourist, you depend on? Where do you belong in the historically sanitized, colonially hued international marketplace in environmental relaxation? In writing about tourism, poverty, and clashing cultures of nature, Kincaid, Ndebele, and Jordan all attempt to negotiate, through memoir and polemic, the minefields of race, class, and gender that confront them on entering a realm of nature industry tourism clearly not designed for them yet to which they can afford class access.

Many of the writers I consider in this book, as well as the three figures whom I acknowledge in my preface—Edward Said, Rachel Carson, and Ramachandra Guha—exemplify in their work the versatile possibilities of politically engaged nonfiction. For one of the enduring passions that informs this book is the special allure that nonfiction possesses for me as a writer, scholar, reader, and teacher. I am drawn to nonfiction's robust adaptability, imaginative and political, as well as to its information-carrying capacity and its aura of the real.[49] Yet a tenacious tendency remains to marginalize nonfiction, to treat it as at best supplementary to "real literature" like the novel or poetry rather than taking seriously its adaptive rhetorical capacities, the chameleon powers that make it such an indispensable resource for creative activism. Indeed, a particular joy of teaching transnational environmental literatures is the vigorous, varied writing on offer from within nonfiction's broad domain—memoirs, essays, public science writing, polemics, travel literature, graphic memoirs, manifestos, and investigative journalism. Some of the writers I consider in the chapters that follow work principally in nonfiction forms, others in fiction, while most of them shuttle strategically and instinctively between the two. At a time when the memoir, in particular, has come under fire for self-absorption, we would do well to remember that the "if-it's-me-it-must-be-interesting" memoir is not the only type. The most effective memoirists, not least environmental ones, find ways to draw on the form's intimate energies while also offering the reader a social depth of field.

Much has been written about the literary right to represent, some of it significant work, some overly elaborate. Clearly power, including representational power, often works at an exaggerated remove. The writers I engage have ascended not just into the literate but into the publishing classes, thereby creating some inevitable distance from the bulk of the impoverished people about whom they write. Yet in the scheme of things, this hardly seems to me the most suspect kind of distance. Relative to the invisibility that threatens the marginalized poor and the environments they depend on, the bridge-work such writer-activists undertake offers a mostly honorable counter to the distancing rhetoric of neoliberal "free market" resource development, a rhetoric that displaces onto future generations—above all through slow violence—the human and ecological costs of such "development."

The interplay between representational authority and displacement matters at a biographical level as well.[50] Most of the writers I discuss—Maathai, Saro-Wiwa, Munif, Kincaid, Jordan, Ndebele, Naipaul, Carson, Richard Rodriguez, Nadine Gordimer, and James Baldwin—were the first in their families to attend college.[51] From the contradictions of sudden class displacement—often compounded by transgressed expectations that attend gender, race, sexuality, or immigrant status—a certain type of public intellectual may arise, someone who has to negotiate the vexing terrain of unfamiliar—and unfamilial—privilege fraught with an anxious sense of collective responsibility. The public role such figures assume is often animated both by an expressive anger and by the fear that their novel, precarious privilege is temporary or illusory—that one misstep may plunge them back into a viscerally remembered familial indigence. What frequently appears, then, is a quest to improvise community, both literal and imaginative, to help counter the isolation that comes from feeling economically, professionally, and psychologically unsheltered by precedent. These tendencies inflect the socioenvironmental and creative sensibilities that distinguish many of the writers in this book. Having extricated themselves improbably from impoverished circumstances—and then seeing their work published in the *New Yorker,* or on being awarded a Ph.D. or even the

Nobel Prize—they stand above the immediate environmental struggles of the poor yet remain bonded through memory (and through their own vertiginous anxieties) to the straitened circumstances from which they or their families recently emerged. Hence, as go-betweens, such writers are at the very least intimate, highly motivated translators.

The challenges of translating across chasms of class, race, gender, and nation is thus viscerally connected to memories of self-translation across dauntingly wide divides, as Tsitsi Dangarembga's bildungsroman set in colonial Rhodesia, *Nervous Conditions*, illustrates so well. The thirteen-year-old rural heroine, Tambu, is granted the unexpected chance to acquire an education when her brother dies and a beneficent uncle decides to divert the money he had committed to his nephew's schooling to his niece instead.[52] In approaching the mission school where she hopes to reinvent herself, the first signal to Tambu of the distance she must travel finds expression through divergent cultures of nature:

> The smooth, stoneless drive ran between squat, robust conifers on one side and a blaze of canna lilies burning scarlet and amber on the other. Plants like that belonged to the cities. They had belonged to the pages of my language reader, to the yards of Ben and Betty's uncle in town. Now, having seen it for myself because of my Babamukur's kindness, I too could think of planting things for merrier reasons than the chore of keeping breath in the body. I wrote it down in my head: I would ask Maiguru for some bulbs and plant a bed of those gay lilies on the homestead in front of the house. Our home would answer well to being cheered up by such lovely flowers. Bright and cheery, they had been planted for joy. What a strange idea that was. It was a liberation, the first of many that followed from my transition to the mission.[53]

Tambu, on the brink of being educated toward middle-class possibility, experiences the garden as a portal into her imminent self-translation, as an ornate reminder of the gap she must leap. Emerging from her uncle's car as (to use her word) a "peasant," she cannot yet see this garden, exotically exempt from human need, as ordinary: it belongs to books, to the wealthy, to those at liberty to treat the earth as an aesthetic canvas.[54] This indigent rural girl thus stands on the threshold of a divided self: she will be admitted to this garden aesthetic and learn to love it, but always with a double vision. She will belong forever to two earths: this second soil of luxurious self-expression but always just beneath it her childhood soil, fraught with survival's urgent chores.

A contortionist concern with representational authority can distract us from the fortitude required by those rare writers who, having escaped familial poverty, can convey an experientially rooted environmentalism that straddles immense divides. It is no coincidence that Jamaica Kincaid alights on Dangarembga's garden descriptions to contrast them with those gardens, lush with assumed access, that she encounters in Henry James.[55] One senses Kincaid looking on as an outsider at James's easy familiarity with dominant upper-class European conventions of horticultural depiction. By creating an alliance with Dangarembga's character, by choosing her as an imaginative coconspirator, Kincaid, the naturalized Caribbean American, denatures James's gardens which, for all their literary floral familiarity, are just that: the kinds of gardens that prevail in a literature written predominantly by those remote from the soil perspectives of the laboring poor.

This recognition scene between an Antiguan-American essayist and a fictional Zimbabwean character speaks to the politics of the unforeseeable imaginative connection, to the far-off, serendipitous chance find that becomes an exhortation.[56] The scene speaks, more broadly, to the unpredictable dynamics of cross-cultural translation that attend the creative circuits of globalization from below, in literature and other cultural forms. We see this process at work in the way activists like Saro-Wiwa, Maathai, Chico Mendes, and Mahatma Gandhi have assumed an allegorical potency for geographically distant struggles. For example, on the tenth anniversary of Saro-Wiwa's execution, anti-Shell activists in County Mayo, a region of Ireland's historically impoverished west, unveiled a vast mural of Saro-Wiwa whom they had adopted posthumously as the iconic transnational figurehead of their local struggle against Shell. The mural displayed a Saro-Wiwa poem translated into Gaelic and the names of the Ogoni Eight executed alongside Saro-Wiwa—that in an Irish community enraged by the imprisonment of the so-called Rossport Five, activists who had nonviolently protested Shell's plans to build a refinery close to their homes. Spill-prone pipelines were to link the inland refinery to offshore drilling sites, thereby jeopardizing the health and livelihood of a fishing and farming community dependent, as in the Niger Delta, on fragile intertidal ecosystems.[57]

Anna Tsing observes similarly how in post-Suharto Indonesia, the Chico Mendes story became for grassroots activists a malleable, inspirational precedent reformulated for local need. So too the largely female tree-huggers who had energized India's Chipko movement entered into Indonesian environmental parlance as a story of gendered resistance to forest stripping by globalizing corporate forces.[58] Even before the Internet and cell phones became widespread, such circulating allegories were aided by traveling environmentalists and by writer-activists—like Vandana Shiva, whose eco-feminist reading of the Chipko movement inflected its

Figure 1 Mural of Ken Saro-Wiwa in County Mayo, Ireland, for a campaign by Irish activists against Shell. Some of his poetry (translated into Gaelic) is displayed, as well as the names of the eight other Ogoni activists executed on November 10, 1995, by Nigerian military personnel. Reproduced by permission of Wikimedia Commons.

[29]

circulation among antiglobalization environmental movements, as well as among NGOs, thereby helping reshape the character of international funding and debate.

Such precedents—whether through iconic figureheads or entire social movements—offer resources of hope in the unequal battle to apprehend, to stave off, or at least retard the slow violence inflicted by globalizing forces. Such precedents help us engage, in all their complexity, the politics of the visible and the invisible, as environmental justice movements—and the writer-activists aligned with them—strategize to shift the balance of visibility both in the urgent present and over the long haul, pushing back against the forces of temporal inattention that compound injustices of class, gender, race, and region.

The Environmental Humanities and the Edge Effect

Field biologists have devised the term "ecotone" to characterize the border zones between adjacent communities of vegetation where (as between, say, grasslands and wetlands) life forms that ordinarily require discrete conditions meet and interact. Ecotones may thereby open up new configurations of possibility (and for some species, introduce new threats) as the transitional areas create so-called edge effects. In university life, we are witnessing an upsurge in these edge effects as interpenetrating fields proliferate at the borders between once separate disciplines, at times creating new dynamic combinations while also, depending on one's perspective, inflicting casualties through habitat fragmentation. In the scholarly ecotone, as in the biological, one may detect an elevated concentration in the sheer variety of life-forms, but at the expense of less-adaptable, specialist species.

How adaptable will the humanities prove in a less specialist environment? In particular, what kinds of connective corridors toward other disciplines can scholars creatively navigate in an intellectual milieu where habitat fracture is becoming increasingly pervasive? Certainly, the environmental humanities are entering a dynamic phase, as the long-established field of environmental history has in recent years encountered the ecocritical terrain of literary studies. We seem to be at a crucial turning point in the contribution literary scholars can make to the ecological humanities and, beyond that, to environmental studies at large.

Critical choices now confront us as scholars and writers reaching out to other fields as we try to consolidate transformative possibilities emerging at the edges of the humanities, the social sciences, and the natural sciences. Influential environmental literary critics, like Lawrence Buell, Wai Chee Dimock, and Ursula Heise have begun to forge innovative connections between literary environmentalism and the sciences around, for example, chaos theory and the premises underlying restoration ecology.[59] What remains less developed, however, are the energizing interdisciplinary possibilities, the unrealized creative bridgework, between environmental literary studies and the social sciences.[60] Such possibilities are overdue for recognition and, to that end, in the chapters that follow I have attempted to strengthen such links.

In so doing, I have drawn on environmental scholarship by anthropologists, geographers, political scientists, and sociologists like Fernando Coronil, Al Gedicks, Ramachandra Guha, Adriana Petryna, Anna Tsing, and Michael Watts. I have drawn inspiration, too, from the writings of leading progressive public intellectuals of our age: John Berger, Mike Davis, Eduardo Galeano, Naomi Klein, George Monbiot, and Rebecca Solnit among them, all of whom have engaged, with ambitious communicative intent, transnational questions arising from the borderlands between empire, neoliberalism, environmentalism, and social justice. I have thereby sought, first, to widen the interdisciplinary avenues available to us and, second, to keep alive a sense of the hugely varied public registers that writers can marshal to testify on issues of world urgency.

When literary studies becomes uncoupled from worldly concerns, we frequently witness, alongside an excessive regard for ahistoric philosophy, an accompanying historically indifferent formalism that treats the study of aesthetics as the literary scholar's definitive calling. Questions of social change and power become projected onto questions of form so that formal categories such as rupture, irony, and bricolage assume an inflated agency through what Anne McClintock has called "a fetishism of form:"

> The question is whether it is sufficient to locate agency in the internal fissures of discourse. [This] runs the risk of what can be called a fetishism of form: the projection of historical agency onto formal abstractions that are anthropomorphized and given a life of their own. Here abstractions become historical actors;

discourse desires, dreams and does the work of colonialism while also ensuring its demise. In the process, social relations between humans appear to metamorphize into structural relations between forms—through a formalist fetishism that effectively elides the messier questions of historical change and social activism.[61]

These concerns have a direct bearing on the relationship between literary forms, forms of socioenvironmental change, and environmental activism. Crucially, how do we as environmental scholars keep questions of political agency and historical change central in order to connect specialist knowledge to broader public worlds in which environmental policy takes shape and within which resistance movements arise? In this book, I have underscored those places where writers, by drawing on literature's testimonial and imaginative capacities, have engaged nonliterary forces for social change. Rather than displacing social agency onto anthropomorphized, idealized forms, I argue that any interest in form must be bound to questions of affiliation, including affiliation between writers and movements for environmental justice.

In addressing slow violence, the environmentalism of the poor, and the role of writer-activists, I have thus sought to integrate reflections on empire, foreign policy, and resistance with questions about aesthetic strategy. It is sometimes argued that ecocriticism's singular contribution to environmental studies ought to be centered on the aesthetic—that an attentiveness to form is the environmental literary scholar's proper bailiwick.[62] But there is a risk in this if the aesthetic gets walled off as a specialist domain, severed from the broader sociopolitical environmental contexts that animate the forms in question. The more exacting challenge, it seems to me, is how to articulate these vital aesthetic concerns to socioenvironmental transformation. Clearly, genre study remains a pertinent component of our inquiries into the complex interface between aesthetic forms and forms of socioenvironmental change. As Wai Chee Dimock and Lawrence Buell have argued succinctly: "the importance of affect in environmental writing highlights the function of genre as a point of transit—a kind of switch mechanism—in the reversible hierarchy between the local and the global."[63] Indeed, some of the most powerful transnational environmental writing, from Sinha and Roy to Munif and Saro-Wiwa, has arisen at those transit points where genre inventively mediates foreign policy, nation-state violence, and local resource rebellions.

Postcolonialism and Superpower Parochialism

The most conceptually ambitious and influential figures within the ecocritical turn have been Buell and Heise, who deserve special credit for the reach and rigor of their innovative work, which has powerfully reshaped the priorities of literary studies and the environmental humanities more broadly. Buell and Heise are both Americanists by expertise and inclination. My background, and hence my approach, is somewhat different; my training is in postcolonial studies and, as such, the 'elsewheres' that fringe their work constitute my intellectual foreground.[64]

From a postcolonial perspective, the most startling feature of environmental literary studies has been its reluctance to engage the environmental repercussions of American foreign policy, particularly in relation to contemporary imperial practices. To be sure, this failing is not restricted to literary studies but has dogged the environmental humanities more broadly. Ramachandra Guha, while applauding the groundbreaking work by American environmental historians, has lamented their tardiness in exploring the transnational fallout of American environmental practices. Similarly, Robert Vitalis, the preeminent historian of U.S.-Saudi petro-politics, has expressed regret that "the U.S. historical profession has not as yet produced any significant tradition of scholarship in American interventionism that is comparable to the 'new social histories' of European imperialism."[65] Indeed, if as Greg Garrard noted in 2004, "the relationship between globalisation and ecocriticism has barely been broached," one should stress that the ecocritical silence around U.S. foreign policy has been especially resounding.[66] Why is it—as I explore in my final chapter—that in American environmental literary studies, transcendental approaches have typically trumped transnational ones?

There are signs that the environmental humanities are beginning to make some tentative headway toward incorporating the impact of U.S. imperialism on the poor in the global South—Vitalis's book *America's Kingdom: Mythmaking on the Saudi Oil Frontier* (2008) is an outstanding instance, as are powerful recent essays by Elizabeth DeLoughrey on the literatures associated with American nuclear colonialism in the Pacific, Susie O'Brien on Native food security, colonialism, and environmental heritage along the U.S-Mexican border, and Pablo Mukherjee's groundbreaking materialist work on Indian environmental literatures.[67] Yet despite such vitally important initiatives, the environmental humanities in the United States remain skewed toward nation-bound scholarship that is at best tangentially international and, even then, seldom engages the environmental fallout of U.S. foreign policy head on. What's at stake is not just disciplinary parochialism but, more broadly, what one might call superpower parochialism, that is, a combination of American insularity and America's power as the preeminent empire of the neoliberal age to rupture the lives and ecosystems of non-Americans, especially the poor, who may live at a geographical remove but who remain intimately vulnerable to the force fields of U.S. foreign policy.

To be sure, the U.S. empire has historically been a variable force, one that is not monolithic but subject to ever-changing internal fracture. The U.S., moreover, has long been—and is increasingly—globalized itself with all the attendant insecurities and inequities that result. However, to argue that the United States is subject to globalization—through, for example, blowback from climate change—does not belie the disproportionate impact that U.S. global ambitions and policies have exerted over socioenvironmental landscapes internationally.

Ecocritics—and literary scholars more broadly—faced with the challenges of thinking through vast differences in spatial and temporal scale commonly frame their analyses in terms of interpenetrating global and local forces. In such analyses cosmopolitanism—as a mode of being linked to particular aesthetic strategies—does much of the bridgework between extremes of scale. What critics have subjected to far less scrutiny is the role of the national-imperial as a mediating force with vast repercussions, above all, for those billions whom Mike Davis calls "the global residuum."[68] Davis's image is a suggestive one, summoning to mind the remaindered humans, the compacted leavings on whom neoliberalism's inequities bear down most heavily. Yet those leavings, despite their aggregated dehumanization in the corporate media, remain animate and often resistant in unexpected ways; indeed, it is from such leavings that grassroots antiglobalization and the environmentalism of the poor have drawn nourishment.[69]

As American writers, scholars, and environmentalists, how can we attend more imaginatively to the outsourced conflicts inflamed by our unsustainable consumerism, by our military adventurism and unsurpassed arms industry, and by the global environmental fallout over the past three decades of American-led neoliberal economic policies? (The immense environmental toll of militarism is particularly burdensome: in 2009, U.S. military expenditure was 46.5 percent of the global total and exceeded by 10 percent the expenditure of the next fourteen highest-ranked countries combined.)[70] How, moreover, can we engage the impact of our outsized consumerism and militarism on the life prospects of people who are elsewhere not just geographically but elsewhere in time, as slow violence seeps long term into ecologies—rural and urban—on which the global poor must depend for generations to come? How, in other words, can we rethink the standard formulation of neoliberalism as internalizing profits and externalizing risks not just in spatial but in temporal terms as well, so that we recognize the full force with which the externalized risks are outsourced to the unborn?

It is a pervasive condition of empires that they affect great swathes of the planet without the empire's populace being aware of that impact—indeed, without being aware that many of the affected places even exist. How many Americans are aware of the continuing socioenvironmental fallout from U.S. militarism and foreign policy decisions made three or four decades ago in, say, Angola or Laos? How many could even place those nation-states on a map? The imperial gap between foreign policy power and on-the-street awareness calls to mind George Lamming's shock, on arriving in Britain in the early 1950s, that most Londoners he met had never heard of his native Barbados and lumped together all Caribbean immigrants as "Jamaicans."[71]

What I call superpower parochialism has been shaped by the myth of American exceptionalism and by a long-standing indifference—in the U.S. educational system and national media—to the foreign, especially foreign history, even when it is deeply enmeshed with U.S. interests. Thus, when considering the representational challenges posed by transnational slow violence, we need to ask what role American indifference to foreign history has played in camouflaging lasting environmental damage inflicted elsewhere. If all empires create acute disparities between global power and global knowledge, how has America's perception of itself as a young, forward-thrusting nation that claims to flourish by looking ahead rather than behind exacerbated the difficulty of socioenvironmental answerability for ongoing slow violence?[72]

Profiting from the asymmetrical relations between a domestically regulated environment and unregulated environments abroad is of course not unique to America. But since World War II, the United States has wielded an unequalled power to bend the global regulatory climate in its favor. As William Finnegan notes regarding the Washington Consensus, "while we make the world safe for multinational corporations, it is by no means clear that they intend to return the favor."[73] The unreturned favor weighs especially heavily on impoverished communities in the global South who must stake their claims to environmental justice in the face of the Bretton Woods institutions (the World Bank, the IMF), the World Trade Organization, and the G8 (now G20) over which the United States has exercised disproportionate influence. That influence has been exercised, as well, through muscular conservation NGOs (the Nature Conservancy, the World Wildlife Fund, and Conservation International prominent among them) that have a long history of disregarding local human relations to the environment in order to implement American- and European-style conservation agendas. Clearly, the beneficiaries of such power asymmetries are not just American but transnational corporations, NGOs, and governments from across the North's rich nations, often working hand-in-fist with authoritarian regimes.

Yet within these resource wars, image, idiom, and narrative are themselves powerful, if unpredictable, resources that regardless of origins can help advance the environmentalism of the poor. As I note in the chapters on Ken Saro-Wiwa and Wangari Maathai, the discourse of environmental justice, borrowed largely from the West (and often through personal exposure to America), is frequently blended with local discursive traditions and, in these melded forms, adaptively redeployed as a strategic resource. Such transnational meldings may prove unstable, but they have become significant forces in the unequal battles waged by the poor as they strive to be seen and heard on an international stage. These hybridized discourses can help afford socioenvironmental struggles an emblematic significance that strengthens their claim on rich-nation media that might otherwise dismiss them as obscurely local conflicts. International attention, in turn, can help afford such movements some protective visibility within their own nation-states (although a backlash of violence may also result). Among those whom Al Gedicks has dubbed global resource rebels, the hybridized, traveling discourse of environmental justice has proven critical in forging both South-South alliances and South-North alliances, not least among those who find themselves pitted against analogous threats—be they giant hydroelectric dams, for example, or toxic tailings.[74]

Moreover, the development of strategic rhetorical common ground, however fragile, has proven critical in attempts to move beyond knee-jerk oppositions counterposing misanthropic rich eco-colonialists against third worlders assumed to be hostile to a narrowly defined environmentalism. By laying claim to the mobile rhetoric of environmental justice, the dispossessed may enhance their prospects of becoming visible, audible agents of globalization from below. It is in the quest for such transnational visibility and audibility that writer-activists may play a critically enabling role.

In cautioning against a narrowing of literary studies that pulls back from the wider world, we need to recognize the radical energies that traditions of postcolonial engagement at their best have encouraged. Debates over the merits and demerits of the term postcolonial are by now quite extended; no value is to be gained from rehearsing them.[75] That said, postcolonial studies at its most incisive remains, it seems to me, an invaluable critical presence in an era of resurgent imperialism, an era in which—sometimes through outright, unregulated plunder, sometimes under camouflage of developmental agendas—a neoliberal order has widened, with ruinous environmental repercussions, the gulf between the expanding classes of the super-rich and our planet's 3 billion ultrapoor. Indeed, the official and informal militarization of resource extraction as well as paramilitary conservation practices in the global South continue to spark or inflame broader conflicts. Such environmentally intensified conflicts become indissociable from the eroded prospects, under neoliberalism, of maintaining sustainable livelihoods, often under marginal conditions. Gargantuan transnational corporations like BP, ExxonMobil, Shell, Freeport McMoran, and Walmart have wised up to the kudos they can gain from greenwashing in the countries of the rich, through high-minded advertisement campaigns, through strategic donations to NGOs and universities, by buying out or intimidating scientists who might testify against the slow violence of their practices, and through rarified talk about being fine stewards of our delicate planet. Meanwhile, back on planet Earth, they persist with their profitable devastation of relatively impoverished, less regulated societies—societies that have little visibility and recognition value in the rich-country corporate media. Such assaults on the livelihoods of the poor are given extra muscle by industry lobbyists who, while greenwashing with one hand, campaign with the other hand to further skew the terms of trade, weakening whatever frail environmental, labor, and human rights, and economic regulations stand between them and a "freer" market. In short, the oil majors and allied transnational corporations are potent, active players in manufacturing the icons and stories that shape popular perception of environmental science and policy.

Against this backdrop, I am leery of the widespread assumption that everything postcolonial studies has enabled can always be assimilated, without loss, to the more ambitious, more contemporary-sounding global studies. The notion of the straight swap—midsized postcolonial for supersized global—is too often accompanied by a blunting of the adversarial edge, the oppositional incisiveness, that has distinguished postcolonial work at its most forceful. World literature studies has become a rich, dynamic field too diverse to characterize simply, but I do feel some concern about how the categorical turn, in literary studies, to world literature often ends up deflecting attention away from the anti-imperial concerns that a materialist postcolonial studies foregrounded. To be sure, we need scholarship and teaching that can address, in transnational terms, territories beyond postcolonialism's conventional reach. But in so doing we should be watchful that surface geographical gains are not marred by political retreat, that neoliberal acts of violence, for example—especially slow violence—are not hastily euphemized as "global flows." In the classroom and beyond, we need to challenge globalization's gung ho cheerleaders. Indeed, the most scintillating work by antiglobalization public intellectuals—Mike Davis, Naomi Klein, Amitava Kumar, Andrew Ross, and Arundhati Roy among them—carries forward postcolonialism's critical energies while moving beyond the field's geographical and analytical limitations.

Among the decisive challenges such critical initiatives face is that of scale: how can we imaginatively and strategically render visible vast force fields of interconnectedness against the attenuating effects of temporal and geographical distance? This is a crucial challenge if we are to generate any sustained understanding of the transnational, intergenerational fallout from slow violence. The task of thinking on such a geographical scale—let alone a temporal one—can seem overwhelming. Indeed, Wendell Berry has warned against the potentially debilitating effects of such large-scale approaches: "The adjective 'planetary' describes a problem in such a way that it cannot be solved . . . The problems, if we describe them accurately, are all private and small."[76] I would argue, however, that although advocating personal environmental responsibility is essential, to shrink solutions to the level of the private and the small is evasive, even if it does constructively enhance one's sense of agency. Planetary problems—and transnational, national, and regional ones—cannot simply be resolved by the aggregated actions of responsible individuals. Institutional actions (and institutionalized inaction) have a profound impact on environmental outcomes, most blatantly in relation to climate change, which no collectivized ethical behavior can combat without backing from well-implemented transnational accords.

Slow Violence and the Production of Doubt

The forces of inaction have deep pockets. Environmental activists face well-funded, well-organized interests that invest heavily in manufacturing and sustaining a culture of doubt around the science of slow violence, thereby postponing policies that would help rein in the long-term impacts of climate change in particular. A coalition of Big Oil, Big Coal, and Big Tobacco, led by ExxonMobil and Phillip Morris, has amassed an army of doubt-disseminators: lobbyists, political consultants, media plutocrats like Rupert Murdoch, right-wing think tanks, fake citizens' groups on Facebook, scholarly reviewers of climate science written by non climate scientists, pseudo-scientific websites, university departments endowed to demonstrate conclusions friendly to Big Oil, Big Coal, and Big Tobacco and to sponsor uncertainty around climate change and, in the case of tobacco, uncertainty about the carcinogenic risks of second hand smoke.[77]

Despite the overwhelming, virtually unanimous, consensus among climate scientists that climate change is happening, is human-induced, is accelerating, and will have catastrophic consequences for human and much nonhuman life on earth, all the misnamed 'denialists' need do is keep ensuring that, in the public's mind, the jury remains permanently out, so that irresolution rules. This is the point underscored by a leaked memo from political consultant, Frank Luntz distributed to Republican activists during George W. Bush's presidency: "Should the public come to believe that the scientific issues are settled, their views about global warming will change accordingly. Therefore, you need to continue to make the lack of scientific certainty a primary issue in the debate."[78] Or, to cite another memo: "Doubt is our product since it is the best means of competing with the 'body of fact' that exists in the mind of the general public. It is also the means of establishing a controversy."[79] Controversy, in turn, plays into the media's standard for-and-against formula for debate, even if that binary skews the consensus radically; even if, as in the case of anthropogenic climate change, 3,000 climate scientists confirm that it is happening and none deny it. The against position thus typically devolves to a right-wing activist with no peer-reviewed climate change publications.

In "Concerning Violence," the opening chapter of *The Wretched of the Earth*, Fanon writes of the role played under capitalism by an army of cultural "bewilderers."[80] The spread of slow violence in our own times has been exacerbated by a lavishly funded army of new bewilderers, those doubt producers and doubt disseminators whose job it is to maintain populist levels of uncertainty sufficient to guarantee inaction. We thus need to recognize that slow violence involves more than a perceptual problem created by the gap between destructive policies or practices and their deferred, invisible consequences. For in addition, slow violence provides prevaricative cover for the forces that have the most to profit from inaction: under cover of deferred consequences, these energetic new bewilderers literally buy time. For the new bewilderers, led by Big Oil and Big Coal, doubt is more than a state of mind—it's a bankable product. In this context, we should acknowledge the role played by a raft of public science writers who are writer-activists in their own way, figures like James Hoggan, Elizabeth Kolbert, Naomi Oreskes, Erik Conway, Andrew Rowell, Tim Flannery, David Michaels, and the incomparable George Monbiot who have followed the money and worked industriously to render visible the clandestine networks that finance doubt.[81]

Of Vampire Squids and Resource Rebels

In 2009, amidst the global economic crash, Matt Taibbi memorably depicted Goldman Sachs as a "great vampire squid wrapped around the face of humanity, relentlessly jamming its blood funnel into anything that smells like money."[82] Within a year his deepwater image of life-sucking avarice would seem an uncanny foreshadowing of petroleum giant BP.

Indeed, Taibbi's vampire squid achieved such popular resonance, I would suggest, because it gave emotional definition to an age, over and above the tentacular reach of any specific transnational corporation. An era of imperial overreach has brought to crisis a Washington Consensus ideology premised on globalizing the "free market" through militarization, privatization, deregulation, optional corporate self-policing, the undertaxation of the super wealthy, ever-more arcane financial practices, and a widening divide separating the gated über-rich from the unhoused ultrapoor within and between nations.

Together these practices have heightened capitalism's innate tendency to abstract in order to extract, intensifying the distancing mechanisms that make the sources of environmental violence harder to track and multinational environmental answerability harder to impose. Such distancing mechanisms include the rhetorical gulf between development as a grand planetary dream premised on growth-driven consumption and its socioenvironmental fallout; the geographical distance between market forces as, to an almost occult degree, production has become disaggregated from consumption; and the temporal distance between short-lived actions and long-lived consequences, as gradual casualties are spread across a protracted aftermath, during which the memory and the body count of slow violence are diffused—and defused—by time.

Yet memory loss is unevenly inhabited. Whether through sustained activism or more sporadic protests, resource rebels and the environmentally disenfranchised have mobilized repeatedly against memory loss, refusing to see their long-term livelihoods abstracted into oblivion, be it through state violence, transnational corporate rapacity, or some combination of the two. The resource rebels who rise up (or dig in for the long haul) express ambitions that may be difficult to achieve but, in the scheme of things, are typically not grand: some shelter from the uncertainties of hunger; some basic honoring of established patterns of agroforestry, fishing, hunting, planting, and harvesting; access to clean water; some prospects for their children; some respect for the cultural (and therefore environmental) presence of the guiding dead. And, if one accepts as a given that traditions are always mutable, resource rebels seek some active participation in the speed and character of cultural change. Failing all that, the rebels may seek compensation directed not at the nation at large (always an unequal abstraction) but at those most intimately affected by the defacement of the living land by the boardrooms of faceless profiteers.

The fraught issue of compensation connects directly with the infrastructural failures of the state: insurrectionary anger is repeatedly stoked when a community experiences technological modernization as extractive theft without service delivery. Under such circumstances, visible reminders of theft through modernity's infrastructural invasions—by oil pipelines or massive hydroelectric dams or toxic tailings from mines—foment rage at life-threatening environmental degradation combined with the state's failure to provide life-enabling public works.[83] Often, as a community contends with attritional assaults on its ecological networks, it isn't granted equitable access (or any access at all) to modernity's basic infrastructural networks—piped clean water, a sewage system, an electric grid, a public transport grid, or schools—utilities that might open up alternatives to destitution. Such communities, ecologically dispossessed without being empowered via infrastructure, are ripe for revolt. Like those Niger Delta villages where children for decades had no access to electricity for studying at night, while above their communities Shell's gas flares created toxic nocturnal illumination. Too dark for education, too bright for sleep: modernity's false dawn.

Writers who align themselves with resource rebellions may help render decipherable the illegible distance between a far-off neoliberal ideology and its long-lasting local fallout. Such writers may serve as *portes-paroles* in an economic order premised on acute inequities in portability—of commodities, factories, jobs, people, and the environment itself. Writer-activists may thereby help expose injustices arising from the global freedom of movement afforded powerful corporations and the Bretton Woods institutions, while swathes of humanity are so ecologically undermined that they are abandoned to the plight of the stationary displaced. Whether as part-instigators or as amplifiers, writer-activists can strive to advance the causes of those who confront turbo-capitalism's assaults on the resources that shape their survival. In confrontations between such typically unequal forces, determined hope is mixed with what John Berger, in the spirit of Antonio Gramsci, has called "undefeated despair."[84]

While honoring the writer's role, I wish to do so without glamorizing it. This role requires incessant compromise and incessant reinvention, particularly given the rapid changes in the technological and geopolitical climate in which writers must act. I should note here that the events I engage in this book are clustered in the period from the early 1980s through the late-1990s—in what one might call neoliberalism's near present.[85] From the beginnings of the Reagan-Thatcher era through the Bhopal disaster, the collapse of communism and apartheid, the first Gulf War, the rise of the Save the Narmada Movement in India, the International Campaign for Justice in Bhopal, Delta's Movement for the Survival of the Ogoni People in Nigeria, Kenya's Green Belt Movement, to Acción Ecológica in the Ecuadorian Amazon, the purview of *Slow Violence* predates two particularly significant environmental developments. First, the full-blown ascent of Chinese authoritarian capitalism, ushering in the Chimerican age as, through entangled rivalry, mutual dependence, and mutual mistrust, an emboldened China has joined an overstretched America as a global force in annexing—and carting off—the very conditions of life. We see this dramatically, for instance, in the 3-million-acre swathe of equatorial forest in the Democratic Republic of Congo that China has bought for a pittance to log and, once logged, has dedicated to monocultural palm oil production, thereby displacing and immiserating the forest's inhabitants. This is all integral to the second scramble for Africa, as the continent's resource maps are redrawn and its riches carved up among Chinese, American, European, Australian, and South African corporations typically working in cahoots with unelected officials or regional brigands. Africa may contain some of the most acute cases of such rampant disregard for socioenvironmental survival in the Chimerican age, but it is far from alone.

Alongside this geopolitical shift we are witnessing the most profound changes in centuries to the technological climate within which writer-activists must operate. In the era on which I focus, "text" was not yet a standard verb. Since then, proliferating nonprint platforms, an upsurge in new media networks, and digital immediacy have transformed the technological milieu within which oppression is inflicted and dissidence expressed—and within which speed is experienced. Among the writers I consider, Indra Sinha is by a long measure the most digitally attuned. His Bhopal novel, *Animal's People*, straddles two eras, as he reconfigures a cold-war event for a twenty-first century obsessed with virtual networks and biopolitics. Triggered by the 1984 Union Carbide disaster and the environmental justice movement that rose from its ashes, Sinha's 2007 fiction can be read as an experiment in linking the protest novel to digitally networked dissent.[86] Indeed, the public life of *Animal's People* as a novel has been powerfully shaped by Sinha's mobile, multimedia approach: on his blog and Web site, for example, he mixes non-fictional testimony from Bhopal survivors with a sardonic visual-and-verbal fantasia of a poisoned city trying to rebrand itself as a tourist paradise.

If the quarter-century lag between the Union Carbide explosion and *Animal People's* appearance marks a shift from predigital to digital activism, the lag also allows Sinha to challenge the conventions of what constitutes a catastrophic event. For the explosion itself plays a relatively minor role in the novel; instead, Sinha focuses on the less obviously eventful aftermath, the slow violence that, by the novel's end, comes to be recognized as the event itself, a violence that has yet to run its course. It is to this novel and Bhopal that I now turn.

I

Slow Violence, Neoliberalism, and the Environmental Picaresque

It is only right, to my mind, that things so remarkable, which happen to have remained unheard and unseen until now, should be brought to the attention of many and not lie buried in the sepulcher of oblivion.

—Anonymous, *Lazarillo de Tormes*

A quarter century ago, Raymond Williams called for more novels that attend to "the close living substance" of the local while simultaneously tracing the "occluded relationships"—the vast transnational economic pressures, the labor and commodity dynamics—that invisibly shape the local.[1] To hazard such novels poses imaginative challenges of a kind that writers content to create what Williams termed "enclosed fictions" need never face, among them the challenge of rendering visible occluded, sprawling webs of interconnectedness. In our age of expanding and accelerating globalization, this particular imaginative difficulty has been cast primarily in spatial terms, as exemplified by John Berger's pronouncement, famously cited in Edward Soja's *Postmodern Geographies*: "Prophecy now involves a geographical rather than a historical projection; it is space and not time that hides consequences from us. To prophesy today it is only necessary to know men [and women] as they are throughout the world in all their inequality."[2]

Yet the legitimate urgency of spatial prophecy should not, in turn, distract us from the critical task—especially for environmental writers— of finding imaginative forms that expose the temporal dissociations that permeate the age of neoliberal globalization. To this end, *Animal's People*, Indra Sinha's fictional reworking of the Bhopal disaster, offers a powerful instance of a writer dramatizing the occluded relationships of transnational space together with time's occlusions. Sinha's novel stands (to adapt Williams's phrase) as a work of "militant particularism," yet it discloses through that radical particularity temporal and spatial webs of violence on a vast scale.[3] Sinha's approach to the aftermath of the catastrophic gas leak at Union Carbide's Bhopal factory in December 1984 throws into relief a political violence both intimate and distant, unfolding over time and space on a variety of scales, from the cellular to the transnational, the corporeal to the global corporate. *Animal's People* can be read as a novel of risk relocation, not just in Susan Cutter's spatial sense but across time as well, for the transnational off-loading of risk from a privileged community to an impoverished one changes the temporal topography of fear in the long term.

The power of *Animal's People* flows largely from Sinha's single-handed invention of the environmental picaresque.[4] By creatively adapting picaresque conventions to our age, Sinha probes the underbelly of neoliberal globalization from the vantage point of an indigent social outcast. His novel gives focus to three of the defining characteristics of the contemporary neoliberal order: first, the widening chasm—within and between nations—that separates the megarich from the destitute; second, the attendant burden of unsustainable ecological degradation that impacts the health and livelihood of the poor most directly; and third, the way powerful transnational corporations exploit under cover of a free market ideology the lopsided universe of deregulation, whereby laws and loopholes are selectively applied in a marketplace a lot freer for some societies and classes than for others.

A neoliberal ideology that erodes national sovereignty and turns answerability into a bewildering transnational maze makes it easier for global corporations like Union Carbide to sustain an evasive geopolitics of deferral in matters of environmental injury, remediation, and redress. Thus, among the many merits of Sinha's novel is the way it gives imaginative definition to the occluded relationships that result both from slow violence and from the geographies of concealment in a neoliberal age.

Slow Violence, Chernobyl, and Environmental Time

Maintaining a media focus on slow violence poses acute challenges, not only because it is spectacle deficient, but also because the fallout's impact may range from the cellular to the transnational and (depending on the specific character of the chemical or radiological hazard) may stretch beyond the horizon of imaginable time. The contested science of damage further compounds the challenge, as varied scientific methodologies may be mobilized to demonstrate or discount etiologies, creating rival regimes of truth, manipulable by political and economic interests. Moreover, the official dimensions of the contaminated zone may shrink or dilate depending on which political forces and which research methodologies achieve the upper hand. What emerges, then, is a contest over the administration of difference between those who gain official recognition as sufferers and those dismissed as nonsufferers because their narratives of injury are deemed to fail the prevailing politico-scientific logic of causation; or for that matter, because they lack the political contacts to gain admission to the inner circle of certified sufferers and thus to potential compensation. These unstable, complex procedures—and hierarchies—of toxic recognition may create novel forms of biological citizenship, as in the long aftermaths of the 1984 Bhopal disaster and the 1986 Chernobyl explosion.[5]

The varieties of biological citizenship that emerged in the aftermaths of Bhopal and Chernobyl were distinct in certain ways, as were the media responses. Chernobyl received far more sustained attention in the Western media for several reasons. First, because of Chernobyl's proximity to Western Europe, it was perceived as an ongoing transnational threat to "us" rather than a purely national threat that could be imaginatively contained as an Indian problem, over there among the faceless poor of the third world. Moreover, during the rise of Reagan's and Thatcher's neoliberal orders, Chernobyl could be directly assimilated to the violent threat that communism posed to the West, a threat that increased calls for heightened militarization and, ironically, for further corporate and environmental deregulation in the name of free-market forces. Bhopal, by contrast, was easier to dissociate from narratives of global violence dominated by a communist/anticommunist plotline, thus obscuring the free-market double standards that allowed Western companies to operate with violent, fatal impunity in the global South. Indeed, Warren Anderson (then Union Carbide's chairman), company lawyers, and most of America's corporate media argued in concert that blame for the disaster was local not transnational in character, ignoring the fact that in the run up to the disaster, the parent company had slashed safety procedures and supervisory staff in an effort to staunch hemorrhaging profits.[6]

In reading *Animal's People* as, among other things, an exposé of these neoliberal double standards, we can recognize Khaupfur as both specific and nonspecific, a fictional stand-in for Bhopal, but also a synecdoche for a web of poisoned communities spread out across the global South: "The book could have been set anywhere where the chemical industry has destroyed people's lives," Sinha observes. "I had considered calling the city Receio and setting it in Brazil. It could just as easily have been set in Central or South America, West Africa or the Philippines."[7]

Chernobyl occurred three years before the Soviet Union's dissolution in 1989, which was also the year John Williamson coined the term "the Washington Consensus" to describe the prevailing ideology that united the World Bank, the IMF, and the U.S. Treasury Department around the preconditions for "development aid" to nations in the global South.[8] The developmentalist, neoliberal ideology of the Washington Consensus became a crucial foreign policy wing of what George Soros would term "market fundamentalism," a broad crusade that would continue to gather force amid the postcommunist ideological uncertainty through demands for deregulation, privatization, and the hacking back of government social programs and safety nets. It was in this neoliberal context that, ultimately, the ailing survivors of both Bhopal and Chernobyl would find themselves sinking or swimming.

From a temporal perspective, the Chernobyl disaster of April 26, 1986, was distinguished by an initial catastrophic security lapse followed by a series of time lapses. The initial catastrophe was spectacular but, in media terms, deferred: eighteen days passed before Mikhail Gorbachev appeared on TV to acknowledge the explosion.[9] Had the Soviet government dispensed nonradioactive iodine pills during that lost time, it could have averted the epidemic of thyroid cancers that only began, en masse, four years later at the time of the breakup of the Soviet Union and the emergence of a Ukraine that was officially independent yet bound in environmental, epidemiological, and consequently economic terms to the Soviet-era nuclear disaster.

The different timelines of mutation—international, intranational, intergenerational, bureaucratic, and somatic—are dizzying even to attempt to map. The prevailing winds carried the radiation plume north over Belarus, across eastern, western, and northern Europe, and beyond. Over time, through toxic drift, the national epicenter of the catastrophe would shift so that Belarus, not Ukraine, would become the country most pervasively polluted.[10] In both countries, radiochemical poisoning coursed through air, water, soil, crops, meat, and mother's milk at divergent speeds. Some symptoms manifested themselves relatively quickly, others appeared most dramatically among children born a decade or more after the disaster struck. The stratified slow violence of the fallout was compounded by the tardiness of the Soviet authorities, whose reflex response was foot-dragging, equivocation, and denial.

Adriana Petryna's anthropological work on post-Soviet Ukraine persuasively demonstrates the complex entanglements between environmental fallout and the socioeconomic fallout of being classified as a sufferer or nonsufferer. Compensation for Chernobyl injuries that rendered a citizen an official sufferer might be a mere $5 per month. But after Washington Consensus-style market liberalization was imposed on Ukraine in 1992, hyperinflation and mass unemployment followed, creating a sudden chasm between economic survivors and economic casualties.[11] In this neoliberal context, official recognition as a Chernobyl sufferer-survivor—and the modest government compensation that ensued—could make the difference between subsistence and starvation for a whole family.[12] The onus of proof fell on Ukrainians to develop, over time, an intimate expertise that was both bodily and bureaucratic. Which symptoms counted and which were discounted by the state? What work history in which officially recognized affected areas (and for how long) would strengthen one's claim for the imprimatur of sufferer? Which doctors, lawyers, and bureaucrats could accelerate one's efforts to enter that inner circle? How could one meet such influential people? Did they need to be bribed?

The ground rules for being counted and discounted kept changing. Even the boundaries of the pollution zones were unstable, shrinking and dilating through a mixture of bureaucratic caprice, economic expediency, and slippery science. So the system required energetic, up-to-date pro-activism on the part of Ukraine's biocitizens as they scrambled to avoid plummeting into economic free fall. A key survival strategy was to fit their life stories, their self-narrations, into the limited generic narratives of suffering that possessed a state mandate from which a small stream of compensation might flow. New categories of identity emerged that—in other societies, in other times—might have remained confined to the domain of private medical records. Instead, a Ukrainian might introduce herself, position herself publicly, by announcing, "I am a mother of a child who is a sufferer. I am an evacuee from Zone Two. My husband is a Chernobyl worker, Category One."[13]

Foreign Burdens: Chernobyl, Bhopal, and *Animal's People*

Within ten days of the Chernobyl explosion, the Soviet authorities had mobilized thousands of Ukrainian coal miners to help with remediation work at the disaster site. One of them, Dmytro, who labored at the site for a month, was later afflicted with pulmonary, cerebral, and cardiac disorders and found to have chromosomal aberrations. In an interview, he portrayed his body's radiation load as a "foreign burden."[14] He was referring—as his interviewer notes—to the sense of harboring an alien, unnatural, and disquieting force within.

But the miner's choice of phrase deserves a second parsing, one directly pertinent to my reading of *Animal's People*. Dmytro had been saddled, I would argue, with a "foreign burden" not just in a somatic but in a geo-temporal sense as well: his post–Soviet Ukrainian body remained under occupation by a Soviet-era catastrophe. For in the case of Chernobyl, not only did the radiological toxicity travel across the national border, but (as the Soviet Union fragmented) the national border traveled across the toxicity. The Ukrainian body politic, though politically autonomous, remained environmentally and epidemiologically dominated by the "foreign burden" of a ghosted country, by a Soviet past that (as Faulkner would have it) was not even past. Through the workings of slow violence across environmental

time, Ukraine's sovereignty was compromised. If the Ukrainian body politic at large was afflicted with the burden of involuntary macro memory,
mutagenic chromosomes at the micro level sustained a Soviet heritage that
prompted Dmytro (and many compatriots) to refuse to reproduce for fear of
a future burdened by an afflicted Ukrainian child.

The concept of the foreign burden offers a productive prism through
which to approach Sinha's novelistic response to the Union Carbide disaster when, one early December night, a cloud of methyl isocyanate gas (in
combination with other toxins) leaked from the company's pesticide factory
in Bhopal. Estimates of those killed immediately vary wildly, from 4,000
to 15,000 people. In the years that followed, scores of thousands of deaths
and life-threatening disabilities were linked to exposure to the gas cloud. By
some estimates, 100,000 residents continue to be afflicted.[15]

Although *Animal's People* is set twenty years after the disaster, the novel
dramatizes the illusion of the singular event: from a narrative perspective,
the events—like the poisons themselves—are suspended in medias res, in a
state of environmental, epidemiological, political, and legal irresolution. If
the unfolding of slow violence across environmental time is typically managed through powerful strategies of distantiation, in Sinha's novel those distancing strategies depend primarily, in geographical terms, on transnational
corporate distance and, in temporal terms, on both the slow emergence of
morbidity and on legal procrastination, which provide prevaricative cover
for the CEOs who wish to exploit time to defuse the claims of the afflicted.
Khaufpur (Sinha's fictional Bhopal) is the "world capital of fucked lungs"; it
is also a place of interminable trials—bodily and legal.[16]

For twenty years the immiserated people of Khaufpur have been trying
to bring the American CEOs of the corporation responsible—named simply as the "Kampani"—to stand trial in India. Thirteen judges have come
and gone in successive trials, but the spectral Kampani bosses keep failing
to materialize, maintaining their oceanic distance from a city infiltrated
and haunted by Kampani poisons. Playing for time, the Kampani resorts
to legal chicanery, political bribery, and backroom deals with India's Minister for Poison Affairs and his colleagues. What emerges, then, is a contest
between the tenacity of corporeal memory and the corrosive power, over
time and space, of corporate amnesia emboldened by a neoliberal regime
of deregulation.

[51]

If Chernobyl's "foreign burden" is an inheritance from an evaporated empire, we may read Khaufpur's burden rather differently as the weight of absentee corporate colonialism, whereby transnational companies internalize profits and externalize risks, particularly in impoverished regions of the global South. However, as a novelist, Sinha cannot afford to be this explicitly polemical. An observation by the Irish writer Eavan Boland is pertinent to the novelistic challenges Sinha must negotiate: "If the voice of a character in a fiction speaks too clearly with the anger and hindsight of an ethical view of history, then the voice may be made louder by argument but grow less convincing through being less imagined. Then both humanity and history can be sentimentalized."[17] Because novels about slow violence suffer from a drama deficit, they risk resorting to sentimentality and political moralizing as substitutes for arresting spectacle and narrative tension. For these reasons some critics, like Anthony Lane, have gone so far as to assert that "eco-drama . . . is a contradiction in terms."[18]

Sinha astutely negotiates this ethical and dramatic minefield without compromising his novel's political energies. He does so by devising a narrator who is at best ambivalent toward the pursuit of justice, yet whose physical form serves as a bodily shorthand for Khaufpur's transnational plight. Through a literal twist of fate—a toxic corkscrewing of his spine—Animal morphed at the age of six from an upright boy into a creature reduced to going around on all fours.[19] When four-footed Animal (now nineteen) transports an ailing child on his back, his posture is precisely that of a beast of burden. Thus the symbolic economy of Animal's body affords Sinha an implicit yet unforgettable image of a body politic literally bent double beneath the weight of the poisoned city's foreign load.

By making an occluded economic relationship physically manifest through his narrator's body, Sinha thus ingeniously resolves the dilemma that Williams posed: how to give a novel a local materiality while exposing the web of transnational forces that permeate and shape the local. In the process, Sinha engages a temporal question that Williams did not specifically address: how do you dramatize the costs of uneven development when their delayed effects are intimate but their genesis is far-off in time?

Animal's People stages a simultaneous inquiry into the border zones between human and animal and the economic boundaries between rich and poor, the ever-deepening, dehumanizing chasm that divides those who can act with impunity and those who have no choice but to inhabit intimately, over the long term, the physical and environmental fallout of actions undertaken by distant, shadowy economic overlords. What does it mean, the novel asks, to belong to the same species—in biological, existential, ethical, and economic terms?

Figure 2 Photograph of "Animal" sculpture. Reproduced by permission of the artist and photographer, Eleanor Stride.

[53]

Orphaned when the Kampani explosion killed both his parents, Animal has little truck with the niceties of belonging. His familial isolation, physical difference, and moral disgust at human inhumanity combine to set him apart. Despite his singularity, however, Animal also serves as a symbolic condensation of the vast army of the economically orphaned, abandoned to their fate by the merciless logic of the neoliberal marketplace.

Animal is a foundling who has morphed into a posthuman changeling, a one-of-a-kind creature spawned by a kind of chemical autochthony. Marooned in the present, Animal views himself as a four-footed species without precedent or the prospect of progeny, the alpha and omega of his kind. We can read him as a new beginning, which (in keeping with the novel's apocalyptic tenor) doubles as the end of time.

Animal has forgotten his childhood human name: it's as remote, as inaccessible as his city's culturally rich, prelapsarian, pretoxic past. From the moment children at the orphanage taunt him for walking like an animal, he embraces the name of his alienation and abasement, scoffing at those, like Zafar (the slum's chief anti-Kampani activist), who suggest that he is not a beast just an "especially abled" human.[20] The catastrophe that has befallen Khaufpur, imposing on the city a radically changed culture of nature, has in the process converted Animal into a figure who insists, "I've no choice but to be unnatural."[21]

His refusal of the natural is redolent of the stance adopted by Chernobyl's self-declared "biorobots" who, through hazardous exposure, inhabited a related gray zone between the human and the posthuman.[22] Four months after the initial Chernobyl explosion, the Soviet authorities sent in robots to remove radioactive debris; when off-the-charts radiation levels rendered the robots dysfunctional, young men were conscripted to replace them. The men recognized they were being treated not as human employees but as "biological resources to be used and thrown out. . . . [S]lated for bio-robotic death."[23] As the Ukrainian director of the Ministry of Health declared, "no one has ever defined the value of a human here."[24] In this context, it is understandable that the young men would insist on their indeterminate status, not as human citizens, but as biorobots destined for the scrap heap of expendable parts. Like Animal, whose humanity was subject to a hostile foreign takeover, the biorobots exemplified the dissolution of the boundaries of their humanity through the slow, corrosive violence of environmental catastrophe.

The Environmental Picaresque,
Abjection, and the Urban Poor

Animal joins a long line of picaros: canny, scheming social outliers governed by unruly appetites, potty-mouthed and scatalogically obsessed, often orphaned outcasts who, drawn from polite society's vast impoverished margins, survive by parasitism and by their wits. The picaro is the abject from which the body and the body politic cannot part. Stigmatized as aberrant and filthy, the picaro embodies everything the socially remote privileged classes, with their ornate rhetoric and social etiquette, seek to contain, repress, and eject. But the picaro keeps resurfacing as a discomfiting reminder of the limits to the social barriers and the studied amnesia that elite society strives to uphold.[25] Julia Kristeva's formulation of the abject thus offers a productive analytic frame for *Animal's People*, a picaresque novel about the dissociative rituals of a neoliberal transnationalism determined to disown, across time and space, the toxic repercussions innate to its practices, repercussions that will return to haunt it.[26]

Sinha's poisoned picaro embodies—at a somatic and a transnational level—the conditions under which, in Kristeva's terms, "the subject finds the impossible within."[27] The unsettling confrontation with the abject entails facing "those fragile states where man strays on the territories of animal."[28] This confrontation with stray territory results in repeated efforts to cast out the threatening traces of animalism from the culture. If we associate abjection with the rupturing of systemic order and sealed identity from within, then Sinha has created in his picaresque Animal a potent compression of disturbing, porous ambiguity, a figure whose leakiness confounds the borders between the human and the nonhuman as well as the borders between the national and the foreign. His presence exposes the limits of disownership: he is an irrepressible, abject reminder of that from which the Kampani—however far off it may seem—can never fully part.

Since the Spanish Golden Age, the picaresque has posed questions about the class and gender politics of crime, contrasting the narrator's peccadilloes with the weightier crimes that society's overlords commit and from which they are structurally exonerated. This passion for interrogating the hypocrisies of criminality—above all, the inequitable definitions of crime—makes the picaresque a promising fit with the priorities of the environmental justice movement. Sinha, in repurposing the picaresque, brings into brilliant focus the environmental, epidemiological, and economic fallout of the terrors that transnational neoliberal lawlessness dispenses in cahoots with corrupt, legally immune local politicians.

The picaresque emerged between 1550 and 1559 in the Spanish Golden Age as a countergenre, a reminder that, for all the infusion into Spain of transatlantic imperial wealth, the great majority of Spaniards remained deeply poor.[29] The genre—most famously in *Lazarillo de Tormes*—was countergeneric in tone as well, rich in bawdy street argot that clattered, in subversive counterpoint, against Spanish as imperial language and against the attendant ascendancy of classical literary forms. The picaresque thus inserted itself into a historical moment when a chasm was opening between the exalted, gluttonous classes with their linguistic refinements and perfumed pretensions and the indigent masses for whom life was an hourly scramble for survival. As in our own age of ballooning CEO golden parachutes soaring above a planet of the slums, the picaro achieves a particular potency as a marginal literary figure, a seldom-heard voice, who belongs nonetheless to the statistical majority. His or her existence depends on quick-witted improvisation coupled to expedient parasitism. As such, the picaro survives, in Michel Serres's fine phrase, as a "tactician of the quotidian."[30]

Within the genre's comedic arc, the picaro typically pursues a quest of upward mobility; in Animal's case that quest becomes an elaborate pun subverting any ethical correlation between moral and physical erectness.[31] He is witheringly dismissive of the artistry with which humans—most notably those in power—perform spectacles of rectitude. From his vantage point on humanity, Homo looks neither *sapiens* nor *erectus*, but a morally debased species whose uprightness is mostly posturing. Animal's bent posture, by contrast, embodies a crushing neoliberal, transnational economic relationship and also marks him as a literal "lowlife," a social and anatomical outlier whose physical form externalizes the slow violence, the unhurried metastases coursing through the community. His penumbral human/posthuman identity places a constant strain on the idea of limits (environmental, economic, ethical, and biological).[32] In refusing the tainted designation "human," Animal remains for most of the novel defiantly otherwise. What one witnesses, then, is Sinha adaptively carrying forward what Giancarlo Maiorino has termed "the antihumanist core of the picaresque."[33]

Together, the antihumanist and parodic strains that permeate the picaresque help Sinha ward off three threats to the dynamism of fictional eco-drama: predictability, sentimentality, and a political outrage or self-righteousness that supplants depth of character. Animal, like most picaros, is not expressly political; he positions himself at an angle to Khaupfur's environmental justice movement and for much of the novel is more troubled by his tenacious virginity than by the toxic tenacity of his environment. Yet, as a product of that environment and as a denizen of the community of the poisoned abject, Animal poses profound questions about the limits and value of the human. He does so, however, not from some concern with abstract justice but from inside the highly unpredictable business of holding body and soul together at street level.

Paradoxically, Animal appears as unique but not exceptional: in his singularity he serves as a synecdoche for the spectrum of mutations to which Khaufpuris have been subjected over time, ranging from the celebrated singer with now-ravaged lungs to the chatty Kha-in-a-jar, a double-headed bottled fetus that envies Animal his external, unbottled freedoms.[34] Unmistakably hypervisible, Animal is also by turns undetectable, passing beneath human eye level in a crowd, allowing him to slip porously, in the picaresque manner, between different social strata.

But there are spatial limits to how far he can venture in his infiltrations and exposes. In a masterstroke, Sinha's deploys Animal's physical form as not just a consequence but a condensation of occluded transnational economic relations. His picaro is literally outlandish, his twisted body the physical manifestation of extraterritorial, offshore capitalist practices. The novel tracks the economics of a transnational regime of contamination by posing questions about the limits to bodily integrity, in both the individual and the nation-state. The Kampani's factory is located yet dislocated, inside India geographically yet elusively afloat, outside the reach (or at least the application) of Indian law. A novel narrated by a human animal—"a beastly boy"— bent out of shape by his foreign load simultaneously questions other forms of mutability, not least the plasticity of ownership, how foreign corporate practices inside India can be owned (for short-term profit) and disowned (for long-term consequences to environmental and human health).[35] To return this dissociative economic logic to a somatic language, we come to see the Kampani as both incorporated and unincorporated into the national body. The Kampani is so compendious, so omnipresent in its effects yet so visibly absent that, at one point, Zafar (leader of Khaufpur's campaign for justice) declares the Kampani's faceless power to be eternal. In that despairing moment, we're given a fused nightmare of neoliberal corporate immunity and corporate immortality.

The picaresque proves uncannily effective at dramatizing another critical dimension to the environmentalism of the urban poor—their relationship to time. Like the picaro, the environmentally embattled slum dwellers are hell-bent on immediate survival, improvising from day to day, from hour to hour. Their temporal element is "now o'clock," their lives subject to the fickle tyranny of the eternal today.[36] Yet collectively, the city's environmentally afflicted are bound in complex ways to past and future through the metamorphoses wrought by toxicity, the pursuit of social justice, and their collective relationship to apocalyptic time. The environmental picaresque of *Animal's People* pivots on two apocalypses: the horrors of "that night" when the interminable narrative of poisoning began and the certainty that over the long haul, as the activist Zafar insists, the poor possess "the power of zero."[37] Global geopolitics may in the short term be skewed against them, but time is on their side: the Kampani has everything to fear from those with nothing to lose. Animal insists as much in the novel's closing lines: "All things pass, but the poor remain. We are the people of the Apokalis. Tomorrow there will be more of us."[38] Animal's final words uncannily echo the end of *Planet of the Slums*, Mike Davis's powerful account of the contemporary neoliberal shantytown world from which, implicitly, the contemporary picaro emerges. "If the empire can deploy Orwellian technologies of repression," Davis warns, "its outcasts have the gods of chaos on their side."[39]

Reflecting on Hurricane Katrina, Michael Eric Dyson writes memorably of "the color of disaster" as integral to the "neoliberal neglect" that has plagued American politics for over twenty years.[40] In keeping with Dyson's stance, we can refuse the unsustainable divide between human disasters (like Bhopal and Chernobyl) and natural ones (like Katrina), dissociating ourselves, for example, from former president George W. Bush's insistence that "the storm didn't discriminate and neither will the recovery effort."[41]

Discrimination predates disaster: in failures to maintain protective infra-structures, failures at pre-emergency hazard mitigation, failures to main-tain infrastructure, failures to organize evacuation plans for those who lack private transport, all of which make the poor and racial minorities dis-proportionately vulnerable to catastrophe. As investigative Indian report-ers, writing for publications like the *Hindustan Times* and *Statesmen* were quick to reveal, the Union Carbide disaster was preceded by a long history of structural neglect and a reckless flouting of elementary safety measures.[42]

If we project Dyson's national "color of disaster" onto a transnational screen, his phrase can be seen—like Animal's apocalyptic final words—to point backward to global crimes of environmental racism (that treat cer-tain communities as more expendable than others) and forward as a global portent. The poor of the world are the uncontainable color of a future that cannot be held in check. Yet there is another way to read that future, as a wager—however idealistic—to those in power to embrace the project of more equitable risk distribution, within the nation and beyond. The South African writer Njabulo Ndebele puts this case most forcefully:

> We are all familiar with the global sanctity of the white body. Wherever the white body is violated in the world, severe retribu-tions follow somehow for the perpetrators if they are non-white, regardless of the social status of the white body. The white body is inviolable, and that inviolability is in direct proportion to the vul-nerability of the black body. This leads me to think that if South African whiteness is a beneficiary of the protectiveness assured by international whiteness, it has an opportunity to write a new chapter in world history. . . . Putting itself at risk, it will have to declare that it is home now, sharing in the vulnerability of other compatriot bodies. South African whiteness will declare that its dignity is inseparable from the dignity of black bodies.[43]

Three points are worth underscoring here. First, that international white-ness provides a second shield for national whiteness, a protective dynamic that has profound consequences for the way slow violence has unfolded across the global stage in a neoliberal age. Second, and relatedly, the internal distance between the inviolable body and the vulnerable body is widened by being routed through international circuits of power. Third, implicit in Ndebele's racial narrative of violation and retribution is the kind of environmental narrative that Sinha's novel tells, whereby a corporate bastion of white power deploys a battery of distancing strategies (temporal, legalistic, geographical, scientific, and euphemistic) in the *longue durée* between the initial catastrophe and the aftermath. Through this battery of attritional, dissociative mechanisms, the transnational corporation strives to wear down the environmental justice campaigns that seek compensation, remediation, and restored health and dignity. Under cover of a variety of temporal orders, the company can hope that public memory and demands for restitution will slowly seep out of sight, vanishing into the sands of time.[44]

Yet the open-ended politics of catastrophic procrastination do not operate in isolation within the corporate realm. What of the roles of the state and science? If Ndebele exhorts the state to "jealously and vigorously protect all bodies within its borders and beyond," he acknowledges this has seldom been the case.[45] In Khaufpur the Chief Minister and the Minister for Poison Affairs, their palms well greased with bribes, provide local cover for the American Kampani while going through the motions of taking seriously the concerns of exposed locals.

The role of science is more complex. In Khaufpur—as in Bhopal—the transnational corporation withheld from the afflicted community details about the chemical composition of the insecticides it was producing at the site, profoundly weakening remedial prospects by denying those exposed precise scientific information. Small wonder that, when an American doctor arrives to open a free clinic in Khaufpur, local activists mount a boycott, viewing her as an agent of tendentious Kampani science—science whose long-term remit is to generate a circular narrative that will confirm the larger narrative of corporate self-exculpation or, at the very least, oil the machinery of doubt. From this skeptical perspective, the scientific process, like the legal one, provides further temporal camouflage, ostensibly uncovering what happened while deferring and occluding any decisive, actionable narrative.

Terror Time and Shadow Kingdoms

Khaufpur, translated from the Urdu, means "city of terror."[46] The city's poorest denizens inhabit a different terror time from the terror time projected by the Kampani. When the slum-dwellers rise up nonviolently to protest the Kampani's inaction, the Kampani, invoking the fallback international rhetoric of terrorism, demands that the protestors be tried in the very Indian courts the company itself has been evading. Back in America, the Kampani engages in corporate antiterrorist training exercises, staging mock abductions and executions of their employees by Khaufpuri "terrorists."[47] Khaufpuris, by contrast, face a clear and present danger of an environmental kind: an immanent and imminent terror, faceless yet physically intimate, percolating through the penumbral time of the aftermath that is also the suspended time of the illimitable in-between.

We all inhabit multiple temporal orders that often coexist in frictional states, shifting and sliding like tectonic plates. The predominance—and our awareness of—some temporal orders as opposed to others is shaped by where and how we live. We need to ask how directly, how forcefully a given community is impacted by the cycles of sun and moon; by ebbing and flowing tides; by shifts in the seasons, stars, and planets; by the arrivals and departures of migratory life; and by climate change in ways that are crosshatched with the migratory cycles of transnational capital, electoral cycles (local, national, and foreign), digital time, and the dictates of sweatshop time. Sinha hints at, for example, the unpredictable interface between digital and seasonal time when Animal discovers the "internest" on a computer.[48] We can gloss his malapropism as fusing different ecologies of time: the "internest" is, after all, where images go to breed.

Animal's People exposes the uneven timelines and multiple speeds of environmental terror: the initial toxic event that kills thousands instantly; the fatal fire that erupts years later, when the deserted but still-polluted factory reignites; the contaminants that continue to leach into the communal bloodstream; and the monsoon season that each year washes abandoned chemicals into the aquifers, repoisoning wells and producing new cycles of deferred casualties. Thus the initial airborne terror morphs into a waterborne terror that acquires its own seasonal rhythms of heightened risk.[49]

Ordinarily, rural subsistence communities—"ecosystem people"—are attuned (and vulnerable) to different ecologies of time from those that impact the lives of the urban poor.[50] This is not to suggest that ecosystem people possess some romantic, timeless, organic bond to the pulse of nature, but rather to acknowledge that their often precarious conditions of survival depend on different combinations of temporal awareness. However, both rural and urban communities share a vulnerability to the vagaries, the haunting uncertainties, of what Ulrich Beck depicts as a "shadow kingdom":

> Threats from civilization are bringing about a kind of new "shadow kingdom," comparable to the realm of the gods and demons in antiquity, which is hidden behind the visible world and threatens human life on their Earth. People no longer correspond today with spirits residing in things but find themselves exposed to "radiation," ingest "toxic levels," and are pursued into their very dreams by the anxiety of a "nuclear holocaust" . . . . Dangerous, hostile substances lie concealed behind the harmless facades. Everything must be viewed with a double gaze, and can only be correctly understood and judged through this doubling. The world of the visible must be investigated, relativized with respect to a second reality, only existent in thought and concealed in the world.[51]

In Beck's depiction this imperceptible shadow kingdom is spatially recessed behind "harmless façades." But his spatial trope warrants a temporal gloss as well: beyond the optical façade of immediate peril, what demons lurk in the penumbral realms of the *longue durée*? What forces distract or discourage us from maintaining the double gaze across time? And what forces—imaginative, scientific, and activist—can help extend the temporal horizons of our gaze not just retrospectively but prospectively as well? How, in other words, do we subject that shadow kingdom to a temporal optic that might allow us to see—and foresee—the lineaments of slow terror behind the façade of sudden spectacle?

We need to question here Beck's assumption that "people no longer correspond today with spirits residing in things," in other words, that the divine and demonic shadow kingdom "of antiquity" has been superseded by the modern shadow kingdom of toxic and radiological hazards. This sequential narrative of threat does not adequately convey the persistent vitality of the numinous within modernity. For the majority of our planet's people (and this is something Sinha brings to life) the two kingdoms of toxic threat and spiritual threat interpenetrate and blend, creating a hybrid world of techno-numinous fears.

Sinha and Carson: Leakages and Corporate Evaporations

Animal's People gives focus to the environmental politics of permeation and duration. Leakages suffuse the novel: gas leakages and category leakages, porous national borders and permeable fetal membranes, the living who are semidead and the dead who are living specters.[52] What, the novel asks across a variety of fronts, are the boundaries of identity? Where do identities part or merge? How much change must an entity (an individual, a community, a corporation) undergo before it can assume the name of categorical difference, drawing a line across time?

On the subject of porous identities, it is worth noting one aspect of the Union Carbide story that Sinha, for whatever reasons, declined to enfold into his novel. In 2001, Union Carbide disappeared through that act of corporate necromancy known as the merger. Dow Chemical bought out Union Carbide, and so the name indelibly associated with disaster evaporated, further confounding the quest in Bhopal for environmental justice, compensation, remediation, and redress. Dow Chemical deployed this nominal vanishing act, this corporate shape-shifting, as a rationale for disclaiming responsibility for a disaster committed by a corporation that no longer exists.[53] If with Chernobyl the environmental fallout outlasted the empire responsible, with Union Carbide the fallout outlasted the transnational company responsible. Thus Soviet imperial fracture and American corporate merger both effectively circumvented or off-loaded historical culpability for the continued slow violence of delayed effects.

The evaporation of Union Carbide exemplifies the gap between the relative immobility of environmentally afflicted populations and the mobility (in time and space) afforded transnational corporations. What the extinct company leaves behind is ongoing proof of the excellent durability of its products; as Animal notes sardonically, the Kampani clearly concocted "wonderful poisons . . . so good it's impossible to get rid of them, after all these years they're still doing their work."[54] The factory may have been abandoned, but the invisible poisons remain dynamic, industrious, and alive—full-time workers around the clock. The far less resilient biota, however, express themselves primarily through the sensuality of absence: "Listen, how quiet," Animal observes as he wanders the factory grounds. "No bird song. No hoppers in the grass. No bee hum. Insects can't survive here."[55] Sinha's rhetorical strategy here—his summoning of ecological carnage through negative presence—echoes "La Belle Dame sans Merci," which Rachel Carson chose as the epigraph to *Silent Spring*: "The sedge is wither'd from the lake, / And no birds sing." Sinha's rhetoric calls to mind, too, Carson's use of negative presence in the controversial "Fable for Tomorrow" that launches *Silent Spring*, where she evokes the plight of a devastated community. In a once harmonious American heartland town (dubbed Green Meadows in an early draft of *Silent Spring*), "[t]here was a strange stillness. The birds, for example—where had they gone? . . . The hens brooded, but no chicks hatched. . . . The apple trees were coming into bloom but no bees droned among the blossoms, so there was no pollination and there would be no fruit."[56]

Both Carson and Sinha give the absence wrought by toxicity a sensory density; in so doing they strike a complex temporal note, through blended elegy and apocalypse, lamentation and premonition, inducing in us a double gaze backward in time to loss and forward to yet unrealized threats. Through this double gaze they restage environmental time, asserting its broad parameters against the myopic, fevered immediacy that governs the society of the catastrophe-as-spectacle.

The blighted community Carson depicts in "A Fable for Tomorrow" did not exist in its entirety, although all the component disasters Carson fed into her composite, fictionalized portrait had occurred at some point somewhere in America. By clustering these scattered microdisasters into a single imaginary community, she sought to counter the dissociative thinking encouraged by the temporal and spatial dispersion of environmental violence, acts that in isolation would pass beneath the radar of newsworthiness.

Like Carson, Sinha has clearly grappled with the imaginative dilemmas posed by the diffusion of slow violence across environmental time. But his response is differently inflected, given that all the disasters he summons to mind had indeed been concentrated in a single community. The problem he tackled, moreover, was one Carson never addressed directly: how some afflicted communities are afforded more visibility—and more access to remediation—than others through the mechanisms of globalization, environmental racism, and class discrimination. This discriminatory distri-bution of environmental visibility—intranationally and transnationally—lies at the heart of Sinha's fictional endeavor.

Almost half a century earlier, Carson had protested that the scattershot victims of "herbicides" and "pesticides" ought to be recognized as victims of indiscriminate "biocides" instead.[57] Sinha develops this idea of biocidal risk in terms redolent of Carson: one old Indian woman, bent double by the poisons, upbraids the Kampani lawyer thus: "you told us you were making medicine for the fields. You were making poisons to kill insects, but you killed us instead. I would like to ask, was there ever much difference, to you?"[58] Yet Sinha departs from Carson in representing "pesticides" as both indiscriminate and discriminatory: their killing power exceeds their tar-geted task of eliminating troublesome insects, but they do discriminate in the unadvertised sense of saddling the local and global poor with the highest burden of risk. Thus, by implication, the biocidal assault on human life is unevenly universal.

Extraordinary Events, Ordinary Forgettings

Looking back at Chernobyl, Hiroshima, Nagasaki, and Bhopal, Petryna laments how "many persons who have survived these large-scale techno-logical disasters have been caught in a long-term and vicious bureaucratic cycle in which they carry the burden of proof of their physical damage while experiencing the risk of being delegitimated in legal, welfare, and medical institutional contexts."[59] Such people, the illiterate poor above all, are thrust into a labyrinth of self-fashioning as they seek to fit their bodily stories to the story lines that dangle hope of recognition (possibly, though elusively), even recompense. In so doing, the poor face the double challenge of invis-ibility and amnesia: numerically, they may constitute the majority, but they remain on the margins in terms of visibility and official memory. From an environmental perspective, this marginality is perpetuated, in part, by what Davis terms "the dialectic of ordinary disaster," whereby a calamity is incor-porated into history and rendered forgettable and ordinary precisely because the burden of risk falls unequally on the unsheltered poor.[60] Such disasters are readily dismissed from memory and policy planning by framing them as accidental, random, and unforeseeable acts of God, without regard for the precautionary measures that might have prevented these catastrophes or have mitigated their effects.

At stake here is the role of neoliberal globalization in exacerbating both uneven economic development and the uneven development of official memory. What we witness is a kind of fatal bigotry that operates through the spatializing of time, by off-loading risk onto "backward" communities that are barely visible in the corporate media. Contemporary global politics, then, must be recognized "as a struggle for crude, material dominance, but also (threaded ever closer into that struggle) as a battle for the control over appearances."[61] That battle over spectacle becomes especially decisive for public memory—and for the foresight with which public policy can motivate and execute precautionary measures—when it comes to the attritional casualties claimed, as at Bhopal, by the forces of slow violence.

We have seen, in recent years, some excellent analytical books about the plight of the international urban underclass by Davis, Jeremy Seabrook, and Jan Breman, among others. However, the kind of visibility such books afford is very different from the visibility offered by a picaresque novel. For even the most eloquent social scientific accounts of the underclass, like social scientific accounts of environmental disaster, veer toward the anonymously collective and the statistical. Such accounts thus tend to be in the same gesture humanizing and dehumanizing, animating and silencing.

The dilemma of how to represent the underclass, the *infrahombres*, stands at the heart of the picaresque tradition. Like *GraceLand*, Chris Abani's superb picaresque novel about ingenious desperation in a Lagos shantytown, *Animal's People* stages a disaggregated irruption of a vivid individual life. Animal, speaking his life story into the Jarnalis's tape recorder, is all charismatic voice: his street-level testimony does not start from the generalized hungers of the wretched of the earth, but from the devouring hunger in an individual belly. If the novel gradually enfolds a wider community—Animal's people—it does so by maintaining at its emotional center Animal, the cracked voiced soloist, who breaks through the gilded imperial veneer of neoliberalism to announce himself in his disreputable vernacular.[62] His is the antivoice to the new, ornate, chivalric discourse of neoliberal "free trade" and "development."

Through Animal's immersed voice, Sinha is able to return to questions that have powered the picaresque from its beginnings. What does it mean to be reduced to living in subhuman, bestial conditions? What chasms divide and what ties bind the wealthy and the destitute, the human and the animal? What does it mean, in the fused imperial language of temporal and spatial dismissal, to be written off as "backward"?[63]

In Animal's day-to-day meanderings, the impulse for survival trumps the dream of collective justice. Yet through his somatized foreign burden—and through the intrepid, blighted lives around him—Sinha exhumes from the forces of amnesia not just the memory of a long-ago disaster but the present and future force of that disaster's embodied, ongoing percolations. The *infrahombres*—those who must eke out an existence amidst such percolations—are, the novel insists, also of this earth. Through his invention of the environmental picaresque, Sinha summons to the imaginative surface of the novel the underclass's underreported lives, redeeming their diverse quirks and hopes and quotidian terrors from what, almost half a millennium ago, Lazaro recognized as "the sepulcher of oblivion."[64]

2

Fast-forward Fossil

Petro-despotism and the Resource Curse

As I fill my tank at the self-service station a bubble of gas swells up
in a black lake buried beneath the Persian Gulf, an emir silently
raises hands hidden in wide white sleeves, and folds them on his
chest, in a skyscraper an Exxon computer is crunching numbers, far
out to sea a cargo fleet gets the order to change course.

—Italo Calvino, "The Petrol Pump"

We are the sons of the Indians who sold Manhattan. We want to
change the deal.

—Abdallah Tariki, former Director of Petroleum and
Mineral Affairs of Saudi Arabia

If the twentieth century has been declared, by turns, the
American Century and the Century of Oil, it is by now manifest that the
twenty-first century will be known as neither.[1] We are heading toward a
multipolar global order that will depend for its survival on belated—and
therefore evermore desperate—responses to uncertain petroleum reserves
and mounting climate change. American hegemony has already peaked
and (whatever the squabbles over the most likely date) peak oil will follow,

ending the dreams of unfettered oil-powered growth that have become inseparable from petroleum's incendiary geopolitics.

In this interregnum between energy regimes, we are living on borrowed time—borrowed from the past and from the future. "Fossil fuels" captures in a phrase this double relationship to planetary time: it suggests, on the one hand, the stratified death compacted over millennia that technology has enabled us to resurrect as the force that drives our fleeting, internal combustion civilization. On the other hand, "fossil fuels" also conveys an aura of antiquatedness, of built-in obsolescence inadequate to future needs. For if the fossil record, as a sedimentary script, has been parsed with a host of competing religious, political, and economic motives toward times past and times to come, what remains certain is its finitude as a source of usable energy. What's equally certain is that the faster we extract and consume our planet's compressed hydrocarbon inheritance the greater the likelihood that our actions will propel us—and other living multitudes—toward an abbreviated collective future as fossils in the making.

If "fossil fuels" resonates with a sense of time borrowed against an exhaustible past and an exhaustible future, the phrase "resource curse" conveys a different, but complementary, doubleness. "Resource curse" holds in taut suspense notions of fortune and misfortune; the phrase also fuses utilitarian and numinous perspectives on Earth, suggesting the vulnerability of the world of solid, useful goods to spiritual force fields—the curses and blessings that can have profoundly material effects. Moreover, "resource curse" compresses huge, fraught questions about ownership: what does it mean to be possessed or dispossessed, politically, economically, and spiritually? What are the repercussions of having mineral belongings that literally undermine a community or society's capacity to belong? And what forces turn belongings—those goods, in a material and an ethical sense—into evil powers that alienate people from the very elements that have sustained them, environmentally and culturally, as all that seemed solid melts into liquid tailings, oil spills, and plumes of toxic air?

The notion of the resource curse hinges on the paradox of plenty, whereby nation-states blessed with abundant mineral wealth are too often concomitantly blighted.[2] As a rule of thumb, the greater a state's reliance on a single mineral resource, the greater the chances that state is undemocratic, militaristic, corruption riddled, and governed without transparency or accountability. Abundant resources are frequently coupled to rampant injustice, fragile economic growth, and low rankings in the United Nations Human Development Index. In strengthening a country's currency, mineral discoveries may render other economic sectors, like agriculture and manufacturing, less competitive, while the boom-bust cycles of mineral markets exacerbate social volatility. There are of course exceptions to these tendencies, but in resource-cursed societies, a mineral strike, though less immediately spectacular than a missile strike, is often more devastating in the long term, bringing in its wake environmental wreckage, territorial dispossession, political repression, and massacres by state forces doing double duty as security forces for unanswerable petroleum transnationals or mineral cartels. In such societies, a highly concentrated revenue stream is readily diverted away from social and infrastructural investment and into offshore bank accounts. The ties between rulers and ruled are typically weak: the despots or oligarchs prefer to depend—for their private wealth, consumer sprees, extravagant military spending, and power displays—on controlling the central resource than on strengthening civic expectations by introducing taxes, elections, and a diversified (and therefore less controllable) economy. Under such circumstances, national cohesion and stability may be jeopardized by exaggerated inequalities. These frequently entail both vertical inequality (a widening class chasm between super rich and ultra poor) and horizontal inequality (a geographical gulf between resource-rich enclaves and the remainder of the country).

That said, the resource curse, when invoked as a free-floating cultural explanation bereft of history, can mislead. Australia and Canada are resource rich but not resource cursed. Is that merely because they are stable, long-established electoral democracies that have avoided the extreme concentrations of power that have blighted monoeconomies like Nigeria, Libya, and Angola? The historical answer is more complicated than that.

The "curse" is in part a spin-off of an international legal system that compromised decolonizing nations' sovereignty over their natural resources. In the 1970s, when efforts to create a New Economic Order collapsed, the European powers and the United States denied newly independent states resource sovereignty by declaring, as Antony Anghie has noted, that such resources were not national in character but belonged to all humanity, by upholding old colonial treaties for resource transfer, and by granting multinational corporations equal international legal standing to third-world states.[3] From Saudi Arabia to Zaire, from Indonesia to Iran, the Western powers typically supported oligarchs, dictators, and military regimes that cooperated with the skewed terms of resource extraction. The Western powers often machinated to topple rulers who objected to these skewed terms. Moreover, Western multinationals typically exerted a disproportionate influence over the terms of extraction with their third world state partners, inhibiting democratic dispensations from developing while exploiting an environmental, health, and labor climate far more lax than the legislative controls corporations were subject to back home. Hence, international law enabled a single multinational to cultivate divergent standards of operation in the global North and South, a double standard that grew out of—and exacerbated—the historical, structural inequities for which the resource curse has become shorthand.

In the global South, oil culture in particular typically brings few new jobs to the locals to replace old forms of communal subsistence jeopardized by fouled water, earth, and air. Multinational oil corporations, seeking a pliable workforce, prefer to import laborers from rival communities or distant lands rather than create jobs for communities most immediately affected by extraction operations. This practice, in turn, impedes labor unions and civic organizations from developing—organizations that could mesh the workplace with the priorities of neighboring communities, whose ostensible resource wealth has reduced them (from the perspective of fossil fuel authoritarians and their partners, the oil majors) to disposable people.

From a literary perspective, the idea of the resource enclave achieves a special resonance, for it depends on a profound act of imaginative disconnection. French foreign policy makers, for example, would sometimes divide Africa into *Afrique utile* and *Afrique unitile*, the gulf between the useful and the useless bits corresponding largely to those enclaves with exploitable resources that could be profitably incorporated into metropolitan capitalist structures and the unincorporated, disposable remainder.[4] The tightly garrisoned useful enclaves would be embedded in—yet materially, militarily, and imaginatively removed from—the destitution that surrounded them.

Such an enclave mindset is inseparable from another form of imaginative dissociation, namely, rent-seeking behavior, attempts to maximize the often immense chasm between the market value of a resource and the costs of its extraction. Economic rent effects a rending gap in the social fabric, as mining transnationals and collaborative local elites treat a nation's "natural" bounty as if it were neither of nor for the nation, but exists as a kind of extraterritorial gravy train. In the global South, these multiple practices of economic and imaginative disconnection foster apprehensive nation-states and apprehensive states of mind, in which rulers readily incline toward the paranoid and the great majority who are excluded from the spoils scramble for survival.

As these forms of dissociation suggest, to address the resource curse requires that we confront the uses and abuses of enchantment. The eminent Polish journalist Ryzsard Kapuscinski captures something of this sentiment in his Iranian book, *The Shah of Shahs*, when he observes how "oil creates the illusion of a completely changed life, life without work, life for free, it expresses the eternal human dream of wealth achieved through a lucky accident . . . in this sense it is a fairy tale and like all fairy tales a bit of a lie."[5] Jose Ignacio Cabrujas, writing from the other end of the world, exclaims over how Venezuela's petroleum state turned into a "magnanimous sorcerer . . . . Oil is fantastic and induces fantasies. The announcement that Venezuela was an oil country created the illusion of a miracle; it created, in practice, a culture of miracles" propelling the nation "toward a hallucination."[6] Thus the oil encounter lends itself to populist fairy tales of sudden bounty that easily sour into volatile disillusionment, as people possessed by outsize dreams find themselves captive instead to outsize military regimes and the disenchantments of a ruined environment.

Abdelrahman Munif and the Oil Encounter

For some eighty years, oil has been responsible for more of America's international entanglements and anxieties than any other industry. In 2009, the United States spent $188.5 billion on imported oil ($95 billion of that from OPEC members alone).[7] According to Princeton economic geographer Roger Stern, in the three decades from 1976 to 1997, the United States spent a further $7.3 trillion on securing its oil supply from the Middle East.[8] Oil remains a primary source both of America's strategic vulnerability and of its reputation as a bully, in the Islamic world and beyond. Our appetite for fossil fuels has created a long history of unsavory marriages of convenience with petro-despots, generalissimos, presidents for life, and fomenters of terrorism. Given this history—given the outsize characters, bloated dreams, unscrupulous alliances, double crossings, insurrections, and repressions, given the soaring and plummeting fortunes, one would have expected that the titanic drama of the resource curse would by now have generated a substantial, ambitious literature.

This leaves us facing a conundrum. Why is it, as Amitav Ghosh has asked, that the oil encounter has failed to generate a literary response comparable in range and depth to that produced in earlier times by the spice trade?[9] Moreover, one should note that Big Oil certainly hasn't produced a literature equal in range or magnitude to that generated by its fossil fuel precursor, King Coal, which inspired Emile Zola, George Orwell, Sinclair, Clancey Segal, and D. H. Lawrence, to name but a few. Given the preeminence of oil in America's destiny, it is startling that not since Sinclair's California saga *Oil!* appeared in 1927 has any author hazarded writing the great American oil novel.[10]

There is, however, one twentieth-century writer who sought, on an unparalleled scale, to give transnational life to the forbidding subject of oil, a writer alive to oil's lubrication of human greed, alive to oil's bewitchments and its disenchanted states, both national and psychological.[11] Between 1984 and 1989 Abdelrahman Munif penned *Cities of Salt*, a sprawling quintet of novels that engages the broad geography and volatile history of the petroleum encounter. The encounter he dramatizes entails the special relationship, or rather, the special deal between our planet's biggest petroleum players: Saudi Arabia, the leading producer; and the United States, the principal consumer. *Cities of Salt* takes shape around the rise of the hydrocarbon despots encouraged, armed, and sustained by American corporate and foreign policy interests. The companion subject of *Cities* is the growing repression and disillusionment of ordinary Bedouins and their intense, if episodic, insurrectionary response. Munif tracks the psychological and cultural disorientation of Bedouins whose lands and lives the two-headed behemoth of empire and petro-despotism has trampled. The novels—especially the fine first volume—deserve to be better known and more widely taught in the United States, not least for their power to illuminate America's fateful entanglements with Islam and for the chance they offer us to rethink the parameters of environmental literature, transnationally and across the frontiers of genre.

The opening volume of *Cities of Salt* spans the period from 1933 to 1953, the very era when Aldo Leopold was enunciating his land ethic, advocating a far-sighted vision of what it means to live responsibly and viably in environmental time.[12] Leopold's ethic was circumscribed, in some ways, by the particularities of America's Jeffersonian traditions; he did foresee, however, that to live as an American in the American century was to be a consumer of historically calamitous proportions. He foresaw, too, how the impact of such unchecked resource consumption would be felt disproportionately abroad. In 1932, one year before an American petroleum corporation signed the first concession agreement in the Persian Gulf, Leopold wrote: "When I submit these thoughts to a printing press, I am helping to drain a marsh for cows to graze, and to exterminate the birds of Brazil. When I go birding in my Ford, I am devastating an oil field, and re-electing an imperialist to get me rubber."[13]

Yet Leopold could do no more than limn these issues in ethical outline from afar. Munif, writing from within the oil encounter's extractive vortex, could give imaginative dimension to the hydrocarbon force fields—the petroleum-driven promises, seductions, coercions, betrayals, and catastrophes—that shaped his region and rippled across the world. Thus his writings—at once historical and premonitory—offer us a unique entry point into one of the twentieth century's defining stories: the rise of a transnational petro-modernity that contained, from the outset, the seeds of its own undoing. What Munif brings to life, in unparalleled detail, is the profound investment of the foreign and domestic petroleum overlords in quashing democratic aspiration and resource sovereignty. Munif conjures, moreover, a huge chorus of disenfranchised voices, some bewildered, some complicitous, others intrepid in their dissidence, yet all outmaneuvered by American and British imperial forces in league with the oil majors and (if sometimes frictionally so) with the petro-despots too.

Munif felt he had been summoned to his theme by the stars: he was born on the very day in 1933 when the Persian Gulf's first concession agreement was signed between the monarch of the newly created Kingdom of Saudi Arabia Abdul Aziz ibn Saud and an American oil corporation, the California Arabian Standard Oil Company. As it transpired, Munif's final book (on Iraqi resistance to imperialism from 1917 to the twenty-first century) would appear just months after the 2003 American invasion of Iraq, giving his life a certain symmetry around empire and oil.

Although he wrote *Cities of Salt* before the term "resource curse" had been coined, Munif has bequeathed us the most expansive novelistic account of the Persian Gulf's early oil conflicts that would bring the resource curse in train. *Cities of Salt* tracks how a nascent transnational oil culture created the foundations for the resource curse, deepening the divide between a narrow class that would become astronomically rich and the uprooted, immiserated masses (from inside and increasingly from beyond the Persian Gulf). Munif's novels remind us of the perception by French economist, Jacques Attali, that ours is a world increasingly divided into rich and poor nomads, into a wandering elite that travels expansively and a disenfranchised poor whose movements are propelled by misery in a quest for basic goods and rights beyond their grasp.[14] This rift between the mobile rich and wretched, disenfranchised nomads is at its most dramatic in the Gulf States, where such discrepancies foster political volatility among people bound by desperation, oil, Islam, and American and European need.

Munif portrayed his novelistic method as the imaginative pursuit of "the deep, internal movement of history," a history indissociably environmental, political, and cultural.[15] Arguably, his greatest gift was for linking oil's hybrid lives as a commodity to the oil-induced movements of human populations across oceans and across deserts. Munif himself was perfectly placed as a witness to displacement, for he was (to adapt Bertolt Brecht's self-portrait) a man given to "changing his country as often as his shoes."[16] A child of the Arab diaspora, Munif was born in Jordan to an Iraqi mother and a Saudi trader who traveled expansively across the region as the race for oil was transforming it. Munif himself led an improbably peripatetic existence, residing in Jordan, Iraq, Egypt, Lebanon, Syria, Yugoslavia, and France.[17] En route he earned a Ph.D. in oil economics from Belgrade University, edited the Baghdad journal *Oil and Development*, and worked in the Syrian oil ministry.

As such, he was ideally situated to enter into the fantasies purveyed by petroleum's manipulative emissaries while also addressing the impact of petroleum—through force and fabulation—on Bedouin oral culture. In Munif's writings about the resource curse, spiritual powers are never immaterial: he is alive to the active energies of the spectral, whether expressed through the opaque enchantments of oil as fetishized commodity or through political resistance inspired by rumors of a shimmering, elusive desert fighter who launches sallies against the foreign dispossessors. Munif is alert, in other words, to the blurring of corporeal and incorporeal powers within the coercive-seductive force fields of oil imperialism, commodity desire, and the insurrectionary forces ranged against them both.

Munif's involuntary and voluntary movements, his exile and his rovings, were accompanied by a rare range of professional experiences whose one binding thread was petroleum. He was an oil industry insider who also knew, from the inside, what it meant to be dispossessed. Saudi Arabia stripped him of his citizenship; his novels were banned in several Gulf States and Egypt for their excoriating satires of the peninsula's oil elite; and in his displacements, he felt vulnerable to the suffocating political gamesmanship that pervaded the region. Yet his empathy for the uprooted preceded his own deracinations: his memoir about his Amman childhood sharply enunciates the impact Palestinian refugees had on his political psyche, as they were driven from their lands by the *nakbah* and streamed into his hometown in the late 1940s, utterly transforming it.

In chronicling his region's oil-induced environmental and cultural upheavals, Munif implicitly distinguishes between the nomadic and the rootless. Nomadic Bedouin culture had been inscribed on the land through movement; theirs was a belonging-in-motion shaped to an arid world. But the deracinations of the oil age plummeted them into a rootlessness that was nomadism's opposite. Driven from their lands, increasingly urbanized, repressed and exploited by a corrupt sepoy class in cahoots with American oil interests, many lower-class Bedouin found themselves culturally humiliated and politically estranged.

Writing and Political Agency

To write against the corrupting intimacies between petro-despots and the oil majors can be a life-threatening enterprise. Ken Saro-Wiwa was executed for doing as much; George Aditjondro, the vocal Indonesian intellectual who wrote fearlessly about his nation's oil-driven authoritarianism, was forced into exile, as was Munif after the Saudis revoked his citizenship and issued threats. Moving from country to country, Munif became, in his words, an "uninvited guest" whose exiled presence could be wielded by the Saudis (and others hostile to his views) against any state that hosted him.[18]

Yet through all those upheavals he refused to temper his outspokenness on the region's root corruptions.

"Our crisis," he once declared, "is a trilogy: oil, political Islam, and dictatorship."[19] *Cities of Salt* was pitched against that trilogy of fused calamities. In *Cities*—and across the broad swathe of his writings—Munif exposed the perfidies of the petro-despots, the spread of the carceral state, and the costs borne by those who (from oases to city streets) clamored for resource sovereignty, political answerability, socialism, civil liberties, or participatory democracy. By shuttling between fiction and nonfiction, Munif exposed the imperial underpinnings of that trilogy of calamities, bearing witness to the ways American and British petroleum powers—whether in competition or collaboration, whether backed by the CIA or MI6 or both—cynically fomented and funded political Islam, propped up petro-despots, helped subvert or assassinate democratically elected leaders, and thwarted street-level efforts to advance a more equitable spread of regional oil wealth.

Munif maintained an insistent belief that writing could be a tool for change.[20] To that end, he adopted a multigenre assault on both the Persian Gulf elites and their foreign collaborators. However, unlike most writers under consideration in this book, Munif's faith in literature's instrumental value was neither integral to his organizational activism (as with Saro-Wiwa, Maathai, and Ndebele) nor supplementary to an already established literary career (as with Roy, Sinha, Carson, and Gordimer). For if Munif turned to literature belatedly (he was forty before his first novel, *Trees and the Assassination of Marzuq*, appeared in 1973), that turn marked a withdrawal from organizational politics and a reentry into politics through a different door. Disillusioned with organized resistance, he determined to become a full-time writer, which he saw as a compensation—albeit in his view an inadequate one—for the social transformations that he'd once hoped the region's radical movements would provide, before they were crushed, corrupted or collapsed through self-immolation.[21]

From his student days onward, Munif had plunged into a dizzying array of political organizations, variously and in combination, socialist, democratic, nationalist, pan-Arabist, and Baathist. But by the late 1960s his faith in movement politics had been exhausted: repression by despotic forces from within and subversion by imperial forces from without had resulted in surging imprisonments, executions, disappearances, torture, and banishments.

Above all, it was the Six Day War that propelled Munif to channel his political energies in a literary direction. Reflecting on the impact of that war, Munif recalled how "the defeat of 1967 pushed [him] toward the novel not as a means of escape but of confrontation. It had an unforgettable effect: to see such a vast area as the Arab world—with all its enormous clamour and slogans—crumble and fall, not just in six days but a mere few hours."[22] In turning to literature during that aftermath, he sought to redeem the oppositional capacities of language from such clamorous sloganeering, a task he undertook through the complementary possibilities offered him by fictional and nonfictional forms.

Munif belonged to a post–World War II generation emboldened by decolonization, inspired by nationalism and socialism, and burdened "with an immense load of dreams and desires for change. . . . But our dreams were greater than our resources."[23] Faced with waning possibilities for organized resistance, Munif envisioned literature as an alternative resource. Perhaps literature might offer some modest counter to the surreal, unmoored worlds of despotism afloat on oil; might offer some anchorage in history, some space for dreaming and for insurrectionary acts of memory, aspiration, and satirical exposé. Munif became a writer-activist, then, through a disengagement from rather than an immersion in movement politics.[24] In this diverted realm Munif secured for himself, amidst the precariousness of exile, some element of imaginative sovereignty and purposeful hope. An unsettled man, literature became his place of displaced possibility.

He found himself writing into the headwinds of ongoing, region-wide crises. He responded with essays, polemics, and manifestos on (among other things) how to reorganize the oil industry.[25] He responded, too, with novels, mostly either allegorical fables steeped in oral tradition or historical epics that blended in semiallegorical elements. This allegorical propensity—and his refusal to name a society that provided the setting for any novel, even when it was recognizably, say, Saudi Arabia, Iraq, or Iran—served a double purpose. On the one hand, it allowed him political deniability. But perhaps more significantly, it marked him as a resolutely regional writer in a transnational (rather than a Thomas Hardy) sense. Munif insisted that his region's commonalities were more striking—and more politically consequential—than its internal differences. He viewed the region as, among other things, one vast carceral state: "the political prison exists from the Atlantic to the

Gulf," he declared, a sentiment that found dramatic expression in his most famous novel, *East of the Mediterranean*, set in a typically unnamed despotic state.[26] In a similarly regionalist gesture, he observed how "the Bedouin oil blessing, which at one time was confined to the desert, has moved to all Arab cities and become the force defining not only politics but culture, ways of life, and the human concerns in this region."[27] These remarks give voice to Munif's paired imaginative obsession with imprisonment on the one hand and movement (upheaval, banishment, exile) on the other: his writings return again and again to the visitations of involuntary immobility and involuntary mobility that have bedeviled his region.

By not specifying the locations of his novels Munif sought to limit the risk that a nation-specific critique could be read as exculpating other equally heinous regimes in the region. His fiction works, as it were, through inverse specificity. By amassing sensory, cultural, geographical, and historical detail he writes against the forces of amnesia, censorship, and repression, creating the impression of whole societies that are, nonetheless, never reducible to themselves. His broad regionalism is underscored by his recurrent commitment to a transnational justice at once cultural and environmental, powerfully established through figurative counterpoints between, on the one hand, oil culture's invisible maneuverings and material excesses; and on the other, the transparent, modest, and regenerative life of the grove.

If the oil realm is geologically subterranean, politically opaque, rife with secret concessions and imperial back room deals, the realm of the grove—whether olive, date, lemon, orange, or almond—is the realm of provender and provenance. Munif was especially alert to the impact of the uprooted grove on human ecology: to trees as bioregional and historical stakeholders, as palpable markers of contested memory, as standard bearers of sustainable life and equally of cultural dignity. His own improbably uprooted life, his profoundly inhabited sense of deracination's rending, intensified his predilection for humanizing his region's trees and for arborealizing its people. That tendency comes to a head in the first volume of *Cities of Salt*, during the intense scenes of first contact between American petroleum prospectors and the people of the oasis, as Munif gives fictional form to the events that would lead to the first American oil company concession in the Persian Gulf, to the completion in 1950 of the Trans-Arabian Pipeline and, in the novel's explosive later pages, to the worker strikes that shook Dhahran in 1953.

[79]

The Oasis as Resource Frontier

The oasis scenes in *Cities of Salt* mark the first skirmishes in an imperial resource war that would bring, not far behind it, the first premonitions of the resource curse. Like many scenes of first contact, this is a war that isn't a war, or at least one that doesn't announce itself as such; initially, it simply appears to involve the arrival of bewildering strangers whose advent gives no inkling of the extensive violence to follow. But we can read the encounter between the oasis community and these newcomers—three American oil prospectors and their two marsh Arab guides—as an epochal, if as yet inchoate, contest between a desert culture historically shaped around water wealth and interlopers following a different wealth script, in which "resource rich" means oil. Hitherto, water (and its dependent trees) had been the foundational bounty—connecting past to future, time to space, place to movement, agriculture to nomadism. In this context, water sustained tradition as what Amiri Baraka once called "the changing same"; it was water that underlay a culture of continuity-within-flux responsive to ecological vicissitudes, a culture infused with cosmological belonging and steeped in a history of nomadic cosmopolitanism.[28]

Over the course of *Cities of Salt* we witness the Americans (in collusion with a far-off emir) uproot this water-based culture and supplant it, without explanation or consultation, with a petroleum-fixated culture.[29] This tectonic shift in resource priorities is accompanied by a profound temporal rupturing: oasis deep time (inseparably cultural and ecological) becomes subordinated to petroleum culture's swaggering sense of an even deeper time, one premised on an apparently infinite geological generosity fueling an apparently infinite future wealth. The newcomers' hubris disdains the idea of limits: the decisive time frame changes from a cyclical, seasonally renewable culture that prizes water time to a culture dominated by oil time's linear narrative, in which concerns regarding sustainability get crushed by an onrushing developmental ideology, purportedly universal in its generosity. ("Wait, just be patient, and all of you will be rich!" the Americans declare upon arrival.)[30] In the background, we have the slow time of hydrocarbon's geological accretions and in the foreground, the accelerated time of petro-modernity's primitive accumulation.

If primitive accumulation generally combines a history "of force, of dispossession, and enclosure," in the case of petroleum, we confront primitive accumulation of a special type.[31] Fernando Coronil, writing in a Venezuelan context, is pertinent here, particularly his incisive thinking about the distinctive character of "nature-exporting societies."[32] Coronil remarks on how "the tension between the natural origin of the nation's finite collective wealth and the private destiny of its social appropriation shaped the contest between democracy and dictatorship."[33] However, in Saudi Arabia, far more acutely than in Venezuela, the oppositional forces were never able to mount a significant democratic challenge because they faced a more daunting set of collusions—between empire, petro-capitalism, and the House of Saud. Saudi Arabia, after all, was a society where in 1947 a U.S. ambassador could boast that America possessed its own "oil colony."[34]

If the etymological ties between nature and nation were deployed in the United States to mythologize the society as "nature's nation," in Saudi Arabia that logic resurfaced in heightened form. Soon after American prospectors had made their first oil strike in the Persian Gulf, the United States oversaw the creation and "independence" of Saudi Arabia; and so, through a gesture of simultaneous decolonization and colonization, an outpost of "nature's nation" was engineered into birth. The new nation's "natural" bounty was promoted from the outset as imminent wealth for all its newly minted "independent" citizens, while simultaneously being privatized by imperial need and familial monopoly. The result was a paradigmatic instance of what Wm. Roger Louis and Ronald Robinson have aptly called "the imperialism of decolonization."[35]

Cities of Salt chronicles the emergence of a nature-exporting, client nation-state premised on ruined ecologies. The novel's thinly disguised Saudi Arabia possesses a natural bounty so vast and monolithic that it inhibits economic, infrastructural, and civic diversity, encouraging instead highly stratified social relations, highly concentrated power, and an international feedback loop of corruption and repression. These inequities are set in motion by the first oil concessions at the desert oases that, like the "purchase" of Manhattan from the Native peoples, bore no earthly relation to the long-term market value of the resource. Thus, in the official narratives, the oasis was typically represented as a remote, "primitive," worthless place redeemed by the arrival of American technology that allowed nature's beneficence to flower.

It might be productive, then, to approach *Cities of Salt* as an unofficial, contrarian imaginative history of the oasis as resource frontier. From this perspective, Munif can be seen to use the technology of the novel—the novel as paperwork—to script petro-capitalism's contradictions, contradictions papered over by American and Saudi public relations that crafted a seamless developmental narrative from which oil imperialism and petro-despotism were both carefully excised. As such, Munif's novels take shape (in form and impulse) as works of disenchantment: they dispel the bureaucratic necromancy whereby Saudi Arabia appeared as an autochthonous nation-state blessed with impeccable natural credentials.

What emerges in Munif's denaturing of the petroleum nation-state is a tension between different geometries of environmental time: at the pre-petroleum oasis, or wadi, a cyclical set of expectations prevails, one that acknowledges both scarcity and replenishment, whereas the official, linear, developmental narrative of the naturally rich nation-state suppresses notions of finitude and stewardship. Thus the twilight of the wadi and the dawning of the petroleum state mark the fall and rise of incompatible cultures of benediction:

> Wadi al-Uyoun was an ordinary place to its inhabitants, and excited no strong emotions, for they were used to seeing the palm trees filling the wadi and the gushing brooks surging forth in the winter and early spring, and felt protected by some blessed power that made their lives easy.[36]

This known, inhabited ecology of good fortune stands in contrast to the unknown fortune that has yet to materialize from the rhetoric of oil riches. When the wadi's representatives travel to their emir to oppose the American presence, he reassures them that "there are oceans of blessings under this soil" and that the foreigners have traveled from "the ends of the earth to help us."[37] We can read this scene as a showdown between different temporal visions as well as divergent ecologies of scale: a showdown between the wadi, a visible place of finite bounty; and the invisible realms—those "oceans of blessings" below and "the ends of the earth" beyond—that are reputedly conspiring, through geological and technological generosity, to put an end to scarcity.

The people of the wadi first experience oil's blessings as violation; the Americans, having probed the soil at Wadi-al-Uyoun, vanish then reappear in "yellow iron hulks."[38] The "unearthly" machines are neither of nor for this earth:

> They descended like ravenous wolves, tearing up the trees and
> throwing them to the earth one after another, and leveled all
> the orchards between the brook and the fields. After destroy-
> ing the first grove of trees, the tractors turned to the next with
> the same bestial voracity and uprooted them. The trees shook
> violently and groaned before falling, cried for help, wailed, pan-
> icked, called out in helpless pain and then fell entreatingly to the
> ground, as if trying to snuggle into the earth to grow and spring
> forth alive again.[39]

The trees had anchored community and enabled a blend of nomadic and
semiagrarian subsistence. As the machines rip up the roots—and routes—of
the culture, they rip through the temporal fabric of oasis ecology, whereby
life returns to the earth for cyclical retreat and regeneration. Furthermore,
the assaults on the oasis set up a conflict between the micropolitical culture
of the once sovereign grove and the transnational macropolitics of concession—in the fullest political, psychological, geological, and environmental
sense of concession.

In the second phase of oil's benediction, the wadi's now homeless people
get displaced to a coastal refinery town, Harran, where they find themselves
housed in furnace-like metal shacks and remade as laborers in a wage economy under foreign mastery. The worker compound is segregated from the
transplanted American suburban enclave—in a Persian Gulf rendition of
Jim Crow.[40] At day's end, the workers part

> like streams coursing down a slope, one broad and one small,
> the Americans to their camp and the Arabs to theirs, the Ameri-
> cans to their swimming pool, where their racket could be heard
> in the nearby barracks behind the barbed wire. When silence
> fell the workers guessed the Americans had gone into their air-
> conditioned rooms whose thick curtains shut everything our:
> sunlight, dust, flies, and Arabs.[41]

Thus the undifferentiated oil blessing becomes institutionalized as class distinction and racial segregation: nature's unbounded bounty becomes incrementally bounded, privatized, partitioned. On the poor side of the wire,

that bounty is reduced to the noises of luxury rising from the far side of the barricade and to the inner noise of yearning.

Inarguably, a romantic strain suffuses Munif's elegiac depictions of the pre-petroleum oasis—as harmonious, almost paradisal, compared to the divided, divisive world that would ensue.[42] Munif falls back on tropes familiar from other postcolonial or neocolonial literatures to project an atmosphere of conjoined ecological integrity and cultural authenticity. Certainly, if in an American context, Shepard Krech has argued that it is historically inaccurate and politically dubious to propagate the myth of the Ecological Indian, one could make a similar case for the dangers of a reductively mythologized Ecological Bedouin.[43] In fairness, Munif does temper his Edenic oasis authenticity by underscoring the droughts, famines, and calamities that have historically beset the place. It is not as if the wadi is a stranger to violence; rather that petro-capitalism's arrival introduces a violence of unprecedented magnitude and irreversible consequences.[44]

If Ken Saro-Wiwa sometimes sought to defend Ogoni rights by mobilizing a dubious discourse of impermeable cultural authenticity, so too Munif's romance with authenticity has some problematic fallout. We witness this, for example, when the textured sympathy he extends to the wadi's cosmopolitan nomads is not extended to the cosmopolitan foreign workers who arrive from Asia and from across the Middle East:

> Once Harran had been a city of fishermen and travelers coming home, but now it belonged to no one; its people were feature-less, of all varieties and yet strangely unvaried. They were all of humanity and yet no one at all, an assemblage of languages, accents, colors and religions.[45]

At moments like this, foreignness per se—whether embodied by American petroleum overlords or by the Yemeni, Sri Lankan, Egyptian, Bangladeshi, and Indian immigrant underclass—gets collapsed into the figuration of loss.

If the elegiac oasis scenes depend on familiar, troubling postcolonial tropes, in Munif's case those scenes assume an autobiographically inflected melancholy. As a child, he traveled widely with his family of small-time traders; their wanderings traversed national divides before the region's nation-states existed. Munif recalls in interview how "we brought flour from Amman to Saudi Arabia and, at the same time, brought salt and dates from Saudi Arabia back to Jordan. This was the specific kind of trade that I did in my youth."[46] During this period, encountering an oasis would have been emotionally momentous for the boy. So Munif had profound familial reasons for nostalgia and rage when he witnessed this tradition of traversal traduced (or at least unrecognizably transformed) by petro-capitalism's dictates.

An abrupt transition from an economy dispersed around nodal oases to a centralized, client nation-state presided over by an oil corporation transforms cultures of exchange—of stories as well as goods. Exchange defines the oasis almost as much as water: an oasis is not an enclave, it is a place where (to adapt James Clifford's terms) rootedness is routed through the constancy of movement.[47] An oasis is a place of passage that blends the agrarian and the nomadic, an ecosystem as way station and thoroughfare. Indeed, without the Bedouin caravans and the flux of nonhuman migrant living forms as well, the wadi would soon wither. So the arrival of visitors at Wadi al-Uyoun is scarcely an isolated event; nor is the wadi a stranger, even, to the visitations of imperialism. Locals recall how during Ottoman times, Jazi al-Hathal and his forces would ambush Turkish invaders who had seized the wadi for themselves, eventually forcing them to withdraw.[48]

What is perplexing about the Americans is the way they exempt themselves from the cultures of exchange that animate the oasis. They arrive with equipment, but no goods to trade and no stories. Possessed of a bewildering incuriosity, they reserve their most intense investigations for the earth below, not the surface people; bewitched by the unseen geology, the Americans remain indifferent to the eco-cultural history. Their presence along the margins of the oasis is acquisitive not inquisitive; the newcomers stand inscrutably outside the wadi's dense culture of narrative and commercial exchange. If Munif's writing about the oasis takes on tones of anticipatory elegy (for an authenticity simplified and heightened in remembrance), he nonetheless conveys the cosmopolitan complexity of oasis culture before it was ecologically, culturally, economically, and psychologically unsettled by an instrumental rationality that saw only fossil fuels and relic people, impedimentary Bedouin who, in the name of civilization, modernity, and profit had to be moved and forcibly remade. ·

[85]

Provincializing America:
Wilderness and the Frontiers of Genre

In 1988, when Peter Theroux's English translation of the first volume of *Cities of Salt* appeared, the most prominent American response came from John Updike, who reviewed it for the *New Yorker*.[49] Updike disliked the novel intensely, for political and formal reasons. The grounds for his distaste are worth examining because they open up large questions about the frontiers of genre in relation to transnational frontier literatures. What would it mean to disturb the conventions of U.S. frontier and wilderness literature through what Anne McClintock has called America's "offshore histories"?[50] To what extent, in engaging a history as vast, as multifarious, as that of the resource curse, is the novel itself an adaptable resource? How, moreover, do the geological, geopolitical, and technological translations of an oral culture's vernacular landscapes into petro-capitalism's official landscapes impact the refraction of oral community through the written technology of the novel? And finally, in the canons of environmental literature, what can we learn from novels that simultaneously globalize and provincialize America, envisioning America from abroad, from the outside in, thereby reconfiguring America's weight in the world?

Updike poses none of these questions, yet the angle of his approach allows us to engage them productively. He bristles at the novel's stance toward America: *Cities of Salt* is suffused with a hostility that shows, he argues, that "the maledictory rhetoric of the Ayatollah Khomeini is nothing new."[51] But Updike's more elaborate quarrel concerns Munif's formal incompetence. Acknowledging the epic potential of the oil theme, Updike laments that this Arab author is "insufficiently Westernized to produce a narrative that feels much like what we call a novel."[52] Here the bogeymen of authenticity and progress narratives both rear their heads again: Updike's proprietary "we" casts Munif as an uncomprehending outsider, peripheral to the central narrative of the novel's development. This Arab is a neophyte; he may get there, but not yet.

The markers of this foreigner's insufficiency, Updike argues, are twofold: he fails at character and he fails at voice. Above all, the novel doesn't work because Munif botches character: "no single figure acquires enough reality to attract our sympathetic interest. . . . There is none of that sense of individual moral adventure . . . which, since *Don Quixote* and *Robinson Crusoe,* has distinguished the novel from the fable and the chronicle; *Cities of Salt* is concerned, instead, with men in the aggregate."[53] The effect, Updike concludes sniffily, is simply "sociological."[54]

Updike thus seeks to give his generic complaint a genealogical authority; Munif, whether out of ignorance or disrespect, has failed to pay homage to the master genealogy. (There is something superbly apposite about Updike's bewildered response to this Arab interloper's unfathomable novel about Arab bewilderment at the unfathomable ways of American interlopers.) Yes, Munif breaks with the dominant traditions of the European and American novel, but his iconoclasm is not wholly eccentric: he is scarcely alone in working with a crowded canvas and with themes of collective transformation. His approach has much in common with Upton Sinclair's hugely populous epic, *Oil!*, which certainly had no use for *Robinson Crusoe* as a viable forebear. Sinclair, like Munif, was imaginatively fired by social convulsions that occur at high speed and on a vast scale: both oil frontier writers were fascinated by the land heists; the snake oil artists; the naïfs and faux-naïfs; the corporate ruthlessness; the economic and imaginative speculation; the surge in wealth and poverty; and the emergence, manipulation, and insurrections of an extraction industry working class. Both writers were fascinated, moreover, by technologies of power, technologies that, in the explosive mix of hope and servitude they deliver, are tinged with an atmosphere of apocalypse. Above all, Munif and Sinclair bear imaginative witness to the collisions (and collusions) between old religious cosmologies and new ones, between the preachers and the preachers of profit, between damnation or paradise in the afterlife and the satanic or redemptive possibilities created by an unearthly oil-rush.

The novelistic strategies that Munif favors are also redolent of those that shape collective fictions of modernization like Emile Zola's *Germinal* (*Cities'* great hydrocarbon forebear) and Ousmane Sembene's *Les bouts de bois de Dieu* (*God's Bits of Wood*). Munif, Zola, and Sembene are fascinated by the germination of revolt, the seeding of collective dissent—whether among coal miners in 1860s northern France, railroad workers in 1940s French West Africa, or Trans-Arabian Pipeline workers in 1940s Saudi Arabia. To this end, all three writers spurn an individual or familial focus, opting instead for a collective approach to character and form as they track across the sprawling canvases of societies in violent flux working class, peasant, and nomadic responses to injustices wrought by the onset of industrial modernity. As such, in recasting historical worker uprisings all three writers also remodel the conventions of the novel, treating orality as an imaginative resource and individual character as secondary to collective metamorphoses. The resultant novels are all positioned at some dramatic interface between capitalism's primitive accumulations, an assailed environment, and an insurrectionary labor movement.

One can be drawn to the ambition of such novels or not; the fact is, they exist and many readers have been moved by them. Updike's genealogical allegiances—and his affective preferences—are quite different: whatever else Updike's novels contain, they eschew multitudes. His native terrain is the sparsely populated crabgrass frontier, where tumult takes the guise of (often almost inaudible) disturbances that rumble through suburbia. Updike's regionalism is internal to the nation and his imagination contoured to a particular strip and social stratum of America's northeast corridor, whereas Munif is a transnational regionalist whose imagination roams from Morocco to Iran. Munif's fascination with epic, tectonic convulsions is at the furthest remove from the assumed solidity—emotionally deep but geographically narrow—that Updike cites as his own creative foundation: "The street, the house where I had lived [in Shillington, PA], seemed blunt, modest in scale, simple; this deceptive simplicity composed the inhabitants' precious, mystical secret, the conviction of whose existence I had parlayed into a career, a message to sustain a writer book after book."[55]

Munif knew no such house. Imaginatively, he was housed and fed by homelessness; he never possessed a categorical nationality or a conclusive homeland. He understood what it meant to live and travel as a problem. He bore witness in his writings to upheaval after upheaval—the *nakbah* that drove Palestinian refugees into Jordan, the Nasserite revolution, the Suez Crisis, the 1967 Arab-Israeli War, the Lebanese civil war, Sabra and Shatila, the Iranian revolution, the intafadah, the Iran-Iraq War, the Persian Gulf War, and the 2003 Iraq War shortly before his death. He felt drawn at a monumental and a micropolitical level to deracination as a theme: to societies and subjectivities rapidly undone and remade, not least at the ruined oasis and in the company town through petro-capitalism's dominion. His profound empathy for uprooted ecologies and communities carried over into his empathy for the refinery town's bewildered workers, betrayed by the oil blessing, workers whose experience of subsistence time had become shrunken and precarious:

> No one knew if they would remain alive or if tomorrow they would find food. True the company paid them, but what they received today was spent on the following day. Prices kept rising from day to day and money was accumulating in a few hands. As for the promises of houses and a comfortable life which Ibn al-Rashid had made them years ago as he herded them from 'Ajara and other places, they had vanished even before Ibn al-Rashid himself. And as for the promises of the personnel office in the company to build houses for the workers to enable them to bring their families over and return home in the evening to wife and children, years had passed without a single house being built.[56]

This is not to suggest that Munif had been unhoused by history in as profound a sense as his fictional refinery town workers. Yet he was sufficiently intimate with statelessness; with censorship; with being threatened, banished, or shunted about by regimes inimical to his voice to have, as his place of imaginative departure, a sense that place itself is fragile, irredeemably provisional, always vulnerable to history's storms.[57] That certain knowledge of uncertainty permeated the way he imagined the environment, social ecologies, and the novel as a form.

When Updike bemoans Munif's failure to deliver the obligatory "individual moral adventure," one senses beneath the surface of that judgment a set of assumptions not just about what a proper novel should look like but, more specifically, about what the frontier novel should look like *a la Americaine*, replete with individualistic male moral adventurers (or homosocial twosomes) riding westward across a panoramic wilderness of boundless threat and boundless promise. To provincialize such sentimental interpretations of the frontier novel entails that we address the allied challenge of provincializing wilderness literature. It feels apposite that the first volume of Munif's quintet, a work enlivened by scenes of cross-cultural misreadings, should itself be known in English through an act of mistranslation— or rather, by an inability to translate the untranslatable. Peter Theroux's

English version assumes the charismatic title of the quintet as a whole—*Cities of Salt*—rather than attempting to find an adequate rendition of Munif's title, '*al-Tih*. When this discrepancy is mentioned at all, '*al-Tih* is briskly translated as "the wilderness." But the Arabic phrase suggests something more resonant, more dynamic than that: '*al-Tih* refers not merely to wilderness as place, but to wilderness as an existential human condition, the state of being lost in the wilderness.[58] This human lostness, this wilderness bewilderment is, I would suggest, vital to the expansive reach and reverberant power of Munif's novel. If '*al-Tih* is a transnational masterpiece of Arab literature, as is conventionally observed, then it also warrants being read with a supplementary set of transnational questions in mind, among them this: how can such a novel help us rethink the conventional parameters of American wilderness literature?

Arabic literature boasts an immense tradition of wilderness literature in which the desert figures variously as a place of obliteration, threat, derangement, prophecy, and purifying promise. Yet the narrative arc of '*al-Tih*—from wadi to refinery town—disturbs any straightforward opposition between oasis civilization and desert barbarism. The most threatening desert marauders, the barbarians out there, are by implication imperialism's primitive accumulators. The full force of the novel's titular bewilderment is felt when the Bedouin characters are thrust into the high-speed, unintelligible chaos of the company town—the urban wilderness that is petromodernity's cultural creation.

By now, a considerable critical literature has accrued in an American context around the constructedness of wilderness—the fencings, the framings, the human evictions and erasures—in short, the cultural heavy lifting that has gone into evacuating cultural history from the concept and experience of wilderness. Munif's '*al-Tih* offers an innovative angle on the enterprise of American wilderness creation by erasure, not in Alaska or Wyoming, but way offshore in the Persian Gulf. What we witness are nomadic Bedouins rapidly remade as settled construction workers and tasked with constructing an urban wilderness that becomes the very condition of their dispossession and historic invisibility. '*Al-Tih* thereby creatively reframes some profound questions, especially this: how can the wilderness novel help us reconceive the dynamic between imperial resource frontiers and the frontiers of genre?

One productive resource for addressing such questions is Robert Vitalis's richly archived history on U.S.-Saudi relations, *America's Kingdom: Mythmaking on the Saudi Oil Frontier*. Although Vitalis does not engage the novel as a genre, he is profoundly engaged, as his subtitle announces, by frontier mythologies. Vitalis uses ARAMCO archives and private correspondence to dispel the myths of American exceptionalism promulgated by the oil consortium's richly funded propaganda machine. The consortium habitually contrasted enlightened American practices in the Middle East with those of the benighted British, using the language of partnership, mutual respect, benign incorporation, development, and nation building to advance the story line that U.S. expansion into the Persian Gulf was anticolonial in spirit and thereby consistent with a long, honorable tradition of sensitive cross-cultural uplift that animated American exceptionalism. Yet as Vitalis succinctly puts it: "America can only be seen as avatar of a more humane twentieth-century abroad against the atavism of European empire by leaving out the unbroken legacy of conquest and subjugation at home."[59]

Vitalis insists that the American West and the Saudi East Coast be read as conjoined frontiers held together by recycled tropes, myths, and political practices adaptively redeployed from the subjugation of Native American tribes to the creation, through coercive treaties and broken promises, of a "sovereign" Saudi nation. By exploring the company's private (and sometimes inadvertently public) utterances, Vitalis reveals how the rhetoric used to vindicate the internal colonization of Native peoples in the American West was reengineered and projected outward to justify an American imperialism that, while waving the banner of enlightened anticolonialism, was securing for itself an oil colony on the Persian Gulf's eastern shores. Many of the same personnel—Oklahoma and Texas oilmen, some doubling as the kind of CIA operatives who machinate in Munif's *The Trench*—adapted the practices of Western mining camps to the oil camps they established in the Persian Gulf. These practices included Jim Crow segregation; racialized pay structures; violent assaults on would be unionizers and civil rights campaigners; and what one oilman termed, in private correspondence, the cultivation of "a Texas herrenvolk atmosphere."[60] In trying to codify their relations to the Arabs and their lands, the oilmen repeatedly analogized to the American "encounter" with Indians back West. Moreover, in order to legitimate their U.S.-dependent petro-oligarchy, the Saudi elite in turn would learn to reinvent their history in terms assimilable to U.S. narratives of benign nation-building, developmental ascent, and glorious progress. (Without, of course, any reference to democracy.) The flag, the national anthem-tooting brass bands, the national costumery were all marshaled for parades of self-determination. ARAMCO public relations man Patrick Flynn, reminiscing about Arab-American relations during the opening decades of the oil encounter, gets positively dewy eyed:

> The early American oilmen coming to Saudi Arabia were extraordinary pioneers. They combined the can-do ingenuity of dedicated Americans with a great affection for the people and their customs. . . . Living with the Bedouins, sharing the hardships of life with the people in the desert and in town, they gained the respect and admiration of the Arabs. . . . The early Americans, it has to be understood, loved the Saudi Arabian people. They loved the country and spent their lives there in dedicated labor. There was no salary that could inspire such an outpouring and sacrifice, only love and affection.[61]

With that said, Franklin Roosevelt could still blithely declare that he "could do anything that needed to be done with Ibn Saud with a few million dollars."[62]

Against such a backdrop we are better positioned to revisit Updike's complaint that Munif was too ignorant of novelistic conventions and insufficiently Westernized to convert his material into a memorable pioneering adventure. Might *Cities of Salt* represent less a missed opportunity than a canny effort to push back, imaginatively and politically, against the frontier novel as heroically individualized pioneer romance? Instead of crafting an adventurer who faces down some Persian Gulf version of the wilderness and Native Americans, Munif summoned to life a radically different kind of historical panorama, a violent conflict on a communal scale, as the uprooted Bedouin fought for ecological subsistence, cultural dignity, and scraps of power against an advancing petro-capitalist imperialism in league with an emergent oligarchic client state.

Orality, Geology, and Writing:
The Technologies of Encounter

The narrative voice of *Cities* (disdained by Updike as that of "a campfire explainer") enables Munif to recast genre by blending elements drawn from oral fabulation into the epic historical novel.[63] *Cities* is not a sustained work of what Jennifer Wenzel (with reference to Nigerian literature) calls petro-magic-realism.[64] Yet if the quintet contains nothing as fully phantasmagoric as, say, "What the Tapster Saw," Ben Okri's story about Niger Delta petro-modernity, *Cities* is peppered with scenes of cross-cultural mistranslation where the inexplicable, the hallucinatory, and the realistic converge. These nodal, often humorous scenes of apparent magic coalesce around technological encounters, as Munif simulates, from a Bedouin perspective, the complex emotions triggered by the arrival of a procession of technologies from beyond all possible belief: the radio, the air conditioner, the generator, the telephone, the thermos, and the automobile. The mixed sentiments the Bedouins feel on encountering these signs taken for wonders—the incredulity, the terror, the yearning—are intensified by the fact that only the Americans and the emir can own such things. The marvels exist but are unavailable; in their enchantments, their bewitchings, they reshape the dynamics of power, labor, and desire, becoming by implication condensations of petro-capitalism's widening chasm between the haves and the never-will-haves.

This otherworlding of American technological practices reaches its apogee in a scene where Munif conveys how geological and spiritual substrates interpenetrate:

> The diabolical Americans, who had come looking for water, why did they continually dig into the earth, never stopping but never taking anything out? The water from the wadi, from Sabha and from the many wells they dug was pumped back into a hole in the ground—why wasn't it given to people? Did the ground hold such ghastly hordes of thirsty jinn, whose screams day and night could be heard only by the foreigners, who had come to quench their thirst? Were the jinn burning in the depths of the earth, and were the Americans pumping the water down to extinguish

[93]

the flames? Was there another world underground, with gardens, trees and men, all clamoring for water?[65]

This scene of mistranslation doubles as a scene of make-believe. Flummoxed by the foreigners' failure to respect water's insuperable value, the oasis dwellers read the ceaseless pumping as a possibly merciful act that quenches invisible, insatiable spiritual need. Incredible technological ritual is thereby folded back into the circle of belief. The locals explain away ecological insanity and ethical insensitivity—the Americans' unproductive pumping fetish and their inhumane profligacy—by speculating that the foreigners are attuned not to water but to some alternate universe below. Only the Americans can hear, as it were, the clamorous substrate, the notes from underground. This scene offers up, then, mistranslation as prescience: before the locals are let in on the underlying oil script, their speculations establish an ominous aura of geological-demonic suffering that foreshadows the traducing of the oasis, when the thirsty cries of gardens, trees and humans—an entire life world—will become inaudible, buried beneath petro-capitalism's crescendo din.

The Americans themselves are engaged in elaborate acts of translation. The first technology that signifies their arrival is the technology of writing, which becomes integral to their incremental appropriation of the wadi and becomes one of their distinguishing rituals.[66] Each day the Americans wander the area, staring at, probing, and measuring the earth; at dusk, they retreat to their tents and stare with equal intent at paper, writing furiously. They bring in boxes of sand and write inscrutable things on them. From the outset, the wadi's denizens perceive this peculiar crepuscular ritual as sinister, most likely a kind of witchcraft.[67] What are they writing? For whom? What does it signify? Why does it happen when the light fades?

We can read these scenes as intimating the twilight of the oasis itself: the writing at day's end is covertly violent, masking its nature and intent, an act that sets in motion an escalating series of overtly violent acts. The power that a geological survey embodies may, of course, be used for positive or destructive ends. But here the implication is that in being written up, the place (and all the life forms that depend on it) is being written off. The prospectors' writing may be petro-capitalism's first act of protoviolence, but it does not constitute a first mapping of the wadi; rather we can read their industrious writing as superimposing an "official landscape" onto a "vernacular landscape."[68] And thus the Americans will soon designate three oil camps outside Harran H1, H2, and H3: the stark, affectless numerical counting, posing as rationality, discounts and overwrites the existing place names and the histories that animate them.[69]

If in his own life Munif turned to writing as a technology of resistance, in *Cities* he dramatizes a less honorable tradition of writing as imperial technology of camouflaged intent—particularly as wielded against predominantly illiterate ecosystem peoples. One notes, more broadly, that this dimension to the politics of writing—writing as scripted obliteration—remains pivotal to the struggles that animate environmental justice movements around the world; central, too, to the author-activists who have written back against the tendency to inscribe whole socioecological communities as superfluous, as primitive obstacles to development, or as nonexistent. This pattern of writing off—and writing back—extends to realms far beyond Munif's novels or the Persian Gulf. First the writer-geologists arrive, then the bulldozers and earthmovers as, step by step, the promise of wealth morphs into a heavily policed, militarized, imperially entangled, resource-cursed authoritarian state.

The wadi's uprooted Bedouin soon find themselves at the violent end of another institutional novelty: a police force, instructed to beat to death if necessary anyone who refuses to abandon their oil-rich oases. Next, the people are moved to the coastal refinery town, their camels are taken away, and a prison is created in which nomads can be jailed for, among other things, the ironic crime of vagrancy. In the sequel to *Cities*, *The Trench*, Munif tracks the sophisticated repressive technologies put in place to defend the collaborative interests of indigenous oil sheiks and the foreign oil barons. By now, with help from the CIA, the paranoid, profligate ruler of America's newly "postcolonial" oil colony has set up a surveillance culture, which he boasts, "can hear ants crawling in the dark."[70] If the first two volumes of *Cities* describe an arc—from the coming of the writer-geologists, through the razing of the oasis, to the internal migrations to the company boomtown, to the petro-despotic carceral state—that arc should be understood as the passage from survey to surveillance.

Among the procession of repressive technologies deployed to secure the surveillance society, writing returns to play a second role in the remaking of state and subjectivity. At the oasis, the Americans had asked few questions; what fascinated them—what demanded writing up—was the earth below, not the people above. But the Bedouins relocated to the urban wilderness of the company town find that the Americans have now turned into big-time questioners: after long interrogations each worker is inscribed into the system, shadowed by a paper trail identity. The bewitchments of writing now include the signature and the identity card: writing has become fundamental to petro-modernity's control of labor and to the administration of difference enforced by a surveillance-cum-carceral culture.

These circumstances in which, far from being a mightier alternative to the sword, the pen becomes a sword supplement, are consistent with dissident Israeli architect Eyal Weizman's observation that territorial domination starts not with bulldozers and tanks but with the notes and sketches amassed by architects and by town planners. Weizman portrays these written plans as a first move toward a "politics of verticality" whereby, as John Berger notes, "the defeated even when 'at home' are being literally overseen and undermined."[71] This formulation is particularly resonant when applied to the resource curse: Munif's first volume portrays a community profoundly undermined in the most literal sense, and his second portrays a displaced, urbanizing community that becomes brutally overseen. This undermined-and-overseen dyad recurs across resource-cursed communities, in the Middle East and far beyond.

The Future Eaters and the Fuel-Fed Fire

When Europeans began to colonize Australia, some aborigines dubbed these unfathomable strangers "the future eaters": the newcomers consumed without replacing, devouring the future at a speed bereft of foresight, hollowing out time by living as if the desert were a place of infinite, untended provision.[72] This image of resource depletion as self-devouring cultural practice resonates with Munif's depiction of that other, far-off first desert encounter between Bedouins and American oil prospectors: there and indeed across the span of his work, Munif writes against the cycles of heedless avarice that imaginatively and materially erode older ecologies of time. Again and again, he returns to interweave the themes of shortsighted political repression and environmental temporal compression.

The future eating that accelerated during the "American" century was unevenly spread between centers of consumption and extraction, an unevenness that intensified inequities, fomented violence, and solidified structural repressions. Early in that century, Upton Sinclair, writing from California (an extraction frontier already mutating into a consumption epicenter) concluded his great hydrocarbon epic with an apocalyptic eruption over the costs exacted by "visions of unearned wealth."[73] Such visions were widening the breach between America's oil-impoverished classes and the nation's oil-enriched: Sinclair cast petroleum as a variety of religious experience that, in rending the earth, rent communities asunder. In so doing, he anticipated on an internal (though never wholly internal) American frontier a divisive dynamic that would soon replicate and mutate internationally, assuming its most exaggerated and politically costly forms in the Middle East.

Yet productive as it is to read Sinclair's *Oil!* and Munif's *Cities of Salt* in epic tandem, what passed for development in those two societies could scarcely have been more remote in their social outcomes. By the mid-1980s, when Munif was completing *Cities of Salt*, California boasted the world's sixth-largest economy; whatever imperial and corporate ties still bound it to the Gulf States, economically diverse California was structurally shielded from the resource curse. However, at that stage, after almost fifty years of oil extraction, Saudi Arabia, which ranked twenty-first in GDP, still ranked only sixty-fourth on the United Nations Human Development Index (a combined measure of democratic, educational, and health achievement and income distribution). That gap of forty-three places between Saudi Arabia's GDP and its Human Development Index was exceeded only by three other nation-states, all so-called oil rich: Oman, United Arab Emirates, and Gabon.[74]

We can thus read *Cities of Salt* as an epic expose of the fictions of sovereignty and development in societies squeezed between petroleum overlords above and the desirable subsoil below. In interview, however, Munif is at pains to point out that it is not modernity per se that he laments but rather the particular mangled form that it assumed in the Arabian peninsula. What he deplores is perhaps best captured by Michael Watts who (reflecting on the Niger delta) writes of petro-capitalism's "geography of intolerance."[75] That geography becomes, in Munif's work, inseparable from petro-capitalism's omnivorous appetite for time. In his fiction and nonfiction alike, Munif expresses a deep perturbation at (in both senses of the phrase) futureless states.

Having lived in five Middle Eastern countries, and having steeped himself in oil history for novels set in the Gulf States and Iran, Munif had a bird's-eye view of the ways in which America's cold-war strategizing converged with American support for tyrannies that helped secure stable access to petroleum. He foresaw how American policies—ranging from connivance through complicity to direct threats, assassinations, and the deliberate fomenting of unrest—increased the probability that uncontrollable blowback would ensue. Munif voiced outrage at the way, during the cold war's final decade, "the people behind fundamentalism's current hard line were recruited as youths, then nurtured in Afghanistan, and ultimately sent on to Bosnia, all with the enthusiastic support of the United States and Saudi Arabia."[76] The jihad was not some atavistic, medieval eruption, but was in large measure the child of modernity in the form of the Soviet-U.S. rivalry, of which control over petroleum reserves was a critical dimension.

Munif once remarked that the double standards of Washington's cold warriors left him nauseated: "They talked of democracy and human rights in the USSR, Eastern Europe and Cuba, but when they reached the Mediterranean coasts, they forgot about democracy. All they thought about was oil."[77] Five years before 9/11, when a bomb blast killed nineteen American servicemen stationed in Saudi Arabia at Dhahran (the basis for Munif's fictional Harran), Munif deplored the attack. He also sought to understand it, warning that America needed "to treat the causes of despair, not merely the symptoms. The United States, obsessed with oil fever and the need to control the oil states, has gone much too far in protecting regimes and individuals unworthy of protection."[78] Unless the United States backed those Muslims who sought to bring economic hope to the disaffected, unless it adopted a more even-handed approach to the Israeli-Palestinian conflict, and unless it closed the military bases in Saudi Arabia that Muslims viewed as symbols of a collective humiliation, Munif feared worse was to come: more violent hijackings of Islam with even more catastrophic consequences.

In essays and opinion pieces, Munif fleshed out as argument the short-sighted cross-cultural dynamics he had brought to life as fiction in *Cities of*

Salt. He insisted that America's obsession with creating client regimes, not equal partners, would exacerbate the region's instability, noting how the client-patron relationship "creates a psychological barrier between [the two sides], and makes it impossible for either to know what is going on in the minds and hearts of the other."[79] Munif's concern with the long-term, destabilizing effects of the resultant cross-cultural opacity permeates *Cities of Salt*. More than a decade after he began that vast work, he felt greater apprehension than ever toward the future: "I speak as a novelist who follows events, and tries to understand them. . . . In my book *Cities of Salt*, I wrote about the dangerous relationship between America and the countries of the Arabian Peninsula. Now it appears that what I imagined and expected—that the salt would dissolve in water—has begun."[80]

In *The Trench* Munif turned to the Qur'an to ring the changes on his imagery of an apocalypse brought on by a self-immolating avarice. That volume's title, Sabry Hafez observes, "alludes to the Qur'anic verse in which the infidel ruler of Mecca casts believers into a pit of fire: 'Self-destroyed were the owners of the trench, of the fuel-fed fire, when they sat by it, and were themselves the witnesses of what they did' (LXXXV, 4–7)."[81] This new religion, which incinerates all before it, is the creed of petro-despotism, marked by uncontrollable rapacity, corruption, brutality, and hypocrisy. The motif of the fuel-fed fire can thus be read as linking conspicuous consumption with its invisible twin, the inconspicuous consumption of irreplaceable oil time as, without hindsight or foresight, the petro-despotic state plunges headlong into the pit of collective self-destruction.

Munif was angered by the lost ground of the Gulf States—the geological, historical, and political lost ground. He was well aware that the energy wars are time wars as well; the temporal debt that the Gulf States had incurred pained him—how they had frittered away their resource wealth, betraying both past and future generations. His own exile—his inhabited impermanence—surely quickened his responsiveness to the soaring and plummeting of historical fortunes, to the unstable, fleeting riches of the petroleum age, an age whose bounty he saw squandered by a failure to provide—at a national, regional, and planetary level—for its own provisionality.

The official, sanitized histories disseminated by the Persian Gulf's rulers and their imperial oil partners were rife with bromides and selective

amnesia. Both parties made a big public relations push to distance themselves from any suggestion of imperialism. The most peculiar instance of
this push is Wallace Stegner's *Discovery! The Search for Arabian Oil*, commissioned by the Arabian American Oil Company in 1955 as part of an effort
to counter Nasserite denunciations of the House of Saud for capitulating to
imperialism and betraying pan-Arabism. Stegner's book, after a sixteen-year
delay, was eventually published in the company magazine, *Aramco World*,
in fourteen installments.[82] Stegner, in the unfamiliar position of writer-for-
hire, nonetheless blithely reads Aramco's history in Saudi Arabia as a mostly
benign extension of America's own mostly benign frontier development, an
extension marked by a "spirit of goodwill and generosity toward the Saudi
Arabs as people."[83] At pains to distance his paymasters from any intimation
of imperial malpractice, Stegner underscores the company's "frequent altru-
ism," its concern with "the total well-being of its employees, both American
and Arab," and how, unlike the British, the Americans refused to retreat into
"aloof enclaves."[84]

Munif's interpretation of this history is closer to that of the "hostile
propagandists" whom Stegner accused of maligning the well-intentioned,
uplifting role that American companies had played in the region.[85] Munif
profoundly mistrusted the whitewashed corporate and petro-despotic grand
narratives of progress: as a postcolonial novelist writing in imperial times,
he recognized, at least implicitly, that failures in the forms of memory are
inseparable from failures of political foresight. Looking back on the myopic
cities of the Arabian Peninsula, he viewed them as relics-in-the-making, as
fossils from a fleeting past. "The tragedy," he declared,

> is not in our having the oil, but in the way we use the wealth it
> has created and in the future awaiting us after it has run out.
> Trees were cut down, people uprooted from their land, the earth
> dug up and oil finally pumped out only to turn people into a
> crowd of open mouths waiting for charity or a crowd or arms
> fighting over a piece of bread and building an illusory future. In
> developed countries like Britain or Norway, the oil 'whim' . . .
> brings a new strength to the community, but in underdeveloped
> countries . . . oil becomes a damnation: a ceiling that screens
> the future from view. In twenty or thirty years' time we shall

discover that oil has been a real tragedy for the Arabs, and these giant cities built in the desert will find no one to live in them and their hundreds of thousands of inhabitants will have to begin again their quest for the unknown. Oil could have been a road to the future . . . but what actually happened is nothing like that. As a result we shall again have to face a sense of loss and estrangement, this time in complete poverty.[86]

Munif's vision of imminent catastrophe viewed retrospectively as ruin makes him read, at times, like a Benjaminian Angel of Progress for the Petroleum Century: blown backwards into a post-oil future he watches the debris of progress pile up before his eyes.

Munif ranks as one of the most mercilessly visionary writers to have engaged imaginatively with the politics of sustainability in its local, regional, transnational and transhistorical dimensions. His obsession with time's tyrannies is more than metaphoric: his work returns, again and again, to the deathly dance between regional petro-despots and imperial petro-capitalists, both quickstepping with eyes determinedly averted from the sorrows of resource finitude. If Munif stands out as an epic chronicler of epic excess, beneath his satires runs an anxiety and a rage at the cultures of petro-amnesia that have erected cities of salt on a vast but delusory wealth, equally shallow in its social distribution and in its vision of inhabitable time. For although *Cities of Salt* spans well over a century, Munif is at heart a chronicler of violent temporal compression. The quintet follows the short road—but the great distance—traversed by Bedouin society as the engines of petro-capitalism propel it at speed through a wilderness of inequity toward a post-petroleum frontier that beggars the imagination.

"Cities of Salt," Munif once explained, "means cities that offer no sustainable existence. When the waters come in, the first waves will dissolve the salt and reduce these great glass cities to dust. In antiquity, as you know, many cities simply disappeared. It is possible to foresee the downfall of cities that are inhuman. With no means of livelihood they won't survive."[87] Munif directs his anger at the Arab States' failure to shore up their future by diversifying their economies; by investing petroleum revenues in infrastructure; and critically, by cultivating a social democratic ethos, replete with a dynamic, resourceful civil society that would better prepare them for an oil-less tomorrow.[88] Yet his choice of apocalyptic idiom—"when the waters come in"—befits an age that is facing those twinned calamities of squandered time: oil's receding tides and the advancing tides of climate change, sped on by our brief, rapacious age of hydrocarbon extraction and combustion.

3

Pipedreams

Ken Saro-Wiwa, Environmental Justice, and Micro-minority Rights

Shell operations still impossible unless ruthless military operations are undertaken for smooth economic activities to commence.

—Nigerian government memo, December 5, 1994

Pity the land that needs heroes.

—Bertolt Brecht

Ken Saro-Wiwa squints at us from the cover of his Nigerian detention diary, the posthumous *A Month and a Day*.[1] His moustache looks precise and trim; his eyes are alight; a gash scrawls across his temple. But it is his pipe that governs the picture. It is an intellectual's accessory, a good pipe to suck and clench, to spew from and lecture with. Saro-Wiwa had expected tobacco to kill him: "I know that I am a mortuary candidate. But I intend to head for the mortuary with my pipe smoking."[2] In the end, it was the other pipes that got him, the Shell and Chevron pipes that poured poison into the land, streams, and bodies of Saro-Wiwa's Ogoni people, provoking him to take up the life of protest that was to be his triumph and his undoing.

Saro-Wiwa believed to the last that his writing would return to haunt his tormentors. Shortly before his execution in the Nigerian coastal city of Port Harcourt on trumped-up charges of murder, he declared: "The men who ordained and supervised this show of shame, this tragic charade, are frightened by the word, the power of ideas, the power of the pen. . . . They are so scared of the word that they do not read. And that will be their funeral."[3] Saro-Wiwa's conviction that the pen is mightier than the goon squad may well sound, to European and North American ears, like an echo from another age. But across much of Africa the certainty persists that writing can make things happen.

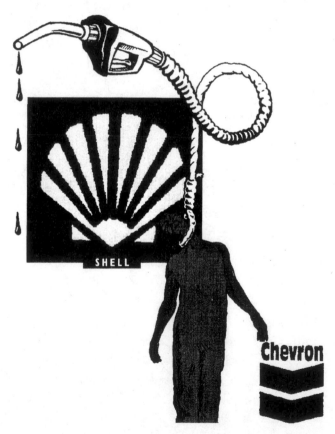

Figure 3 Cartoon protesting Ken Saro-Wiwa's execution. Reproduced by permission of the artist, JR Swanson; and Chris Carlsson, via Processed World magazine.

In one of his final letters from detention, Saro-Wiwa assured his friend, the novelist William Boyd: "There's no doubt that my idea will succeed in time, but I'll have to bear the pain of the moment. . . . the most important thing for me is that I've used my talents as a writer to enable the Ogoni people to confront their tormentors. I was not able to do it as a politician or a businessman. My writing did it. . . . I think I have the moral victory."[4] Elsewhere, he prayed that his work would have as visceral an impact as Andre Gide's 1927 journal, *Voyage au Congo*, which prompted an outcry against Belgian atrocities, helping secure their cessation.[5] Saro-Wiwa saw himself as part of that testimonial tradition, a witness to what he called the "recolonization" of Ogoniland by the joint forces of the oil companies and the Abacha regime.[6] Together the corporations and the regime had transformed the Niger Delta into a Bermuda triangle for human rights.

Saro-Wiwa wrote as a member of what I would call a micro-minority: he was one of 500,000 Ogoni in a nation of some 140 million, composed of nearly 300 ethnic groups. He produced tireless testaments to the devastation of his culture by the oil-driven avarice of vast forces beyond its control. He recognized, however, that the justice of a cause—particularly an African cause—is no reason to believe that it will gain the international attention it merits. As a writer and campaigner, he saw the strategic necessity of analogizing, of turning what he called the "deadly ecological war against the Ogoni" into a struggle emblematic of our times.[7] His prolific writings thus lay the ground for a broader estimation of the global cost, above all to micro-minorities, of the ongoing romance between unanswerable corporations and unspeakable regimes.

Micro-Minorities and the Delta of Death

The problem of competitive ethnicity is widespread in Africa, but it is particularly acute in Nigeria. The roots of the problem derive from the British invention of Nigeria in 1914. The British historian Lord Malcolm Hailey once described Nigeria as "the most artificial of the many administrative units created in the course of European occupation of Africa."[8] When Nigeria gained independence in 1960, it kept its improbable borders with the result that almost 300 ethnic groups were clustered under the umbrella of one nation-state. For most of the five decades since independence, this formidably diverse society has suffered under military rule. Unelected officials from the three largest ethnic groups—the Yoruba, the Igbo, and the Hausa-Fulani—have totally dominated national politics.

For Nigeria, 1958 had the makings of an auspicious year. Independence was on the horizon; Chinua Achebe's classic novel *Things Fall Apart* appeared, auguring great things—since realized—for the nation's literary future; and on February 17, 1958, the first tanker bearing Nigerian crude for export departed from Port Harcourt, destined for the Shell refinery at the mouth of the Thames.[9] What could and should have been for the Niger Delta's oil minorities the beginnings of great promise augured instead a poisonous future. Who could have dreamed in 1958 that four decades and $600 billion of oil revenues later, some 90 million Nigerians would be surviving on less than a dollar a day? And that Nigeria would rank below Haiti and Congo on the United Nations Human Development Index, a composite gauge of life expectancy, education, and income?[10] Even those figures don't capture the plight of the Ogoni and the delta's forty other oil micro-minorities: their environment has become so despoiled that supplementing that daily dollar with untainted crops and fish has become untenable.

The Ogoni constitute approximately 0.4 percent of the Nigerian population. Thus, like the other micro-minorities who dwell in this delta the size of England, the Ogoni lack the political leverage and constitutional protections to lay claim to the wealth that has been stripped from their land. Nigeria's independence initially promised a measure of economic justice for micro-minorities: the 1960 constitution required that the government return 50 percent of any mining revenues to the region of extraction.[11] But instead of the 50 percent constitutionally due to them, the Ogoni have been awarded a mere 1.5 percent, and in effect not even that.[12]

As a rule of thumb, the greater a nation's reliance on a single product for its economic survival, the higher the chances that that society is riddled with corruption and afflicted by profoundly skewed income distribution. Nigeria's dependence on oil is absolute: it constitutes 96 percent of Nigeria's export revenue and generates 80 percent of government income.[13] Thus Nigerian oil (of which the United States buys 40 percent) has readily become a precondition of and a byword for militarization. The petro-state has given rise, moreover, to a society in which 85 percent of oil wealth goes to a mere 1 percent of the populace, almost none of whom belong to the micro-minorities who inhabit, ingest, and inhale the eco-logical devastation.

Shell is by far the largest foreign stakeholder in the Nigerian econ-omy, owning 47 percent of the oil industry. Its joint venture partner in the petroleum business during Nigeria's most draconian years was the Abacha regime. Yet Shell representatives have repeatedly declared that they exercise no influence over Nigeria's rulers; Europe's largest oil cor-poration has thereby ducked behind the brutalities of its militaristic finan-cial partners. Such an arrangement means that Shell and other foreign oil corporations can maintain their desired technological presence while, under cover of deference for national sovereignty, they continue to act as ethical absentees.

This arrangement has also enabled Shell to ignore appeals by the Ogoni, the Ijaw, the Ikwerre and other neighboring micro-minorities for a share of oil revenues, a measure of environmental self-determination, and economic redress for their devastated environment. For Shell, Chevron, and the other oil majors operating in the delta, these are internal, Nigerian matters that belong to a sovereign realm inaccessible to corporate influence. But the record suggests otherwise: Chevron, for example, has acknowledged trans-porting Nigerian forces to quell uprisings in the oil camps of Rivers State.[14] Shell has imported arms for the Nigerian police, paid retainers to Nigerian military personnel, and made boats and helicopters available to them in assaults against protestors.[15] This is all integral to what one former Shell scientist has dubbed "the militarization of commerce"—an apt designation, if ever there was one, of resource extraction procedures under neoliberal-ism across the global South.[16]

By the time Saro-Wiwa was executed, the Nigerian military and Mobile Police force had killed 2,000 Ogoni through direct murder and the burning of villages.[17] Ogoni air had been fouled by the flaring of natural gas, their croplands scarred by oil spills, their drinking and fishing waters poisoned. Although Shell was driven out of Ogoniland in 1993, it simply moved on to other parts of Nigeria's once lush delta of death. Meanwhile, the Shell legacy continues to seep into the environment and bodies of the local farming com-munity that, unlike the international corporation, has nowhere else to go.

One witness described the aftermath of an oilfield explosion near the Ogoni village of Dere as an ocean of crude oil moving swiftly like a great river in flood, successfully swallowing up anything that comes its way. Cassava farms, yams, palms, streams, and animals for miles on end. There is no pipeborne water and yet the streams, the only source of drinking water are coated with oil. You cannot collect a bucket of rain water for the roofs, trees and grass are all covered with oil. . . . Men and women forced by hunger have to dive deep in oil to uproot already rotten yams and cassava.[18]

In the words of a second witness: "We can no longer breathe natural oxygen; rather we inhale lethal and ghastly gases. Our water can no longer be drunk unless one wants to test the effect of crude oil on the body."[19] The flaring of vast volumes of gas meant that villagers spent their nights beneath an artificial sun: "The people were used to having 12 hours of day and 12 hours of night. But now their position is worse than that of the Eskimos in the North Pole. For while nature gave the Eskimos six months of daylight followed by six months of night, Shell-BP has given the Dere people about ten years of continuous daylight."[20] Subsistence farming and fishing are the mainstays of these delta communities, yet they have received no compensation for the devastation of resources on which they utterly depend.

The half million Ogoni retain nominal ownership of most of their densely populated territory. But since oil extraction began over sixty years ago, they have suffered massive subterranean dispossession. Shell, Chevron, and successive Nigerian regimes have siphoned $30 billion worth of oil from beneath Ogoni earth.[21] Yet the locals still find themselves lacking a hospital, electricity, piped water, basic roads, housing, and schools. The community has found itself, in the fullest sense of the word, utterly undermined.

Neocolonialism and Instrumental Aesthetics

Faced with the neocolonial politics of mineral rights in the Niger Delta, Saro-Wiwa continued to believe that written testimony, backed by activism, could make a difference. Like many African authors before him, he recognized that in a society with frail democratic forces and a thin intellectual elite, interventionist writing required versatility and cunning.[22] His life as a public intellectual was distinguished by his astute sense of strategy.

Saro-Wiwa was alert to shifts in audience and occasion, locally and internationally; he would adjust his register and focus accordingly. He produced over twenty books across an ambitious spread of genres: novels, plays, short stories, children's tales, poetry, histories, political tracts, diaries, satires, and newspaper columns. *Sozaboy: A Novel in Rotten English*, a witty and wrenching book about life in the Nigerian Civil War, is an iconoclastic work in patois, daring and brimful of fine writing.[23] But across Anglophone West Africa, Saro-Wiwa achieved his greatest renown as the creator of the TV comedy hit *Basi and Company*: 30 million Nigerians tuned into it during prime time on Wednesdays. Saro-Wiwa wrote 150 episodes of *Basi*, a robust satire with a moralistic edge.[24] The series satirizes the street scammers and wide-boys who are such a feature of the Lagos life Saro-Wiwa loved and loathed. ("Living in Lagos," Saro-Wiwa wrote, "is an invention in itself and no one, I repeat, no one who lives in it can fail to be touched by its phoniness.")[25] But after the death of one of his sons in 1992, Saro-Wiwa cut back on his TV and literary activities. He single-mindedly devoted himself to the Ogoni cause, becoming the chronicler of his people's genocide and, finally, a death-row diarist.

Saro-Wiwa's generic versatility, his belief in an instrumental aesthetics, and his obsession with land rights place him in an established tradition of African writing.[26] Yet there the similarities end. For in East and Southern Africa, such tendencies have been routinely associated with writers whose anticolonialism—or anti-neocolonialism—has been inseparable from their socialism.[27] One thinks, for instance, of Ngugi wa Thiong'o's *Barrel of the Pen* and Mafika Gwala's essay "Writing as a Cultural Weapon" (which became the credo for a generation of South African writers).[28] Saro-Wiwa, by contrast, cultivated a deeply international sensibility while standing outside any lineage of African socialism. He was the first African writer to articulate the literature of commitment in expressly environmental terms: "[T]he environment is man's first right," he wrote in a letter smuggled from a Nigerian jail.[29] Yet as a successful owner of a small business—successful enough to send a son to Eton—he was never anticapitalist per se. He did, however, find himself painfully well placed to protest one of the signal developments of the 1980s and 1990s: the consolidation and increasingly unregulated mobility of transnational corporations. Five hundred corporations, Shell among them, now control 70 percent of global trade.[30]

As a micro-minority intellectual in an impoverished African country, Saro-Wiwa viewed deregulation as a synonym for corporate lawlessness of the kind that had ruined Ogoniland. But it is a testament to Saro-Wiwa's savvy sense of strategy that his political protests went well beyond the devastation of his homeland. While passionately centered in that cause, he came to situate it in a wider, global frame. He began to criticize corrosive international tendencies: above all, how in third-world countries weakened by structural adjustment, unregulated transnational firms and the national soldiery are at liberty to vandalize the weakest minority communities.

Saro-Wiwa appreciated the improbability of converting an injustice against a small African people into an international cause. His strategic response was to scour the wider political milieu for possible points of connection. In the preface to *Genocide in Nigeria* (1992), for instance, he takes heart from three contemporary developments: "[T]he end of the Cold War, the increasing attention being paid to the global environment, and the insistence of the European Community that minority rights be respected, albeit in the successor states to the Soviet Union and in Yugoslavia." But, he worried, "It remains to be seen whether Europe and America will apply to Nigeria the same standards which they have applied to Eastern Europe." His doubts have proved well founded.[31]

Unconventional War by Ecological Means

A Month and a Day includes a record of Saro-Wiwa's imaginative efforts to capitalize on these new forms of international attention. Initially, both human rights groups and ecological groups proved equally unreceptive to the Ogoni cause. An African intellectual claiming ethnocide by environmental means? Saro-Wiwa seemed, at first, eccentric and unplaceable. At Boyd's prompting, he decided to contact Greenpeace. They replied, quite simply, that they did not work in Africa.[32] Amnesty International, for their part, said they could only take up the Ogoni cause if the military was killing people or detaining them without trial, a process that had yet to begin. Saro-Wiwa responded with frustration: "The Ogoni people were being killed all right, but in an unconventional way."[33] As he later elaborated:

> The Ogoni country has been completely destroyed by the search for oil. . . . Oil blow-outs, spillages, oil slick and general

pollution accompany the search for oil. . . . Oil companies have flared gas in Nigeria for the past thirty-three years causing acid rain. . . . What used to be the bread basket of the delta has now become totally infertile. All one sees and feels around is death. Environmental degradation has been a lethal weapon in the war against the indigenous Ogoni people.[34]

Appeals to minority and environmental rights both gained ground in the 1990s, but there was little precedent in Africa for their simultaneous invocation. Despite the early unresponsiveness of Greenpeace, Amnesty International, Friends of the Earth, and Survival International, Saro-Wiwa persisted in arguing that the Ogoni were victims of an "unconventional war" being prosecuted by ecological means. Undeterred, he sought to educate himself further through travel. An odyssey through the rupturing Soviet Union confirmed his sense of a growing international context for the articulation of minority claims. A visit to Colorado gave him access to an environmental group that had successfully salvaged a wilderness from corporate and governmental assaults.[35] These experiences persuaded Saro-Wiwa that his incipient Movement for the Survival of the Ogoni People (MOSOP) would be well served by linking minority rights to environmental rights. Through a young Dutch lawyer, Michael van Walt van der Praag, long active in the Tibetan cause, Saro-Wiwa made contact with the Unrepresented Nations and Peoples Organizations.[36] This gave him access to the United Nations Working Group on Indigenous Populations, which he addressed in Geneva in 1992. (That same year, another Ogoni leader, Chief Dr. H. Dappa-Biriye, spoke at the Rio Earth Summit on behalf of the delta peoples.) Saro-Wiwa discovered that "in virtually every nation-state there are several 'Ogonis'—despairing and disappearing peoples suffering the yoke of political marginalization, economic strangulation or environmental degradation, or a combination of these."[37] The parallel tracks of Saro-Wiwa's self-education had finally converged. From 1992 onward, the combined appeal to minority and environmental rights became fundamental to the MOSOP campaign. Human rights and ecological groups that had once found the Ogoni campaign enigmatic now became its most adamant international supporters. Friends of the Earth, Greenpeace, Amnesty International, Human Rights Watch/Africa, International Pen, Abroad, and the Body Shop all rallied to the cause.

These developments gave Saro-Wiwa's campaign a resonance it had previously lacked and challenged stereotypes about environmental activists: that they are inevitably white, young, middle-class Europeans or Americans who can afford to hug trees because they have been spared more desperate battles. Saro-Wiwa's campaign for environmental self-determination may well prove historically critical to the development of a broader image of ecological activism. Just as we witnessed how the sometimes rarefied concerns of middle-class white feminists in the 1970s gave way in ensuing decades to a more internationally diverse array of feminisms, locally led and locally defined, so too we are now seeing indigenous environmentalisms proliferate under pressure of local necessity. As the spectrum of what counts as environmental activism expands, it becomes harder to dismiss it as a sentimental or imperial discourse tied to European or North American interests. Nor does the case for this diversification rest, any longer, solely on Amazonian or Indian examples.

Saro-Wiwa understood that environmentalism needs to be reimagined through the experiences of the minorities who are barely visible on the global economic periphery, where transnationals in the extraction business—be it oil, mining, or timber—operate with maximum impunity. Environmental justice became for him an invaluable concept through which to focus the battle between subnational micro-ethnicities and transnational macroeconomic powers. As an Ogoni, suffering what he called Nigeria's "monstrous domestic colonialism," Saro-Wiwa was in no position to trust the nation-state as the unit of collective economic good.[38] Instead, he advocated a measure of ethnic federalism in which environmental self-determination would be acknowledged as indispensable to cultural survival. After the "judicial murder" of Saro-Wiwa and the eight other accused, public outrage tended to divide into those who primarily condemned the Abacha regime and those who condemned Shell.[39] For Saro-Wiwa, however, the blame was indivisible. He consistently represented the Ogoni as casualties of joint occupying powers: the transnational oil corporations and a brutal, extortionate Nigerian regime. Shell, meanwhile, sought to put a positive gloss on this relationship, with public relations primers like "Nigeria and Shell: Partners in Progress."[40] But the regressive character of the relationship is more accurately portrayed by a leaked Nigerian government memo addressing protests in Ogoniland. Dated December 5, 1994, it reads: "Shell operations still impossible unless ruthless military operations are undertaken for smooth economic activities to commence."[41]

This ruthless smoothing of Ogoniland was embarked on in a spirit of racism and ethnic hatred. Again, Saro-Wiwa resisted the temptation to reduce his people's suffering to either term.[42] Shell's racism is manifest: in Africa, the company waives onshore drilling standards that it routinely upholds elsewhere. Indeed, 40 percent of all Shell oil spills worldwide have occurred in Nigeria.[43] When operating in the Northern hemisphere—in the Shetlands, for instance—Shell pays lucrative rents to local councils; in the Niger Delta, village authorities receive no comparable compensation.[44] A 1995 World Bank report noted that 76 percent of the natural gas resulting from petroleum production in Nigeria was flared (at temperatures of 14,000 degrees Celsius), while in Britain only 4.3 percent and in the United States a mere 0.6 percent was flared. This toxic practice foreshortened the life expectancy of the delta peoples. Children, moreover, who had no access to electricity to read or learn by also had no experience of night, as they lived 24/7 beneath the blazing false sun of interminable flares, as if in some seasonless equatorial rendition of an Arctic summer.[45] In the mid-90s, when flaring from Nigeria's oil fields was pumping 12 million tons of methane and 35 million tons of carbon dioxide into the atmosphere annually, it was argued by some that this was the single greatest contributor worldwide to climate change.[46] (In this one regard at least, the oil corporations did not discriminate.) Given this backdrop, the irony was not lost on the Ogoni that Shell was winning awards in Europe for environmentally sensitive conduct—north-south greenwashing, par excellence.[47]

But Shell's racial double standard would have been inoperable without brutal backing from a Nigerian regime whose record on minority rights verged on the ethnocidal. General Abacha's dreaded Mobile Police force—which Nigerians dubbed the "Kill and Go Mob"—responded violently to peaceful protests by the Ogoni and their delta neighbors. After an anti-Shell rally in January 1993 drew several hundred thousand Ogoni, the police razed twenty-seven villages. Two thousand Ogoni were killed and 80,000 displaced.[48] Saro-Wiwa has likened the fate of the Ogoni during the oil rush to their fate during the Nigerian Civil War of 1967, when a conflict erupted between the nation's dominant ethnicities.[49] This battle over oil territory left the Ogoni flattened "like grass in the fight of the elephants."[50] Ten percent of all Ogoni died in a war that was not of their making, a calamity that drove home for Saro-Wiwa the distinction between minority and extreme minority status.[51] A micro-minority was powerless to influence national events, particularly in a society run on principles of kleptocratic militarism. The wealth that flowed beneath Ogoniland was wealth in name only: historically, it brought poverty, injustice, and death, as outsiders stampeded for oil. A quarter century after the civil war, Saro-Wiwa's despair about Nigeria continued to deepen because the nation's rulers had "the hearts of stone and the brains of millipedes; because Shell is a multinational company with the ability to crush whomever it wishes; and because the petroleum resources of the Ogoni serve everyone's greed."[52]

The International Response

The fact that the Ogoni have been casualties of racism and ethnic hatred may help, in a peculiar way, to explain the low-key American response to the executions. The outcry in Britain, South Africa, and France was far more vocal and sustained. In the British case, this is understandable: Shell is an Anglo-Dutch conglomerate, and British coverage of Africa has traditionally been stronger than America's because of the colonial ties. (For similar reasons, the reverse is true of Latin American news.) But there was more to the American media's relative indifference to the executions than that. In U.S. political discourse, racial oppression and minority discrimination typically function as identical terms. This makes it difficult for liberal or minority Americans to condemn in a single breath an African regime for oppressing its own minorities and a European corporation for racism against Africans. Randall Robinson, director of TransAfrica, the African-American foreign-policy lobbyists, met with a ruptured response to his appeal for U.S. sanctions against Nigeria similar to those imposed on South Africa. Many African-American leaders, among them, Louis Farrakhan—who visited Lagos and gave the Abacha regime his blessing—argued that it was divisive to campaign against any African government.[53]

But Saro-Wiwa never enjoyed the luxury of such long-distance compunctions. He insisted that the Ogoni were joint casualties of a brutal European racism and an equally brutal African ethnocentrism. He never hesitated to make such controversial connections. As he wrote in his prison diary, skin colour is not strong enough to stop the oppression of one group by another. Sometimes it reinforces oppression because it makes it less obvious. White people oppressing blacks in South Africa draws instant condemnation because it is seen to be racism. But black upon black oppression merely makes people shrug and say, "Well, it's their business, isn't it?"[54]

Saro-Wiwa repeatedly called for international measures—like those that had helped end apartheid—against a Nigerian regime that he deemed equally heinous.[55] The two countries rank as the powerhouses of the continent: South Africa boasts Africa's largest economy and Nigeria the second largest, as well as being the continent's most populous nation. At the time of Saro-Wiwa's appeal for international intervention, the image of these two giants had undergone a sharp reversal. For over thirty years, Nigeria had stood as Africa's leader in the antiapartheid campaign. But just as South Africa, under Mandela's leadership, was finally moving beyond apartheid, so Nigeria was sinking to its antidemocratic nadir.[56]

By the time the fifty-two Commonwealth nations met in Auckland, New Zealand, in November 1995, South Africa and Nigeria's standing had largely been reversed. South Africa was present at a Commonwealth gathering for the first time in thirty-five years. And triumphantly so, in the magisterial form of Nelson Mandela. Previously the ritual object of Commonwealth condemnations, South Africa was now, by virtue of Mandela's moral gravitas, the de facto commonwealth leader. Nigeria, by contrast, had become a potential new pariah. The Commonwealth, the United States, and the European Union were all goading Mandela to take the lead in Africa. Nigeria was to be his first major foreign policy test.

On arriving at the summit, Mandela voiced his opposition to isolating Nigeria, advocating quiet negotiations instead.[57] The Nigerian regime responded, almost immediately, by hanging Saro-Wiwa and the Ogoni Eight. Mandela instantly became the target of outrage. Wole Soyinka charged him with appeasement, likening his "quiet diplomacy" toward the Nigerian junta to Reagan and Thatcher's notorious policy of "constructive engagement" toward the apartheid regime.[58] Professor Kole Omotoso, one of the swelling ranks of Nigerian exiles who had found refuge in South Africa, agreed: "Those who know my country know how irrational and illogical the military regime is. There wasn't a chance that it would respond to what Mandela called 'softly-softly.'"[59] Saro-Wiwa's lawyer protested angrily to Mandela, "Were quiet diplomacy pursued in South Africa . . . I doubt you would be alive today."[60]

Mandela's tragic misreading of the Abacha regime and the threat to Saro-Wiwa can best be understood in terms the ANC's historical sentimentality toward Nigeria. Many of South Africa's new political and cultural elite had found refuge in Nigeria in the 1960s, when it was emerging as a bulwark against apartheid and colonialism. Those exiles included eminents like the academic and writer, Ezekiel Mphahlele, and the South African deputy president, Thabo Mbeki. It is no coincidence that Mbeki became South Africa's chief negotiator in the country's "softly-softly" response to the Abacha coup. He seemed to confuse South Africa's historic debt (and his own personal one) to the Nigerian people with a debt to Nigeria's rulers, even when they had deposed an elected government and enjoyed no popular mandate whatsoever. At the Commonwealth summit, Nigerian human rights activist Innocent Chukwuma stressed the wrongheadedness of this confusion. Calling for an international ban on Nigerian oil, Chukwuma pointed out, "The proceeds from oil revenue are going into private accounts. They don't even get to the people."[61] In 1994 alone, $12 billion worth of oil went missing from government accounts.[62]

The South African failure to provide international leadership against Abacha also needs to be understood in terms of the ANC's "fetish for compromise."[63] This fixation had enabled Mandela to maneuver the ANC into power and to avert the civil war that just before the South African elections had begun to look menacingly imminent. But he misjudged the Nigerian political climate: Abacha was more ruthless than De Klerk, and Nigeria lacked the dense matrix of civic bodies, trade unions, and other democratic organizations that exerted pressure on the apartheid regime while Mandela negotiated a compromise.[64]

If Saro-Wiwa's execution triggered a national political scandal for Mandela's government, it also quickened the flow of Nigerian exiles and refugees into South Africa. These included intellectuals, journalists, and democratic activists. In perhaps the surest sign of the about-face in Nigerian-South African relations, Johannesburg became a prominent outpost of the Lagos-based Democratic Alternative, of the Saro-Wiwa support campaign, and of the international boycott of Shell. Where ANC activists had once plotted against apartheid in Lagos and Kano, thirty years later, Nigerian democrats were mobilizing in Johannesburg for the overthrow of the Abacha regime. Thus the Ogoni "judicial murders" brought into focus the critical vulnerability of Africa's micro-minorities, as well as the shifting prospects for democracy on the continent.

Micro-Minorities and the Resource Curse

Some years back, the Philippine government placed an ad in *Fortune* magazine that read: "To attract companies like yours, we have felled mountains, razed jungles, filled swamps, moved rivers, relocated towns . . . all to make it easier for you and your business to do business here."[65] The Philippines is just one of a succession of poor nations to have wooed transnationals in a manner indissociably catastrophic for the environment and micro-minorities. This process has been most acutely damaging in the equatorial belt that girdles the earth's midriff from Ecuador, Bolivia and Brazil; through Surinam and Guyana; on through Nigeria, Cameroon, the Central African Republic, Gabon, and Congo; to the Philippines, Malaysian Borneo, Indonesia, and New Guinea. This belt contains a unique concentration of ethnic minorities for simple ecological reasons. Rich equatorial ecosystems encouraged the development of a higher concentration of self-sufficient cultural groups than was possible in less fertile regions. Today most of these ethnic groups exist as micro-minorities in undemocratic, often destitute nation-states that register in the global economy principally as sites for the unregulated extraction of oil, minerals, and timber. It is thus no coincidence that indigenous environmentalism has burgeoned most dramatically in this zone, as micro-minorities battle for the survival of their land-dependent subsistence cultures.

The plunder and terror suffered by the Ogoni have been mirrored in other mineral-rich equatorial regions, West Papua, Ecuador, and Peru among them. West Papua has an even higher concentration of minorities than the Niger Delta. And, like the delta peoples, West Papuans have the curse of wealth—some of the world's richest deposits of copper and gold—seaming beneath their land. They face a similar alliance between an occupying military power and an unscrupulous transnational corporation.

The same Indonesian regime responsible for the third worst genocide of the twentieth century, in East Timor, colonized West Papua with a brutality that killed 43,000 indigenous people. Their accomplice in that endeavor was the Louisiana-based mining transnational Freeport McMoran. After the arrival of Freeport in 1967, the indigenous people endured detention without trial, torture, forced resettlement, disappearances, the plunder of their mineral wealth, and the uncompensated degradation of their environment.[66] Freeport's private security officers and the Indonesian military on occasion combined to shoot and kill unarmed indigenous protesters. In an alliance even more devastating than that between the Abacha regime and Shell, the Indonesian regime and Freeport pursued ethnocide as a condition of mandatory development. James Moffett, Freeport McMoran's chairman, himself seemed confused as to whether such "progress" was a life-giving or death-dealing business. In Moffett's proud words, "Freeport is thrusting a spear of development into the heart of West Papua."[67] In this deadly battle, the micro-minorities fought back in a language that melded new modes of environmental defiance with a more traditional reverence for the land. As one Amungme leader put it, "Freeport is digging out our mother's brain. That is why we are resisting."[68]

Some of these acts of environmental defiance have begun to take effect: for example, in the oil-rich Oriente Region of Ecuador, where Texaco devastated Indian territory in a manner similar to Shell's despoliation of Ogoniland. Oriente drinking water, fishing grounds, soil, and crops have all been polluted. According to the Rainforest Action Network, Texaco spilled 17 million gallons of crude oil in the Oriente, leaving a toxic legacy that has caused, as in Ogoniland, chronic health problems for the residents.[69] Here again, the seepage of oil-contaminated waste resulted from the jettisoning of procedures that are standard for onshore drilling in the Northern hemisphere. The appeal of the Oriente and Ogoniland is precisely the prospect of profits without interference or limits. As one petroleum geologist working in the Oriente put it: "I want to stamp on the ground hard enough to make that oil come out. I want to skip legalities, permits, red tape, and other obstacles. I want to go immediately and straight to what matters: getting that oil."[70]

Ecuador's Acción Ecológica led a successful national boycott of Texaco and has helped drive the corporation from the region. In addition, a coalition of indigenous federations, mestizos, grassroots environmentalists, and human rights groups pursued an innovative avenue of redress, filing a $1.5 billion class action suit in New York against Texaco. The suit earned the support of Ecuador's Confederation of Indigenous Nationalities, the country's largest Indian organization. Following the Ecuadorian example, a group of Ogoni villagers decided to sue Shell for $4 million for spillages that had robbed them of their livelihood.

Joseph Conrad and Colonial Buccaneering Redux

The ravaging of West New Guinea, the Oriente, and Ogoniland testifies to the growing inequity between subnational minorities and transnationals that have enjoyed enhanced mobility and experienced diminishing controls since neoliberalism's ascent in the 1980s. Third-world governments are often joint partners in the regional plunder or worse than useless at regulating transnationals that are more powerful than the states themselves. One result has been a reversion to concessionary economics in which forested or mineral-rich areas are sold for a song. It is in this context that Saro-Wiwa's talk of recolonization and his invocation of Andre Gide's Congo journal begin to sound eerily apposite. When Shell can pump out $30 billion worth of oil and the trade-off for the locals is disease, dispossession, military occupation, massacres, and an end to self-sustaining fishing and agriculture, the process seems more redolent of late nineteenth-century colonial buccaneering than it does of twenty-first century international economics. But if the idea of the nation-state continues to lose any vestige of popular appeal through a failure to deliver local benefits, and if rulers lack the will or the resources to command a national polity, the continent's poorest countries will continue to fall prey to a twenty-first-century version of nineteenth-century concessionary economics, unhampered by regulations or redress. The nation-state will become ever more marginal to deals negotiated between local chiefs and transnationals, an imbalance in bargaining power if ever there was one. A German diplomat recently foresaw as much: "In the twenty-first century German ambassadors and CEOs heading for Africa may again be authorized to sign treaties of cooperation with whatever coastal kings or leaders are able to assert some sort of control over the interior."[71]

Under such circumstances, the kleptocrats and soldiery in the nominal capital will still demand their palm greasing, while locally, the chiefs request their crude version of the same. Such practices are already widespread. During Abacha's rule, for example, a group of foreign explorers arrived by ship at the head of a marshy river near the Niger Delta village of Sangama. They sought to establish a station there. After lengthy bartering with a local chief, they settled on his cut: he would receive £1,000 sterling, twelve bottles of cognac, and twelve bottles of gin. But as the foreigners pushed deeper into the hinterland, they found villagers blocking their river route with a barricade of palm fronds and canoes. The explorers' leader felt bewildered and betrayed. He reported, "There were about a hundred people ahead of us. If we'd pressed ahead we would have risked killing them. So we took a boat and went back to get Chief Jumbo."[72]

More bargaining, more demands. Another £300 changed hands, a further bottle of gin, an agreement to repair a building. The chief sacrificed a goat to the water gods; the barricade was lifted; the foreigners passed through. If they weren't pulling an oil rig in tow, this could be have been an entry from Gide's Congo journal or the opening scene of a lost Conrad novel.

Over a century has passed since Conrad immortalized in fiction the unregulated plunder that he witnessed in the Congo. In a gesture of imaginative cynicism, he christened the worst of these plunderers the Eldorado Expedition. They were "sordid buccaneers: reckless without hardihood. . . . To tear treasures out of the bowels of the land was their desire, with no more moral purpose at the back of it than there is in burglars breaking into a safe."[73] Over great swathes of Africa and much of the global South, Eldorado Expeditions are rising from the dead. They are still the self-declared standard-bearers of progress and are still tearing at the bowels of the earth. Today one finds in their motley ranks a mix of international and indigenous colonialists. Not least in Nigeria of which Saro-Wiwa once remarked in exasperation, "there is no such country. There is only organized brigandage."[74]

We have witnessed in the past two decades the accelerated extraction of African minerals, oil, and timber in many of the continent's least stable nations: Liberia, Gabon, Congo, Central African Republic, Nigeria, Mali, Niger, Chad, Sierra Leone, Mauritania, and Angola among them. (South African mining corporations, buoyed by their postapartheid legitimacy, have come to compete in this terrain against European, American, Australian, Canadian, Chinese, and Brazilian outfits.) However, in most of these shaky African nations, concessionary economics, kleptocratic rule, structural adjustment, and corporate deregulation mean that irreplaceable minerals and forests are being lost for little national gain and at considerable local ruin. We are seeing a repartitioning of Africa into what French colonialists used to call *l'Afrique utile* and *l'Afrique inutile*: this time "capital 'hops' over 'unusable Africa,' alighting only in mineral-rich enclaves that are starkly disconnected from their national societies."[75] It is in this climate that Saro-Wiwa's campaign against the destruction of micro-minorities through the devastation of their environment has proven to be a harbinger of a much broader discontent. He seemed to intuit as much at his tribunal, as he looked back on his life with an otherworldly eye: "I will tell you this, I may be dead, but my ideas will surely not die."[76]

The Gospel cadences to Saro-Wiwa's prophecy are consistent with the Passion play the Nigerian junta inadvertently helped create. Saro-Wiwa was no messiah. He was a courageous man who stood outside the conventions of corruption but who could also be testy, inflexible, self-aggrandizing, and subject to overweening ambition. The junta took this very mortal and internationally obscure activist, gave him a stage trial, and turned him through execution into a martyr. They thus amplified his cause and—as happens with martyrs—simplified it in his favor. ("Living people grow old but martyrs grow younger," the Palestinian poet Mourid Barghouti once observed.)[77] Saro-Wiwa instantly became larger and longer than life. The word flashed around Lagos and Port Harcourt that he had refused to die, that it had taken five hangings to kill him. As a final precaution against his posthumous revenge, the regime stationed armed guards at the cemetery. They had orders to shoot anyone seen approaching the grave to pay homage or claim relics.

Saro-Wiwa understood far better than his adversaries that you can't crucify ideas, that there are some things which cannot be resolved by a show of force. Abacha and his sidekicks were exasperated by the unruliness of language, by its refusal to submit to military control. In countries like Nigeria where official brutality and paranoia feed off each other, unofficial writing begins to assume the status of latent insult. Thus journalists, writers, and intellectuals are singled out for harassment, detention, torture, and execution often as much for what they represent as for anything they say. But Africa's muscle men who seek to shackle language and criminalize imaginings only flatter writers with their fears. While Abacha was naïve enough to believe that murdering Saro-Wiwa would silence him, another African autocrat, Kenyan president Daniel arap Moi, was simultaneously seeking to stamp out subversive fantasy. He had a journalist arrested for "the crime of imagining the death of the president."[78] This was surely the high-water mark for the dictatorial tendency to equate fantasy with political treason.

Abacha clearly had no conception of the cost of creating a martyred writer, an image with considerable pulling power in the media—doubly so after the fatwa against Salman Rushdie. The threat of censorship typically raises the hackles of journalists and writers because they are professionally invested in freedom of speech. From this viewpoint, the execution of a writer on false charges is more than just another human injustice; it also becomes, as Harold Pinter observed, "the most brutal form of censorship."[79] It was predictable, therefore, that the image of Saro-Wiwa as writer-martyr would provoke intense journalistic outrage as well as the most vocal literary protest since the Rushdie affair. Pinter, Soyinka, Boyd, Chinua Achebe, Ben Okri, Fay Weldon, and Arthur Miller were just a few of the writers who spoke out publicly against Abacha and Shell.[80] So in death Saro-Wiwa extended—surely, beyond his imaginings—the remarkable coalition of international interests he had begun to forge while alive, an alliance that brought together environmentalists, minority rights advocates, antiracists, opponents of corporate deregulation, and defenders of free speech. Whether his principles ultimately prevail will depend as much on the future of this coalition as on the timeliness of the ideas themselves. Otherwise, the pipe-puffing activist, with his tenacious faith in democracy, nonviolence, and the power of the pen, will lose yet further ground to the figure (in Michael Watts's image) of "the masked militant armed with the ubiquitous Kaloshnikov, the typewriter of the illiterate."[81]

Forms of Inheritance, the Inheritance of Loss

At Saro-Wiwa's funeral, his eldest son, Ken Saro-Wiwa Jr., followed his father's express instructions, placing two copies of Ken Sr.'s books in the coffin alongside his favorite pipe. As the coffin was lowered into the tomb, the attendant crowd surged forward and, for a moment, Saro-Wiwa Jr. felt certain he would be swept into his father's grave. The incident speaks powerfully to the son's lifelong fear of the all-devouring cause, the cause that had swallowed his father and threatened to swallow the next generation as well. More broadly, the incident speaks to the risks and quandaries that attend the martyr-focused cause as a political figurehead's pragmatic leadership enters the realm of mythic potency through the manner of his death. The immortal corpse, the one true body of the cause, can become a powerful political asset but also stand dauntingly in the path of those who wish to take the struggle forward in new ways, for new times. Rival claimants—all anonymous by comparison—will clash, sometimes violently, over who has the right, by birth or principle, to take up the hero's mantle. For those who follow, after martyrdom, what next?

This question looms over the life and writings of Ken Saro-Wiwa Jr., his father's anointed but initially reluctant legatee. Saro-Wiwa Jr.'s memoir, *In the Shadow of a Saint*, which closes with that image of the son teetering above his father's gaping grave, stages a searching engagement with the forms of inheritance.[82] This often-anguished, internally riven book allows us to open up vexing questions, at once political and aesthetic, about activist nonfiction: questions about individual creativity and movement answerability, about originality and reiteration, about self-revelation and self-concealment. Read in tandem, *A Month and a Day* and *In the Shadow of a Saint* offer contrasting routes into the maze of nonfiction forms that activist-writers can draw on in pursuit of their political and literary ends.

A Month and a Day is an unruly, polyvocal work, a nonfictional collage, in which Saro-Wiwa tacks back and forth among a raft of genres: diary, memoir, journal, manifesto, advocacy journalism, ethnography, and satire, throwing in for good measure some transcribed speeches and a bill of rights. The book's disorderly syncretism is partly circumstantial: most of it was spliced together under the stresses of Saro-Wiwa's confinement in a Port Harcourt prison. Yet one senses in the irreverent, breathless bricolage something tactical as well, the propulsive urgency of colliding forms as Saro-Wiwa strives to fit into a single book an ill-fitting set of causes by binding together, in unprecedented ways, an African commitment to environmental and human rights, to micro-minority justice, and to exposing the slow violence of what he judges to be attritional ecological genocide. The result is a book without a clear narrative itinerary or stable voice, structurally diffuse yet inventively affiliative and unwavering in its political energy.

Despite the word "diary" in the subtitle, *A Month and a Day* is at best a fitfully personal book; the private Saro-Wiwa disappears for long stretches, and when he reappears he does so primarily as an outsize public persona in a way that renders him opaque. We can read his son's memoir, in part, as a questing, ambiguous protest against his father's vanishing acts—as a parent and as a writer. Saro-Wiwa Jr. uses the memoir's intimate potential to push back against a certain self-aggrandizing impersonality that comes with the heroizing territory of the cause. As he wrestles with his political and familial inheritance, Saro-Wiwa Jr. strives to humanize his remote, complex father—to put mortal flesh on his immortality—without diminishing what he stood for. This requires a layered exhumation, as the son seeks to unearth the father whom he'd lost in life to a higher cause and then lost a second time to "judicial murder" and then a third time, after death, to sainthood. In exhuming his father Saro-Wiwa Jr. must also exhume himself from beneath the weight of the familial, inherited cause so that ultimately he can embrace the commitments that his father had chosen for him, but on his own terms. That embrace is fraught with ambivalence at first because, while growing up, his chief competitor for his father's scarce time and affection was that most voracious rival sibling, the Ogoni cause itself.

Saro-Wiwa Jr.'s decision to become an *écriture engagée* himself compounded his predicament. What he had long feared was the already-scripted life, in which he was destined from birth to be his insurrectionary father's compliant shadow act, a fear intensified by his father's afterlife as the martyred essence of the noble, untouchable cause. "I grew up in a political house, and it had turned me off politics. When many of my friends were looking for a political cause because they were tired of living uncomplicated lives, I just wanted an uncomplicated life because I was tired of living a political cause."[83] It was his father's detention that propelled the son—who had spent most of his life in England and Canada—into politics and political writing.

Saro-Wiwa Jr. walks a line between intransigence and deference as he creates a testament that is, in a double sense, a resistance memoir: he revolts against the emotional costs imposed on a household where political revolt was the iron-fisted orthodoxy, while also carrying forward the cause that shaped his father's life and sealed his fate. If it is originality that he prizes as a writer, Saro-Wiwa Jr. the activist must first defer such ambitions, as he recapitulates the arc of his father's—and his people's—grievances, citing amply from his father's work. But the memoir takes a decidedly individual turn as he travels to meet the children of mythic freedom fighters—some martyred, some still monumentally alive—like Nelson Mandela, Steve Biko, and Aung San Suu Kyi. He shares, with the small band of saints' children, the strange struggle to reconcile a parent's ethical stature as the hallowed face of justice with the absences, the aloofness, the familial dysfunction, and to find in all of that some measure of resistant loyalty. In looping back to embrace his father's commitment to environmental justice and micro-minority rights, Saro-Wiwa Jr. draws strength from literary precedent as well: while campaigning for his father's release, he carries with him Nadine Gordimer's great novel, *Burger's Daughter*, which charts the quest, by an antiapartheid hero's daughter, to find a way of circumventing the abstracted icon of her father while pursuing her own half-chosen, half-inherited commitment to the justice of his cause.[84]

In his pursuit of environmental justice, Saro-Wiwa Jr. sought to do an end run around the dysfunctional Nigerian state. He took up the cause as writer and speaker on the international human rights circuit but also, critically, as a lead plaintiff in a fourteen-year-long case against Shell for complicity in his father's execution and for paying soldiers who had committed human rights abuses in Ogoniland. On June 9, 2009, days before the trial was due to begin in New York, Shell settled out of court, agreeing to pay $15.5 million, mostly into a trust fund for the Ogoni people.[85] The plaintiffs had filed under the Alien Tort Claims Act of 1789, which the Supreme Court ruled in 2004 could be used to try in American courts foreigners accused of crimes against humanity overseas. There is a satisfying symmetry to learning that the Alien Tort Claims Act was originally introduced in the eighteenth century to combat piracy, given the piratical practices of the Shell-Abacha partnership under a system that Saro-Wiwa once condemned as "organized brigandage."[86]

Saro-Wiwa Jr. saw the settlement as a victory that he believed would have pleased his father: "[F]rom a legal perspective, this historic case means that corporations will have to be much more careful."[87] However, the legacy of the case may be more complicated than that. Most large corporations sued under the Alien Tort Claims Act have, like Shell (and like the oil giant Unocal, charged with using slave labor to build a pipeline across Burma in the 1990s) settled out of court, leaving no clear trail of legal precedent. Moreover, when MOSOP activists ejected Shell from Ogoniland in the 1990s, the company left without conducting any cleanup and continued to operate with environmental impunity in the wider, increasingly volatile delta area. The costs of environmental reparation for the slow violence that has permeated the delta and its inhabitants are incalculable: the World Wildlife Fund has put out a figure of $6 billion, but really there's no telling.[88]

Before the settlement, Ledum Mittee, who assumed the leadership of Saro-Wiwa's MOSOP movement, insisted that the Ogonis were still waiting for an apology from Shell: "[T]hey should be able to look us in the face and say 'We're sorry for what we have caused you to go through as a result of all these years.' It's quite important to us."[89] Likewise, Tompolo, leader of MEND (the Movement for the Emancipation of the Niger Delta)—the largest, most ethnically diverse of the increasingly diffuse and increasingly militant groups that have proliferated in MOSOP's wake—demanded, in addition to greater resource control, at the very least an apology from Shell and the Nigerian military.[90] Yet in settling the court case, Shell denied any wrongdoing, deeming with outrageous condescension the out-of-court settlement for $15.5 million "a humanitarian gesture."[91]

Many of the delta's oil minorities, exiled from their subsistence cultures by ruined land, by dead-fish waterways, by government attacks and by multiplying uncontrollable militant groups, have gravitated toward the city of Port Harcourt. There, write Ike Okonta and Oronto Douglas,

> hunger leads to anger, and the crushing poverty and marginalization of communities, in contrast to the oil resources that are rightly theirs, provide the trigger. A war of all against all ensues: youths against elders, whom they accuse of selling out to Shell; community against community in competition for scarce Shell contract work; and communities against Shell and the federal government, who deny that their actions have driven the Nigerian people into a dark, impossible corner.[92]

Twenty years ago, Saro-Wiwa foresaw this dire turn in an essay called "The Coming War in the Delta." "The Delta people," he warned, "must be allowed to join in the lucrative sale of crude oil . . . only in this way can the cataclysm that is building up in the Delta be avoided. Is anyone listening?"[93] In the aftermath of his "judicial murder" the wider world listened for a time, but one wonders who exactly is listening anymore. Apart, that is, from the Mongolian leader who, when oil was recently discovered in his territory, declared, "[W]e do not want to become another Nigeria."[94] Fresh oil strikes in Ghana and Uganda have prompted similar responses: exhilaration tempered by fears of letting loose unanswerable, unspeakable forces that rip through the socioenvironmental fabric, leaving behind a Niger Delta redux.[95]

4

Slow Violence, Gender, and the Environmentalism of the Poor

Ah, what an age it is / When to speak of trees is almost a crime /
For it is a kind of silence about injustice!

—Bertolt Brecht, "An die Nachgeborenen" (To posterity)

Kenya's Green Belt Movement, cofounded by Wangari
Maathai, serves as an animating instance of environmental activism among
poor communities who have mobilized against slow violence, in this case,
the gradual violence of deforestation and soil erosion. At the heart of the
movement's activism stand these urgent questions: What does it mean to
be at risk? What does it mean to be secure? In an era when sustainability
has become a buzzword, what are the preconditions for what I would call
"sustainable security"? And in seeking to advance that elusive goal, how can
Maathai as a writer-activist working in conjunction with environmentally
motivated women from poor communities, most effectively acknowledge,
represent, and counter the violence of delayed effects?

Maathai's memoir, *Unbowed*, offers us an entry point into the complex,
shifting collective strategies that the Green Belt Movement (GBM) devised
to oppose foreshortened definitions of environmental and human security.
What emerges from the GBM's's ascent is an alternative narrative of national

security, one that would challenge the militaristic, male version embodied and imposed by Kenya's President Daniel arap Moi during his twenty-four years of authoritarian rule from 1978 to 2002. The Green Belt Movement's rival narrative of national security sought to foreground the longer time-line of slow violence, both in exposing environmental degradation and in advancing environmental recovery. At the same time, *Unbowed* provides us with an entry point into some challenging questions about the movement memoir as an imaginative form, not least the relationship between singular autobiography and the collective history of a social movement.

The Green Belt Movement had modest beginnings. On Earth Day in 1977, Maathai and a small cohort of likeminded women planted seven trees to commemorate Kenyan women who had been environmental activists.[1] By the time Maathai was awarded the Nobel Peace Prize in 2004, the movement had created 6,000 local tree nurseries and employed 100,000 women to plant 30 million trees, mostly in Kenya, but in a dozen other African countries as well.[2] The movement's achievements have been both material—providing employment while helping anchor soil, generate shade and firewood, and replenish watersheds—and symbolic, by inspiring other reforestation movements across the globe. As such, the Green Belt Movement has symbolized and enacted the conviction that (as Lester Brown has stressed in another context) "a strategy for eradicating poverty will not succeed if an economy's environmental support systems are collapsing."[3]

Early on, Maathai alighted on the idea of tree planting as the movement's core activity, one that over time would achieve a brilliant symbolic economy, becoming an iconic act of civil disobedience as the women's efforts to help arrest soil erosion segued into a struggle against illicit deforestation perpetrated by Kenya's draconian regime. Neither soil erosion nor deforestation posed a sudden threat, but both were persistently and pervasively injurious to Kenya's long-term human and environmental prospects. The symbolic focus of mass tree plantings helped foster a broad alliance around issues of sustainable security, a set of issues crucial not just to an era of Kenyan authoritarianism, but to the very different context of post-9/11 America as well, where militaristic ideologies of security have disproportionately and destructively dominated public policy and debate.

The risk of ignoring the intertwined issues of slow violence and sustainable security was evident in many American responses to the March

2003 invasion of Iraq, which was widely represented as a clean strategic and moral departure from the ugly spillages of total warfare. Even many liberal commentators adhered to this view. Hendrik Hertzberg, writing in the *New Yorker*, declared that

> [w]hatever else can be said about the war against the Iraqi dictatorship that began on March 19th, it cannot be said that the Anglo-American invaders have pursued anything remotely resembling a policy of killing civilians deliberately. And, so far, they have gone to great tactical and technological lengths to avoid doing it inadvertently. . . . What we do not yet know is whether a different intention, backed by technologies of precision, will produce a different political result.[4]

This war, Hertzberg continued, was not the kind that "expanded the battlefield to encompass whole societies."[5] Like most American media commentators at the conflict's outset, Hertzberg bought into the idea that so-called smart bombs exhibit a morally superior intelligence.[6] Yet, depending on the ordnance and strategies deployed, a quick "smart" war may morph into a long-term killer, leaving behind landscapes of dragging death. Precision warfare that has receded into memory often continues, through its active residues, to maim and slaughter imprecisely for generations.

The battlefield that unobtrusively threatens to encompass whole societies is of direct pertinence to the conditions that gave rise to Kenya's Green Belt Movement. The movement emerged in response to what one might call the violence of staggered effects in relation to ecologies of scale. From the perspective of rural Kenyan women whose local livelihood has been threatened by soil erosion's slow march, what does it mean to be secure in space and time? As Maathai notes,

> during the rainy season, thousands of tons of topsoil are eroded from Kenya's countryside by rivers and washed into the ocean and lakes. Additionally, soil is lost through wind erosion in areas where the land is devoid of vegetative cover. Losing topsoil should be considered analogous to losing territory to an invading enemy. And indeed, if any country were so threatened, it

would mobilize all available resources, including a heavily armed military, to protect the priceless land. Unfortunately, the loss of soil through these elements has yet to be perceived with such urgency.[7]

What is productive about Maathai's reformulation of security here is her insistence that threats to national territorial integrity—that most deep-seated rationale for war—be expanded to include threats to the nation's integrity from environmental assaults. To reframe violence in this way is to intervene in the discourse of national defense and, hence, in the psychology of war. Under Kenya's authoritarian regime, the prevailing response to soil erosion was a mix of denial and resignation; the damage, the loss of land, went unsourced and hence required no concerted mobilization of national resources. The violence occurred in the passive voice, despite the regime's monumental resource mismanagement.

Maathai's line of reasoning here can be connected to activist writings from elsewhere in the global South, most strikingly to Vandana Shiva's advocacy for soil security as a form of environmental justice.[8] Shiva's arguments are inflected with the distinctive history in India of the Green Revolution, peasant resistance to industrial agriculture, and the battle against transnational corporate plant patenting, but her insistence on broadening our conception of security is consistent with the stance that underlies Maathai's soil and tree politics.

Soil erosion results in part, of course, from global forms of violence—especially human-induced climate change, to which rural Kenyan women contribute little and can do very little to avert. But the desert's steady seizure of once viable, fertile land also stems from local forms of slow violence—deforestation and the denuding of vegetation—and it was at those junctures that the Green Belt women found a way to exert their collective agency. As the drivers of the nation's subsistence agriculture, women inhabited most directly the fallout from an environmental violence that is low in immediate drama but high in long-term consequences.

Resource bottlenecks are difficult to dramatize and, deficient in explosive spectacle, typically garner little media attention. Yet the bottlenecks that result from soil erosion and deforestation can fuel conflicts for decades, directly and indirectly costing untold lives. Certainly, if we take our cues from the media, it is easy to forget that, in the words of the American agronomist Wes Jackson, "soil is as much a nonrenewable resource as oil."[9] International and intranational contests over this finite resource can destabilize whole regions. Soil security ought to be inextricable from national security policy, not least in a society like Kenya, which has lost 98 percent of its anchoring, cleansing, and cooling forest cover since the arrival of British colonialists in the late nineteenth century.[10] Together transnational, national, and local forces—climate change, an authoritarian regime's ruthless forest destruction, and rural desperation—fueled the assault on human and environmental security that the Green Belt Movement recognized as inextricably entangled. That threat had its roots in a colonial history of developmental deforestation, most memorably evoked in Ngugi wa Thiong'o's epic novel *Petals of Blood*, where an elder remarks how "the land was covered with forests. The trees called rain. They also cast a shadow on the land. But the forest was eaten by the railway. You remember they used to come for wood as far as here—to feed the iron thing. Aah, they only knew how to eat, how to take away everything."[11] Despite Ngugi's forceful critique of colonial and neocolonial land politics, his novels tend—as Laura Wright notes—to fall back on an essentialist feminizing of the soil, replete with oppositions between a precolonial virginal purity and neocolonialism as prostitution.[12] One of the key challenges facing Maathai, as a writer and activist, was how to dramatize the gendered dynamics of Kenyan land politics without submitting to the sentimental essentialism that mars Ngugi's novels. To understand the angle of her approach requires that we engage the metaphoric underpinnings of the GBM's gender and civic politics.

The Theatre of the Tree

The Green Belt Movement's achievements in engaging the violence of deforestation and soil erosion flowed from three critical strategies. First, tree planting served not only as a practical response to an attritional environmental calamity but to create, in addition, a symbolic hub for political resistance and for media coverage of an otherwise amorphous issue. Second, the movement was able to articulate the discourse of violent land loss to a deeper narrative of territorial theft, as perpetrated first by British colonialists and later by their neocolonial legatees. Third, the Green Belt Movement made strategic use of what one might call intersectional environmentalism, broadening their base and credibility by aligning themselves with—and stimulating—other civil rights campaigns that were not expressly environmental, like the campaigns for women's rights, for the release of political prisoners, and for greater political transparency.[13]

The choice of tree planting as the Green Belt Movement's defining act proved politically astute. Here was a simple, pragmatic, yet powerfully figurative act that connected with many women's quotidian lives as tillers of the soil. Soil erosion and deforestation are corrosive, compound threats that damage vital watersheds, exacerbate the silting and desiccation of rivers, erode topsoil, engender firewood and food shortages, and ultimately contribute to malnutrition. Maathai and her allies succeeded in using these compound threats to forge a compound alliance among authoritarianism's discounted casualties, especially marginalized women, citizens whose environmental concerns were indissociable from their concerns over food security and political accountability.

At political flashpoints during the 1980s and 1990s, these convergent concerns made the Green Belt Movement a powerful player in a broad-based civil rights coalition that gave thousands of Kenyans a revived sense of civic agency and national possibility. The movement probed and widened the fissures within the state's authoritarian structures, clamoring for answerability within what Ato Quayson, in another context, calls "the culture of impunity."[14]

The theatre of the tree afforded the social movement a rich symbolic vocabulary that helped extend its civic reach. Maathai recast the simple gesture of digging a hole and putting a sapling in it as a way of "planting the seeds of peace."[15] To plant trees was to metaphorically cultivate democratic change; with a slight vegetative tweak, the gesture could breathe new life into the dead metaphor of grassroots democracy. Within the campaign against one-party rule, activists could establish a ready symbolic connection between environmental erosion and the erosion of civil rights. At the heart of this symbolic nexus was a contest over definitions of growth: each tree planted by the Green Belt Movement stood as a tangible, biological image of steady, sustainable growth, a dramatic counterimage to the ruling elite's kleptocratic image of "growth," a euphemism for their high-speed piratical plunder of the nation's coffers and finite natural resources. Relevant here is William Finnegan's observation, in a broader international context, that "even economic growth, which is regarded nearly universally as an overall social good, is not necessarily so. There is growth so unequal that it heightens social conflict and increases repression. There is growth so environmentally destructive that it detracts, in sum, from a community's quality of life."[16] Certainly, there is something perverse about an economic order in which the unsustainable, ill-managed plunder of resources is calculated as productive growth rather than a loss of GNP.

Within the metaphoric groves of "growth," we have witnessed a huge spectrum of literary tree politics. Bertolt Brecht, from his Danish exile in 1939 most memorably lamented the dark times he lived in, times of "terrible tidings": "Ah, what an age it is / When to speak of trees is almost a crime / For it is a kind of silence about injustice!"[17] The poem that bears those words— "An die Nachgeborenen" (To posterity or To the unborn)—has sometimes been invoked by those who wish to distinguish the hard, clear clarion call of radical politics from the soft claims of environmentalism. Yet Brecht was clearly writing into a particular cultural moment—into an ascendant fascism, a powerful strain of blood-and-soil German romanticism implicated in Nazism's ascent. As Kenya's Green Belt Movement testifies, there are other eras when, for the sake of the unborn, we need to talk about trees with unremitting urgency; indeed, when to be silent about trees is to become complicit in an injustice to posterity.

To plant trees is to work toward cultivating change, in the fullest sense of that phrase. In an era of widening social inequity and unshared growth, the replenished forest can offer an egalitarian, participatory image of growth—growth as sustainable over the long haul.[18] The Moi regime vilified Maathai as an enemy of growth, development, and progress, all discourses the ruling cabal had used to mask its high-speed plunder. Saplings in hand, the Green Belt Movement returned the blighted trope of growth to its vital, biological roots.

To plant a tree is an act of intergenerational optimism, a selfless act at once practical and utopian, an investment in a communal future the planter will not see; to plant a tree is to offer shade to unborn strangers. To act in this manner was to secede ethically from Kenya's top-down culture of ruthless short-term self-interest. (Kenyan intellectuals used to quip that under Moi *l'etat c'est Moi*.)[19] A social movement devoted to tree planting, in addition to regenerating embattled forests, thus also helped regenerate an endangered vision of civic time. Against the backdrop of Kenya's winner-takes-all-and-takes-it-now kleptocracy, the movement affirmed a radically subversive ethic—an ethic of selflessness—allied to an equally subversive timeframe, the *longue durée* of patient growth for sustainable collective gain.

By 1998, the Moi regime had come to treat tree planting as an incendiary, seditious act of civil disobedience. That year, the showdown between the Green Belt Movement and state power came to a head over the 2,500-acre Karura Forest. Word spread that the regime was felling swathes of the public forest, a green lung for Nairobi and a critical catchment area for four rivers.[20] The cleared, appropriated land was being sold on the cheap to cabinet ministers and other presidential cronies who planned to build luxury developments on it —golf courses, hotels, and gated communities. Maathai and her followers, armed with nothing but oak saplings, with which they sought to begin replanting the plundered forest, were set upon by guards and goons wielding pangas, clubs, and whips. Maathai had her head bloodied by a panga; protestors were arrested and imprisoned.

The theatre of the tree has accrued a host of potent valences at different points in human history: both the planting and the felling of forests have become highly charged political acts. In the England that the Puritans fled, for example, trees were markers of aristocratic privilege; hence on numerous occasions, insurrectionists chopped or burned down those exclusionary groves. After the Restoration, notes Michael Pollan, "replanting trees was regarded as a fitting way for a gentleman to demonstrate his loyalty to the monarchy, and several million hardwoods were planted between 1660 and 1800."[21] By contrast, early American colonists typically viewed tree felling as an act of progress that could double as a way of improving the land and laying claiming to it.

Since the early 1970s, a strong but varied transnational tradition of civil disobedience has gathered force around the fate of the forest. In March 1973, a band of hill peasants in the isolated Himalayan village of Mandal devised the strategy of tree hugging to thwart loggers who had come to fell hornbeam trees in a state forest on which the peasants depended for their livelihood. This was the beginning of a succession of such protests that launched India's Chipko movement. Three years later, in the Brazilian Amazon, Francisco Chico Mendes led a series of standoffs by rubber tappers and their allies who sought to arrest uncontrolled felling and burning by rancher colonists.[22] In Thailand, a Buddhist monk was jailed when he sought to safeguard trees by ordaining them, while Julia Butterfly Hill achieved celebrity visibility during her two-year tree sit to protest the clear-cutting of endangered California redwoods.

What distinguished the Green Belt Movement, like the Chipko movement before it, was the way that activists protesting deforestation went beyond what would become standard strategies of environmental civil disobedience in the global North (sit-ins, tree hugging, or chaining oneself to a tree). For the Kenyan and Indian protestors, active reforestation became the primary symbolic vehicle for their civil disobedience. Under an undemocratic dispensation, the threatened forest can be converted into a particularly dramatic theatre for reviving civic agency because it throws into relief incompatible visions of public land. To Kenya's authoritarian president, the forest was state owned, and because he and his cronies treated the nation as identical to the state, he felt at license to fell national forests and sell off the nation's public land. To the activists, by contrast, the forest was not a private presidential fiefdom, but commonage, the indivisible property of the people. The regime's contemptuous looting of Karura Forest was thus read as symptomatic of a wider contempt for the rights of the poor.

The Green Belt Movement's campaign to replant Karura assumed a potency that reverberated beyond the fate of one particular forest; their efforts served as a dramatic initiative to repossess, for the polity, not just plundered public land and resources, but plundered political agency. Outrage over the Karura assaults soon swelled to students and other disaffected groups in Nairobi, until the regime was forced to suspend its attacks on both the women and the trees. In this way, the theatre of the tree fortified the bond between a beleaguered environment and a beleaguered polity.[23]

For those who perpetrate slow violence, their greatest ally is the protracted, convoluted vapor trail of blame. If slow violence typically occurs in the passive voice—without clearly articulated agency—the attritional deforestation of Karura and other public lands offered a clearer case of decisive accountability than, say, soil erosion. The Green Belt Movement's theatre of the tree inverted the syntax of violence by naming the agents of destruction. Through the drama of the axed tree and the planted sapling, Maathai and her allies staged a showdown between the forces of incremental violence and the forces of incremental peace; in so doing they gave a symbolic and dramatic shape to public discontent over the official culture of plunder. Ultimately, Maathai saw in the culture of tree planting a way of interrupting the cycle of poverty, a cycle whereby, as she put it, "poverty is both a cause and a symptom of environmental degradation."[24]

Colonialism, Mau Mau, and the Forest in National Memory

In using the theatre of the forest to reanimate political debate around ideas of sustainable growth, grassroots democracy, erosion of rights, and the seeds of change, Maathai and her resource rebels also tapped into a robust national memory of popular resistance to colonialism—above all, resistance to the unjust seizure of land.[25] Maathai's memoir doesn't engage this question of anticolonial memory directly, but it is surely pertinent to the political traction that her movement attained given the particular place of the forest in Kenya's national symbolic archive of resistance. The confrontation, during Moi's neocolonial rule, between the forces of deforestation and the forces of reforestation was played out against the historic backdrop of the forest as a redoubt of anticolonialism, a heroic place that, during the Mau Mau uprising from 1952 to 1958, achieved a mythic potency among both the British colonialists and those Kenyans—primarily Kikuyu—who fought for freedom and the restitution of their land.[26]

In the dominant colonial literature about Mau Mau (political tracts, memoirs, and fiction), the forest appears as a place beyond reach of civilization, a place of atavistic savagery where "terrorists" banded together to perform degenerate rites of barbarism.[27] For those Kenyans who sought an end to their colonial subjugation, the forest represented something else entirely: it was a place of cultural regeneration and political refusal, a proving ground where resistance fighters pledged oaths of unity, above all, an oath to reclaim, by force if necessary, their people's stolen land.

The forest thus became the geographical and symbolic nexus of a peasant insurrection, as a host of Kenyan writers, Meja Mwangi, Wachira, Mangua, and Ngugi wa Thiong'o among them, have all testified.[28] From an environmental perspective, *A Grain of Wheat*, Ngugi's novel of the Mau Mau uprising, is particularly suggestive. As Byron Caminero-Santangelo

observes, most of the novel's British characters work at the Githima For-
estry and Agricultural Research Station, an institution whose official aims
are to advance agriculture and conservation, but which was founded "as
part of a new colonial development plan."[29] The novel unfolds in part, then,
as a clash between rival cultures of nature: between nature as instrument of
colonial control (under the guise of development) and nature as a sustaining
animist force, an anticolonial ally of Mau Mau forest fighters pledging oaths
of liberation.[30]

The gender politics of all this are complex and compelling. In the
1950s, the forest served as a bastion not just of anticolonialism but of war-
rior masculinity. Thirty years later, it was nonviolent women, armed only
with oak saplings and a commitment to civil disobedience, who embodied the political resistance to neocolonialism. So the showdown at Karura
reprised the anticolonial history of forest resistance in a different key: now
the core fighters—Maathai's "foresters without diplomas"—were female
and unarmed.[31] Does this double rescripting of resistance help explain the
particularly vicious backlash against the women from Kenya's male political establishment?

Intersectional Environmentalism,
Gender, and Conservation

The colonial backdrop to the achievements of the Green Belt Movement
surfaces not just through the memory of Mau Mau forest fighters but also
through the contrast between colonial conservation and what one might
call intersectional environmentalism. Maathai was never a single-issue
environmentalist: she sought, from the outset, to integrate and advance the
causes of environmental, women's, and human rights by engendering stronger civic institutions. The Green Belt Movement emerged in the late 1970s
under the auspices of the women's movement: it was through Maathai's
involvement in the Kenya Association of University of Women that she was
first invited to join a local Environment Liaison Centre and from there was
approached by representatives from the United Nations Environmental Programme, which led in turn to ever-widening circles of international access.[32]

Maathai's intersectional approach to environmental justice contrasted
starkly with the dominant colonial tradition of conservation, which had

focused on charismatic megafauna.[33] That sharply masculinist tradition—in Kenya and, more broadly, in East and Southern Africa—was associated with forced removal, with colonial appropriation of land, and with an antihuman ecology. That tradition remains part of Kenya's economic legacy, a legacy associated not just with human displacement but with local exclusion from elite cultures of leisure. In ecological as in human terms, Maathai's angle of approach was not top down: instead of focusing on the dramatic end of the biotic chain—the elephants, rhinos, lions, and leopards that have preoccupied colonial hunters, conservationists, and foreign tourists—she drew attention to a more mundane and pervasive issue: the impact of accumulative resource mismanagement on biodiversity, soil quality, food security, and the life prospects of rural women and their families.

As Fiona Mackenzie's research reveals, the grounds for such resource mismanagement were laid during the colonial era when conservationist and agricultural discourses of "betterment" were often deployed in the service of appropriating African lands. Focusing on colonial narratives about the environment and agriculture in the Kikuyu reserves between 1920 and 1945, Mackenzie traces the effects of the colonial bureaucracy's authoritarian paternalism, of what James C. Scott calls "the imperial pretensions of agronomic science."[34] Not least among these deleterious effects was "the recasting of the gender of the Kikuyu farmer . . . through a colonial discourse of betterment that was integrally linked to the reconstruction of agricultural knowledge."[35] Thus—and this has profound consequences for the priorities of the Green Belt Movement—colonial authorities failed to acknowledge women as primary cultivators. This refusal had the effect of diminishing the deeply grounded, adaptable knowledge (both ecological and agricultural) that women had amassed.

Maathai's refusal to subordinate the interwoven questions of environmental and social justice to the priorities of either spectacular conservation or industrial agriculture has proven crucial to the long-term adaptability of the GBM, allowing the movement to regenerate itself by improvising alliances with other initiatives for sustainable security and democratic transformation. Although it was the theatre of tree planting that initially garnered Maathai and her allies media attention and international support, they expanded the circles of their activism, mobilizing for campaigns that ranged from the release of Kenya's political prisoners to debt forgiveness for impoverished nations. The Green Belt Movement's intersectional strategy helped integrate issues of attritional environmental violence into a broad movement for political answerability that, in turn, helped lead to democratic elections in Kenya in 2002.

The positioning of the GBM at the crossroads between environmental rights and women's rights makes historic sense. Women in Kenya have born the brunt of successive waves of dispossession, dating back to the late nineteenth century, when the British colonialists shifted the structures of land ownership to women's detriment. Previously, land had belonged inalienably to the extended family or clan; with the introduction of colonial taxation that same land became deeded to a male deemed to be head of the household. As taxation forced more and more Kenyans into a wage economy, and as (first under colonialism and later under neocolonial structural adjustment) cash crops like tea, coffee, and sugar cane shrank the arable land available for food production, women became disproportionately marginalized from economic power. In the resultant cash economy, men typically owned the bank accounts.[36]

Rural women suffered the perfect storm of dispossession: colonial land theft; the individualizing and masculinizing of property; and the experience of continuing to be the primary tillers of the land under increasingly inclement circumstances, including soil erosion and the stripping of the forests. As forests and watersheds became degraded, it was the women who had to walk the extra miles to fetch water and firewood; it was the women who had to plough and plant in once rich but now denuded land where, without the anchorage of trees, topsoil was washed and blown away. In this context, the political convergence of the campaigns for environmental and women's rights in Kenya made experiential sense: women inhabited the betrayals of successive narratives of development that had brutally excluded them. The links between attritional environmental violence, poverty, and malnutrition was a logic they lived. So when the Moi regime laid claim to Karura Forest and Uhuru Park for private "development" schemes, Maathai was able to mobilize women who had historically been at the raw end of plunder that benefited minute male elites, be they colonial or neocolonial in character.

It is a measure of the threat that this intersectional environmentalism posed that in 1985 the regime demanded (ultimately without success) that the women's movement and the green movement disengage from one another.[37] What the regime foresaw was that these women tending saplings in their rural nurseries were seeding a civil rights movement that could help propel a broader campaign for an end to direct and indirect violence in the name of greater political answerability.

The repeated showdowns between the GBM-led civil rights movement and Kenya's authoritarian regime offer a salient reminder that, for all the elaborate, often invaluable theorizing about cosmopolitanism and globalization, the nation-state remains a potent actor, in societies as diverse as Kenya, Venezuela, Indonesia, China, and India. Yet in much contemporary environmental thinking in the humanities, the nation-state is either overlooked entirely or treated as a quaint anachronism. The struggles and successes of the GBM clearly cannot be understood outside the particular dynamics of Kenya's national authoritarianism. That said, they also cannot be viewed solely within a national frame: local and global geopolitics contributed in complex, often unpredictable ways. For if the forces arrayed against the movement were primarily from the ruling national elite, the resources Maathai drew on combined a national memory bank of anticolonial resistance, meticulously local forms of organization and cultural knowledge, and expansively transnational alliances. On the one hand, the Green Belt Movement recognized that, to operate in a country where sixty-two languages are spoken, it was essential to work with teams of women fluent in the local tongue, conversant with local power dynamics, and possessing local environmental knowledge. On the other hand, the movement gained indispensable traction through support from the United Nations and Scandinavian funders.

The United States played a complex role, as it would in the rise of Ken Saro-Wiwa's Movement for the Survival of the Ogoni People. If one of Saro-Wiwa's primary adversaries was American petro-giant Gulf Chevron, operating collaboratively with Nigerian authoritarianism, in Kenya (a detail Maathai omits from her memoir) the American government refused to turn the screws on President Moi because they perceived him as a friendly authoritarian and valuable ally close to the volatile Horn of Africa. That said, both Maathai and Saro-Wiwa traveled to the United States and drew inspiration from the civil rights and environmental campaigns they witnessed there. That inspiration was profoundly personal but it was also—and crucially—rhetorical, granting each a vocabulary that helped them achieve an international resonance for what might otherwise have remained obscure campaigns for environmental justice for their nation's or region's poor.

In 1960 Maathai became one of 600 Kenyans airlifted to the United States under the Kennedy program. (When she published her memoir she couldn't have foreseen how consequential that 1960 program would be: accompanying her on that airlift was a young Kenyan named Barack Obama on scholarship to the University of Hawaii.) As a beneficiary of the Kennedy airlift, Maathai got to study at a small college in Kansas; she proceeded for her graduate work to the University of Pittsburgh and, while there, was energized by listening to Martin Luther King at the height of his powers, an experience that contributed to her intersectional attitude to movement politics, whereby she would envisage environmentalism as one wing of a broader civil rights campaign. A few years after returning to Kenya, she and her early collaborators chose Earth Day to launch the GBM. She thus drew inspiration from her exposure to the civil rights movement and from a decisive event in the organizational history of the American environmental movement, while simultaneously adapting to Kenyan circumstances both of those animating precedents. In both instances, moreover, a movement's ascent was intimately connected, in sometimes complicating ways, with an iconic figurehead, be it Martin Luther King or Gaylord Nelson. What Maathai could not have foreseen was the way the relationship between her iconic visibility and anonymous collective action would compound her vulnerability to attack.

Collective Activism and Genres of the Self

Maathai's account of her sojourn in the United States is shaped by a series of conventions, as the chapter title, "American Dream," suggests. Those conventional pressures surface most forcefully in *Unbowed* in the domain of genre: if her first book, a little-noticed manual on the Green Belt Movement, had a collective center, by the second book, a memoir commissioned by an American publisher in response to her Nobel Prize, she clearly felt greater pressure to recast that collective history as a personal journey with a singular autobiographical self as its gravitational center.

Maathai was one of seven women who founded the Green Belt Movement, yet in *Unbowed* the other women never achieve any definition as characters. I observe this less as a criticism than as a way of signaling the intractable dilemmas that attend the movement memoir.[38] To underscore this point: after Nelson Mandela emerged from prison, Little, Brown and Company paid him a high six-figure advance for his autobiography. On becoming president, he predictably fell behind with his writing, so his publisher dispatched an American ghostwriter to help speed things along. The ghostwriter discovered, to the publisher's consternation, that Mandela's autobiography had advanced with only a smattering of "I's"; his preferred, default personal pronoun was "we" as in "we, the ANC." The ghostwriter was tasked with disaggregating that movement "we" and channeling it into an "I" story that American readers and *Oprah* viewers would recognize and respond to. For Maathai, as for Mandela, the single-authored movement memoir raises profound representational dilemmas intricately entangled with transnational power imbalances in the publishing industry—entangled, too, with the genre expectations of projected readers, who reside mostly in the global North. Maathai's 2004 Nobel Peace Prize—and with it, the publishers' investment in a celebrity memoir—intensified the pressure on the writer to recast a collective struggle in largely personal terms. Under such circumstances, to testify is to confirm certain genre expectations and thereby to shape the way political movements, not least environmental justice movements, are narrated and remembered.

Although *Unbowed* is subtitled "A Memoir," that someone odd designation seems symptomatic of the mood of American publishing in the early 21st century, when "memoir" was a hipper, more saleable category than the fusty-sounding "autobiography" to which *Unbowed* more properly belongs. The memoirs that boosted the genre's visibility, sales, and cultural cachet— Kathryn Harrison's *The Kiss*, Mary Karr's *The Liar's Club*, Frank McCourt's *Angela's Ashes*, Marya Hornbacher's *Wasted*, Dave Pelzer's *A Child Called It*, Augusten Burrough's *Running with Scissors*, and James Frey's *A Million Little Pieces*—typically focused on a specific trauma (addiction, incest, bulimia) and had a narrow social frame, centered on familial dysfunction. They were written by unknown figures and read largely for their intimate, sometimes scandalously, confessional tone. By contrast, *Unbowed* unfolds across a vast social canvas, is focused on a dysfunctional nation-state rather than a dysfunctional individual or family, and is authored by a woman of international renown. If this is a "misery memoir" then the primary source of that misery is a patriarchal, authoritarian nation-state and the solution is not some personal twelve-step plan but collective dissidence which, in the writing, gets routed through an iconic individual life.

By contemporary American memoir standards, *Unbowed* is wholesome, quite private, even withholding. As such the book has more in common with the older autobiographical tradition of, say, Ben Franklin, where the focus is on the grand sweep of a lifetime's accomplishments. Maathai is less prone to self-hagiography than Franklin, but she is similarly inclined toward extracting lessons, even parables, from experiences: that hard work pays off; that, in her words, she needed "to pull myself up by my bootstraps;" how the values instilled in her as a child stood her in good stead; how morality and optimism will see off adversity. In contrast to most contemporary American memoirists, Maathai represents her childhood and family as profoundly functional to the point of being idealized. Pitched somewhere between *The Autobiography of Benjamin Franklin* and Nelson Mandela's *Long Walk to Freedom* (with an environmental, feminist twist), Maathai's narrative is didactic and solution-oriented. In her complex balancing act between self-effacement and heroic self-fashioning, she has to translate, at every turn, her selfhood into forms amenable to her largely American audience.

Environmental Agency and Ungovernable Women: Carson and Maathai

Wangari Maathai and Rachel Carson each sought, in their different cultural milieus, to shift the parameters of what is commonly perceived as violence. They devoted themselves to questioning shibboleths about development and progress, to making visible the overlooked casualties of accumulative environmental injury, and to mobilizing public sentiment—especially among women—against the institutionalized deceptions and profitable complicities of a male power elite. Both writer-activists questioned the orthodox, militarized vision of security as sufficient to cope with the domino effects of exponential environmental risk, not least the intergenerational risk to food security.[39] Indeed, both saw the militarization of their societies—cold-war America of the late 1950s and early 1960s and Moi's tyrannized Kenya of the 1980s and 1990s—as exacerbating the environmental degradation that threatened long-term stability (locally, nationally, and transnationally).

Retrospectively, it is easy to focus on the achievements of these two towering figures: the social movements they helped build, the changes in legislation and public perception they helped catalyze, Maathai's Nobel Peace Prize, the selection of *Silent Spring* as the most influential work of nonfiction of the twentieth century. Yet it is important to acknowledge the embattled marginalization and vilification both women had to endure at great personal cost in order to ensure that their unorthodox visions of environmental violence and its repercussions gained political traction. Their marginality was wounding but emboldening, the engine of their originality.

Carson and Maathai were multiply extra-institutional: as female scientists (anomalies for their time and place); as scientists working outside the structures and strictures of the university; and as unmarried women. On all fronts, they had to weather ad feminam assaults from male establishments whose orthodoxies were threatened by their autonomy.

Although Carson had a master's degree in biology, financial pressures and the pressures of caring for dependent relatives had prevented her from pursuing a Ph.D. Her background was in public science writing; she had no university affiliation, at a time, one should add, when only one percent of tenured scientists in America were women.[40] But by the time she came to embark on *Silent Spring,* her best-selling books on the sea had given her some financial autonomy. Carson's institutional and economic independence freed her to set her own research agenda, to engage in unearthing, synthesizing and promoting environmental research that had been suppressed or sidelined by the funding priorities of the major research institutions, whose agendas she recognized as compromised by the entangled special interests of agribusiness, the chemical and arms industries, and by the headlong rush to profitable product development.

Carson's detractors questioned her professional authority, her patriotism, her ability to be unemotional, and the integrity of her scientific commitment to intergenerational genetic issues, given that she was a "spinster." "Why is a spinster with no children so concerned about genetics? She is probably a Communist," a former U.S. Secretary of Agriculture intoned.[41]

Hostile reviewers dismissed Carson's arguments as "hysterically over-emphatic" and as "more emotional than accurate."[42] The general counsel for Velsicol, a Chicago chemical company, accused Carson of being under the sway of "sinister influences" whose purpose was "to reduce the use of agricultural chemicals in this country and the countries of western Europe, so that our supply of food will be reduced to east-curtain parity."[43] Other commentators deduced that "Miss Rachel Carson's reference to the selfishness of insecticide manufacturers probably reflects her Communist sympathies."[44] Carson's nemesis, the chemical industry spokesman Dr. Robert White-Stevens (who gave twenty-eight speeches against *Silent Spring* in a single year) opined that "if man were to faithfully follow the teachings of Miss Carson, we would return to the Dark Ages."[45] In the ultimate vilification of Carson as embodying a model of irrational female treachery, a critic in *Aerosol Age* concluded that "Miss Carson missed her calling. She might have used her talents in telling war propaganda of the type made famous by Tokyo Rose and Axis Sally."[46]

Twenty-five years on and Maathai's opponents were brandishing even more outrageous ad feminam threats and insinuations against an autonomous female scientist who threatened the political and environmental status quo. Maathai was not a "spinster," but she was a divorcée, a label her opponents wielded against her relentlessly. Like Carson, she was represented as overly emotional and unhinged, an unnatural woman, uncontrollable, unattached, without a husband to rein her in and keep her (and her ideas) respectable. If the chemical-agricultural establishment sought to dismiss Carson, who lacked a Ph.D., as unqualified to speak, Kenya's power elite tried to discredit Maathai—the first woman in East or Central Africa to receive a doctorate in any scientific field—as suspiciously overqualified, as a woman who had to be brought down because she was overreaching.[47] When she led the protests against government plans for the private "development" of Uhuru Park, one parliamentarian declared, "I don't see why we should listen to a bunch of divorced women." Another politician portrayed her as a "madwoman"; a third threatened to "circumcise" her if she ever set foot in his district.[48]

As a highly educated woman scientist, an advocate of women's rights, and a proponent of environmentalism for the poor, Maathai was vulnerable, on multiple fronts, to charges of inauthenticity and, like Carson, of unpatriotic behavior. A Kenyan cabinet minister railed against Maathai as "an ignorant and ill-tempered puppet of foreign masters."[49] Another criticized her for "not being enough of an African woman," of being "a white woman in black skin."[50] Such critics typically adhered to a gender-specific nativism: as Maathai notes,

Kenyan men freely adopted Western languages, Western dress, and the technological trappings of modernity, while expecting women to be the markers and bearers of "tradition."[51] President Moi (who imprisoned Maathai several times) chastised her for being "disobedient"; if she were "a proper woman in the African tradition—[she] should respect men and be quiet."[52]

As Kwame Anthony Appiah has observed, the charge of inauthenticity is an inherently unstable one:

> Nativists may appeal to identities that are both wider and narrower than the nation: to 'tribes' and towns, below the nation-state; to Africa, above. And, I believe, we shall have the best chance of re-directing nativism's power if we challenge not the rhetoric of the tribe, the nation, or the continent, but the topology that it presupposes, the opposition it asserts.[53]

This is certainly borne out in Maathai's case: she fell foul of proliferating "uns"—un-African, un-Kenyan, un-Kikuyu, unpatriotic, ungovernable, unmarried, unbecoming of a woman. But through her intersectional environmentalism she sought to circumvent the binaries of authentication. One strategy she used to sidestep such oppositional topologies was to seek out local environmental practices that were consistent with but not necessarily reducible to notions like biodiversity, the commons, and ecological stewardship. So, for example, Maathai recounts the Kikuyu injunction against cutting down fig trees which, with their widespread root systems and broad canopies help anchor sandbanks and shade vulnerable streambeds.[54] That injunction, passed down to her in childhood by her grandmother, serves in her narrative to foreshadow the green values that, on returning from America, she rescripts in the discourse of environmental science. As a "been-to" (a returnee from the West) and a go-between, Maathai ends up tacking back and forth strategically between nativist declarations ("I'm a child of my native soil") and invocations of a cosmopolitan science.[55] By positioning herself as a transnational patriot with deep local roots, and by assiduously striving to reconcile her commitment to Kenya and to planetary values, Maathai seeks to deflect charges of treachery. So, too, she is careful not to articulate her views on women and tradition through a universalized feminism, but by invoking counter-currents within Kikuyu cultural practices.

In these ways, we witness Maathai actively trying to defuse the accusation that her behavior is unwomanly and that her purported triple betrayal (of her gender, her culture, and her nation) is indissociable from her role as a Westernized agent of "green imperialism."

The vehement attacks on Maathai and Carson are a measure both of institutionalized misogyny and of how much is at stake (politically, economically, and professionally) in keeping the insidious dynamics and repercussions of slow violence concealed from view. While personally vulnerable, Maathai and Carson were threatening because they stood outside powerful systems of scientific patronage, academic intimidation, and silencing kickbacks. Their cultural contexts differed widely, but their extrainstitutional positions allowed them the scientific autonomy and political integrity to speak out against attritional environmental violence and help mobilize against it.

Quotidian Terrors

If Maathai's nativist detractors sought to discredit her as an enemy of national development, , when awarded the 2004 Nobel Peace Prize she faced, a different style of criticism from abroad. Carl I. Hagen, leader of Norway's Progress Party, typified this line of aggressive disbelief: "It's odd," Hagen observed "that the [Nobel] committee has completely overlooked the unrest that the world is living with daily, and given the prize to an environmental activist."[56] The implications of Hagen's position are clear: nineteen months into the Iraq War and, amidst the war in Afghanistan, the wider "war on terror," and tumult in the Middle East, Congo, Sudan, and elsewhere, to honor an environmentalist for planting trees was to trivialize conflict resolution and to turn one's back on the most urgent issues of the hour.

Maathai, however, sought to recast the question of urgency in a different time frame, one that challenged the dominant associations of two of the early twenty-first century's most explosive words: "preemptive" and "terror." The Green Belt Movement focused not on conventional ex post facto conflict resolution but on conflict preemption through nonmilitary means. As Maathai insisted, "many wars are fought over natural resources. In managing our resources and in sustainable development we plant the seeds of peace."[57] This approach has discursive, strategic, and legislative ramifications for the "global war on terror." Most of our planet's people face more immediate terrors than a terrorist attack: creeping deserts that reduce farms to sand; the incremental assaults of climate change compounded by deforestation; not knowing where tonight's meal will come from; unsafe drinking water; having to walk five or ten miles to collect firewood to keep one's children warm and fed. Such quotidian terrors haunt the lives of hundreds of millions immiserated, abandoned, and humiliated by authoritarian rule and by a purportedly postcolonial new-world order. Under such circumstances, slow violence (often coupled with direct repression) can ignite tensions, creating flashpoints of desperation and explosive rage.[58]

"Local disasters," writes Wai Chee Dimock, "are the almost predictable side effects of global geopolitics. They are part of a larger distributive pattern—a pattern of unequal protection that Ulrich Beck calls the global 'risk society'—with the risk falling on the least privileged, and being maximized at just those points where the resources have been most depleted."[59] Dimock is reflecting here on the impact on the poor of the prelude to and the aftermath of Hurricane Katrina, yet her words apply with equal force to contemporary Kenya and many other societies in the global South, where structures of slow violence sustain tinderbox conditions that cynical political elites can readily ignite at great cost to a society's systemically disenfranchised.

Perhaps to Hagen and others like him, tree planting is conflict resolution lite; it lacks a dramatic, decisive, newsworthy military focus. But Maathai, by insisting that resource bottlenecks impact sustainable security at local, national, and global levels, and by insisting that the environmentalism of the poor is inseparable from distributive justice, has done more than forge a broad political alliance against Kenyan authoritarian rule. Through her testimony and through her movement's collective example, she has sought to reframe conflict resolution for an age when instant cinematic catastrophe has tended to overshadow violence that is calamitous in more insidious ways. This, then, is Wangari Maathai's contribution to the "'war on terror'": building a movement committed, in her words, to "reintroducing a sense of security among ordinary people so they do not feel so marginalized and so terrorized by the state."[60]

5

Unimagined Communities

Megadams, Monumental Modernity, and Developmental Refugees

The highest expression of dignity can be summed up in the single word "No!"

—Dai Qing, "China: Rivers and Dams,"
Goldman Environmental Prize speech

If the idea of the modern nation-state is sustained by producing imagined communities, it also involves actively producing unimagined communities. I refer here not to those communities that lie beyond the national boundaries but rather to those unimagined communities internal to the space of the nation-state, communities whose vigorously unimagined condition becomes indispensable to maintaining a highly selective discourse of national development. Narratives of national development are partial narratives that depend on energetically inculcated habits of imaginative limit, habits that hide from view communities that inconvenience or disturb the implied trajectory of unitary national ascent. Assaults on a nation's environmental resources frequently entail not just the physical displacement of local communities, but their imaginative displacement as well, indeed on the prior rhetorical and visual evacuation of those communities from the idea of the developing nation-state. This imaginative work of expulsion typically predates the arrival of the police, the dogs, the lorries, the bulldozers, and the engineers. Thus the direct violence of physical eviction becomes coupled to an indirect bureaucratic and media violence that creates and sustains the conditions for administered invisibility. The result is what I have called spatial amnesia, as communities, under the banner of development, are physically unsettled and imaginatively removed, evacuated from place and time and thus uncoupled from the idea of both a national future and a national memory.

We witnessed a classic instance of this process with the invention, under apartheid, of what were called "surplus people." Largely women and children, these "surplus people" were deemed superfluous to the labor market and to the idea of national development and were forcibly removed or barred from cities.[1] Trucked to remote rural areas—the so-called "dumping grounds"—they were "resettled" in overcrowded conditions, with no viable means of sustenance. The consequences—human and environmental—were disastrous. Crucially, the dynamics of forced removal depended both on direct police violence and on the administration of an imaginative violence whereby certain communities were designated indispensable to the nation and others designated expendable and driven—literally trucked—out of sight. This invention of surplus people through the conjoined processes of imaginative expulsion and forced removal was far from unique to apartheid South Africa. Indeed, the production of ghosted communities who haunt the visible nation has been essential for maintaining the dominant narratives of national development, a process that has intensified during the era of neoliberal globalization. The intertwined processes of imaginative and physical eviction have assumed a particularly dramatic force around the construction of megadams, those iconic structures of monumental modernity that serve to concretize the idea that developing nations are "catching up," as evidenced by spectacular, televisable, soaring feats of world-class engineering.

When it comes to narratives of resource development—whether of water, oil and gas, minerals, or forests—the people recast as "surplus" are most often rural, or at least people sent ricocheting between rural and urban desperation. Often they are ecosystem people, dependent for their survival on the seasonal cycles of adjoining ecosystems and therefore often living in circumstances of necessarily adaptable mobility. In many instances, their relationship to the land is historically deep but legally informal. Thus their imaginative expulsion from narratives of national development is facilitated by the frequent lack of official title deeds to the ecosystems that have sustained them for centuries or, in some cases, millennia.

In considering the unimagined communities cast into shadow by the looming imaginative edifice that is the megadam, we may usefully append to the idea of surplus people two other notions: "developmental refugees" and "uninhabitants." The anthropologist Thayer Scudder coined the term "developmental refugees" to convey the calamitous fallout of megadams (largely World Bank funded) that he had charted for decades in the global South.[2] Scudder estimated the number of people displaced by such dams at somewhere between 30 million to 60 million.[3] Almost without exception such displacements have resulted in declining key barometers of quality of life: nutrition, health, infant mortality, life expectancy, and environmental viability. Even the World Bank itself determined in a 1994 study that of 192 dam resettlement projects it had funded, only one had involved adequate compensation and rehabilitation for those resettled.[4]

The "developmental refugee" is a poignantly paradoxical figure. Development implies positive growth, ascent toward a desirable end; refugee implies flight from a grave threat—in this case, the threat of development-inflicted destitution or even, when it comes to megadams, of drowning. In horizontal terms, the notion of the developmental refugee holds in tension an official, centripetal logic of national development on the one hand and on the other, a terrifying, centrifugal narrative of displacement, dispossession, and exodus. In vertical terms, the megadam as icon of national ascent becomes coupled to the descending prospects of communities that have become ecologically unmoored, cut off from a drowned commons that, however modestly or precariously, had proffered a diverse diet, a livelihood, and a sustained temporal identity of continuity within change. In the wake of the megadam such communities are, in the most literal sense, inundated by development.

The idea of "developmental refugees" overlaps with another paradoxical notion, that of the "uninhabitant." The term surfaces in an interview Rebecca Solnit conducted for her superb essay on the Nevada Test Site (in *Savage Dreams: A Journey into the Landscape Wars of the American West*).[5] The essay stands as a powerful attempt to counter the cold-war reinvention of the Nevada Desert as an empty, isolated space, sealed against culture and memory. Solnit repopulates the emptiness by bringing into focus the people who had been turned into ghosted casualties of a federal project of imaginative self-enclosure that concealed them from view: the downwinders and the Western Shoshone on whose territory the nuclear tests were conducted, as well as their Soviet counterparts, the nomads of the Kazakhstan Desert/Semi-Palatinsk, people whose lands, culture, and rights Soviet explosions decimated during the violently contrapuntal rivalry from cold-war nuclear "development." *Savage Dreams* offers a transnational bridge between those two desert spaces, both spaces of amnesia predicated on imaginative evacuations.[6]

There is an especially telling incident in Solnit's nuclear journey that becomes central to the question with which this chapter began: what is the relationship between an actively imagined national community and actively unimagined communities on which the idea of national development depends? While traveling through southern Utah, 150 miles east of the Nevada Test Site, Solnit encounters a downwinder, Janet Gordon, who has lost many family and friends prematurely from cancer. The area Gordon and her family inhabited was largely Native land. Yet in the build-up to the nuclear explosions, this land was officially declared "a virtually uninhabited area." "We became," Gordon observes in a mordantly resonant phrase, "virtual uninhabitants."[7]

Gordon's phrase is readily adaptable to the imaginative force field of the megadam, for it holds in equipoise ideas of presence and absence—absence not as originary but as imposed through a war against presence, as inhabitants drop off official maps and plummet into zones of invisibility. People like the Nevada Test Site's Western Shoshone were evacuated not just from their lands but from public awareness—two intimately entangled processes of forced removal.[8] Other residents of the area, like the Gordons, were not physically removed but had their status downgraded from inhabitants to virtual uninhabitants: they were and were not there, existing in a kind of vaporized dwelling.

This violent conversion of inhabitant into uninhabitant has been a recurrent trauma amidst the spread of gargantuan dams across the so-called developing world. People viewed as irrational impediments to "progress" have been statistically—and sometimes fatally—disappeared. The story behind Guatemala's Chixoy Dam forcefully illustrates this. To quell opposition to the dam and to speed up the clearing of the submergence zone, in March 1980 Guatemalan paramilitary units conducted a series of massacres, slaughtering 378 Maya Achi Indians. The brutality took a bloody, local form, but the decisive players were the invisible, bloodless transnational collaborators with the Guatemalan dictatorship: the World Bank and the Inter-American Development Bank who buttressed the dam with their loans. Their endeavors, in turn, were made possible by a consortium from American, Swiss, and German engineering consultants who declared in their feasibility report that "in the tract of the study . . . there is almost no population."[9] Thus, with the stroke of a pen, 3,400 "Project-Affected People"—including many who would soon be murdered for development—became virtual uninhabitants.[10]

Megadams and the Countersublime

Given America's historic role as megadam pioneer, it is perhaps predictable that so many of the twentieth century's most vocal literary opponents of hydraulic hubris—John Muir, Edward Abbey, Wallace Stegner, and David Brower—would be concentrated in the United States. All these writers, significantly, lived in the lightly populated American West and all were associated primarily with a wilderness ethic. But in the twentieth century's final year, a quite different strain of literary opposition to gargantuan dams rose to prominence with the publication of Arundhati Roy's "The Greater Common Good," the first in a volley of polemics she launched against the serial damming of India's Narmada River. Some 3,000 dams were slated for the river and its tributaries, including thirty megadams; most notorious was the mammoth Sardar Sarovar Dam, which became a symbolic focus for activists from the Narmada Bachao Andolan (Save the Narmada Movement), led by Medha Patkar, a cause that Roy's voice helped amplify nationally and internationally.

The historical timing, geopolitical circumstances, and rhetorical strategies of Roy's classic essay set it apart in significant ways from the dominant strains of American anti-megadam literature. First, "The Greater Common Good" is a post–cold war essay whose backdrop is the hegemonic rise of neoliberal globalization, dominated by a single superpower in cahoots with the G8, and the corresponding ascent of an antiglobalization movement.

("The Greater Common Good" appeared in 1999, the year of the Seattle WTO protests.) A second major difference between Roy's invective and most American anti-dam writing derives from a historical and geographical shift in the global big dam industry. By 1999, India had become the world's third most prolific dam builder. Roy sought to expose the collusions between a fascist strain of Hindu nationalism at home and neoliberal globalizers, notably the megadam boosters at the World Bank and in the Western-based dam industry that, one notes, like the tobacco industry was shifting its exploitative center of gravity to the global South, where huge profits could be accumulated in conditions where health, safety, and environmental regulations were absent, lax, or poorly enforced.

The third, critical difference is this: the giant dams Roy opposed were located in rural areas densely populated with subsistence farmers, areas quite unlike the thinly peopled hinterland of the American West. Roy's rhetorical strategies are thus remote from those associated with the traditions of the wilderness ethic. Instead, her approach borrows from and advances the rhetoric of an international environmental justice movement that did not exist in any comparable form during the years when Edward Abbey, much less John Muir, was writing.

We can ground these differences by contrasting the strategies and circumstances of the Save the Narmada movement (and Roy's writerly role within it) to those that characterized the mid-1960s movement—in which both Abbey and Brower were prominent—opposing Glen Canyon and other Colorado megadams. The driving spirit behind the loose alliance of monkey wrenchers and desert rats in the American West was anarchist; their strategic vocabulary was drawn from the wilderness sublime, a discourse that enfolded elements of eulogy and elegy. The wilderness sublime became inseparable from a contest over the rhetoric of the monumental: a clash between transcendent engineering and a transcendent geology invested with awe and grandeur. For Brower, "the most beautiful place in all the region of Glen Canyon was a cavernous space, under the vaulting rock walls, that had been named the Cathedral in the Desert."[11] Brower, like Abbey, became a public relations maestro in the vernacular of the countersublime: "Lake Powell is a drag strip for power boats . . . The magic of Glen Canon is dead. Putting water in the Cathedral in the Desert was like urinating in the crypt of St. Peter's."[12] An anti-dam coalition placed an advertisement in the

New York Times that asked, "Should we flood the Sistine Chapel so tourists can get nearer the ceiling?"[13]

Such strategies depended on a Manichean, trans-Atlantic split between a cultural and a natural sublime, whereby Europe's soaring, hallowed architecture became shorthand for Culture and the American West's soaring, geological edifices shorthand for Nature or, more specifically, Nature's Nation. Thirty years on, in the Narmada Valley, such polarities were unfeasible for political, historical, and topographical reasons. At stake in the Narmada were literal temples not metaphoric ones, temples to be drowned, alongside the villages they had served for centuries, by the monsoon waters that rose higher each year with the ever-rising dam walls. When Roy writes that the Narmada dams were causing the "submerging of culture," she refers to the inundation of densely populated village cultures inextricable from floodplain ecosystems in "the only valley in India, according to archaeologists, that contains an uninterrupted record of human occupation from the Stone Age."[14] This is a far cry from the inundation of symbolic temples of nature whose paradigmatic witness is an antisocial, often misanthropic man roaming a wilderness in resplendent solitude.

The aesthetic contrasts embedded in all this are deeply informed by divergent economic structures. The contest over the Colorado dams remained internal to the United States: the economics of the megadams was federally managed and nationally contained. By contrast, the damming of the Narmada Valley—as is typical in the global South, from Panama, Guatemala, and Belize to Cameroon, Cambodia, and Krygystan—was dependent on transnational funding structures of neoliberal globalization. Hence the Sardar Sarovar became an iconic battle with ramifications far beyond India. This is where Roy, for all her contentiousness within India, became an indispensable translator for international audiences of the wider implications the Narmada Valley struggle had for environmental justice movements elsewhere. She assumed this role by exposing the global machinery of the big dam industry, the paradigmatic plight of downstream tribals, the ecological costs and the connection of all of these elements to a hegemonic neoliberal global order.

If, as I am suggesting, big dams themselves are (beyond any possible utility) a kind of national performance art, it was the genius of Abbey and his gonzo anarchists to recognize the dam wall as a blank staging ground for outsize guerilla theatre that could be projected into the homes of the first television nation. Abbey viscerally understood the high-stakes politics of spectacle and counterspectacle. The massive dam face represented the monumentalism of national modernity, but it could also represent—especially amidst 1960s cold-war paranoia—the monumentalism of the apocalypse. Onto the blank canvas of the televised dam wall could be projected a nation's outsize hopes, but also its outsize fears. Long before one could Photoshop nuclear explosions into the landscape, Abbey and his fellow gonzos unfurled a 300-foot sheet of black polyurethane down the face of Glen Canyon wall. This plausible crack, picked up with alarm by television stations, linked the elegiac anger of anti-dam anarchists to an apocalyptic visual rhetoric. If the death of Glen Canyon became a leitmotif in Abbey's writing, perhaps for legal reasons, his activist response is generically divided, vacillating between nonviolent anti-dam activism in his nonfiction and violence in his fiction. The closest he comes in his nonfiction to advocating direct anti-dam violence—what one might euphemistically call the informal decommissioning of Glen Canyon Dam—occurs in *Desert Solitaire*, where he fantasizes about "the loveliest explosion ever seen by man, reducing the great dam to a heap of rubble in the path of the river. The splendid new rapids thus created we will name Floyd E. Dominy Falls."[15] However, in his most celebrated novel, *The Monkey Wrench Gang*, Abbey moves beyond both fantasy and gonzo theatre and has his eco-anarchists push the lever that detonates the wall.

The Politics of Visibility, the Politics of Scale

Two epochal Indian environmental events occasioned Roy's decision to redirect her creative energies from fiction toward the polemical, interventionist essay. The desert nuclear tests the BJP government conducted in May 1998 (and to which Pakistan responded in kind) were followed in February 1999 by an apparently unrelated development: after a four-year legal stay, the Supreme Court of India gave the go ahead to resume construction on the Sardar Sarovar Dam on the Narmada River. With two small essays on two outsize subjects—the megaweapon and the megadam—Roy launched her second career as an international writer-activist, whose central preoccupations are the politics of visibility, distance, and scale. What she alighted on, in these pre-9/11 essays, was the way a populist visual rhetoric of nationalism—a visual rhetoric one might describe as fusing the technological sublime with the sacralizing of spectacle—expressed and helped enable a fascist turn in India. That turn diminished the rights of the citizenry, widened the gap between haves and have-nots, and quickened the centralizing of economic power and privilege. Roy's instincts for this dynamic foreshadowed what would become one of her signature, expansive themes over the next decade: during the post-9/11 "war on terror," she would rail in essay after essay against how a hubristic global, neo-liberal order was widening the gulf, inside the nation and beyond, between development's beneficiaries and its casualties. To borrow Gadgil and Guha's useful opposition, the gulf was widening, in particular, between India's omnivores and its ecosystem people.

By pairing her essays on India's nuclear tests and the Narmada Valley dams, Roy sought—controversially—to bring big dam building into the domain of violence. Through these essays, Roy gives focus to a larger drama: the way India's outsize, self-assertive modernity depends on rendering invisible stories of national exclusion. As such, her interrogation of what counts as modernity becomes inseparable from her tenacious attentiveness to the conjoined politics of scale and the politics of invisibility.

Together, Roy's paired essays on the bomb and the megadam pose one central question: at the turn of the millennium, what did it mean to be a major modern nation? Or rather, what did it mean, as a nation, to *display* modernity? The detonation of a "Hindu" bomb became a spectacle staged simultaneously as a declaration of great nation status, via the mastery of science and nature, and as a supernatural portent: "'The desert shook,' the government of India informed us . . . 'The whole mountain turned white,' the government of Pakistan replied . . . One scientist on seeing [the blast] said, 'I can now believe stories of Lord Krishna lifting a hill.'"[16] On both sides of the border the bombs set off serial media explosions of national self-aggrandizement expressed through the languages of the technological sublime, national religious destiny, and a virile jingoism: "We have proved we are not eunuchs any more." "We have superior strength and potency." "These are not just nuclear tests, they are nationalism tests."[17] The convergence of the technological sublime, manifest destiny, and a hubristic, jingoistic refusal of limit has, of course, its own variant in the entangled nuclear and hydrological histories of the American West. "What do you do," Wallace Stegner asks, "if you are a nation accustomed to plenty and impatient of restrictions and led westward by pillars of fire and cloud? You try to engineer it out of existence."[18] The very notion of the Bureau of Reclamation is suggestive of such national hubris: the federal agency was tasked not with claiming the desert through megadams and irrigation, but with reclaiming it, as if the arid West were once fertile federal property wrongfully seized by sinister desert forces.

In both Roy's nuclear and her megadam essays, one senses a mistrust of her government's outsize technological assertions of India's modernity, of the way these purportedly unifying spectacles of imagined community have been predicated on violent habits of imaginative disconnection—what I am calling the nation's unimagined communities. The much-vaunted survivable nuclear war against Pakistan rested on just such a dissociative fantasy: that contiguous nations sharing sky, air, and water could avoid being radiated and poisoned in unbounded ways when citizens on both sides of the nuclear divide were also ineluctably regional citizens of an unpartitioned Earth. One senses a similar turn in "The Greater Common Good," wherein Roy exposes the imaginative disconnect between "the most ambitious river valley development project ever conceived in human history" and the human and ecological disasters that flow from that grandiose project of national reengineering.[19]

Roy's radical, controversial move was to view the Indian government's nuclear and hydrological hubris as two versions of a single mindset rather than divide them into a purely malign and a purely benign spectacle of modernity.[20] Her conjoining of her antinuclear and antimegadam polemics suggests this explicit pairing can help shift our perspective on what qualifies as modernity. This—at least implicitly—is one alternative definition of modernity: "The orbits of the powerful and the powerless spinning further and further apart from each other."[21] As William Finnegan observes in another context, "It is simplistic, even misleading, to talk about whole nations as winners or losers under the current globalization regime, since there are, in every country, significant groups of both winners and losers."[22] Thus, at the heart of Roy's exposé of the megadam as a grandiose, highly selective, divisive fiction of Indian modernity lies an integrative ambition: the desire to imagine the Narmada Valley dams not just from the distant orbit of the powerful modernizers (those who, in her words, conduct "imperialism by email") but from the more intimate orbit of the powerless as well, that is, from the vantage point of those whom we might variously call modernity's surplus people, its developmental refugees, and its virtual uninhabitants.

The Writer-Activist and the Submergence Zone

At the heart of Roy's polemical method is the very writerly subject of imaginative limit. If her nuclear essay engages the quandary of how to give sensory definition to the unimaginable—the more or less evenhanded disaster of atomic apocalypse—the companion essay protesting the mass damming of the Narmada River engages the imaginative dilemmas posed by an unequally distributed catastrophe. Here the primary quandary becomes how to bring into imaginative focus threatened communities and ecosystems rendered invisible by the celebratory developmental rhetoric that gushes from big dam technocrats, cabinet ministers, World Bankers, and media moguls. The World Bank, a larger-than-life character in Roy's nonfiction, made an early, premonitory cameo appearance in *The God of Small Things*, when Estha strolls "along the banks of the river that smelled of shit and pesticides bought with World Bank loans."[23] The very notion of the World Bank, one notes, contains a dead aquatic metaphor. Banks shore up investments, control streams of capital and global flows. If we pause to reflect on the submerged metaphor of the World Bank, we see that a river runs through it.

Across scores of essays, Roy returns to the connection between the tyranny of scale and the politics of a violent invisibility. These have become the signature subjects—the great binding themes—of her writings on environmental justice, globalization, empire, and the war on terror. It is no accident that, in the triumphal aftermath of *The God of Small Things*, she turned to confront the secular and religious gods of mammoth things: the World Bank, the International Monetary Fund, the World Trade Organization, the American empire, the Murdoch empire, religious fundamentalism, the war on terror, nuclear proliferation, and the megadam. Her novel's outsize success had bestowed on Roy a sudden, unexpected visibility that she chose to channel into challenging the largely opaque collusions between transnational and national forces that imperil the weave of human and biotic communities. Her essays acknowledge that the mechanisms of these giant, shape-shifting forces are difficult to track, visualize, dramatize, and expose—and hence successfully oppose—not least when they promote the megadam as a munificent, luminous icon of triumphal national progress, a bright beacon on the road to great nation status.

In contrast to the encomiums that greeted the Hoover Dam, Roy's approach to India's most iconic megadam focuses not on the scale of the modern edifice but on the scale of the very modern forced removals it incurs. The dam's outsize dimensions are easily calculable yet, symptomatically, the outsize dimensions of the displacements remain unknown. A direct relationship emerges between the massive imaginative displacement required to sustain the developmental fantasy of a benign, redemptive dam and the imaginative displacement required to suppress the fate of the human and nonhuman casualties of the "submergence zone." The bureaucratic euphemism of the "submergence zone" itself suggests the drowning out of developmental refugee voices, voices rendered inaudible by the floodwaters of gung-ho developmental rhetoric.

Roy's obsession with the politics of scale and the politics of visibility call to mind a similar preoccupation in the writings of John Berger, one of our most astute contemporary writer-activists on the links between neoliberal globalization and the transnational devastation of place, as community and ecosystem. In his preoccupation with ways of seeing and not seeing—with the invisibility industry—Berger is especially insightful on the violence wrought by the rationalizing developmental rhetoric of the zone:

> Extensive areas which were once rural places are being turned into zones. The details of the process vary . . . The initial dismembering, however, always comes from elsewhere and from corporate interests pursuing their appetite for ever more accumulation, which means seizing natural resources (fish in Lake Victoria, wood in the Amazon, petrol wherever it is to be found, uranium in Gabon, etc.), regardless of to whom the land or water belong . . . People in such zones lose all sense of residence . . . Once this has happened, to restore any sense of domesticity takes generations. Each year of such accumulation prolongs the Nowhere in time and space.[24]

Berger's outrage is directly pertinent to the transformation of places of residential subsistence and ecological complexity into hydrological zones and submergence zones that, in the violence of their euphemized effects, are second cousins to the so-called sacrifice zones of military strategy. The patriotic-cum-technocratic discourse of zones displaces place, creating conditions for the transformation of inhabitants into surplus people, barely visible beside the seductive image of the megadam as a towering miracle of achieved modernity.

When refugees are severed from environments that have provided ancestral sustenance they find themselves stranded not just in place but in time as well. Their improvised lives in makeshift camps are lives of temporal impoverishment. When a megadam obliterates a flood plain whose ebb and flow has shaped the agricultural, fishing, fruit and nut harvesting—and hence nutritional—rhythms of a community, it also drowns the past: the submergence zone swallows place-based connections to the dead, the dead as living presences who move among past, present, and future, animating time with connective meaning. It is in this sense that I read Berger's warning of the generations it would take to rebuild "domesticity." For if forced removal involves agonizing adjustments to bleak accommodation, unfamiliar ecologies, and typically barren, hostile terrain, it involves the additional challenge posed by temporal violence: how to survive in a truncated, severed present, torn by involuntary displacement from the numinous fabric that had woven extended meaning from time-in-place.

As one of the most sensational, visually arresting spectacles of development, the megadam readily deflects attention from the undertow of violent underdevelopment that follows in its wake, especially in densely populated societies like India and China. The construction of Sardar Sarovar, Roy argues, involves "an unacknowledged war." Symptomatically, no official figures for the casualties of this war exist. The problem is not that such people have been reduced to statistics but that they've been reduced to nonstatistics, a whole different level of dehumanization—indeed, one definition of surplus people. To gain a more textured sense of the conversion of inhabitants of "hydrological zones" into uninhabitants who (if represented at all) figure as backward impediments to the developmental advancement of the nation proper, we need to consider the specific violent and nonviolent strategies deployed.

Five main strategies have been used to deny the rights of "hydrological zone" inhabitants. The first is the blunt threat of direct violence: forced removal at military or paramilitary gunpoint or via the barrel of a dam. (Here is Morarji Desai, addressing villagers in the submergence zone of the Pong Dam in 1961: "We will request you to move from your houses after the dam comes up. If you move, it will be good. Otherwise we shall release the waters and drown you all.")[25] The second strategy (often used in tandem with direct violence) involves a rhetorical appeal to selective self-sacrifice: your loss, your suffering is for the greater good—a heroic offering on the pyre of national development. (Here is Nehru, in 1948, exhorting the communities about to be dispossessed by the Hirakud Dam: "If you suffer, you should suffer in the interest of the country.")[26]

The third strategy for denying "hydrological zone" inhabitants their rights and diminishing their visibility involves the indirect violence of euphemism and acronym. The official terminology favored by the World Bank (for decades the core backer of megadams in the global South) is PAPs—Projected-Affected People. This bloodless, technocratic, deviously neutral term obscures the fact that those affected are inevitably negatively affected—often doomed—by the project in question. "Project affected" translates as involuntary eviction, loss of land, community dispersal, and plummeting life prospects. To cut through the pseudoneutrality of such bureaucratic jargon, big dam opponents have preferred a more direct language that underscores the violence involved, advancing terms that range from "oustees" (an Indian neologism that has since garnered international currency) to Scudder's "developmental refugees."

In a fourth strategy the rights of those inhabiting a projected submergence zone may be dismissed on the grounds that such people are culturally inferior—or indeed lack any culture to speak of. This strategy did not end with the waning of direct colonialism: in postindependence India, the Adivasis, or tribals, who together with the Dalits make up the majority of oustees have been treated as expendable because they're widely viewed as culturally contemptible and marginal to the core Hindu nationalist parameters of Indian civilization, although the Adivasis' presence in India long predates Hinduism's advent.[27] I. M. Shah, a leading engineer in the Sardar Sarovar, advocated sterilizing all Adivasis, while Vidhut Joshi of Gujarat's Gandhi Labour Institute argued that "a culture based on lower level of technology and quality of life is bound to give way to a culture with superior technology and higher quality of life. This is what we call development."[28]

The treatment of such people as inconveniencing anachronisms in a globalizing economy is often vindicated through fused discourses of environmental and cultural utilitarian control, whereby the convergent unruliness of "irrational" river people and an "irrational" river must be straightened out and channeled into a national culture of rational development. We thereby witness—and this is far from unique to India—a combined assault on an "unregulated" river and purportedly "lawless" people. Such communities can be readily dismissed as living benighted lives; they belong, in the fullest sense of the dead metaphors, to a cultural backwater not the national mainstream.[29]

The plight of river-reliant Adivasis and Dalits leads us to the fifth strategy for abrogating the rights of those dispossessed by hydrological megaschemes. For the question of cultural recognition—of what counts as a culture—is intimately connected to the question of what counts as belonging. The Adivasis—and indeed most oustees in the global South—do not have title deed to the riverbanks, floodplains, river-dependent forests, and catchment areas that have sustained them, in some cases for millennia. Such people may belong to the land but, within a Lockeian logic of private property, the land doesn't belong to them. Thus in terms of the right to remain (not to speak of the right to just compensation) they can readily be cast as uninhabitants, residual presences from a precapitalist era whose anachronistic criteria for dwelling may be overridden by the legal logic of private property as self-development within a larger narrative of national development. In these terms, oustees can be displaced without being dispossessed.

For floodplain people, as for desert people, to live adaptively on the land through cycles of mobility makes environmental and nutritional sense. One can assert that much without romanticizing ways of living that are often arduous, fraught with danger, and at times result in mismanaged resources. Recession agriculture, for example, which depends on a river's seasonal vagaries, may involve a deeply cultural but always approximate environmental dynamic. However, the perils of mobile adaptation to the risky, unpredictable provisions of river and flood plain and the forests they sustain pale beside the perilous life of the megadam refugee.

In Lockeian (and in Jeffersonian) terms, to dwell in movement is an unacceptable, uncivilized, irrational contradiction: you are improving neither the physical land nor yourself and, by extension, you're failing to advance the national interest. What counts as productive, legitimate, bureaucratically authenticated residence thereby becomes inextricable from the politics of visible self-improvement and the civilizational spectacle of the nation. Thus, through the logic of a selective enlightenment that discriminates against environmentally viable mobility, a deep temporal belonging is made shallow by the designation "informal residents." From there, borrowing from the pervasive discourse of the global "war on terror," it is only one rhetorical step to downgrading "informal residents" who protest eviction to the status of "insurgents."

Through the invention of emptiness—emptiness being the wrong kind of presence—"underdeveloped" people on "underdeveloped" land can be rendered spectral uninhabitants whose territory may be cleared to stage the national theatrics of megadams and nuclear explosions, those certifiable acts that mark the "developing" nation's ascent into modernity's pantheon. Emptiness is an industry that needs constant rhetorical replenishment: the promotion of megadams depends on such emptying out, on actively administered invisibility. Within the dynamics of invisibility and hypervisibility, the myths of emptiness generate unimagined—or at the very least, underimagined—communities. The rationalizing logic of forced removal and resource theft thereby suppresses an environmental justice variant of Walter Rodney's insight: that underdevelopment is not as an original condition of backwardness crying out for modernization, but in large measure an inflicted condition, the legacy of a very modern external plunder by far-off forces.

In the national and transnational resource wars, a double paradox asserts itself. First, in what one might call the resource law of inverse longevity, the longer a people have dwelled in an area in a condition of mobile adaptation, the less they officially belong there, their tenure rendered precarious by a Lockeian logic of what counts as belonging. Their residence, if acknowledged at all, can be dismissed as extralegal. Second, in what one might call the resource law of inverse proximity, the closer people live to the resources being "developed," the less likely they are to benefit from that "development," be it water from megadams or oil pumped from beneath their lands.

Megadams and the Limits of Postcolonialism

The twentieth century was the century of the megadam: in 1900, no dam on our planet was higher than fifteen meters; a hundred years later, there were 36, 562 dams that exceeded that height.[30] This headlong rush not just to control the great rivers of the world but to control them with gargantuan structures had two primary political contexts. The first was the cold war, which saw the superpowers vying to demonstrate greater scientific and engineering supremacy, in the hydrological as in the nuclear domain. The megadam, like the mushroom cloud, made an awesome, cinematic statement of superpower prowess in the race to be the übermaster of natural mastery.[31]

Decolonization became the second primary political motor behind the proliferation of megadams. Nasser, Nkrumah, and Nehru were all seduced by the symbolism of epic dams at a time when these leaders were striving to give material solidity to a newly acquired state of independence.[32] Grandiose dams (like the High Aswan in Egypt and the Akosombo in Ghana) assumed a national psychological significance over and above their pragmatic promise. If the dam wars between the United States and the Soviet Union became one front in a cold-war rivalry for visible technological supremacy, in the newly independent nations of the global South the fervor for megadams became expressive of a different rivalry, one infused with an anxious politics of emulation: whatever our old colonial masters can do, we can do as well. Unlike, say, a rise in literacy rates or life expectancy, megadams served as highly visible, spectacular statements that new nations were literally soaring toward development by mastering rivers and reaching for the sky.

Constructions on such a scale rendered material the trope of nation building: to erect a megadam was literally to concretize the postcolonial nation's modernity, prosperity, and autonomy. No nation boasting such solid grandeur could be dismissed as backward or puny. Each dam was simultaneously an act of national self-assertion—independence writ large across the landscape—and an act of natural conquest. "Nasser and his associates," notes John Waterbury, "could no longer regard the dam as simply a big engineering project, but rather came to hold it up as the symbol of Egypt's will to resist imperialist endeavours to destroy the revolution." Such redemptive symbolism gained populist traction, as crowds flocked to the

Egyptian parliament crying "Nasser, Nasser, we come to salute you; after the Dam our land will be paradise."[33]

Yet ironically, in economic and political terms, these glamorous hydrological regimes of independence doubled as invisible statements of dependence that threw into question the very condition of postcolonialism itself. Literally and metaphorically, the glittering prestige projects of the megadams depended on submergence: of disposable people and ecosystems, but also on the submerged structures of dependence that lay beneath the flamboyant engineering miracles. For the megadams of the South depended on vast loans (typically from the World Bank, the United States, or the Soviet Union) that shackled new nations with high debt loads. Moreover—as in cases like the High Aswan and the Akosombo—where the pressures of cold-war competition and postcolonial aspiration converged, the dams unleashed torrents of political indebtedness to the first- and second-world superpowers. Structures of collusion arose between elites in the first, second, and third world around a related dynamic of invisibility: spectacular megadams require megafunding that offer seductive opportunities for masking gigantic graft.

The Hoover Dam became the gold standard in the rush to emulation.[34] In harnessing the Colorado, it unleashed a torrent of international imitators who took as their canvases the Volga, the Nile, the Niger, the Zambezi, the Yangtze, the Yellow, and the Parana, to name but a few of the most monumental. Although the Oregon Dam soon surpassed the Hoover Dam in scale, it was Hoover that established what became one of the signature discursive features of megadams, namely the contest over the language of transcendence. Hoover gave body to both practical purpose and aesthetic ideals by marrying a miraculous feat of American hydraulic engineering to a sublime spectacle of grandeur.[35] From Hoover onward, megadams became places where the transcendentalisms of religion, nation, science, and art would converge. In this spirit Nehru would proclaim that "dams are the Temples of Modern India," and (in what was then Southern Rhodesia) the boosters of Kariba Dam would marvel at that "glorious castle in the sky."[36] Kariba as transcendental feat of engineering was accompanied by Kariba the transcendental rescue epic—christened Operation Noah—to save the inundated valley's megafauna from drowning. (The eponymous documentary became a nature classic.) Lost in the mix, overshadowed by the glorious sky castle and by Operation Noah, were the 57,000 displaced Gwembe Tsonga, forcibly driven from the valley they had inhabited for centuries and dumped in distant, semiarid terrain, amidst unfamiliar and nonsustaining ecologies.

Small Forms and the Disease of Gigantism

In his latter years, Nehru, formerly enamored of big dams as statements and vehicles of independence, became disenchanted with them, recognizing them as travesties of scale, destructive of local bonds and failing to deliver on their outsize promises. Addressing the Central Board of Irrigation and Power in November 1958, Nehru concluded:

> For some time past, I have been beginning to think that we are suffering from what we may call "the disease of gigantism." We want to show that we can build big dams and do big things. This is a dangerous outlook developing in India . . . the idea of big— having big undertakings and doing big things for the sake of showing that we can do big things—is not a good outlook at all.[37]

The sustainable future, he continued, lay in "the small irrigation projects, the small industries and the small plants for electric power." Nehru's prescient volte-face critiqued the seductive—yet typically inefficient and destructive—forms of modernity engineered on a vast scale.

During the high era of neoliberal globalization, the "disease of gigantism" manifested itself in concrete and on paper: the physical hubris of giant dams was accompanied and enabled by an insufficiently studied, yet potent cluster of outsize genres of writing, prominent among them the World Bank feasibility study and the environmental impact report. (The latter, in the global South, was ordinarily ex post facto, published well after dam work had begun.) This issue of genre and scale is of direct pertinence to Arundhati Roy's turn to the essay as a small, nimble form that allowed her to take on the weighty, leaden genres that gave ballast to the culture of the megadam and, beyond that, to the culture of developmental gigantism. Her quarrel with the genre of the report had several facets to it: she loathed the form, the diction, the voice, and the way all three colluded to render inaccessible what ought to be public knowledge. As a writer, this was her primary contribution to the NBA and to the international environmental justice movement: to expose the insidious, traumatic violence inflicted on the most vulnerable, human and nonhuman, by the affectless language of technospeak. "Language is the skin of my thought," Roy observes. "At The Hague I stumbled on a denomination, a subworld, whose life's endeavor was entirely the opposite of mine. For them the whole purpose of language is to mask intent . . . They breed and prosper in the space that lies between what they say and what they sell."[38]

Roy returns obsessively to that space between: that distance—of diction, genre, and geopolitics—that concentrates power and dissipates responsibility.[39] Her writings against the "disease of gigantism" speak into that gap, speak to the calamitous consequences, especially for ecosystems and ecosystem people, of development as remote control. The contest over access—to resources, power, and audiences—prompted Roy to shift her creative center from the novel to the essay, a form that allowed her to participate more directly and flexibly in the showdown between social movements, a showdown that acquired a generic dimension whereby the agile personal essay was set against the ponderous, strategically impersonal epic report.

Roy's essays stage intimate assaults on the calculated opacity, the profoundly consequential tedium, of the technocratic report that camouflages violence while clearing a path for it in a language scoured of emotion. Extrapolating from her style, one can posit a connection between the uninhabited language of forum speak, policy speak, boardroom speak, and environmental impact speak and the failures of imagination that scour "hydrological zones" of life, replacing threatened living forms with virtual uninhabitants.

In all her writing, Roy teases out the relationship between distance and transgressive intimacies that cross chasms of caste, class, gender, nation, region, and religion. Her concern with the abstracting of life by distance reflects her concern with hierarchies of visibility: the seen and the unseen, the tangible and the untouchable. If Roy writes against distance in many forms, one crucial variant is the distance between the incorporeality of corporate power and its convulsive, material effects. This gap poses particular challenges for the environmental justice movement, hence her call for writers

> who can translate cash-flow chards and boardroom speeches
> into real stories about real people with real lives. Stories about
> what it's like to lose your home, your land, your dignity, your

past, and your future to an invisible force. To someone or something you can't see. You can't hate. You can't even imagine."[40]

Roy thus turns to the essay as a form that, in temporal and sensory terms,
holds the promise of the immediate, of a quick, inhabited retort to the
unimaginable—and unimaginative—culture of the colossus. In this spirit,
she calls for an art committed to undoing verbally and bureaucratically
inflicted absence: "[A]n art that makes the impalpable palpable, makes the
intangible tangible, and the invisible visible. An art which can draw out the
incorporeal adversary and make it real. Bring it to book."[41]

In bringing to book the deadly, long-distance administration of living rivers via the silted language of the hydro-bureaucrat's report, Roy repeatedly
returns to questions of narrative monopoly. The shrinking of knowledge to
expertise and the centralizing of power—not least the power to tell—renders us unsighted, making it harder to inhabit the lived consequences of
neoliberalism's densely rationalized developmental narratives.

Roy's vocal tactics, by contrast, are expressly decentered. There's a
productive instability to her voice that keeps her audience off balance. She
belongs, in that sense, to the tradition of the lyric essay as environmental
polemic, a tradition that includes figures as diverse as Edward Abbey and
Jamaica Kincaid. All of them are cantankerous, rowdy, irreverent, but also by
turns tenderly specific, interspersing a lyricism of the sentence and a lyricism
toward living forms with blasts of sarcasm, parody, hyperbole, vehemence,
and blunt anger. All three writers are exponents of what Raymond Williams
called "militant particularism," but all are equally exponents of the calculated
overgeneralization. In the process, they jettison any ambition of directing the
essay's formal possibilities toward building a quiet, readerly rapport, far less
universal admiration. By seceding from what one might call the emotionally
miniaturist tradition of the essay, Roy, Abbey, and Kincaid explode the form
with outsize sentiments directed at outsize adversaries: developers, the tourist industry, empire, the World Bank's hydrological regimes.

If, as I've suggested, Roy's defining subjects are the politics of visibility, distance, and scale, one witnesses through her activism a showdown
between two highly engineered spectacles of modernity—the megadam and
the megacelebrity, in this case a Booker Prize-winning author and icon of
Indian national cultural pride. By appending her garlanded visibility to the

environmental justice movement that opposed the Sardar Sarovar Dam, Roy plunged headfirst into the political quagmires of representation and displacement. She would be duly accused, among other things, of celebrity showboating, of ethical egotism, of impetuous self-involvement, of strategic naïvety, and of squandering her novelistic gifts on mere polemics.[42] Some of these charges were specific to turn-of-the-millennium Indian politics, others echo familiar accusations against novelists, from James Baldwin to Nadine Gordimer, who have activated the essay's polemical possibilities to advocate for political causes. Through her celebrity persona, Roy found herself in a paradoxical position: she represented the distance of privilege, so had to strive to surmount the suspicions that distance provoked by grounding her credentials through the Andovar movement. Moreover, while arguing for the devolution of the power to narrate, she herself would have to ward off charges that she was recentering narrative authority through her hypervisibility.

In contrast to writer-activists like Ken Saro-Wiwa and Wangari Maathai, Roy was not a founding member of an environmental justice movement but a late affiliate. This complicated the fraught politics of representation and left her more vulnerable to attack on grounds of privilege, insensitivity, and usurpation. However, she persisted in using her celebrity visibility to try to amplify the cause of the Narmada River's resource rebels. Moreover, she became a vital translator in four ways. First, she translated an impenetrably technocratic discourse into more accessible language and story lines. Second, she gave an Indian story an international audience of an order it would not otherwise have achieved. Third, alongside the NBA, Medha Pratkar, and Vandana Shiva, she articulated the battle over the Narmada River megadams to the international water wars, helping make the Narmada campaign an iconic struggle. Fourth, Roy placed destructive hydrological regimes in the broader transnational contexts of neoliberalism's ascendant hegemony and the international opposition to that ascent. Through this last act of translation, Roy became, alongside Naomi Klein, the primary invigorating voice for a whole new generation of antiglobalization activists.

Monumental Modernity, Ecological Democracy

Collectively, the notions of surplus people, developmental refugees, and uninhabitants give us a language for contesting the narrative of the redemptive megadam as spectacular symbol of rational deliverance from irrational rivers and irrational cultures. At stake is submergence: of communities, ecosystems, and voices, as the emissaries of gigantism seek to drown out the narrative diversity that would expose the short-lived, impossibly contradictory combinations of permanent plenitude such emissaries promise in the name of a forward-thrusting (but selectively delimited) nationalism. But the megadams are transients, temporary sojourners in the long life of the river. All too often, they silt up, spread salination, poison the soil. They are also steeped in well-timed deceits: in 1985, the World Bank estimated the Sardar Sarovar project would displace 33,000 people; eight years later, with the dam safely underway, the Bank reestimated the displaced at 320,000.

George Perkins Marsh recognized as far back as 1874 that large hydrological schemes redistribute more than water: "The tendency of irrigation as a regular agricultural method is to promote the accumulation of large tracts of land in the hands of single proprietors, and consequently to dispossess the smaller land-holders."[43] Patrick McCully, our own age's nonpareil critic of outsize dams, underscores this point: "The story is a familiar one from Rajasthan to California. Irrigation schemes are promoted with the promise of land to the tiller, but end up delivering it to the absentee landlord."[44] Often, those not driven away end up as bonded laborers on what formerly was their own land.

Big dams are thus diversionary in a triple sense. They divert water—and through water, land—from the powerless to the powerful. But they also divert attention, their glistening enchantments throwing into shadow unimagined communities. One recalls, in this spirit, Roy's portrait of globalization as "like a light which shines brighter and brighter on a few people and the rest are in darkness, wiped out. They simply can't be seen. Once you get used to not seeing something, then, slowly, it's no longer possible to see it."[45]

Vandana Shiva is right: "[T]he water crisis is an ecological crisis with commercial causes but no market solutions . . . Ending the water crisis requires rejuvenating ecological democracy."[46] For that to be achieved we have a long way to go. As I write, the all-too predictable script of hydrological hubris is repeating itself in Ethiopia, in an unequal battle between resource omnivores and ecosystem peoples. Dam work has begun on the Omo River: the contract for the dam, which will create the second-largest reservoir in sub-Saharan Africa, was signed for almost two billion dollars with an Italian dam construction company. No tenders were made and the first environmental impact report was published two years after the dam's construction had begun. The procedures were so scandalously immoral that even the World Bank withdrew its funding, leaving the government of Ethiopia—one of the world's poorest, most debt-laden nations—saddled with a shortfall of over $500 million.

The Omo River megadam may deliver electricity and graft to the capital's elite, but the downstream tribes whose livelihoods and ecosystems are most at risk will be left literally and metaphorically in the dark. Informed by a BBC reporter of the imminent damming of their river, they declared they would take up arms against the government. (The tribes in Ethiopia's impoverished southwest are awash with arms that have flooded in from the neighboring conflict in southern Sudan.) One elder observed that the survival of his people depended on three rocks that hold up the pot: cattle; crops grown on higher ground in the rainy season; and in the dry season, floodplain (recession) agriculture. If the river is narrowed and controlled from above, two of those rocks will be removed: "[T]he pot will topple over and my people will starve." The most probable scenario is this: the deadening of the river's seasonal pulse will provoke resource wars among the heavily armed tribes who live downstream from development.[47]

This hydrological story—as happens so often—doesn't end at the border. The Omo River drains into the largest lake in northern Kenya, where tribes find sustenance through a blend of fishing, cattle herding, agriculture, and hunting. Once the dam throttles the inflow of fresh water, the vast lake (whose salinity is already rising) will become fatally salty, unfit for humans, cattle, wildlife, crops, and fish. The ecosystem—and the cultures of ecosystem peoples dependent on it—are at risk of collapse. Together, the dam and the conflicts it stirs up on both sides of the border will result in new waves of developmental refugees.

Despite the formidable odds, sometimes diverse, creative coalitions between local and international activists successfully turn back the megadam juggernaut. When in the late 1980s the Brazilian government, emboldened by a $500 million World Bank loan, announced plans for a massive hydroelectric project on the Xingu River, eleven Indian nations were slated for displacement by flooding. Al Gedicks recounts how the chief of one of those nations, Paulinho Paiakan of the Kayapo, his cousin Kube-I, and Darrell Posey (a North American ethnobiologist who had long worked with the Kayapo) seeded a powerful trans-tribal and international oppositional alliance.[48] In an effort to blunt their initiative, the Brazilian government charged the two Kayapo leaders (along with Posey) with contravening a law that banned foreigners from criticizing the government. Under an astonishing statute, native peoples, who had inhabited the Amazon for millennia, could be designated as foreigners and therefore subject to the gagging measure. Thus the threat of physical expulsion from their lands by flooding was compounded by the imaginative and legal expulsion of the Kayapo from the idea of the nation. But these uninhabitants fought back successfully: 600 native leaders from across the Americas descended on the proposed dam site in protest and, after an international outcry, the World Bank cancelled the loan.

That insurrection bought the Kayapo and allied Amazon tribes some time: two decades, to be precise. For as I write, the Xingu River water wars have begun all over again. In August 2010, Brazil's former president, Luiz Inácio Lula da Silva, authorized construction on the $11 billion Belo Monte Dam on the Xingu, throwing into jeopardy the future of the Kayapo and a score of other tribes. Belo Monte—slated to be the world's third largest dam and a destructive monster of gargantuan inefficiency—is catalyzing yet again a vital coalition of resource rebels.

6

Stranger in the Eco-village

Race, Tourism, and Environmental Time

[Conservation biologists and political ecologists] tend to speak entirely past each other. . . . Conservation biologists segregate nonhumans; political ecologists too often take them for granted as resources for human use. Instead, we might want to look at how species and populations slip in and out of markets, in and out of cultural attention, and in and out of a whole spectrum of not-yet-fully-described interactions between humans and nonhumans.

—Anna Tsing, *Friction: An Ethnography of Global Connection*

Anna Tsing, one of our most incisive thinkers about globalization and the environment, may be writing here about Indonesia, but her insights can be productively adapted to South Africa, where the segregations of humans from nonhumans have long been implicated in the violent segregations of humans from humans. South Africa's traumatic history of colonial conquest, land theft, racial partition, and racist conservation places particular pressure on those conservation biologists, political ecologists, writers, and activists committed to reimagining, during the postapartheid era, their society's inherited cultures of nature.[1]

This transformative task is rendered more urgent by South Africa's rare environmental significance: only two nations, Brazil and Indonesia, surpass it in biodiversity. South Africa thus combines, in combustible form, extreme ecological wealth and a postapartheid legacy of extreme economic and territorial inequity. A major flashpoint for the tension between these extremes remains the game reserve, that contradictory, potentially lucrative, historically troubled space that promises encounters with the "timeless" Africa of charismatic megafauna yet risks reinscribing the society's dominant culture of nature as racially exclusive and hostile to political transformation. Against this backdrop, we need to explore what I call racialized ecologies of looking in relation to environmental amnesia. This environmental dynamic between seeing and not seeing, between remembering and forgetting, is forcefully exemplified by the game reserve. But it has a broader pertinence to the challenges of reconciling environmental justice, political transformation, biodiversity, and touristic expectations that have been shaped by the international marketing of nature.

Across much of southern and East Africa, game reserves and "native" reserves have shadowed each other historically in the interdependent administrations of conservation, leisure, and labor. The noun "reserve" may refer to either a sanctuary or a place of involuntary confinement—a refuge or a cage. This double valence carries a special force in South Africa, suggesting both spaces reserved for environmental protection and the "native" reserves (precursors to the Bantustans) that served as holding pens in the circuits of migrant mine labor. Because South Africa's ecologies of enclosure are ghosted by traumas of forced removal, the destiny of the game reserve—within what Njabulo Ndebele calls the postapartheid "liberation of leisure"—remains inextricably bound to the racial dynamics of sanctuary and trespass, memory and amnesia, visibility and invisibility, looking and looking away.[2]

To illuminate these dynamics I trace in this chapter four journeys, one autobiographical, two nonfictional, and one fictional. Collectively, these journeys track the temporal and racial performances of "wild Africa" through the transnational questions that contour them, not least the international tourist feedback loop whereby the lucrative global branding of charismatic megafauna as quintessentially South African shapes both tourists' expectations and the nature industry that greets them. Such circular expectations, I suggest, can inhibit expanded access to what have been painfully exclusive spaces and retard a broader commitment to biodiversity that isn't reducible to—and is sometimes incompatible with—the spectacular concentrations of megafauna that drive South Africa's nature industry.

Canned Lions and an Eternity of Bush

In the run-up to Nelson Mandela's election in 1994, South Africa experienced considerable white flight. One of the less-noted side stories was a surge in megafauna for sale—lions, elephants, crocodiles, hippos, and the like—sent to market by emigrating whites who had shut down their circuses and private zoos. At the time, I was covering the election in the country's Eastern Province and heard word of a wildlife entrepreneur, J. P. Kleinhans, who had converted his sheep farm into a hybrid space—half game reserve, half hunting lodge. I sought him out upon hearing rumors that some of the seventy lions in his reserve had been purchased on the white-flight black market and that he was charging foreign trophy-hunters top dollar to shoot dangerous African animals that were in fact "canned lions," circus retirees put out to the carnivore's equivalent of pasture.

Kleinhans greeted me with a hearty air of practiced informality: "J. P. Kleinhans, just call me J.P., Texas style." His huge palm in the center of my back, he steered me into the lodge lobby where I found myself surrounded by lion, buffalo, hippo, warthog, bush pig, and a dozen species of antelope, all in half-body mounts, stampeding toward me through whitewashed walls.

Following him through a second door, I entered arguably the world's most voracious master bedroom. Mounted carnivores massed everywhere—across the floor, through the air, obscuring windows. The bed was surrounded. A leopard slunk by the pillow, as if waiting for husband and wife to drop their guard and dip into sleep. A lioness pushed past some jackals squabbling over first rights to the kill. Above the bed hung a vulture with eight-foot wings, beak tilted down, glassy eyes wide, searching the duvet for any whiff of carrion or death. What kind of person, I wondered, would choose to wake to vulture talons, to stagger from some convulsive dream into a hyena's huge, mocking teeth?[3]

As we stepped outside, beyond his theatre of risk, Kleinhans made a tentative allusion to the slur of domesticity that had adhered to his lions. "I've been to the States to hunt. But let me tell you, man, it's different there. Their animals, compared to ours, they're all so tame." We were soon bumping across the thornveld in his jeep, Kleinhans recounting how his son and a school friend had survived a recent mauling by some lions—"just over there." As he spoke, I felt an anxious determination in him that the tired, AARP lion that had spent its life leaping meekly through circus hoops be crushed by that other figurative lion, the untamable, almighty king of beasts, whose rule since time immemorial had terrorized the African bush. Kleinhans, as a wildlife image manager, was clearly fearful that the reputation of his lions (including his lionesses) was being feminized. It was, after all, the aura of explosive risk that would give his lions, male and female, their commercial teeth. His economic survival and male dignity depended on decommodifying the purportedly canned lions in order to recommodify them as a different product—pure, uncanned embodiments of a snarling, timeless African authenticity that couldn't be bought elsewhere.

"Almost anything Africa has got to offer," Kleinhans interjected, "you can kill it here, right here at Wolwekloof. The Americans love this place. One client, he told me, he'd traveled all over—Masai Mara, Zambia, Namibia, Kruger Park. But he said here at Wolwekloof, for the first time, he'd touched the real Africa."

Kleinhans had no blacks working at his game lodge: "My wife and me, we made enough sons to do the job. I don't need blacks here." (His wife and female relatives took care of domestic chores—the cleaning, cooking, and secretarial side of things.) At the very moment of black empowerment in the society at large, Kleinhans was creating a racial and temporal enclave, a timeless island outside a time of change. His brochure promised his American (and Russian, Italian, German, and Canadian) clients an "exclusive" experience—a word that resonated in complex ways in a country whose psychic and physical landscapes bore deep scars of enclosure and expulsion.

Many of his American clients, he noted, loved to bag their lions with crossbows. I pictured the scene as he described it: Kleinhans picks up his client at the airport, drives him to the lodge, where he enacts some ersatz bow-and-arrow hunt, half in the spirit of Iron John, half National Geographic pigmy, while accruing, before being whisked back to the airport, both a trophy lion and an indelibly African adventure shielded from any inconveniencing encounter with living Africans.[4]

It would be easy to read Wolwekloof as a straightforward narrative of atavistic, Afrikaner self-enclosure, of a racially and historically threatened

man barricading himself against history, democracy, and black empowerment. But to that narrative we must add a complicating twist. If the postapartheid turn disturbed Kleinhans, he also recognized in it fresh business
opportunities. With foreign tourists and hunters pouring in under Mandela,
Kleinhans could capitalize on resilient mythologies of international white
masculinity for which the lion hunt could serve as a seductive, profitable
shorthand. In creating a racio-temporal island in a sea of black majority
rule he was simultaneously reaching out to an oceanic white wildlife kill-
or-consume culture that stretched beyond the nation. By internationalizing
his parochialism, Kleinhans was articulating himself to the white call-and-
response of the charismatic megafauna touristic feedback loop.

Foreign hunter-tourists could be fierce in their demands; and what they
demanded was the prospect of an ancient African ferocity, embodied not
only in the king of beasts but in the landscape's untamed visage too. These
projected desires had solidified around Kleinhans's alfalfa problems, which
were compounding his canned lion problems. His clients kept grumbling
about an alfalfa field on a distant farm visible from one corner of the lodge.
The field spoiled the experience, they said; it didn't look African. In order to
expunge from view agriculture's domestic taint, Kleinhans was busy erecting new accommodation for his hunter-tourists—"Zulu" huts on a hillside
that guaranteed panoramic vistas unsullied by labor, human necessity, or
food production.[5] Like the reed baskets, masks, and beadwork that adorned
the lodge, his "Zulu" huts would foster the ambience of a cultural village
sans villagers. By swiveling the view, Kleinhans could now provide his tourists with the sight lines they demanded, guaranteeing them a genuine simu-
lacrum of foreign visual expectations of an authentic Africa.

"Don't get me wrong," Kleinhans said, tipping back his Elk Lodge base-
ball cap. "I like the American. But the thing about the American is you have
to speak his language. What the American wants when he comes here is an
eternity of bush."

I stood with him at that hilltop "Zulu" hut looking down at the bushveld
scene he'd laid out for his clients: a seemingly endless temporal panorama of
undying purity that his hunters could enter to make their kills.

Six months after visiting the lodge, I read in a local newspaper that
Kleinhans and a Texan client had heard a distant ruckus one night: two lions
brawling. The men had driven to the fight where Kleinhans attempted to

distract the warring lions by throwing them some donkey meat. When that failed, he walked toward them shouting and waving before trying to part them with bare hands. The lions turned on him and mauled him to death.

Kleinhans died a performer in the transnational theater of Wild Africa on a stage crowded with anxieties about race, white manhood, domesticity, class, risk, and authentic wilderness, a stage that was both "timeless" and suffused with the historical uncertainties of an emergent postapartheid order. He sought to stave off that order—and capitalize on it—by aligning himself, economically and psychologically, with the eco-archaic expectations of the Pretoria-Fort Worth axis.

Kleinhans's eldest son, Adolf, made an announcement to the press: "We will not kill these lions that killed our father." (In other words, the lions would not be singled out for punitive execution but would be available, as per normal, for commercial killing.) Within this family tragedy, something else emerged: through his unwitting martyrdom Kleinhans had left a legacy of killer lions. The ferocious manner of his death had cleansed his animals—and the enterprise his sons inherited—of any domestic taint. Who now would dare claim he was defrauding foreign hunters with toothless circus retirees masquerading as Wild Africa?

Looking back at my encounter with Kleinhans on this volatile historical cusp, I am returned to Donna Haraway's classic essay "Teddy Bear Patriarchy," in which she links, during a time of American social upheaval, Teddy Roosevelt and Carl Akeley's hunting expeditions to censored performances (in the field and in museum dioramas) that betray profound racial, class, and gender anxieties. I am returned not just to her account of how anything that might complicate a narrative of individual white male hunter heroics was cropped from photographs and narratives, but also to the connection she makes between the uneasy representational artifice of the transnational African hunt as theatre of risk and a nation's racial and gender panics.[6]

The Postapartheid Game Lodge and Ecologies of Looking

Not long after my encounter with Kleinhans, in the newly democratic South Africa of the mid-1990s, the fiction writer and essayist Njabulo Ndebele visited a game lodge in his native land for the first time, a venture he reflects on in his essay "Game Lodges and Leisure Colonialists."[7] Ndebele describes entering the game lodge at a dynamic moment in his society's transformation, yet finding himself cocooned in a temporal enclave, sealed against the environment of political change. Intent on leisure, Ndebele is haunted instead by "the damning ambiguities of the black tourist."[8] Ndebele is not alone in writing about the leisurely stresses, the wrenching ambiguities, of the ancestrally colonized tourist vacationing in an erstwhile colony. The comparison with black travelers to the Caribbean—like Jamaica Kincaid and June Jordan—is particularly suggestive given the pervasive marketing of the islands as, like the game lodges, free-floating Edenic enclaves of natural time, unmoored from historical memory, clock-time, and the time of labor.

The white game lodge is a classic instance of what Anne McClintock terms an anachronistic space, a space marked as noncoeval with the world around it and whose implication in modernity is suppressed.[9] But here the spatial anachronism does not simply mark the game lodge as "backward" in a progress discourse indebted to a tendentiously selective imperial enlight-·enment; instead, the lodge's refusal to acknowledge the contemporary renders it an atavistic space in denial of South Africa's democratic transformation while simultaneously capitalizing on that transformation. We can read the game lodge, then, as a manifestation of the postapartheid nation's suddenly expansive modern tourist industry and as a racialized and naturalized fortress against that very modernity. It is into this contradictory temporal domain that Ndebele steps.

In its antimodern dimension the lodge exists as a temporal enclave in a double, layered sense: the temporal styles evoked are both historically colonial (self-effacing servants vanishing into the bush, white campfire camaraderie, male tales of derring-do) and eternally natural (a time outside of time, before and after the human, when megafauna rule—Kleinhans's "eternity of bush"). Crucially, for our purposes, the game lodge locates itself in the postapartheid marketplace by selling a blended aura of colonial time and prehuman natural time.

Ndebele arrives as a visitor from the future present, a postapartheid pioneer. As a white-collar black wildlife tourist, his arrival at the game lodge gates is a harbinger of change, an intimation that the racialized ideology of fortress conservation is pregnable. His presence is historic in an enclave from which history has been banished; he disturbs the sealed domain of white men playing games of bushveld risk, implicitly reminding them of risk in a wider form—those political transformations that may, however, come in tandem with opportunities. (Ndebele wonders whether the whites around the campfire view him as someone with usable political connections to the ascendant black power elite.)[10]

In class terms, Ndebele too now belongs at the lodge. But the politics of his belonging are fraught with temporal contradictions. As an indigenous tourist from a newly arrived future, he also bears in his person reminders of the past; his presence points forward and backward in time: forward to the anticipated incursions of an excluded black majority into white nature enclaves, and backward to an ancestral history of being territorially *dislodged* by game lodges and other conservation projects that, while modest in relation to the country's broader history of forced removal, nonetheless created, under the banner of wildlife conservation, dispossessed conservation refugees.[11] Ndebele's presence thus renders visibly political the apolitical posture of the game lodge as natural sanctuary from politics.

We can read Ndebele's position as that of a man who has ventured abroad in his own country, an inner émigré in a white nature industry whose marketing premise is the managed wildness of the eco-archaic. His complex pursuit of leisure in this environment—and his concomitant existential stresses—are linked to what I call the ecologies of looking, that is, the interconnected webs of looking and being seen in a context where the idea of the natural predominates. Ndebele has come to relax and look: to peer through his binoculars, alongside these other folk, at the charismatic megafauna, at the spectacles of the wild. But his own spectacular presence disrupts the smooth optics of tourism.

By inserting himself into a tableau of neoapartheid time, amidst those he calls by turns "leisure colonialists" and "leisure refugees," Ndebele makes whiteness visible.[12] He does so by unsettling the temporal and physical insularity of the archaic game lodge, which operates as both a nostalgic, amnesiac space of white refusal of apartheid's aftermath and a contemporary expression of postapartheid South Africa's reintegration into global tourist networks.

Ndebele himself, however, is also profoundly unsettled. We can read the layered self-consciousness into which he finds himself propelled as a kind of bushveld version of Fanon's "Look, a Negro"; that moment when, on encountering the white world, Fanon observes: "I took myself far off from my own presence. . . . It was no longer a question of being aware of my body in the third person but in a triple person. . . . I was responsible for my body, for my race, for my ancestors."[13] But inside the game lodge, a black tourist like Ndebele isn't just under observation and self-observation; he has forked out good money to be observed. As he notes sardonically, "he pays to be the viewer who has to be viewed."[14] (It's rhetorically apposite—a measure of Ndebele's self-anthropologizing self-estrangement—that much of the essay is written as third-person autobiography.)

Ndebele has long been troubled by what is sacrificed, imaginatively, to the pressures of spectacle. In the 1980s, amidst a brutal apartheid state of emergency, he published two controversial essays that questioned what he saw as the subservience of much South African writing to the Manichean dictates of spectacular racial violence. Those essays—"The Rediscovery of the Ordinary" and "Redefining Relevance"—lamented a literary bias toward "the predictable drama between ruthless oppressors and the pitiful victims," a bias that contracted and calcified the imaginative "range of explorable experience."[15] This "hegemony of spectacle" seduced many writers into focusing on a predictable apartheid-antiapartheid agon that obscured a whole spectrum of ordinary experience, thereby producing a literature deficient in complex interiority, deficient in inflected historical awareness, and neglectful of the fabric of everyday life. Skewed by international pressures to produce a recognizable black-on-white agon, Ndebele argued, the prevailing literary imagination tended to marginalize rural black lives in communities that might never encounter a white person from one year to the next.

I read "Game Lodges and Leisure Colonialists" as an extension of Ndebele's early preoccupation with both the spectacular costs of spectacle and the rediscovery of the ordinary. The essay asks, at least implicitly, what would it take for a black South African to enter the game lodge as an unspectacular, unwatched, *ordinary* tourist, thereby transforming what I'm calling the ecologies of looking? Second, how can the temporal enclave of the rural game lodge be reintegrated into a postapartheid national imaginary? Third, just as the international market for the Manichean conventions of apartheid-antiapartheid showdowns may have narrowed the South African literary spectrum, in what ways does the international tourist feedback loop of demand and satisfied desire narrow, through repetitive reinforcement,

South Africa's viable cultures of nature? Returning to Anna Tsing's call for reconciling the priorities of conservation biologists and political ecologists, we can recognize in Ndebele's essay a quest to rediscover the ecological ordinary—those quotidian interactions between humans and nonhumans that move beyond the racialized theatre of the eco-archaic.

Like the Caribbean paradise, the game reserve is shaped as a sanctuary from labor and from history's brutality; here history's corrugations have been Botoxed from nature's visage. In the temporal enclaves of the island refuge ringed by ocean and in the game reserve ringed by electrified fences, the tourist is guaranteed full immersion in the eco-archaic, which is not to be confused with the historical. To enter this refuge is to enter a charmed space that is segregated, among other things, from the history of its own segregation.

For black tourist-writers, from June Jordan and Jamaica Kincaid to Ndebele, this stage-managed amnesia becomes a special source of disorientation and outrage. A direct relationship emerges between a suppressed history of dispossession and the black visitor's embattled self-possession. "How is it [Ndebele asks] that a simple quest for peace and restoration turned into an unexpectedly painful journey into the self?" He finds himself "pushed into a state of simmering revolt."[16]

What surfaces for Ndebele, like Jordan and Kincaid before him, is a vexed relationship to labor, both historically and in the present. The violent labor histories that shaped the colonial landscapes of the Caribbean and South Africa were inseparable from forced removals, whether trans-Atlantic or internal to the white settler nation-state (via first the Native reserves and later the Bantustans). Given this anguished history, all these writers are angered by the labor-intensive production of labor's illusory absence, an absence critical to the eco-archaic's role in producing a sweat-free, soft-focus, natural tranquility that appears at once effortless and untouched by human history.[17]

In the touristic present, the fraught issue of labor resurfaces through the prism of class, which complicates whatever racial identification the vacationing writer may feel with those who tiptoe around him or her in roles of unobtrusive service. Ndebele is plunged into anguished inner debate on how to relate to paradise's servants: if he fraternizes with them, will his dignity be compromised in the eyes of the white tourists? How do the servants view him? How much is the correct amount to tip?

In the Bahamas, Jordan, a Harlem-born daughter of Jamaican immigrants, finds herself veering between, on the one hand, a gendered, racial identification with local women and, on the other, a discomfiting acknowledgement that a class chasm separates her from the structurally invisible women who service her hotel room. Indeed, the most deeply characterized Bahamian woman in Jordan's essay is the spectral Olive, the maid whose performance Jordan is urged to grade at the end of her stay in paradise without ever having met her. In thinking through her relationship to Olive's labor, Jordan concludes that sharing a common racial adversary is an insufficient source of shared identity.[18] When Kincaid revisits her natal Antigua as a naturalized American, the question of labor—past and present—renders her apoplectic. How, she exclaims, can the emancipated descendants of slaves celebrate the Hotel Training School "which teaches Antiguans how to be good servants"?[19]

At the heart of the history-labor-nature quandary stands the vexed issue of transport—as ancestral racial journey, as aesthetic convention, and as touristic affect. Ndebele, Jordan, and Kincaid, all shadowed by histories of forced removal, find themselves unable to enter, in any straightforward way, the sublime as portal to a "natural" state of transport. Given their ancestral histories—and given the suppression of those histories in the temporal enclaves of eco-archaic amnesia—Ndebele, Kincaid, and Jordan all find themselves resistant to being unselfconsciously "carried away."

The uneasy circuits of sublime pleasure are directly related to another dilemma: What does it mean, in the fullest sense of the phrase, to be *absorbed* by nature? In terms of a post-Enlightenment ecology of spectatorship, how are Kincaid (an anticolonial botanical enthusiast) and Ndebele (an avid anti-apartheid bird-watcher) to circumnavigate the repressive legacy of racial classification that figured their ancestors as "natural"? White nature tourists, I would suggest, have less troubled access to sublime natural absorption in a post- or neocolonial environment because they can experience their whiteness as an unselfconsciously unclassified state. Ndebele, by contrast, is painfully alive to the problematics of natural union and a historically freighted politics of looking: "[W]hen [black tourists] go game viewing, it is difficult not to feel that, in the total scheme of things, perhaps they should be out there with the animals, being viewed."[20]

The presence of these animals is critical. In the tourist cultures of the Caribbean, Eden typically figures as a garden—a sanctuary from history and labor, but a sanctuary without predation.[21] By contrast, the African Edens of the southern and East African tourist industries are shaped around the presence—and managed threat—of charismatic megafauna, which becomes the primary guarantor of encounters with the timeless and the pristine.[22] This has profound gender implications: the African Eden must be scoured not only of history and labor but also (as we've seen in the case of Wolwekloof) of the taint of domesticity, the stigma of the tame. As a result, the cultural spectacle around African Edens has a strongly masculine tilt: the white game guides, the black trackers, the bush pilots all carry forward—adapted for the contemporary global marketplace—a neo-Victorian obsession with risk (or at least with saleable performances of risk's illusions).[23]

Stranger in the Village

James Baldwin's "Stranger in the Village" may seem an unlikely text to enfold into an analysis of game reserves, racialized tourism, and environmental time. Yet in light of the discussion of Kleinhans and Ndebele, we can glean from Baldwin's classic essay productive insights into racialized ecologies of looking and the role that cultures of nature play in modernity's civilizational power plays. Some forty years before Ndebele arrived as a solitary, improbable novelty at the game lodge gates, Baldwin spent the first of several sojourns in a Swiss Alpine village that he portrayed as a "white wilderness."[24] He had been forewarned that "he would probably be a 'sight' for the village," and his essay offers a far-reaching meditation on invisible visibility, on how it feels—and what it means culturally—to be a "sight" unseen. Baldwin, like Ndebele after him, is thrust by the stresses of racialized leisure into a state of spectacular self-consciousness.[25]

Baldwin's anger and insight flow from his experience of what one might call empowered parochialism. The Swiss villagers have never encountered a black person before; they lead untraveled lives, holed up in their icy redoubt, severed from the larger world. Yet Baldwin recognizes these hyperparochial people are powerfully connected in their severance, unconsciously emboldened by the broad currents of Western culture—Dante, Michelangelo, the cathedral at Chartres—that afford them an assumed racial superiority and ease.

What makes Baldwin's essay so suggestive in tandem with Ndebele's is the acuity with which both writers expose the profound resistance—local, national, international—to the temporal and geographical incorporation of blackness into modernity. Baldwin is treated in the village as a "suspect late-comer"; despite his experiential cosmopolitanism he is made to feel more tangential to the vast temporal and spatial flows of Western culture than the most illiterate, cut off Swiss villager.[26]

Unlike Baldwin in blindingly white rural Switzerland, Ndebele doesn't have to travel far—just assume the mantle of local time traveler—in order to be exoticized as an oddity in a blindingly white South African rural enclave. If Ndebele too remains, for now, alone and improbable, he is writing decades later than Baldwin, on a very different historical cusp. Yet, when Ndebele exclaims that "the entire world of contemporary tourism carries no intuitive familiarity" for him, we sense a kindred indignation to Baldwin's anger at the energy it takes to stake out for himself a space in a modernity organized around his anachronistic yet constitutive exclusion.[27] The challenge Ndebele faces is to reclaim—and ultimately reimagine—the game lodge's overdetermined modern nature, a modern nature in denial of its modernity. Ndebele's insights can be read as supplementing Baldwin's in this essential way: it is not only the architectural, literary, artistic, and musical cultures of the West that have historically been wielded as weapons of black exclusion (largely through denied coevalness and denied hybridity), but the cultures of nature as well, including the culture of wildlife tourism, whereby a provincial whiteness is fortified by white pilgrims from abroad.[28] The game lodge becomes, then, a site of "provincial cosmopolitanism," to adapt Amitava Kumar's phrase.[29] Thus Wild Africa, while purporting to represent civilization's antithesis, simultaneously freights whiteness with another kind of cathedral ballast.

Both Baldwin's and Ndebele's "white wilderness" essays assail a diehard, historically dominant culture's determination to keep living in denial, to sustain an unsustainable condition of contorted innocence. For the Europe of the 1950s, black people—over there in the colonies—could remain at an abstract remove: "[I]n effect," Baldwin notes, "the black man, as a man, did not exist for Europe."[30] American whites of that era, he adds, proved even greater contortionists, "still nourish[ing] the illusion that there is some means of recovering the European innocence, of returning to a state in which black men do not exist."[31] The postapartheid South African game lodge—as sanctuary of illusory innocence and eco-archaic return—depends on an even less plausible theatre of denial, given the accession of the black majority to political power.[32] Buoyed by performances of ecological elegy and arrested time, the game lodge serves as the last great hope of a mono-chromatic nostalgia that wishes away the cultural, economic, and political transformations of the society in which it is embedded. If, in Baldwin's clos-ing assertion in his 1953 essay, "[t]his world is white no longer, and will never be white again," how much more decisively his voice echoes four decades later in a nation where a black majority, for the first time in world history, had voted a white supremacist regime out of office.[33]

From Leisure Refugees to the Ultimate Safari

Nadine Gordimer's short story "The Ultimate Safari" follows a group of ref-ugees from Mozambique's civil war on a fugitive, perilous trek across South Africa's largest and most celebrated wildlife preserve, the Kruger National Park. The story centers on the experiences of traumatized cross-border trav-elers at the furthest remove from Ndebele's "leisure refugees" and Klein-hans's foreign tourists craving their "eternity of bush." Inside the Kruger Park, the Mozambican refugees find themselves plunged, unguided, into a time outside of time, into a bewildering, life-threatening timelessness from which, if they are to survive, they must extricate themselves. "The Ultimate Safari" carries forward my concern with rival ecologies of time, with the politics of mobility, and with the racialized politics of looking.

Gordimer has a penchant for ironizing tourist industry boilerplate in the titles of her stories, for instance, calling her most brilliant exposé of a racist consciousness "Good Climate, Friendly Inhabitants." "The Ultimate Safari" bears as its epigraph an advertising pitch that appeared in a British newspaper: "The African Adventure Lives On . . . You can do it! The ulti-mate safari or expedition with leaders who know Africa." Gordimer's story pivots on the ambiguity of "ultimate," which can imply either "nonpareil" or "final." The tourist-ad safari is pitched as unbeatable, the adventure of a lifetime, while her fictional refugees' safari, which trades the frying pan of the Mozambican civil war for the fire of foreign human and animal threat, risks becoming terminally ultimate.

The Kruger Park, over eighty years old and roughly the size of Israel, stretches for 220 miles along South Africa's eastern perimeter with

Mozambique.[34] This megafauna-rich game park is symbolically central to South Africa's conservation history, wilderness mythology, and tourist industry. Yet it is also multiply liminal, serving during the Mozambican civil war that lasted from 1975 until 1991 as an overdetermined border zone: between a Marxist postcolonial state and its anticommunist apartheid neighbor, between black majority rule and white minority supremacy, between the cultures of tourist leisure and migrant labor, and between the animal and the human.[35] This liminal overdetermination has a profound temporal dimension as well, bringing into frictional proximity animal time, tourist time, refugee time, the spiritualized time of white supremacy, and revolutionary utopian time, all represented as noncoeval on this particular cusp of modernity. If Yellowstone were located at Nogales or El Paso, it would loosely approximate the convergence of charismatic megafauna, tourist leisure, cross-border desperation, militarization, and clandestine flight that have crisscrossed Kruger's history.

The Kruger Park of Gordimer's story—especially when read alongside her little-known essay on the park as frontier—takes shape as a place of contrasting visible and ghosted movements of animal herds, herds of tourists, civil war refugees, conservation refugees, and migrant laborers shuttling back and forth between Mozambique and the South African gold mines.[36] By selecting as her narrator a ten-year-old refugee, Gordimer grants her story a potent affective energy and intimacy. But the little girl's perspective is necessarily limited in its grasp of the broader political implications of the journey, which we can productively situate in the ideological history of Kruger Park, a history that dramatizes the complicity between the rise of a white supremacist capitalism and an eco-archaic bushveld aesthetic.

Almost a century ago, the Transvaal legislature banned blacks from owning guns and hunting dogs, transforming game, notes Jane Carruthers, from "an economic resource available to everyone, to a commodity reserved for the ruling white group."[37] This ban—in the name of conservation—compounded the multipronged squeeze on rural African subsistence living, rendering it increasingly precarious. In the dominant colonial conservationist mythology, the nineteenth-century decimation of game resulted primarily from the cruel, uncontrolled slaughter of wildlife by rural Africans, whereas historically the prime culprit in that butchery was an imported European ethos of killing as an ennobling sport, an ethos that, backed by advanced weaponry that Africans lacked, severed hunting from the need for protein and hide clothing and the need to safeguard crops, herds, and flocks from animal predation.[38] The racially skewed hunting laws had a malign impact on African nutrition, subsistence livelihoods, and food security. Together with the creation of national parks like Kruger and (to a far greater extent) the creation of congested native reserves and the imposition of taxes, such laws drove more and more blacks into the capitalist economies of the mines and white agriculture.[39] The racialized discourse of wildlife scarcity (mapped in temporal terms as an ethical difference between "backward" and "advanced" peoples) was thus profoundly entwined with the discourse of labor scarcity in a rapidly modernizing economy.[40]

The colonial rescripting of wildlife scarcity as a black problem—which helped rationalize the early twentieth-century creation of national parks—depended on demonizing blacks as barbarous poachers whose relationship to wildlife was one of illegality and threat while depending, conversely, on mythologizing whites as stewards of nature whose conservationist principles evidenced a wider civilizational superiority. This explosive history of land theft and unequal access to wildlife as resource (whether for hunting or, later, tourist revenue) helped harden stereotypes of the white conservationist and the black poacher that continue to hamper environmental efforts today, with many black South Africans still viewing wildlife as rivals for water, food, and grazing land.

South Africa's game reserves are thus historically ensnarled in a tangle of elegiac narratives around vanishing wildlife, vanishing land, vanishing livelihoods, and vanishing labor. Neither the game reserve nor the native reserve was represented as coeval with South Africa's white, mining-driven modernity, yet both were products of that modernization: the game reserve as a hypervisible space of "ancient" wildness administered for touristic consumption, the native reserve as an anachronistic space structured around invisibility, where crowded human suffering and attendant ecological calamity were concentrated in "out of the way" places.[41] In terms of a national progress narrative, the mutually constitutive discourses of racial and natural purity were mapped onto both game reserves and native reserves. Game reserves were represented as positively archaic—unimproved places where whites could venture for spiritual renewal—whereas native reserves were negatively archaic, places set aside for the uncivilized.

As Jane Carruthers observes in her superb history of Kruger Park, the white nationalist regime, confronted with international condemnation when apartheid was imposed in 1948, invoked its caring conservationist ethos—with Kruger Park as primary showpiece—as evidence that South Africa belonged to the community of civilized nations.[42] Carruthers's most astute insight is her recognition that during the 1940s and 1950s, before the ascent of international tourism to South Africa, the idea of the national park helped foster a unifying ideology of white nationalism between historically antagonistic English and Afrikaans South Africans. That ideology drew on two quite discrete, mutually distrustful traditions: British colonial conservation and the Afrikaner mythology of themselves as a chosen people in a God-given land. Post-1948, a trip to the Kruger National Park could be promoted as a spiritual pilgrimage for both Afrikaner and English whites, as in the words of National Parks Board public relations director, R. J. Labuschagne:

> Exalted personages of the past have ever fled to nature for meditation and solitude: Christ climbed the Mount of Olives . . . Solomon repeatedly exhorts mankind to return to nature; President Kruger [of the Transvaal Republic] spent three days on the Magaliesberg in silent meditation . . . It is for this reason that the [white] South African nation undertakes the yearly pilgrimage to the Kruger National Park.[43]

Here Labuschagne deploys, in the service of white unity, the well-established colonial trope of the topographically and socially elevated white male communing in solitude as the monarch of all he surveys. But he also mobilizes the religious archaic—the images of Christ and Solomon—to advance a racially exclusive touristic modernity. We witness here a paradoxically archaic modernity that exhorts white tourists to "return" to nature as a patriotic exercise, an individually and collectively elevating pilgrimage of renewal which is routed both through a Christianized antiquity and through a racially exclusive romantic sublime.[44]

In the late 1980s, when Mozambique was gripped by civil war and South Africa by antiapartheid uprisings, Gordimer visited the frontier zone formed by southern Mozambique, Kruger Park, and the neighboring Bantustan of

Gazankulu.[45] In an astutely materialist account of her untouristic explorations, she reads that frontier wilderness as a cultural space shaped by land wars, militarization, and migrant labor. Since the late nineteenth century, Mozambique has remained the primary foreign labor reserve for South Africa's mines.[46] At the northern end of Kruger Park, a giant baobab tree served for decades as the primary recruiting station for tens of thousands of Mozambican men who were certified, dipped in disinfectant, and carted off to the mines. At this site the cultures of labor, militarism, tourism, and nature converged and interpenetrated: "Although it is within the Kruger Park," writes Gordimer,

> the road leading to the TEBA [the Employment Bureau of Africa] site is barred, like the many roads which now lead to concealed military camps rather than viewpoints for observing the animals. Nevertheless, I got there, passing buck and warthog along deserted tracks. High up overlooking the convergence of the three frontiers was a scene out of Conrad: buried in tropical trees, low buildings where men were received, fed, medically examined, signed up and transported; . . . a dark-browed thatched mansion surrounded by a moat of huge-leaved plants, with a magnificent wild fig tree thrust, like a tower, through the structure.[47]

To this complex ecology of spectatorship we must add another invisible layer. When this northern region was incorporated into the Kruger Park in the 1930s, the Tsonga-speaking Makuleke were driven from their land. Some of these conservation refugees ended up, after decades of resistance, in the Shangaan-Tsonga "ethnic homeland" of Gazankulu, others fled to Mozambique. By the late 1970s and 1980s, a reverse border-crossing was underway; this time the Shangaan were in flight not from conservation violence in South Africa but from South African-fomented military violence in Mozambique. By the late 1980s, refugees were streaming into Gazankulu at the rate of 1,000 a month. To get there, most had to breach first the Kruger Park's 11,500-volt electric fence, then a backup razor-coiled fence, and then the park itself. In short, this "timeless" place has been repeatedly crisscrossed by the convulsive movements of desperate humans historically uprooted from their land, whether by conservation, war, or the ethnic engineering of the Bantustans.

It is one such convulsive movement that Gordimer imagines in "The Ultimate Safari," which we can read as a fictional companion piece to the sociopolitical frontier essay she published fourteen years earlier. The unnamed ten-year-old war orphan who recounts her group's via dolorosa across the Kruger Park tells a story that becomes, among other things, about tourism without tourists, the perspectival antithesis of Kleinhans's "Zulu" village without villagers. If Ndebele's essay focuses on the dilemmas of the hypervisible black middle-class tourist encircled by a white nature industry, Gordimer's story dramatizes the fears of ultra-poor Africans whose lives depend on passing unseen through the white nature industry's commercialized zone of animals.

The girl's journey through time, megafauna, and the bush stands in blunt contrast to the pilgrimage toward a spiritually regenerative white race-time promulgated by Labuschagne and his ilk. "To get there," she recalls,

> we had to go through the Kruger Park. We knew about the Kruger Park. A kind of whole country of animals—elephants, lions, jackals, hyenas, hippos, crocodiles, all kinds of animals. We had some of them in our own country, before the war (our grandfather remembers; we children weren't born yet) but the bandits kill the elephants and sell their tusks, and the bandits and our soldiers have eaten all the buck. There was a man in our village without legs—a crocodile took them off, in our river; but all the same our country is a country of people, not animals. We knew about the Kruger Park because some of our men used to leave home to work there in the places where white people come to stay and look at the animals.[48]

The girl's great trek from her lost "country of people" to the "whole country of animals" gathers force from a potent, if implicit, contrast with the journey the tourists have undertaken. In the country of animals that the girl is entering, humans remain unseen: the story alludes to the tourists who exist only as voices and cooking smells wafting through the animal night from the far side of the rest camp fence. Though constituted by the same modernity, these two contiguous groups live trespass, risk, and animal time in radically different modalities.

As I have argued, white tourists purchase the frisson of trespass into a "timeless" animal zone, a memorable, risk-simulating adventure in an eco-archaic world liberated from history. However, those other foreigners, thrust into the "whole country of animals" by history's convulsions, seek to survive risk and trespass by laboring to remain invisible in the historical present, by passing through the elephant grass undetected (by game wardens, border police, lions), by moving "like animals among the animals, away from the roads, away from the white people's camps."[49] If the Kruger Park is pitched to tourists as an opportunity to "get close" to wildlife, for the refugees human-animal intimacy depends on a deeper kind of interspecies recognition. The girl and her fellow travelers, in their transnational trespass, have also crossed over into the border zone of the human animal—where knowledge gleaned from other species can offer lifesaving pointers to where water and food are and how to achieve a deeper camouflage, a safer invisibility.

As they traverse this border zone, the tourist and the refugee exist in different states of transport. The Kruger Park promises the tourist the excitement of a safely managed plunge into the deep time, the eco-archaic, of the purely animal. (Suspense typically hinges on seeing or not seeing one of the Big Five—lion, elephant, rhino, leopard, and buffalo—that have proven indispensable to the branding of South African tourism.) The refugee's temporal experience, however, is quite different: the perilous passage through a time zone dedicated to tourists and animals doubles as a portal, not into a suspended past, but into a suspended future. These two groups of transients from opposite ends of the spectrum of voluntary and involuntary mobility pass each other like ships in the night, freighted with radically different hopes, radically different experiences of national park space-time, and radically different visions of what constitutes escape.

On their ultimate safari, the Mozambicans' collective egress represents a history-driven descent into timelessness, though one quite remote from the fenced, managed timelessness of the tourist domain. When right-wing bandits scorched their Mozambican village church and schools, the girl and her siblings began to lose their footing in the institutional rhythms of calendrical time. Thereafter, as they flee through "the country of animals," the days lose their names and traction; the old, structured rhythms of a now-destroyed village time give way to an improvised survival dependent on reading sun, sky, and animal behavior.

The Mozambicans, their known world razed by civil war, are not so much moving toward as moving away. "Away" becomes the story's signature word: "We wanted to go where there were no bandits and there was food. We were glad to think there must be such a place; away," the girl declares, "we started to go away, again."[50] When they finally reach a refugee camp beyond the park, she fantasizes about living "in a real house again, with no war, no away."[51]

Away: between the lines the reader fills in the complexities of that abrupt, complex word, connecting it to a double discourse of escape that exposes the chasm between the tourist-ad's promotional blurb and the little girl's voice. Away: as in getaway, sanctuary, refuge, retreat, terms that take on diametrically opposed valences depending on whether leisure or terror is the propulsive force, depending on whether you're in temporary flight from your white-collar workweek or intent on the hard labor of flight through electrified fences into a time that has lost all shape.

Having survived the wildlife reserve, the girl finds sanctuary in a refugee camp that we can assume (extrapolating from hints in Gordimer's short story and her essay) is located in the Gazankulu Bantustan. By story's end the girl has been living there for over two years, in a vast, overcrowded tent that rises in implicit counterpoint to the tented rest camps of the leisure colonialists. The refugees have thus exchanged the suspended time of transit through the national park for the suspended time of the refugee camp, a provisional place that, within the symbolic economy of the story, can never quite serve as resolution or destination.

Gloria Anzaldua has famously observed that

> borders are set up to define the places that are safe and unsafe, to distinguish us from them. A border is a dividing line, a narrow strip along a steep edge. A borderland is a vague and undetermined place created by the emotional residue of an unnatural boundary. It is in a constant state of transition. The prohibited and the forbidden are its inhabitants . . . those who cross over, pass over, or go through the confines of the normal.[52]

When, I would add, that "unnatural boundary" is marked by a national park that embodies a national culture of nature, the borderland can become a site of redoubled violence in its militarized severance of natural from unnatural and native from foreign.[53]

This fierce severance pertains powerfully to the Shangaan, the trans-frontier people to whom Gordimer's narrator clearly belongs.[54] On entering the refugee camp in the Bantustan, the girl

> was surprised to find they speak our language; our grandmother told me. . . . Long ago, in the time of our fathers, there was no fence that kills you, there was no Kruger Park between them and us, we were the same people under our own king, right from our village we left to this place we've come to.[55]

The refugees' journey thus retraces a continuity that persists only in the unfenced past of oral memory, before this threshold people was culturally and territorially severed, first, by the map separating Portuguese colony from Boer Republic, and later by conservation's electrified fence that delimited the beginning of South Africa's national and national-nature space.[56] The Shangaan were left straddling the divide.[57]

As a transfrontier people—who can be capriciously designated by South Africans as either "us" or "them"—the Shangaan have suffered from new forms of vulnerability in recent years, becoming targets of brutal assaults and expulsions. During the wave of xenophobic killings and shack burnings that swept through the shantytowns of Johannesburg and other South African cities in 2008, Shangaan, both South African and Mozambican, were targeted as "foreigners," who (in the all-too-familiar-scapegoating) were deemed "criminal elements" who "come over here" to steal our jobs, our women, our shacks, our things.

This often violently enforced postapartheid discrimination between the "authentically" national and the undesirable foreign is ironically waived when it comes to the commodified performances of memory and amnesia on which the tourist industry depends. The carved wooden animals, the soapstone sculptures, and the masks that American, European, and Japanese tourists carry home as authenticating mementoes of their South African game-park trip overwhelmingly derive from beyond South Africa's borders, especially from Mozambique and Zimbabwe, but also from Ghana, Congo, Senegal, Nigeria, and Cameroon.[58] Immigrants who risk everything crossing borders, fences, national parks, and hostile communities may be branded as undesirable others in their persons, yet play an indispensable role in the circuits of desire of the international tourist feedback loop. For it is these artists and vendors from "away" who serve as the primary purveyors of an ersatz indigeneity through the rebranding of their artifacts as "South African" memorabilia. The carved elephants, lions, hippos, and other charismatic megafauna they sell in the condensed form of the commodity icon authenticate the tourist's "ultimate safari" into the eco-archaic.

International Recolonization?

Whether the space of the game reserve can be repossessed, imaginatively and experientially, will depend on at least four critical factors. First, how will the reserves be impacted by government policies toward land restitution? Second, what role will the ascent of black tourism play in reshaping South Africa's nature industry? Will game reserves become alluring destinations to black tourists or remain alienating reminders of racial entitlement, dispossession, and apartheid atavism? Third, how sustainable will rural ecotourism initiatives prove? Will they offer broad-based economic opportunities and draw on cultures of nature outside the purview of neocolonial conservation? Finally, how will international forces—the feedback loops of global tourism and the pressures exerted by European and American-based conservationist NGOs—shape South Africa's environmental priorities?

Hector Magome and James Murombedzi, two incisive analysts of these policy dilemmas, have expressed a profound skepticism toward the international role: "If the dominant agenda is conventional biodiversity conservation, the political expediency that facilitates the decolonization of nature at the national level will cause its re-colonization at the international level."[59] This remains a real, active risk. That said, however, the primary driver behind the South African conservation systems, both state-run and private, has tended to be the lucrative, easy sell of spectacular megafauna rather than biodiversity. The latter, from a tourist perspective, is often unspectacular and therefore "boring."[60] As Kleinhans's alfalfa problem suggests, for many foreign tourists, mixed-usage landscapes (which blend agriculture, subsistence, and conservation) are anathema, unappealing as spectacle and insufficiently severed from the domestic and the familiar. Yet, for all the complexities that the coexistence of pastoralists, agriculturalists, and wild-life entails, such hybrid uses of land can play an essential part in the long run to help dissolve the resilient, Manichean perception of blacks as poachers (or encroachers) and white environmentalists as humane toward animals but inhumane toward people. Amidst the land squeeze, increased mixed usage will be a necessary component of efforts to reconcile water, food, and eco-system security for humans and nonhuman life-forms. The alternative is unsustainable: powerhouse international NGOs in cahoots with stereotypi-cal tourist demands for Wild Africa driving subsistence farmers and ecosys-tem people off the land.

In its unevenly postapartheid mode, South Africa has to contend with the civilizational clout of powerful national and international ideologies of nature. These are potentially mutable ideologies, to be sure, but nonetheless etched into the nation's physical, psychic, and economic landscapes. These lingering legacies of political subjugation and territorial appropriation (but-tressed by the civilizational discriminations of colonial progress narratives) have been used to rationalize unequal access to land, wildlife, and leisure while erecting a vast international marketplace around charismatic mega-fauna and the eco-archaic. What is acutely at stake in understanding South Africa's environmental dilemmas is that they point, in critical form, toward more generalized global crises around land access, food security, resource wars, biodiversity, tourism, and the place of amnesia in the racial politics of the international wildlife marketplace.

In our quest to transform colonialism's temporal and spatial legacies, a profound tension often arises between economic, historical, and psycho-logical impulses. How much change, how fast, at what cost to whom, and when? The strategic answers will vary according to the specific frictions or collaborations between global forces, local and national power structures, and what Tsing calls "the sticky materiality of practical encounters."[61] Let Ndebele, surveying the game lodge, have the final word: "The ambiguities and choices are difficult, even painful. Now we want to throw off the psy-chological burden of our painful past; now we want to hold on to it. . . . We think: there is no peace for those caught in the process of becoming."[62]

7

Ecologies of the Aftermath

Precision Warfare and Slow Violence

The war has used up words; they have been weakened, they have
deteriorated like motor car tires; . . . we are now confronted with
a depreciation of all our terms . . . that may well make us wonder
what ghosts will be left to walk.

—Henry James in interview, March 21, 1915

One day my Sunday School teacher, Mrs. Graff, read the Noah's
Ark story aloud to our class. When she came to the part about the
floodwaters drying up, she held the book open to the picture of the
sturdy, gleaming ark surrounded after the flood by the lush green
trees and colorful plants, all under the beautiful rainbow in the sky.

The entire class was entranced except for Joel, the boy sitting
beside me.

Joel stared at the picture our teacher held up and yelled suddenly.

"WHERE ARE ALL THE BODIES?!?"

Our teacher looked puzzled and annoyed. She put her book
down.

"WHAT BODIES, JOEL?"

"THE BODIES!" he cried. "WHERE ARE ALL THE BODIES
OF THE PEOPLE AND THE ANIMALS THAT DIED IN THE
FLOOD?!?"

—Ellen O'Grady, *Outside the Ark: An Artist's
Journey in Occupied Palestine*

What is a war casualty? The answer appears painfully obvious. It asserts itself less through argument than through visceral photographs: a torso shredded by a roadside bomb; a bloodied peasant spread-eagled in a ditch; a soldier, cigarette dangling nonchalantly, crashing his boot into a dead woman's head. Yet such images account only for immediate, visually arresting fatalities. What about those casualties that don't fit the photographic stereotypes, casualties that occur long after major combat has been concluded, casualties whose belatedness and dispersal make them resistant to dramatic packaging? The media, in thrall to speed and spectacle, lacks the attention span to follow war-inflicted catastrophes that take years or generations to exact their toll. After official victory has been declared, how do we track the persistence of unofficial hostilities in the cellular domain, the untidy, attritional lethality that moves through the tissue, blood, and bones of combatants and noncombatants alike, moving through as well the living body of the land itself?

As Joel's disquiet over the shiny, rainbow version of Noah's rescue narrative suggests, stories—tightly framed for time, space, and point of view—are convenient places for concealing bodies. Stories of the aftermath are protracted, convoluted, messy, open ended, and often discomforting to tell, particularly when—whether it's Noah's ark or the 1991 Gulf War—the official narrative frame is unequivocally triumphalist. The Gulf War offers a dramatic instance of how challenging it can be to narrate the ecology of the aftermath because America's corporate media represented that war as a spectacular achievement of speed and untainted victory—a strategically, technologically, and ethically decisive war, the nation's anti-Vietnam. Yet the Gulf War was, at the same time, the conflict that gave us Gulf War syndrome and—less remarked upon—the first conflict in which depleted uranium munitions were deployed on a large scale. It was thus a war of profound narrative contrasts: between the crisp story line that marches briskly toward victory and the diffuse, laborious story about slow violence, about convoluted scientific proof and the politics of risk, a story that fans out into the open-ended, uncertain ecologies of the aftermath.

Public debate is overdue on war's hidden human and environmental costs, a debate that acknowledges major shifts in the ways that contemporary wars kill. Military euphemisms like "precision" warfare, "surgical" strikes, "smart" wars, "depleted" uranium, and "miracle drones" have helped legitimize recent high-tech conflicts while concealing their long-term toxic and radiological impact. The rhetoric of precision lulls us into regarding the fatalities of war as swift, immediate killings. But ironically, the increasing reliance of American and British forces on the discourse of "precision" coincides with the integration of "depleted" uranium into their missiles, bullets, and tank armor.

Ever since the 1991 Gulf War, a new kind of fatal environmental imprecision has been built into "precision" warfare, for that war was history's first depleted-uranium conflict. Arguably, not since Hiroshima and Nagasaki have humans unleashed a military substance so tenaciously hostile to life itself. Depleted uranium (DU) possesses a durability beyond our comprehension: it had a radioactive half-life of 4.51 billion years. When it enters the environment, DU effectively does so for all time, with consequences that are resistant to military metrics, consequences that we are incompetent to judge.

In our age of depleted-uranium warfare, we have an ethical obligation to challenge the military body counts that consistently underestimate (in advance and in retrospect) the true toll of waging high-tech wars. Who is counting the staggered deaths that civilians and soldiers suffer from depleted uranium ingested or blown across the desert? Who is counting the belated fatalities from unexploded cluster bombs that lie in wait for months or years, metastasizing into landmines? Who is counting deaths from chemical residues left behind by so-called pinpoint bombing, residues that turn into foreign insurgents, infiltrating native rivers and poisoning the food chain? Who is counting the victims of genetic deterioration—the stillborn, malformed infants conceived by parents whose DNA has been scrambled by war's toxins? The calculus of any conflict needs to at least acknowledge such environmental casualties, even if they cannot be quantified. Such casualties may suffer slow, invisible deaths that don't fit the news cycle at CNN or Fox, but they are war casualties nonetheless.

Fractal Wars and Surgical Tropes

The 1991 Gulf War is widely acknowledged as a benchmark moment in the representation and experience of war. It was, in Paul Virilio's influential formulation, the first "fractal war":

With modern techniques and new logistics of perception, the
battlefield of the Gulf War also developed within the field of perception. It appeared to be a local war, in the sense that its battlefield was very small compared with the Second World War.
However, considering its representation, it was a worldwide
war. . . . So, on one hand, *there was a local war of small interest, with
very little human loss on one side, with very little consequences*, but on
the other hand, there was a unique field of perception operating.
Unlike the Vietnam War, it was a worldwide war, live, with all
the special effects of course, the data processing supervised by
the Pentagon. . . . So, yes, this war happened, more on a screen
than on the ground. *It happened more on the TV screen than in the
reality of the battlefield.* To that extent, one can say that real time
defeated real space. (my emphases)[1]

What appeared so novel about this war was its aura—its manipulated
aura—of virtual immediacy. Here was a "real-time" war conducted and
viewed at high speed in the present tense, a "smart" war projected through
myriad networks onto linked screens in the bomber's cockpit, on TV, and
the Internet, giving the potent sensation of instant access and total, continuous immersion. Perceptually, the Gulf War was high definition, yet episte-
mologically it was blurry, suggesting a radically new turn in what James Der
Derian has dubbed the "military-industrial-media-entertainment network."[2]

Yet commentators on the Gulf War, whether technophile or techno-
phobe, whether dazzled or appalled, have consistently represented it as a
war of speed, brief in historical time and instantly available (though through
complex mediations) as spectacle. Virilio, for example, glosses over the war
on the ground as inconsequential, local, and quick; the war's only long-term
significance derives from its impact on the logistics of the perceptual battlefield. However, this critical fixation with the ethics of the war's potent technological innovations has overshadowed inquiries into the environmental and
epidemiological ethics of its duration. A preoccupation with the paradoxes of
the Gulf War's mediated immediacy has made this a particularly challenging
war to represent in terms of the *longue durée* of the ecological aftermath.

We can give this difficulty the traction of story by embarking on a road
trip in the company of two very different guides who ventured independently

down the same paved two-lane transnational highway in the same week early in March 1991. The highway stretches north from Kuwait City through the border town of Safwan and from there on to Basra, Iraq's primary port. Both our guides traveled that road to Basra soon after American bombers had incinerated retreating Iraqi convoys in what became known as the "turkey shoot" on the Highway of Death.

Our first guide is writer Michael Kelly, whose award-winning *Martyr's Day: Chronicle of a Small War* (1993) has won acclaim as the finest work of American war literature since Michael Herr's *Dispatches* and has been hailed (alongside Anthony Swofford's *Jarhead*) as the literary masterpiece of the first Gulf War.[3] Kelly, a former editor of the *New Republic* and *National Journal* who would go on to edit the *Atlantic Monthly*, offers a visceral account in *Martyr's Day* of the charred bodies and tanks strewn along the Highway of Death. As a reporter, he observes this spectacle of carnage with something bordering on relief:

> The Gulf War was an experience disconnected from itself, conducted with such speed and at such distances and with so few witnesses that it was, even for many of the people involved, an abstraction. It was difficult for the Americans, who had done their killing almost entirely from afar, to feel a connection with those they killed, or with the act of killing.[4]

Kelly belongs to the camp of Gulf War commentators who suffered from pixilation fatigue; afflicted by the vertigo of the virtual, he was disturbed by the war's fusion of video game presence with corporeal absence, its mixture of closeness and distance that made it feel both instant and elusive even, he suggests, to the killers themselves.

Traveling the Highway of Death, Kelly finally comes eye to eye with the intimate, bodily certainties of war. He has stepped outside the infosphere and into a carnal space where war residues penetrate the nostrils and coat the skin. "For miles and miles," he observes, "the roads were rich with the physical realities of war, glutted with the evidence of slaughter and victory. They became the great circuit board of the Gulf War, where the disconnectedness stopped."[5]

From Kelly's vantage point, then, the Highway of Death marks the end of the road. This is the terminus he has been craving, a place of convergent finalities, where the war has exacted its last fatalities, where certain victory has been achieved, and where the feedback loop of bloodless mediation has been trumped by the raw materiality of a corpse-strewn highway. Here, finally, he can slough off the deranging enchantments of the virtual and, standing on the carnal terra firma of American triumph, find the empirical, experiential, and narrative closure he has yearned for.

Our second guide, traveling down that same road that very week, is a woman named Carol Picou, who ventured there in a very different capacity. First Sgt. Picou was serving as a combat support Army nurse working with a mobile hospital unit. A seventeen-year veteran of the U.S. military, she helped open a field hospital alongside the highway and for fifteen grueling days treated the injured and retrieved the Iraqi and Bedouin dead, clambering in out of those same incinerated tanks that for Kelly marked his sense of an ending.[6] Within days of her departure from this scene, Picou's skin starting to erupt in black spots; soon she lost control of her bladder and her bowels. She came to depend permanently on a catheter and diapers. After her return to America, over the months and years that followed, she developed thyroid problems and squamous cancer cells in her uterus; she developed immunological dysfunction and encephalopathy. Three years after her stint on the Highway of Death, tests found dangerously elevated levels of uranium in her urine. Not until a barrage of afflictions had jeopardized her life did Picou first heard the phrase "depleted uranium" and begin to learn of the threat its residues could pose.

"Depleted" is a lulling word: place it in front of robust nouns like "energy" or "ambition," and "depleted" saps them of their vigor. Not so depleted uranium. It poses a terrible radioactive and chemical threat that actively endangers soldiers, civilians, and the environment itself. Despite that reassuring "depleted" in its name, depleted uranium possesses 60 percent of natural uranium's radioactivity. During the Gulf War alone, American troops fired weapons containing 340 tons of depleted uranium. According to British professor of medicinal chemistry Dr. Malcolm Hooper, this contributed significantly to making the Gulf War "the most toxic war in Western military history."[7] In Hooper's measured opinion, depleted uranium is "a new weapon for indiscriminate, mutually-assured destruction."[8] The United Nations Commission on Human Rights, moreover, has classified depleted uranium munitions with nuclear, biological, and chemical weapons as "weapons of indiscriminate effect." Although German scientists first researched DU's military potential in the 1940s, for a half century it was kept off the battlefield. Not until the 1991 Gulf War was depleted uranium integrated into conventional warfare, thereby adding a new fatal kind of environmental imprecision to "precision" warfare. How did such an unethical radioactive substance become enfolded, from the Gulf War onward, into the landscape of modern warfare and into the ecology of war's aftermath?

Why, Carol Picou asked, had she and her unit not been warned of depleted uranium's potential radiological and chemical perils before entering those heavily polluted battle zones? Why had the U.S. military not outfitted them with protective gear, these nurses on their mercy mission, working inside and alongside tanks incinerated by depleted uranium-tipped munitions? In retrospect, Picou worried about the fierce desert winds that her unit had encountered while tending to the injured, winds that had whipped up the desert dust and with it, unbeknownst to her, suspended depleted uranium particles.

Picou's unit included 300 troops. Of those, 150 worked along the front line on the Highway of Death; the other 150 remained in the rear. By 1996, five years after the Gulf War's official end, of the 150 members of Picou's unit who worked on the Highway of Death forty were seriously ill and six had died. By contrast, the 150 who had stayed back from the front line had remained healthy. On learning that some returning veterans had started to father or conceive children missing an eye or an ear or a thyroid gland, that children were being born with flippers instead of arms, Picou, who had done so much to heal war's casualties, decided to have her tubes tied.

The Department of Defense discharged Carol Picou in March 1996, five years after her return from the Highway of Death. She was dismissed with "Bowel and Bladder Incontinence—Etiology Unknown." According to the document that terminated her service, the barrage of illnesses she suffered from was "non-combat-related."[9] She was thus denied the kind of pension that servicewomen and men injured in the battlefield secured. Her decisive dismissal on the basis of a medically indecisive narrative further undermined Picou's physical and financial prospects. Beneath the camouflage of slow violence, and despite soaring uranium levels in her urine five years after combat, Picou's catastrophic physical collapse was dissociated entirely from the environment of war.

For Michael Kelly, the road to Basra marked the end of a pilgrimage, the moment when he could find relief in a triple termination: to the Gulf War's virtual disconnectedness, to the war itself, and to the murky humiliations of America's Vietnam syndrome.[10] For Picou, by contrast, that same highway was where her personal and professional termination would begin, the place where the war's corporeal disconnectedness would begin in earnest. For Picou, the Highway of Death marked the onset of a different kind of disconnection—between her body's collapse and her struggle to be believed as she plunged into an unending battle to win official military acknowledgement as a postcombat war casualty. For Picou, by March 1991 the Gulf War had barely begun.

In ignoring the unfolding of slow violence across environmental and epidemiological time, Kelly, like Virilio, accepted the Gulf War's face-value brevity. The title of Kelly's book—*Martyr's Day: Chronicle of a Small War*—underscores this image of a miniconflict tidily contained, a conflict he dubs the "Hundred Hour War."[11] When he revisits his book eight years after publication to add a post-9/11 foreword, Kelly mounts an argument that would become widespread in rationalizing the then imminent 2003 Iraq War, namely, that a direct line could be drawn between the Gulf War's sanitary brevity, America's cutting-edge precision materiel, and American military humanitarianism:

> The Gulf War wasn't named a war. It was named an operation—Operation Desert Storm. An operation is not a war; it is a surgical event. It is something the definitional purpose of which is limited: get in, get the tumor, get out. . . . The Gulf War was run as an operation, and as an operation it worked very well . . . The troops went in and removed the tumor from Kuwait, which was the sole goal of the operation. Few people got killed. (And in "few," I am including an assessment of Iraqi deaths, which were much higher than Allied deaths, but remarkably low considering the lethal capacity of Iraq's enemy; the Gulf War was the first important demonstration of the ability of the new American military to exploit its overwhelming technological superiority to produce a historic contradiction in terms—effective humanitarian war.)[12]

The notion that surgical strikes, precision warfare, and smart bombs exhibit a morally exact intelligence is understandably widespread.[13] In America, we are primed to view contemporary life as an incessant, accelerating series of technological upgrades, each promising more marvels than the last. Inside this progress narrative, the cults of speed, novelty, and spectacle can seem to generate their own innate morality. It is easy, in such a technological climate, to grant each new weapons system an enhanced ethical potency.[14]

What Kelly fails to observe in retrospect is the shadow of imprecision trailing behind those luminous technologies of precision streaking across the sky, a shadow that for months, years, decades, generations would jeopardize the lives of random civilians through the lethal legacies of incinerated munition depots, depleted uranium, and unexploded cluster bombs. Quick causal leaps from "technological superiority" to "effective humanitarian war" allow no place for what Hiroshima journalist Akira Tashiro terms war's discounted casualties.[15] Kelly's ornate surgical metaphor is especially inapt, given the carcinogenic risks associated with depleted uranium wars: the same "surgical" technologies used to remove the Iraqi "tumor" are instrumental in tumor spread. What kind of surgeon operates with instruments so radioactive that they may catalyze literal cancers in the name of metaphorically excising them?[16]

More apt is Rachel Carson's metaphor of the "unselective bludgeon," which she invokes to describe purportedly target-specific insecticides.[17] Writing in the aftermath of death-camp science and the science behind Hiroshima and Nagasaki, Carson was all too aware how readily the civilizational rhetoric of progress and precision could cloak barbarous consequences. In exposing the long-term perils of unchecked techno-boosterism, she stressed how often the precision pitch relies on reckless promises of miraculous, merciful selectivity.

Kelly, in advocating an ethics of corporeal intimacy over the confounding paradoxes of virtual distance, succumbs to an environmentally obsolete image of war as spectacle. What he observes is not a luminous victory for both America and unmediated empiricism, but rather unwittingly the mirage of war's end. A visible precision—readily framed as instant spectacle—may mask a devastating imprecision, invisible and inhumane, dispersed across the desert sands and across the sands of time. In trusting the authority of his eyes to bring the war to closure, Kelly fails to acknowledge the chemical and radiological perils that lie ahead for Iraqis; for the region's water, earth, and air; for creatures domestic and wild; for the region's crops; and for American troops as well. Beyond the vanishing point of Kelly's sight line stretches the prospect of months, years, generations of epidemiological and environmental threat, a threat that Carol Picou, for one, would come to know with a different kind of intimacy, the intimacy of her own disintegrating organs and crumbling bones. Entering those incinerated tanks along the Highway of Death, Picou unknowingly entered a new phase of that "small war" to which her body's cells would bear corrosive witness.

Hysteria, Millenarianism, and Slow Violence Disavowed

In the aftermath of the Gulf War, the forces of epidemiological disavowal gained an ally from an unexpected quarter: Princeton literary scholar Elaine Showalter. Showalter, best known for her brilliant, pathbreaking work on the cultural production of gendered madness, adjudged in her book *Hystories* that Gulf War syndrome was the result of a media-stoked millennial hysteria. Showalter maintained that with the millennium's approach, Americans were especially susceptible to social panics, hence the rise of alien abduction, Satanic ritual abuse, multiple-personality syndrome, the recovered-memory movement, and Gulf War syndrome—all of them, in her view, millennial epidemics of hysterical disorders and imaginary illnesses, and all virally transmitted through the media.[18]

Gulf War syndrome could thus best be understood as a hysterical "plotline" that gave shape and meaning to the war neuroses of returning veterans:

> Patients learn about diseases from the media, unconsciously develop the symptoms, and then attract media attention in an endless cycle. The human imagination is not infinite, and we are all bombarded by these plot lines every day. Inevitably, we all live out the social stories of our time.[19]

Gulf War syndrome thus becomes little more than a feedback loop in which "psychogenic symptoms" generate stories, which in turn generate further self-identifying victims.[20] As a fin-de-siècle hysterical script, Gulf War syndrome, like alien abduction and Satanic ritual-abuse stories, thereby becomes part of a media-transmitted psychological plague. Showalter dismisses objections to her theory as evidence of resistance to psychology itself: "A century after Freud, many people still reject psychological explanations for symptoms; they believe psychosomatic disorders are illegitimate and search for physical evidence that firmly places cause and cure outside the self."[21]

Despite its idiosyncratic millennial-media spin, Showalter's argument is continuous with a slew of narratives of disavowal that are quick to dismiss or trivialize causes "outside the self." What such narratives downplay is the way each war generates a distinctive, historically specific chemical, radiological, epidemiological, and environmental legacy. As the technologies of war shift, so does the composition of the aftermath. Showalter, obsessed with the millennium's media prelude, deflects attention away from the aftermath in all its textured chemical and radiological specificity.

Moreover, if Gulf War syndrome (or more accurately, Gulf War illness) really were expressive of a fin-de-siècle media-induced panic and had no root environmental causes, then the moment for that panic has long passed: the millennium has come and gone, as have the "media-stoked millennial panics." Yet the number of veterans reporting Gulf War illness continues to soar. In 1997, when Showalter published her book, some 60,000 U.S. Gulf War veterans were afflicted; by 2008, eight years after the uneventful passing of the millennium, that number had surpassed 175,000.[22] The inhabitants of the Basra region, where depleted uranium weaponry was used extensively during the Gulf War, share some disturbingly similar symptoms to America and Britain's ailing veterans. Are we to believe that the Basrans also contracted these symptoms from America's millennial media? After NATO planes deployed depleted uranium-tipped missiles in the Balkan Wars, returning European troops reported a high incidence of "peacekeeper's syndrome," again with strong epidemiological similarities to the symptoms suffered by Gulf War veterans and the Basrans. All three groups experienced, in particular, spikes in leukemia, renal collapse, and birth deformities. While the science on this remains incomplete—indeed, it has in many instances been insufficiently investigated or obstructed—the overlapping tendencies in the epidemiological aftermath of depleted uranium wars are cause, at the very least, for a more precautionary approach.

By insisting that Gulf War syndrome is the creation of millennial panics, the mass media, and veteran hysteria, Showalter excludes from the

realm of explanation battlefield environmental forces. Her line of thinking thereby shrinks the spatial and temporal frames of the aftermath; it is
a line of thinking readily reconciled with the military's dismissal of cases
such as Carol Picou's: "etiology unknown, not combat-related." Surely we
can acknowledge the power of "plot bombardment" without losing sight
of the less metaphoric battlefield bombardment that profoundly shapes the
bodily aftermath?

Showalter, like others in the disavowal camp, displays a naïve, unwar-
ranted faith in the commitment by the Departments of Defense and Veterans
Affairs to a thorough, well-funded investigation. The historic track record of
such organizations—most notably, toward atomic veterans and casualties of
Agent Orange—gives ample grounds for skepticism. The U.S. military has
a long record of dissimulation on such matters, a record of "it's all in your
mind" dismissals, of foot dragging and of underfunded, half-hearted science.
For twenty years it dismissed the physiological effects of Agent Orange as a
grand hallucination. Similarly, it would take the U.S. military until 2008—
seventeen years after the official end of Kelly's "small war"—to acknowledge
that Gulf War illness exists and has material chemical causes.[23]

Temporal Camouflage and the Politics of Belatedness

As we have seen, the proponents of "smart" wars often market them as
humane because they appear to promise not just greater accuracy but
greater brevity. However, the Iraq War that began in 2003 complicated
that assumption, exposing the chasm between a hygienically "smart" war
and the messy hazards of a drawn-out, urban guerilla conflict. Innumer-
able commentators, of course, have made this point. However, they typically continue to overlook the way the specific technologies that purport
to shorten a conflict may delay, disperse, and therefore extend "precision"
warfare's ecological impact. Such technologies, when they compromise the
environment, morph into long-term killers, creating landscapes that inflict
lingering, off-camera casualties. Time itself becomes the ultimate cover-up,
a dependable ally in camouflaging "smart" warfare's sprawling toll.

Environmentalists routinely face the quandary of how to convert into
dramatic form urgent issues that unfold too slowly to qualify as breaking
news—issues like climate change and species extinction that threaten in

slow motion. Any environmentalist who seeks to tally the delayed-action casualties of "precision" warfare labors under a similar disadvantage. How many years, how many decades, how many generations will he or she be granted to come up with an always-approximate count that includes war's after-dead? Since 1991, depleted-uranium ordnance has been deployed in Afghanistan, Bosnia, Kosovo, Kuwait, Serbia, Somalia, and Chechnya and—in unprecedented quantities—during the 2003 war in Iraq. Given depleted uranium's 4.51 billion-year half-life, what can counting even mean?

War deaths from environmental toxicity demand patient, elaborate proof. Spikes in renal collapse; infertility; leukemia; testicular, brain, and breast cancers; and clusters of infant malformations are harder to link to war's technologies than a bullet through the head. The military statistician can simply count corpses within a given place and time, subdivide those columns into combatants and civilians, then draw a line beneath his sums. Such calculations conform tidily to our preconceptions about the time frame within which a war is waged. However, to view war through the prisms of ecological time and genetic mutation demands a different ethical attention span. Uranium, after all, is genotoxic and chemically alters DNA.[24]

An earlier generation of environmental historians first addressed this problem of the relationship between changing military technologies, official disavowal, and belated casualties. Thomas Whiteside's *The Withering Rain: America's Herbicidal Folly* and John Lewallen's *Ecology of Devastation: Indochina* (both published in 1971) launched the by now extensive literature on the protracted lethality of Agent Orange.[25] In 1982, Harvey Wasserman and Norman Solomon's *Killing Our Own: The Disaster of America's Experience with Atomic Radiation* detailed the catastrophic long-term impact of atmospheric nuclear testing on America's "atomic soldiers."[26] The turn to depleted-uranium warfare and the unprecedented proliferation of cluster bombs demands that we revisit the question of who counts as a casualty. Who is counting the veterans slain or disabled by environmentally transmitted "friendly fire" and the deferred casualties among refugees returning to poisoned, radiated landscapes, both groups harboring the illusion that the war is safely behind them?

What accounts for depleted uranium's sudden surge in military popularity? As a by-product of nuclear testing and nuclear power, depleted uranium is extremely cheap—indeed, better than free. A half century of nuclear-weapons and nuclear-power production has left the Department of Defense with more than a billion pounds of nuclear waste in storage. The Department of Defense is delighted to off-load some of that waste onto arms manufacturers, gratis, in the form of depleted uranium. The result is a seductive kind of alchemy: weapons manufacturers magically cut their production costs while the Defense Department magically rids itself of a five-alarm waste product that no American wants buried in their backyard. The result is a kind of antienvironmental recycling that converts highly toxic waste into even more deadly explosive forms.

In a classified acknowledgement of depleted uranium's perils, Britain's Atomic Energy Authority warned that, in the Gulf War's wake, depleted uranium could enter the food chain and cause a half million premature Iraqi and Kuwaiti deaths.[27] By expanding its depleted-uranium arsenal, America is effectively exporting nuclear waste to foreign soil—nuclear waste that contains traces of plutonium, for which there are no safe levels. This nuclear waste also contains the uranium isotope 236, which does not exist in nature and has caused concern among epidemiologists. Dr. Michael Kilpatrick, a leading Pentagon spokesperson on DU has asserted that "our studies in the United States over fifteen years have not shown depleted uranium going from soil into groundwater."[28] However, as Dan Fahey notes, several scientific studies have refuted Kilpatrick's claim by demonstrating the seepage of DU into aquifers and ecosystems:

> Depleted uranium dumped into a pit at the Starmet (formerly Nuclear Metals) manufacturing plant in Concord, Massachusetts, has leached through the soil into groundwater. The State of Massachusetts permits drinking water to contain up to 29 micrograms of uranium per liter, but test wells at the Starmet site have measured levels up to 87,000 micrograms of uranium per liter water. A recent study found DU in the sapwood and bark of oak trees on the Starmet site; the DU was apparently transferred to the sapwood through uptake of contaminated groundwater.[29]

Foreign war zones may appear far-off and, yes, foreign civilians (and the environments on which they depend) bear the brunt of the noxious load. However, they do not bear that load alone: as we have seen, American and British troops also become victims of depleted uranium's slow-motion slaughter.

The Pentagon loves depleted uranium not just because it's free, but also because the metal's density gives it a high penetrative capacity. That means depleted-uranium munitions can be fired from greater distances, ensuring improved "kill range" and thereby purportedly helping keep U.S. troops out of harm's way. But such reasoning depends on a myopic notion of "harm's way" and "kill range"; both euphemisms demand an environmental gloss.[30] For we need to measure a weapon's "kill range" not just across battlefield space but across ecological and genetic time as well.

When a depleted-uranium warhead strikes a metal target, the depleted uranium spontaneously combusts, releasing minute glass particles in aerosol form. These so-called ceramic aerosols, despite the aesthetic elegance of that phrase, give off no scent, so troops and civilians alike inhale them unknowingly. Because ceramic aerosols emit radiation in potentially lethal doses, if they enter your lungs or if you ingest them or if they seep into a cut, you're at grave risk of developing life-threatening renal carcinoma, leukemia, lymphomas, or any one of multiple cancers. Most cancers take five to thirty years to incubate.

Narrating the Aftermath: The Challenges of Scale

In February 1991, on the eve of the Gulf War, the nuclear scientist Leonard A. Dietz warned of catastrophic consequences if the United States and its allies introduced depleted-uranium weaponry to the battlefield.[31] Dietz's prescient appeal was ignored. As a consequence the Gulf War has left in its wake radioactive landscapes that will continue, for untold years, to wage widespread, random warfare. When Dietz cautioned against integrating depleted uranium into conventional warfare, his alarm was grounded in experience. During the late 1970s, he was employed to monitor depleted-uranium levels outside an Albany factory that produced cannon shells for the Air Force. New York state authorities, on learning that radiation levels near the factory had reached ten times permissible state standards, shut down the plant. The subsequent cleanup cost more than $100 million.

Dietz underscored the hypocrisy of such stringent domestic regulation when the United States was creating in the Gulf an infinitely more toxic environment for its troops and for the region's inhabitants. Shortly after the Gulf War began, Dietz observed: "To protect the health of Americans, we shut down a factory for discharging the equivalent of about two 30mm shells into the atmosphere per month. How can we justify using a million such shells in Iraq and Kuwait, most of it in only four days of war?"[32]

Major Doug Rokke, former director of the Bradley Radiological Laboratory in Fort McLellan, Alabama, makes a similar argument to Dietz. Rokke was tasked with leading an operation to clean up American military vehicles shipped back to the United States in the Gulf War's aftermath. That clean up, Rokke notes, took four years. What does that indicate about the toxic threat those war-exposed vehicles posed, not to speak of the long-term threat to the environment whose toxicity went untreated?[33]

No sooner had military victory been declared in the Gulf War than the public relations battle was joined to shield depleted uranium materiel from environmental critiques that might jeopardize its future in the United States' arsenal. On March 1, 1991, Lt. Col. M. V. Ziehmn of the Los Alamos National Laboratory sent out this memo to all officers in the field:

> Depleted Uranium penetrators were very effective against Iraqi armor . . . but there has been and continues to be a concern regarding the impact of DU on the environment. Therefore, if no one makes a case for the effectiveness of DU on the battle-field, DU rounds may become politically unacceptable and thus, be deleted from the arsenal . . . I believe we should keep this sensitive issue at mind when after-action reports are written.[34]

On receiving this memo in Kuwait where he was leading his meticulous effort to scour vehicles of DU residues before shipping them back to the United States, Rokke read it as an unambiguous instruction to self-censor: "[W]e want this stuff—don't write anything that might make it difficult for us to use it again."[35]

Pentagon officials closed ranks around a public insistence that DU was environmentally innocuous. Former Pentagon spokesman Dr. Michael Kilpatrick was especially vocal and insistent: depleted uranium, he declared, is "a lethal but safe weapons system. . . . I think we can be very confident that what is in the environment does not create a hazard for those living in the environment and working in it."[36] But sometimes a less decisive view slipped through. "The military benefits are so much larger compared to any health problems," Colonel James Naughton declared,

> [w]e feel we have to use it. It's radioactive—I wish it wasn't, but I can't change the laws of physics. The issue is, once you've had a hit, once you're involved in the catastrophic failure of the tank, did the crew survive long enough to really care whether it was tungsten or depleted uranium that hit them? Anyone who does should count themselves damn lucky. I'm sure every one of them would thank God that they lived forty years to contract lymphoma.[37]

What Naughton acknowledges openly here is a two-speed lethality, the difference between what I call cold- and hot-war casualties. Here, as is typically the case, the immediate risk in the heat of battle trumps the violence of deferred effects. But as Carol Picou, Doug Rokke, and veterans in their thousands—not to mention far greater numbers of Iraqis—already knew in their soft organs and in the marrow of their bones, you can become a post-combat war casualty in well under forty years. As Major Rokke explains:

> Four years after the first Gulf War I was blowing 432 micrograms of uranium per liter of urine. That's 5,000 times the permissible level. I was pissing fire . . . My immune system is fucked up. I get endless rashes, open sores that bleed, renal problems. My kidneys are gone to crap, my lungs have gone to crap, my bones are crumbling. My teeth break off and fracture. Uranium replaces calcium. Chemistry 101.[38]

To revisit Michael Kelly's title, a chronicle of Rokke's "small war" requires a different type of attention span and more fine-grained narrative strategies. The slow, invisible ousting of calcium by uranium in the body isn't compatible with the triumphal narrative arc that leads, ineluctably, to the tank-and-corpse scene that delivers a satisfying terminus to Kelly's victory quest. We need counternarratives that locate the Highway of Death circa March 1991 as not a scene of finality, but an early moment in a far longer story of slow violence, of random, unofficial hostilities fought out in the cellular theatres of a physically dispersed aftermath. The task facing both epidemiologists and environmentalists is how to track and recount the winding, concealed metamorphoses of sequestration.

The narrative challenges posed by slow violence of this kind are challenges of catastrophic miniaturism, as the difficulty of narrating temporal duration is compounded by the difficulty of narrating physical scale. "What would constitute adequate protection?" Rokke asks of depleted uranium. "There is none. This stuff is 21 microns. It's smaller than the inner diameter of a red blood cell. We don't have respiratory filters anyplace that can stop it short of a space suit."[39] These microscopic temporal narratives of preentry threat and postentry mutation are amplified by a spatial threat that, again, passes beneath the levels of naked eye detection. Pentagon spokesmen have asserted that because depleted uranium is heavier than lead, it lies where it falls and can't pose a mobile risk. But as research by Dr. Dietz and others has shown, the particles in question are so minute—finer than talcum powder—that they can attach themselves to miniscule particles of sand and become readily resuspended in desert winds. Thus, Dietz concludes, "the fallout range of airborne DU aerosol dust is virtually unlimited."[40]

The spatial and temporal carry of this threat, together with the extreme physical scales across which it operates (from the cellular to the transnational) compound the challenge of producing simple, readily communicative narratives of risk. What we need is stories of anticipation based on the emerging science. The science itself is inescapably slow and has been further slowed by an official reluctance to commit funds to long-term, in-depth research. However, this much we know: studies show that DU is carcinogenic, causes tumors and DNA damage, crosses the blood-brain barrier, deposits in the brain, deposits in the lymph nodes and testes, can cross the placenta, and enters the fetus.[41] Alexandra Miller, a radiobiologist with the Armed Forces Radiobiology Research Institute in Bethesda, Maryland, has discovered direct evidence that radiation from DU can damage chromosomes. Miller observes that when assaulted by depleted uranium "the chromosomes break and the fragments reform in a way that results in abnormal joins. Both the breaks and the joins are commonly found in tumor cells."[42] On the basis of her research she has expressed concern that the chemical and radiological effects of DU were reinforcing each other and, moreover, that

DU was causing indirect damage to so-called bystander cells, that is, cells adjoining those that were directly hit.

Home and Away

If the Gulf War is any measure, we can anticipate an even more widespread, protracted epidemic of belated casualties following the war in Iraq that began in 2003, given the considerably greater volume of depleted-uranium munitions deployed by American and British troops and the lengthier duration of the official war itself. But this judgment is based on more than just the comparative volume of DU munitions used. For the Gulf War was essentially a desert conflict, whereas the later war was decidedly more urban, so that densely populated areas suffered direct exposure to chemical and radiological risk.

The gravity of this urban risk startled Scott Peterson, a reporter for the *Christian Science Monitor*, when in May 2003 he began taking Geiger counter readings at sites across Iraq:

> Near the [heavily bombarded] Republican Palace where US troops stood guard and over 1,000 employees walked in and out of the building the radiation readings were the hottest in Iraq, at nearly 1,900 times background radiation levels. Spent shell casings still littered the ground.[43]

If the 2003 war involved heightened urban exposure, there was another critical difference in the deployment of depleted uranium by U.S. and British forces. Whereas most Gulf War troops, like Carol Picou, had never even heard of depleted uranium, much less the threat it posed, by 2003 army training manuals insisted that anybody who came within seventy-five yards of any blown-up tank or spent shells had to wear respiratory and skin protection. The manuals also warned that "contamination will make food and water unsafe for consumption."[44]

The U.S. military, however, continued to send out mixed messages on depleted uranium's threat. One report from the U.S. Army Environmental Policy Institute asserted: "If DU enters the body, it has the potential to generate significant medical consequences."[45] Yet when questioned about the spike in cancers reported in Basra, where the Gulf War's heaviest bombardment had occurred, director of the Pentagon's deployment health support directorate Dr. Michael Kilpatrick responded unequivocally: "To the question, could depleted uranium be playing a role, the medical answer is no."[46]

How were troops and their families—not to mention Iraqis permanently domiciled in the area—supposed to reconcile such contradictory messages? While U.S. troops in the 2003 war had received warnings about the hazards of getting closer than seventy-five yards to scorched tanks and spent munitions without respiratory and skin protection, Iraqi civilians had received no such warnings. The implications are clear. When Scott Peterson was roaming Baghdad with his Geiger counter he happened to pause by a roadside vegetable stand and chatted with a woman selling parsley, mint, and onions. Five yards away from her vegetable stand stood the scorched hulk of an Iraqi tank; some children were frolicking inside. When Peterson entered the tank, his Geiger counter started singing, registering almost 1,000 times normal background radiation. Peterson asked the vegetable vendor how often the children play inside the tank. She shrugged and replied, "Every day."

Because Iraqi civilians received no official warnings about depleted uranium, and because no one has claimed responsibility for postwar cleanups, this scene is replaying itself across Iraq, as a whole army of dead tanks tempts bored children to turn them into instant jungle gyms. Let's call one of the children playing in that radioactive tank beside the vegetable vendor Ahmed. Like most children, Ahmed yearns to be taken seriously. The tank offers him that chance, the chance to leapfrog into imaginary adulthood, to get behind the wheel of this mighty machine, steer it, fire fantasy shells at fantasy enemies. Day after day Ahmed and his friends return to that tank beside the parsley vendor to reinvent themselves as battlefield heroes. But unbeknownst to Ahmed or his family, he is fighting two wars at once: the war game inside his head, and another long-term war, a hide-and-seek with mortality itself.

Did Ahmed cut himself on the tank's jagged metal? Did he lick a finger, wipe or pick his nose, or breathe in DU particles? If so, he may have unwittingly enlisted as a child soldier to fight in a real biological war, waged slowly, silently against his kidneys, his lungs, his lymph glands, or his thyroid—his blood, bones, chromosomes all under fire.

In the language of the Geneva Conventions, DU has been condemned as a "weapon of indiscriminate effect," yet its effects are not entirely indiscriminate. Its increasing military popularity threatens children most directly: children are ten to twenty times more sensitive than adults to radiation's cancerous risks. Once DU passes into the water system, it travels from there into mother's milk, gathering concentration as it goes, contributing to the cancer clusters among children that were recorded in the Gulf War's aftermath, particularly in the heavily bombarded Basra region. In 2002, eleven years after that war's official end, Basra hospitals reported a tenfold increase in birth defects and miscarriages.[47] When Democratic congressman, doctor, and child psychiatrist Jim McDermott visited Iraqi hospitals in September 2002, he was told by a resident obstetrician that "'the average Iraqi woman giving birth no longer says, "Is it a boy or a girl?' She asks, "Is the baby normal or abnormal."'"[48] "It would be a tragedy," McDermott concluded, "for us to bring democracy to Iraq and leave in our wake a horrendous cloud of nuclear waste."[49] Within six months of McDermott's visit, the country would be subjected to a second depleted-uranium war, as tanks and planes unleashed another long dying under cover of a cloud of rhetoric about "precision."

Under such circumstances, the boundaries between the domestic and the foreign, home and away, are impossible to maintain. American and British troops are drawn disproportionately from communities that (by their own countries' standards) are poor; their fates crisscross the fates of those poor from global South war zones who must inhabit, long term, the uranium-compromised aftermath. Many wives and girlfriends of returning Gulf War veterans complained repeatedly that when making love to their husbands and boyfriends, they experienced a ferocious burning in their genitals. For years these women were ridiculed, some for suggesting that Gulf War syndrome could be transmitted through semen. Recent research suggests these women were only partly wrong. The burning is a sign that a lover's semen is polluted with uranium. Research also points to a connection between uranium-polluted semen and increased levels of endometriosis among veterans' sexual partners. Thus depleted uranium munitions may launch a preemptive strike against both semen and the womb. This is the other ultimate sacrifice—sacrificing in perpetuity one's procreative prospects and the integrity of one's DNA.

One man's precision-guided missile is another man's weapon of indiscriminate destruction. With depleted uranium, we're not talking about rogue missiles that accidentally shred a marketplace or a wedding party. We're talking about the triumphant, pinpoint strike that doubles as a chaotic weapon, a weapon that haphazardly strikes down civilians who, whether under some future tyranny or future democracy, just happen to live downwind in time.

From Landmines to Cluster Bombs

In 1932, almost sixty years before the first Gulf War, the Indian Nobel laureate Rabindranath Tagore boarded a plane and flew over Iraq during a British attempt to put down an anticolonial rebellion from the air. He was availing himself of a novel technological perspective: British aerial bombings in Iraq and Afghanistan during the late 1920s and 1930s foreshadowed the way the airplane would reshape the politics, ethics, and aesthetics of military distance during the mass bombings of civilians during World War II. On landing in Baghdad, Tagore met the chaplain at the local British air force base and observed: "[T]he Christian chaplain informs me that they are engaged in bombing operations on some Sheikh villages. . . . The men, women and children done to death there meet their fate by a decree from the stratosphere of British imperialism—which finds if easy to shower death because of its distance from its individual victims."[50]

Tagore's insight into the military power of distance remains as resonant as ever in our age of "precision" warfare, above all, with the advent of the drone. The stratosphere Tagore writes of is susceptible to multiple interpretations: as a measure of the technological distance between the pilot and his invisible victims, as a measure of the geographical distance between imperial metropolis and invisible colony, and as a measure of the numbing emotional distance between the trigger act of killing and the earthly consequences far below. The emotional sanitation of war involves, in entangled ways, technological, geographical, temporal, and linguistic strategies for distancing. Particularly in our age of slow-acting "precision" weapons delivered from afar, we're readily distracted from the violence of deferred effects—those causal chains stretched thin by time. Stretched thin not just by technologies of instant spectacle but also by the forces of linguistic dissociation, those regiments of euphemism, prominent among them depleted uranium and cluster bombs.

Humans have long relied on a combination of verbal, geographical, technological, and temporal distance to shield themselves from the enormity of what Walt Whitman called war's "red business."[51] How in a democracy could wars possibly be sold, justified, perpetuated without the softenings of euphemism? ("Death," Donald Rumsfeld once noted, "has a tendency to encourage a depressing view of war.")[52] Each conflict brings together new euphemisms, new technologies, new strategies of temporal and geographical displacement that help us keep suffering at arm's length, allowing us to live in states of denial distinctive to our age. One crucial displacement of this kind involves the official efforts to segregate—linguistically and thereby ethically—the barbarous landmine from the humane cluster bomb that, together with depleted uranium, has become a signature weapon in the contemporary battlefield discourse of "precision."

Landmines have accrued a public stigma, especially since Princess Diana's much-publicized walk through an Angolan minefield in 1997. Later that year, 150 nations signed the Ottawa Landmine Treaty, which barred the further production, transfer, and use of mines—"weapons of indiscriminate effect." In conflicts over the past two decades (the Balkans, Afghanistan, Iraq, and Lebanon), America, Britain, and their allies have phased out landmines and relied increasingly on cluster bombs instead. Especially in the United States, the cluster bomb has attracted less scrutiny and generated far less public indignation than the landmine. While the landmine has been denounced as backward and barbarous, the cluster bomb has become associated with the era of advanced "smart" wars, wars whose technological sophistication offers the promise of a merciful, civilized precision. The United States has not only used cluster bombs in more conflicts than any other nation, it has also become the most vocal advocate of this technology's purportedly indispensable and humane intelligence.[53]

The cluster bomb has become a pivotal actor in the story of smart warfare's shadow casualties—casualties that result from what one might call precision's death lag. The rise of the cluster bomb has largely corresponded to the decline in the reputation of the landmine, ever more widely condemned as an environmental and ethical pollutant. In 1993, the U.S. Department of State adjudged landmines to be "perhaps the most toxic and widespread pollution facing mankind."⁵⁴ The scale of landmine pollution remains forbidding: 100 million unexploded mines lie inches beneath our planet's skin. Each year they kill 24,000 civilians and maim many times that number. They kill and maim on behalf of wars that ended long ago; they kill and maim as if in afterthought, spreading social and environmental havoc. In neither space nor time can mine-terrorized communities draw a clear line separating war from peace.

The British government under former Prime Minister Tony Blair rallied behind American efforts to maintain a decisive moral divide between landmines and cluster bombs. Blair signed the 1997 Landmine Treaty, but he showed no ethical qualms about deploying cluster bombs. On the eve of the 2003 invasion of Iraq, Blair's Defense secretary, Geoffrey Hoon, defended cluster bombs as legitimate, conventional weapons that his troops would be at liberty to use. Likewise, questioned about cluster bombs that the United States dropped on Afghanistan, former American Deputy Secretary of Defense Paul Wolfowitz offered a blunt retort: "[W]e have to win this war and we'll use the weapons we need to win this war."⁵⁴

How distinct are the humanitarian and environmental repercussions of landmines and cluster bombs? To address this question, we need to ponder the terms themselves, for when it comes to waging war, the softenings of euphemism are no less dispensable than military hardware. Landmines aren't called landmines in military jargon. The technically correct term is anti-personnel mines, to distinguish them from mines that target tanks and other vehicles. "Anti-personnel," however, is one of those verbal fudgings that under the guise of technocratic exactitude obscures what it purports to reveal. "Anti-personnel" is a faceless word, a word without hands or feet or arms or legs.

According to the U.S. Air Force Dictionary, "anti-personnel" means "designed to destroy or obstruct personnel."⁵⁶ But who are these personnel that the mines are so anti? An Afghan girl, late for school, who takes a short cut across a hill. A Vietnamese herder, dreaming of dinner, while rounding up his pigs. An Angolan peasant clambering down a riverbank to fill her water jug. A Laotian farmer, stooping to harvest his rice, who reaps blindness and amputation instead.

Webster's defines "personnel" as "the body of persons employed in an organization."⁵⁷ So to call mines "anti-personnel" flatters their accuracy by implying that they target an organization, military or otherwise. Yet four-fifths of landmine casualties are civilians: mostly peasants and, dispro-portionately, children. Children's spontaneous energy and their craving for play make them particularly vulnerable. For this reason, in heavily mined northern Somalia, mothers took to tethering their toddlers to trees. Human ingenuity has devised some 270 varieties of landmine, yet not one that can discriminate between a soldier's tread and the footfall of a child.

Peasants cannot tend their crops or flocks without moving through their land. But to the mine's undiscerning eye, all movement is enemy movement: any human or other mammalian body above a certain weight is adjudged to be a body in uniform—personnel in need of blowing up. Long after the troops have returned home, long after a war's soldiers have been demobilized, the landmine maintains its unblinking vigilance. It is there to do its duty—even if ten, twenty years too late, retaliating against an enemy as unspecific as humanity itself. These are not anti-personnel mines, they are anti-person mines.

"Cluster bomb" is an even more insidious misnomer than "anti-personnel mine." What distinguishes cluster bombs is less their clustering than the dis-persal of their malign effects. Whether ground launched or dropped from planes, these munitions are indeed clustered at the moment of dispatch, but their impact across space and time is scattershot. Part of what's at stake here is a numbers game. Take, for example, the Pentagon's declaration that it dropped or fired 10,800 cluster bombs during the first, pre- "mission accom-plished" phase of the Iraq War. (The British deployed another seventy such bombs.) Using the most conservative of official dud rates, 5 percent, this would suggest to the casual observer that some 550 coalition bombs failed to explode on impact, posing a long-term, landmine-like threat. In a country the size of Iraq, 550 unexploded munitions is a modest number. So the offi-cial American and British figures would seem consistent with the protocol in the Geneva Conventions barring the use of disproportionate firepower and weapons of indiscriminate effect.

However, to tally cluster bombs the way we tally landmines amounts to false accounting. A cluster bomb only remains a single weapon for a few sec-onds after it is dispatched, until its canister bursts open to deliver (depend-ing on the model) scores or hundreds of bomblets. Each bomblet, in turn, explodes (on impact or when touched) to release a hail of sharp metal shards that can kill or injure people up to 150 yards away.

Here's how the Human Rights Watch Report, *Off Target*, describes the impact of the bomblets delivered by the CBU-130, a cluster bomb the U.S. Air Force first deployed in Afghanistan in 2001:

> The CBU-103's bomblets . . . are soda can-sized yellow cylinders. Each one of these "combined effects munitions" represents a triple threat. The steel fragmentation core targets enemy troops with 300 jagged pieces of metal. The shaped charge, a concave copper cone that turns into a penetrating molten slug, serves as an anti-armor weapon. A zirconium wafer spreads incendiary fragments that can burn nearby vehicles.[58]

Let's do the math. Each CBU-103 contains 202 bomblets, and each bomblet harbors 300 jagged pieces. In other words, a single cluster bomb can dispatch 63,600 potentially lethal pieces driven outward by the blast wave at ballistic speed. The destructive capacity of the molten cone and incendiary fragments amplifies this threat.

Viewed this way, the coalition's use of 10,870 cluster bombs during the first phase of the 2003 Iraq War appears less restrained. Those bombs strewed 2 million bomblets across Iraqi cities, villages, deserts, and fields. According to Human Rights Watch, a minimum of 100,000 bomblets failed to explode on impact. Given that some American ground-launched cluster weapons had dud rates as high as 22 percent, the war's final figure could be closer to a half million potentially live failures. The threat posed by each of those 100,000 to a half million live failures then needs to be multiplied by 300 jagged shards.

What did all this look like from the ground?

Mohamed Moussa, who lives in al-Hilla (sixty miles south of Baghdad), described to a British reporter how, on March 31, 2003, a hailstorm of silvery objects "like small grapefruit" descended from tumbling white canisters onto his neighborhood. "If it hadn't exploded and you touched it, it went off immediately," he said. "They exploded in the air and on the ground and we still have some in our home, unexploded."[59]

That same day those "grapefruit" killed 38 civilians and injured 156 in al-Hilla alone.

It is at this point, after the initial civilian toll, that the dud bomblets are reincarnated as landmines in all but name. Their passive-aggressive presence has the power to rend a community's social, agricultural, economic, and environmental fabric. Generals like to refer to cluster bombs euphemistically as "situational obstacles," meaning they can be used to impede the progress of enemy troops by boxing them in. But when, in defiance of the Geneva Conventions, American, British, Israeli, and Russian forces have fired cluster bombs into populated areas, the failed offspring of those bombs become, long term and en masse, "situational obstacles" to life itself.

In Iraq, to speak of the shards of memory is to make metaphor material again. The unexploded remnants of war have assumed the sedimentary character of that nation's layered conflicts. Landmines from the epic Iran-Iraq War continue to pose a hazard, their threat redoubled by thousands more (planted by both sides) during the Gulf War. The 24 million cluster munitions the allies dropped on Iraq in 1991 have compounded this hazard. How many of them continue to strew fear across the landscape? Not to speak of the further load (from both coalition cluster bombs and Saddam Hussein's mines) that has polluted Iraq's land and waters since the onset of the 2003 war.

The problem in Afghanistan—our planet's most heavily mined nation—is similarly stratified. As in Iraq, the 1980s proved to be a dire decade for landmine pollution in Afghanistan. The Soviet occupiers left the country densely seeded with mines, turning immense huge swaths of the nation into what Lydia Monin and Andrew Gallimore have called "the devil's gardens."[60] The country's Taliban-era internal conflicts and American and British cluster bombing during the 2001–2002 war added to that deathly crop.

Wherever troops use cluster bombs and/or landmines, a tangle of economic, humanitarian, and environmental crises typically results. National reconstruction and the safe return of refugees are impeded; medical resources become overstretched; rural dwellers face a diabolical choice between abandoning their pastures or fields and risking death or mutilation; amidst a degraded environment, pressure on the land increases, fueling further rounds of conflict. These developments often lead to rapid deforestation and the slaughtering of wildlife. We can witness all these convergent ill effects, for example, in Angola—a lush, once agriculturally self-sufficient country whose economic and medical fabric continues (despite the official end of a twenty-five-year-long civil war) to be overstrained by 5 million landmines and the world's highest per capita population of amputees. In Angola, desperate, displaced rural peoples have hacked down much of the country's woodlands and decimated its once rich and varied game.

Most people forced to adjust to living amidst unexploded ordnance are rural and surviving off the land. Across the mined globe, people have found colloquial ways to convey the mad morphing around them of the land's former fecundity: "the devil's gardens," Cambodia's "killing fields," Iraqi descriptions of cluster bomblets as strange, mutant fruit appearing in the wrong groves—deadly oranges and grapefruits dangling from palm trees. This sense of the earth's munificence taking a demonic turn was evident in the language of the Vietnam War as well: the Vietcong dubbed two early American cluster bomblets (the CBU-24 and the BLU-3) the guava and the pineapple. And in a particularly resonant coinage in terms of the violence of deferred effects, the Vietcong nicknamed another brand of cluster submunition the "lazy dog": that pseudo slumberer who takes his time to rouse himself and bite.[61]

The submunitions that cluster bombs dispense are often gleaming and colorful—inquisitive children readily mistake them for toys or food. Some bomblets resemble striped soda cans, others green baseballs or cigarette lighters. During the war in Afghanistan, Allied planes dropped two types of smallish yellow objects: cluster bomblets and humanitarian rations. Eventually, pamphlets explaining the difference had to be dropped too, after humanitarians warned that children would simply see yellow, reach for the false food, and be blown up.

This was not some freak tragedy but a predictable disaster that gets reenacted every time imprecise weapons are deployed in another so-called precision war. During and after the Afghanistan War, 69 percent of casualties from unexploded ordnance were under eighteen. And in the aftermath of the first Gulf War, 60 percent of such casualties in southern Iraq had yet to turn fifteen. A UNICEF report has estimated that there is one landmine for every twenty children on earth, a figure that doesn't even include the untold number of quasi landmines in the form of cluster bomblets.[62]

Like most forms of pollution, cluster bomb and landmine pollution is only semirandom. Just as in Western nations toxic waste sites tend to be placed near poor or minority communities, so too unexploded ordnance pollution is concentrated in the world's most impoverished societies, Afghanistan, Cambodia, Laos, Somalia, Angola, Mozambique, Vietnam, Somalia,

Nicaragua, and El Salvador among them. Because the burden of lethal war residues is unevenly distributed between wealthy and poor nations, the physical liberty to forget the wars themselves is also unevenly distributed. As the list above suggests, many of the world's most heavily mined societies were once cold-war battlefronts, where the superpowers fanned, funded, and armed internal conflicts, often through proxy armies. Many of these countries—destabilized, overarmed, and undermined—have descended into serial warfare. In such societies, where landmines continue to inflict belated maimings and after-deaths, the post- in post–cold war has never fully arrived. Instead, whole provinces inhabit a twilight realm in which everyday life remains semimilitarized by slow violence and in which the earth itself must be treated with permanent suspicion, as armed and dangerous.

Our planet's 100 million leftover landmines approximate in number the combined residents of California, New York, Texas, Florida, and Pennsylvania. Except that the mines are over there, not over here. As Cyrus Vance and Herbert Okun have noted:

> If children walking to school or playing in a field in Manhattan, Maine, or Monterey were having their legs blown off, the U.S. government would certainly be doing everything possible to stop it. This is happening, however, in foreign places where medical care is often almost nonexistent, and physical labor is necessary for survival.[63]

It costs roughly 100 times more to remove a landmine than to lay it. The case of Kuwait after the Gulf War illustrates the human and financial toll that mine clearance exacts. The bill for clearing that minute, New Jersey-sized country of unexploded landmines and cluster bombs came to $800 million. And before the clearance was complete, those mines had slaughtered several hundred Kuwaiti civilians, 100 bomb disposal workers, and 100 American soldiers. The figure for deminers and American troops alone exceeds the total number of U.S. forces killed during Desert Storm.

Eighty-four countries now suffer from landmine and/or cluster bomb pollution. Most are far larger and far poorer than Kuwait. As a result, for example, it took demining agencies fourteen years to clear just 754 square kilometers in Afghanistan. The International Committee of the Red Cross estimates that between 9 million and 27 million landmines and bomblets remain embedded in Laotian soil and streams alone—relics of the huge load that U.S. forces dropped on Laos, Cambodia, and Vietnam between 1964 and 1973 and during the subsequent civil foment. How are Laotians to forget the twenty-first-century threat, as immediate as ever, from cluster bombs and landmines that rained down on them—in American time—during the era of President Johnson?

The slow violence of unexploded munitions exacerbates the problem of political accountability. In the aftermath of war, political changes occur far faster than environmental recovery. There remains little incentive for an administration to spend taxpayer money cleaning up lethal detritus left behind in far-off countries from a predecessor's war.

In 2004, the Bush administration issued a new landmine policy that put a greater distance between the American position and international efforts to universalize the 1997 Mine Ban Treaty. Bush's policy reversed a prior U.S. commitment to sign that treaty by 2006 if alternative weapons were identified. The administration's revised stance permitted the United States to deploy long-lived "anti-personnel" mines in Korea and self-destructing mines anywhere in the world. With "self-destructing mines," another euphemism—and another form of temporal camouflage—has arisen. As Human Rights Watch has observed, self-destructing mines may take up to nineteen weeks to become inactive.[64] And a significant number malfunction, resulting in the usual unpredictable mix of live and dead duds, a mix that continues to pose a humanitarian hazard to civilians that requires painstaking demining.

No single nation or administration is responsible for the ongoing cluster bomb and landmine crisis. However, it does seem especially hypocritical for an American administration to campaign vocally for fetal rights while its advocacy of "precision" weapons was wreaking ruin on the unborn, who months or years later would inherit an environment that treated them, anachronistically, as enemy personnel. It is equally disturbing that the Obama administration—despite advance pledges to change course on landmines—has adhered to the Bush-era policies.

In November 2003, ninety-two countries (including the United States) approved a treaty obliging nations to clean up cluster submunitions and other explosive remnants at war's end. This, the first disarmament treaty the former Bush administration endorsed, could potentially help narrow the gap in international law between landmines and cluster bombs. The treaty was a first step toward acknowledging that cluster bombs, while classed as conventional weapons, often behave more like landmines— weapons of indiscriminate effect that contravene the Geneva Conventions. The treaty marked a tentative first step toward addressing postwar obligations. However, it has no preemptive force in a world where cluster munitions and landmines still proliferate, with lethal fecundity, faster than they can be removed. The Pentagon continues to argue that it can produce smart-weapon solutions to the cluster bomb problem, in the belief that dud levels can be reduced to as little as 1 percent. (That's far below the 14 to 22 percent failure rate of America's ground-launched cluster munitions during the 2003 Iraq War.) However, the fine print in the Pentagon's position remains chilling. It insists that in future wars American forces will continue to include in their weapons mix old cluster ordnance, what the Pentagon calls "legacy" munitions (as if they were irreplaceable heirlooms). Those "legacy" reserves are huge: the American military has stockpiled more than a billion cluster submunitions of extremely variable antiquity and inaccuracy, like the Rockeye cluster bombs developed during the 1950s and deployed in the Vietnam War and again in the 1991 Gulf War. In both Vietnam and the Gulf, Rockeyes continue to inflict long-deferred twenty-first-century deaths and injuries.

Mistrust and enduring animosity are the ultimate legacies of so-called legacy munitions. In Iraq and Afghanistan, as in Indochina, American cluster bombing has alienated many of the very civilians that the military purported to be liberating, by instilling in their midst a material dread that outlasts the bounds of victories and defeats. As a Church of England spokesman has put it: "You will not win the hearts and minds of a people if, in your effort to provide them with a better future, your real legacy is to be associated with hidden deaths and hideous wounds for years to come."[65]

Imprecise intelligence makes even supposedly precise bombs dumb. In 2003, the United States fired rumor-guided cluster bombs into urban Iraqi neighborhoods where someone or other from the CIA's "blacklist" was alleged to be hiding. Time after time, the rumor came to nothing and civilians took the hit. Formidable human, meteorological, and environmental obstacles exacerbate the inaccuracy of these weapons. For instance, pilots hoping to avoid enemy fire may drop their bomb load from inappropriately high altitudes, expanding the broad footprint over which the bombs scatter. (This has happened in the Balkans and Afghanistan.) Wind drift may drag the bomblets off course. Cluster munitions, furthermore, explode most consistently when they strike hard surfaces like roads. Soft surfaces—sand, marshy areas—result in high live failure rates, a recurrent problem if one is waging desert wars. As the cluster canister disgorges its bomblets, and as the detonating bomblets in turn spew out their jagged pieces, the dispersal area widens along with the scope for inaccuracy. The resulting imprecision in space is compounded by temporal imprecision, as the remnants maintain their assaults beyond war's end.

One of the strongest currents of American optimism flows from Thomas Jefferson's vision of land as the most prudent investment, an investment that benefits both the individual and the nation. You can mint more money, Jefferson observed, but you cannot mint more land. Yet that credo seems less certain when one considers a nation like Cambodia, where 4 million to 7 million active mines and uncounted cluster submunitions have rendered half the country unsafe. To demine Cambodia would amount to a miraculous land-minting scheme, effectively doubling the country's size without conquering a neighbor.

In terms of military strategy, landmines and cluster bombs are both "area denial weapons." The problem is that, too often, "area denial" persists into the so-called postwar era, shrinking the viable earth and straining its resources. As a first step toward alleviating this scourge, we need to acknowledge landmines and cluster bombs as two versions of one problem; we need to recognize the ease with which cluster bombs become de facto landmines under cover of a pseudonym.

Fifty-seven nations now possess cluster munitions and sixteen have deployed them, the United States most extensively. Ideally, we should be campaigning for a universal ban on both air- and surface-delivered cluster bombs. But given the daunting pervasiveness of these weapons, it may be more pragmatic to endorse Human Rights Watch's initial demand that as a first step, all obsolete, high-failure legacy munitions be outlawed. This move needs to be supplemented by a moratorium on newer ordnance until a dud rate of less than 1 percent can be demonstrated. But the ultimate goal should be to outlaw all cluster bombs as weapons of indiscriminate effect.

To achieve such a goal, we will first have to start dismantling the whole delusory rhetorical domain of "smart wars" and "precision" warfare.

We need to demand, moreover, that the former Bush administration's regressive landmine policy be overturned, for the sake of children and adult civilians in as yet unimagined wars, and for the sake of an environment that remains compromised wherever landmines and cluster bombs congregate. In the words of Kenneth Anderson, director of the Arms Project of Human Rights Watch: "The effects of landmines as a pollutant in the environment are just now beginning to be understood. . . . all of society pays, over and over again."[66] The same society-wide payments are exacted by cluster bomblets—those landmines in masquerade.

The Highway of Harm

Again and again with furrowed brows, our leaders pledge to keep "our troops out of harm's way." But the highway of harm is broad and long, stretching beyond the sight lines of the generals and beyond any single generation. As nurse Carol Picou learned, the Highway of Death is a deceptive road that dips and rises through convoluted switchback narratives of disavowal, a road that, despite it's simple two-lane surface, is traveled unwittingly at many different speeds.

At least seventeen nations have bought depleted-uranium weapons from the United States since they were first showcased during the Gulf War. As these weapons and cluster bombs become increasingly enfolded into contemporary warfare, we have an ethical responsibility to redraw the boundary between the war survivor and the war casualty. People may outlast a given conflict, but if untold thousands die deferred war deaths, what kind of justice is it to call them survivors?

In our age of depleted-uranium shells and cluster bombs, "smart" wars become wars of ecological folly as we turn soil, air, and water and into slow weapons of mass destruction, wielded unremittingly against ourselves. Armies move on, as do our memories, but a deeper memory remains lodged in the earth. Despots may be deposed, but environmental mayhem outlives regime change.

One of the greatest challenges we now face is to reinstate a more expansive vision of what it means to be secure. What time span will we allow to define our national security and our security as a species? At home and across the planet, in wartime and in peace, environmental safeguards must be reasserted, safeguards on which our health, freedoms, and international standing depend. The fixation on meeting terrorism with high-tech military terror has shrunk our vision of what constitutes sustainable security. If we improved the fuel efficiency of America's cars and light trucks by a mere 2.7 miles per gallon, we would be liberated from the need to import any oil from Saudi Arabia. Such a bold, but feasible move to conserve energy would also help reintegrate a viable environment into our vision of how to protect America in the long term.

Americans cannot afford to shrink military threats to the future to the real but reductive threat of terrorism. If we continue to glorify poisonous weapons of fake precision, belated war deaths will become increasingly widespread, as will the political consequences of the accompanying blow-back rage. We will face an unbounded war, as the planet itself metastasizes into a combatant: the ultimate, toxic hyperpower, a force of random, abiding retribution.

We need to find (as Rachel Carson did some fifty years ago) new ways to tell the slow-moving stories about the long dying; about last year's cluster bombs that turn into next year's killers, about depleted uranium that treats as its arbitrary enemy the child of a child as yet unborn. Carson insisted it was impossible to nourish democracy on a diet of dead rivers and poisoned fields. Her warning applies to any vision of long-term social stability, whether at home or abroad. If a war leaves in its wake terrifyingly polluted lands and mangled genetic codes, any victory will be pyrrhic, as death by indirection becomes the ultimate form of friendly fire. No homeland can be secure if we convert the earth into a biological weapon that threatens biology itself. We're all downwinders now, some sooner than others.

8

Environmentalism, Postcolonialism, and American Studies

We may be living in post-colonial times, but we are not yet living in post-imperial times.

—Linda Colley, "What Is Imperial History Now?"

What would it mean to bring environmentalism into a full, productive dialogue with postcolonialism? These two fields have emerged in recent decades as among the most dynamic areas in literary studies, yet their relationship has been, until very recently, dominated by reciprocal indifference or mistrust. Unlike many initiatives within literary studies (reader response theory, say, or deconstruction), environmental studies and postcolonial studies have both exhibited an often-activist dimension that connects their priorities to movements for social change. Yet for the most part, a broad silence has characterized environmentalists' stance toward postcolonial literature and theory while postcolonial critics have typically been no less silent on the subject of environmental literature. What circumstances shaped this mutual reluctance? And what kinds of intellectual initiatives might best deepen an overdue dialogue that is belatedly starting to emerge?

In other areas of the humanities and social sciences—notably environmental history, cultural geography, and cultural anthropology—a substantial body of work arose much earlier in the borderlands between postcolonial and environmental studies, work that recognized, among other things, the political and cultural significance of the environmentalism of the poor.[1] Yet within literary studies, a critical discipline for both the environmental humanities and postcolonial studies, such crossover work was long inhibited by a widespread assumption that the subjects and methodologies of the two fields were divergent, even incompatible, not least in their visions of what counts as political.

Let me turn to the events that first set my thinking on these issues in motion. In October 1995, the *New York Times* Sunday Magazine featured a cover story by Jay Parini entitled "The Greening of the Humanities."[2] Parini described the rise to prominence of environmentalism in the humanities, especially in literature departments. At the end of the essay, he named twenty-five writers and critics whose work was central to this environmental studies boom. Something struck me as odd about the list, something that passed unmentioned in the article: all twenty-five writers and critics were American.

This unselfconscious parochialism was disturbing, not least because at that time I was involved in the campaign to release Ken Saro-Wiwa, the Ogoni author who was being held prisoner without trial for his environmental and human rights activism in Nigeria.[3] Two weeks after Parini's *New York Times* article appeared, the Abacha regime executed Saro-Wiwa, making him Africa's most visible environmental martyr. Here was a writer—a novelist, poet, memoirist, and essayist—who had died fighting the ruination of his Ogoni people's farmland and fishing waters by European and American oil conglomerates in cahoots with a despotic African regime. Yet it was apparent that Saro-Wiwa's writings were unlikely to find a home in the kind of environmental literary lineage outlined by Parini. The more ecocriticism I read, the more this impression was confirmed. I encountered some intellectually transforming books by Lawrence Buell, Cheryll Glotfelty, Harold Fromm, Daniel Payne, Max Oelschlaeger, Scott Slovic, and many others.[4] Yet such books tended to canonize the same self-selecting genealogy of American authors: Ralph Waldo Emerson, Henry David Thoreau, John Muir, Aldo Leopold, Edward Abbey, Annie Dillard, Terry Tempest Williams, Wendell Berry, and Gary Snyder. All are authors of influence and accomplishment, yet all are drawn from within the boundaries of a single nation. Environmental literary anthologies, college course Web sites, and special issues on ecocriticism revealed similar patterns of predominance. Accumulatively, I realized that literary environmentalism was developing, de facto, as an offshoot of American studies. Moreover, the environmental justice movement, the branch of American environmentalism that held the greatest potential for connecting outward internationally to issues of slow violence, the environmentalism of the poor, and imperial socioenvironmental degradation remained marginal to the dominant purview of environmentalism that was becoming institutionalized through the greening of the humanities.

The resulting national self-enclosure seemed peculiar: one might surely have expected environmentalism to be more, not less, transnational than other fields of literary inquiry. It was unfortunate that a writer like Saro-Wiwa, who had long protested what he termed "ecological genocide," could find no place in the environmental canon.[5] Was this because he was an African? Was it because his writings revealed no special debt to Thoreau, to the wilderness tradition, or to Jeffersonian agrarianism? Saro-Wiwa's writings were animated instead by the fraught relations between ethnicity, pollution, and human rights and by the equally fraught relations between local, national, and global politics. It was futile, he recognized, to try to understand or protest the despoiling of his people's water, land, and health within a purely national framework. For Ogoniland's environmental ruin resulted from collaborative plunder by those he dubbed Nigeria's "internal colonialists" and by the unanswerable, transnational power of Shell and Gulf Chevron.[6]

Saro-Wiwa's canonical invisibility in the United States was all the more telling given the role that America played in his emergence as an environmental writer. The United States buys half of Nigeria's oil, and Gulf Chevron has been a significant Ogoniland polluter.[7] More affirmatively, it was on a trip to Colorado that Saro-Wiwa witnessed a successful environmental campaign to stop corporate logging.[8] This experience contributed to his decision to mobilize international opinion by voicing his people's claims not just in the language of human rights but in environmental terms as well. Yet it was clear from the prevailing ecocritical perspective in literary studies that someone like Saro-Wiwa—whose environmentalism was at once profoundly local and profoundly transnational—would be bracketed as an African, the kind of writer best left to the postcolonialists.

I became aware, however, of a second irony: that postcolonial literary critics had, in turn, shown scant interest in environmental concerns, regarding them (whether explicitly or implicitly) as at best irrelevant and elitist, at worst as sullied by "green imperialism."[9] Saro-Wiwa's distinctive attempt to fuse environmental and minority rights, I realized, was unlikely to achieve much of a hearing in either camp.

These, then, were the circumstances that got me thinking about the mutually constitutive silences that persisted for so long between environmental and postcolonial literary studies. Broadly speaking, four main schisms appeared between the dominant concerns of postcolonialists and ecocritics. First, postcolonialists tended to foreground hybridity and cross-culturation. Ecocritics, on the other hand, historically were drawn more to discourses of purity: virgin wilderness and the preservation of "uncorrupted" last great places.[10] Second, postcolonial writing and criticism was largely concerned with displacement, while environmental literary studies tended to give priority to the literature of place. Third, and relatedly, postcolonial studies tended to favor the cosmopolitan and the transnational.[11] Postcolonialists were typically critical of nationalism, whereas the canons of environmental literature and criticism developed within a national (and often nationalistic) American framework. Fourth, postcolonialism devoted considerable attention to excavating or reimagining the marginalized past: history from below and border histories, often along transnational axes of migrant memory. By contrast, within much environmental literature and criticism, something different happened to history. It was often repressed or subordinated to the pursuit of timeless, solitary moments of communion with nature. Such timeless transcendentalism was shadowed by a durable tradition within American landscape writing of erasing the history of colonized peoples through the myth of the empty lands. Postcolonialist critics were wary of the role that this strain of environmental writing (especially wilderness writing) has played in burying the very histories that postcolonialists sought to unearth.

The Place of Displacement:
Cosmopolitanism and Bioregionalism

Postcolonial critics have been understandably discomforted by preservationist discourses of purity, given the role such discourses have historically played in the racially unequal distribution of post-Enlightenment human rights. In the context of a romantic primordialism, the colonized, especially women, have been repeatedly naturalized as objects of heritage to be owned, preserved, or patronized rather than as the subjects of their own land and legacies. Once cultures have been discursively assimilated to nature (not least through the settler tradition of viewing the United States as "nature's nation"), they have been left more vulnerable to dispossession—whether in the name of virgin wilderness preservation or the creation of nuclear test zones. If, in J. M. Coetzee's terse assessment, "it is certainly true that the politics of expansion has uses for the rhetoric of the sublime," that expansionist thrust found a potent set of story lines and images in the traditions of American exceptionalism animating the work of foundational American studies thinkers like R. W. B. Lewis, Henry Nash Smith, and Perry Miller.[12] In Donald Pease's succinct formulation,

> those images interconnect an exceptional national subject (American Adam) with a representative national scene (Virgin Land) and an exemplary national motive (errand into the wilderness). The composite result of the interaction of these images was the mythological entity—Nature's Nation—whose citizens believe, by way of the supreme fiction called natural law, that the ruling assumptions of their national compact (Liberty, Equality, Social Justice) could be understood as indistinguishable from the sovereign power creative of nature.[13]

Of critical concern within such narratives of naturally-supernaturally predestined nation building was who got cast as which kind of "natural man" and "natural woman."

Autobiographical divergences sharpened intellectual differences between postcolonial and ecocritics over the politics of purity, place, nation, and history. The preeminent critics associated with postcolonialism—Kwame Anthony Appiah, Homi K. Bhabha, Edward Said, Sara Suleri, Gayatri Chakravorty Spivak, and Gauri Viswanathan, among others—have lived across national boundaries in ways that have given a personal edge to their intellectual investment in questions of dislocation, cultural syncretism, and transnationalism. Conversely, the most prominent American environmental writers and critics are mononationals with a deep-rooted experiential and imaginative commitment to a particular regional locale: Vermont for John Elder, the Sierra Nevada for Gary Snyder, Appalachian Kentucky for Wendell Berry, southern Indiana for Scott Russell Sanders, and Utah in Terry Tempest Williams's case. These regionally rooted national writers were adaptively carrying forward the place commitments evinced in the New England writings of Thoreau and Robert Frost and in Willa Cather's Nebraska.

The tension between a postcolonial preoccupation with displacement and an ecocritical preoccupation with an ethics of place needs to be further situated in terms of cosmopolitanism on the one hand and bioregionalism on the other.[14] Bioregionalism, in Parini's words, entails a responsiveness to "one's local part of the earth whose boundaries are determined by a location's natural characteristics rather than arbitrary administrative boundaries."[15] Gary Snyder and ecocritics John Elder, David Robertson, and David Orr are all vocal advocates of a bioregional ethic. Orr connects ecological destruction to the way people can graduate from college "with obligations to no place in particular. Their knowledge is mostly abstract, equally applicable in New York or San Francisco."[16] (His comment evidences the antiurban bias that permeates much bioregional thinking.) In a similar vein, Elder argues that "the traditional model in education has been cosmopolitanism. I've come to prefer a concentric and bioregional approach to learning . . . It makes sense—educationally—to begin with local writing; then you expand, adding layers of knowledge."[17]

There is much to be said for a bioregional approach: it can help instill in us an awareness of our impact on our immediate environment, help ground our sense of environmental responsibility. However, from a postcolonial perspective, a bioregional ethic poses certain problems, for the concentric rings of the bioregionalists more often open out into transcendentalism than into transnationalism. All too frequently, we are left with an environmental vision that remains inside a spiritualized and naturalized national frame.

Much of the American imaginative and critical literature associated with bioregionalism tends toward a style of spiritual geography that is premised on what I call spatial amnesia. Within a bioregional center-periphery model, the specificity and moral imperative of the local typically opens out not into the specificities of the transnational but into transcendental abstraction. In this way, a prodigious amount of American environmental writing and criticism makes expansive gestures yet remains amnesiac toward non-American geographies in which America is implicated, geographies that vanish over the intellectual skyline. The spatial amnesia that often attends a bioregional ethic has temporal implications as well: whether through the legacies of wars or our outsize consumerism, we have a history of forgetting our complicity in slow violence that wreaks attritional havoc beyond the bioregion or the nation.

The environmentalist advocacy of an ethics of place has all too often morphed into hostility toward displaced people. Edward Abbey's rants against Mexican immigrants, Mary Austin's anti-Semitism, and the Sierra Club's disastrous referendum on zero immigration all evidence a xenophobic strain running through American ethics-of-place environmentalism.[18] With the Sierra Club in mind, Richard Rodriguez has noted how the weeping Indian in the public service commercial first became an environmental talisman and then, in a grim historical irony, was invoked against the immigrant descendants of Indians heading north from Mexico and Central America.[19] Sometimes such hostility toward the displaced tilts over into a kind of Malthusian sublime, as in Snyder's suggestion that the project of wilderness restoration would require ninety percent fewer humans.[20] D. H. Lawrence, in "Mountain Lion," similarly elects himself to the traditions of wilderness West Malthusianism by declaiming: "I think in this empty world there was room for me and a mountain lion / And I think in the world beyond how easily we might spare a million or two humans / And never miss them."[21] Typically, here, the human cull begins with those dispensable, anonymous, invisible inhabitants who reside in the "the world beyond," never with any culling of the poetical, wilderness-expanded egotistical male self.

An exclusionary ethics-of-place can easily lapse into jingoistic transcendentalism, as in an essay that the Montana writer, Rick Bass, wrote in defense of southern Utah's Red Rock country. "The unprotected wilderness of the West," Bass declared,

> is one of our greatest strengths as a country. Another is our imagination, our tendency to think rather than to accept—to challenge, to ask why and what if, to create rather than to destroy. This questioning is a kind of wildness, a kind of strength, that

many have said is peculiarly American. Why place that strength in jeopardy? To lose Utah's wilderness would be to strip westerners and all Americans of a raw and vital piece of our soul, our identity, and our ability to imagine . . . The print of a deer or lion in the sand, in untouched country, as you sleep—it is these things that allow you, allow us, to continue being American, rather than something else, anything else, everything else.[22]

In trying to rally Americans to a worthy preservationist cause, Bass may be resorting here to what Spivak calls "strategic essentialism."[23] After all, it is the American people's representatives who will determine the fate of Red Rock country. But such essentialism, strategic or otherwise, comes at a cost, for Bass aggrandizes and naturalizes the American national character in ways that are politically perturbing. How do we square his intimation that creative questioning is "peculiarly American" with many Americans' widespread, unquestioning ignorance of the disastrous consequences (not least environmental consequences) of much U.S. foreign policy? Bass's position is predicated on, among other things, a failure of geographic imagination—a kind of superpower parochialism. If your frame is Red Rock country, the United States may seem quintessentially a nation of questioners who seek to "create rather than to destroy." But from the vantage point of the 1 million Vietnamese still suffering the health consequences of Agent Orange or from the perspective of vulnerable micro-minorities in Nigeria, Ecuador, or West Papua—places where extraction industry colossi like Gulf Chevron, Texaco, and Freeport McMoran run rampant—a reluctance to destroy may not seem as definitive an American value. We should temper Bass's blinkered eco-nationalism with Aldo Leopold's sobering reminder of what else it means, in environmental terms, to be an American: "When I go birding in my Ford, I am devastating an oil field, and re-electing an imperialist to get me rubber."[24]

Moreover, Bass's exaltation of the American as pure imagination—a higher soul in search of "untouched country"—has a dubious settler lineage. It is precisely such thinking that has impeded the American environmental movement's efforts to diversify its support base. As African American eco-activist Jennifer Oladipo observes, "the terms *environmentalist* and *minority* conjure two distinct images in most people's minds. . . . Religion, capitalism, and even militarism learned ages ago to reach actively across the racial spectrum. In terms of winning over minorities, they have left environmentalism in the dust."[25] The "untouched country" pitch is unlikely to help the U.S. environmental movement match, in the field of diversity, the U.S. military's attainments.

From the perspective of North America's First Peoples, the white soul-dream of "untouched country" has been a source of dispossession and cultural erasure. It contributed, classically, to the Ahwahneechee's eviction from Yosemite as part of Yosemite's reinvention as "pure wilderness."[26] Invoking "the print of a deer or lion in the sand" as a timeless icon of an all-American spirituality thus fits uneasily with the historical imprint of internal colonialism on the West, most dramatically the imprint left by the Indian wars.

For people relegated to the "unnatural" margins of nature's nation—like gay minority writers Richard Rodriguez and Melvin Dixon—the wilderness experience can look ominously purified (as opposed to pure). In his ironically titled essay "True West," Rodriguez describes how, setting off on a hike, three minutes beyond the trailhead, he hears rustling in the bushes. Instead of experiencing transcendental uplift, he fears ambush by "Snow White and the seven militias."[27] And in *Ride Out the Wilderness*, poet-critic Dixon has chronicled how for African Americans, wilderness has been associated with the travails of exile: it is more a place of eviction and historical hauntings than of redemptive silences.[28] On the subject of race, gender and "the fields of memory," poet and essayist Camille Dungy has this to say:

> If memory is home, I am a long way from hope. I have escaped
> and am running. I have to remember what has been said: I am
> black and female; no place is for my pleasure. How do I write
> a poem about the land and my place in it without these memo-
> ries: the runaway with the hounds at her heels; the complaint
> of the poplar at the man-cry of its load; land a thing to work but
> not to own?[29]

The poet Ed Roberson expresses similar hauntings bluntly: "American trees had ropes in them."[30]

To observe all this is not to dismiss ethics-of-place environmentalism out of hand, but rather to render visible a particular lineage of variously misanthropic, jingoistic, xenophobic, racially blinkered, gender entitled, and amnesiac celebrations of wilderness that mark an imaginative failure while masquerading as elevated imaginings. Clearly the emotional power generated by attachments to place can be an invaluable resource for environmental mobilization. Yet having said that, we need to recognize how such attachments do not possess any inherent politics: they can induce a conservative, bigoted environmental ethic or a progressive, inclusive one.

Our intellectual challenge surely is how to draw on the strengths of bioregionalism without succumbing to what one might term eco-parochialism. Here we should heed the call by British environmentalist Richard Mabey for a less brittle, less exclusionary environmental ethics. As Mabey writes, "the challenge, in a world where the differences between native and stranger are fading, is to discover veins of local character which are distinctive without being insular and withdrawn."[31] Yet in response to the blurring of the distinction between native and stranger we have frequently witnessed a defensive tendency to naturalize rootedness and stigmatize as alien people who are perceived to look or talk differently. Precisely this kind of defensiveness prompted Paul Gilroy, in a British context, to question the racial implications of Raymond Williams's ethics of place.

Williams (whose *Country and the City* stands as an influential precursor to ecocriticism) championed what he called "rooted settlements" or "natural communities." These were communities in which "lived, worked and placeable social identities" provided anchorage against the dislocating effects of global capitalism and the abstractions of national identity.[32] However, Williams's advocacy of "natural communities" was accompanied, on occasion, by a suspicion not just of capitalism's dislocating effects but of dislocated people themselves, as when he expressed sympathy for local resistance in rural British communities to "the most recent immigrations of more visibly different peoples."[33] It was insufficient, Williams argued, to say these newcomers "are as British as you are," because that was to invoke "a merely legal definition of what it is to be British . . . . Any effective awareness of social identity depends on actual and sustained social relationships. To reduce social identity to formal definitions . . . is to collude with the alienated superficialities of 'the nation.'"[34] Writing from a more cosmopolitan, postcolonial perspective, Gilroy voiced alarm at such sentiments. He pointed out that Williams's vision of "natural community" meant that minority immigrants and their British-born descendants would find themselves typecast as innately foreign and treated as second-class citizens.[35] How many generations, one might ask, does it take for the "visibly different" to get upgraded to "natural" members of the national community?

The terms of this exchange are directly pertinent to the project, still in its infancy, of giving environmental literary studies adequate international dimension.[36] Gilroy's unease with the implications of Williams' remarks dramatizes the need for us to recuperate, imaginatively and politically, experiences of hybridity, displacement, and transnational memory for any viable spatial ethic. Postcolonialism can help diversify our thinking beyond the dominant paradigms of wilderness and Jeffersonian agrarianism in ways that render ecocriticism more accommodating of what I call a transnational ethics of place.

Let me situate this ethics through a second disagreement, this time involving two writers rather than two critics. Its importance lies in the symptomatic terms of the engagement but also in the rarity of a regional American writer engaging in depth with a transnational postcolonial writer. The prolific southern Indiana essayist Scott Russell Sanders has written powerfully about the scars of displacement in American history, scars left by the slave trade, the Indian wars, and the ravenous power of developers who wrench the rural poor from their familial places. In the tradition of Aldo Leopold and Wendell Berry, Sanders proceeds to track the ecological, spiritual, and community damage inflicted by an American tradition of moving on. He proselytizes instead for "staying put," and in an essay of that title, takes Salman Rushdie to task for celebrating cosmopolitan displacement without gauging the environmental, psychic, and neighborly costs.[37] Two statements by Rushdie rankle in particular: his assertion that "to be a migrant is, perhaps, to be the only species of human being free of the shackles of nationalism (to say nothing of its ugly sister, patriotism)" and his celebration of migrant hybridity in these terms:

> The effect of mass migrations has been the creation of radically
> new types of human beings: people who root themselves in ideas
> rather than places, in memories as much as in material things;
> people who have been obliged to define themselves—because
> they are as defined by others—by their otherness; people in whose

deepest selves strange fusions occur, unprecedented unions between what they were and where they find themselves.[38]

Sanders quite justly questions whether immigrants are indeed unshackled from chauvinistic prejudice; people who have moved a lot can be just as bigoted as those who have stayed put. But in disparaging people who refuse to root themselves in place, Sanders is ultimately on shakier ground.

My empathy for aspects of both Sanders' and Rushdie's positions flows from the antithetical forms of marginalization to which the two writers were subjected. I described Sanders as a "regional writer"—a badge of pride for some, but also grounds for belittlement by the bicoastal and transatlantic sensibilities that make the big decisions along the London-New York-Los Angeles Anglophone cultural axis. If you're regional—and especially from some region in the Midwest flyover zone—you're innately minor league, irredeemably provincial, paradoxically unplaceable in your rural placedness.[39]

From that perspective, Rushdie's musings about migrant hybridity must seem, for a writer like Sanders, buttressed by an offputting cosmopolitan entitlement. Yet Rushdie, before he won the Booker Prize, was an immigrant who, while possessing class advantages, faced profound racial obstacles. He is of Paul Gilroy's generation: both came of age to the soundtrack of Enoch Powell's "rivers of blood" speech, with its imprecations against the "rising peril" of immigrants who were unassimilable to the British nation. Rushdie, like Gilroy, became a minority public intellectual against the hostile backdrop of Thatcher's rise to power. During that era a minority writer or intellectual could not hazard a rural, place-based English identity—staying put close to the land—without suffering the most profound alienation and discrimination, more intensely than in metropolitan London.[40]

Although Sanders strives to be evenhanded, his land-ethic intolerance keeps resurfacing. He traces—pure speculation—John Berryman's suicide to his "dogma of rootlessness."[41] Sanders stacks the decks with his choice of classist terms, condemning "vagrancy" and "drifters." Symptomatically, in explicating the higher ethic of staying put he doesn't engage the possibility of an urban commitment to place, not least among landless renters. In a turn that typifies a powerfully canonized strain of American environmental writing, Sanders draws a direct line between deracination on the one hand and, on the other, a dereliction of duty and poverty of being that are simultaneously civic, ethical, spiritual, and environmental. "To be landless," he asserts, "is not to lack property but to lack responsibility."[42] And "only by knocking against the golden calf of mobility, which looms so large and shines so brightly, have I come to realize that it is hollow. Like all idols, it distracts us from the true divinity."[43] And so hybridity and mobility move to the deficit side of the ecological register, as displacement is trumped yet again by a place-based—indeed, place-dependent—environmental transcendentalism.

Postcolonial Pastoral and Environmental Double Consciousness

A transnational ethics of place can help us integrate into the powerful conventions of pastoral the violence beneath colonial and postcolonial uprootings. As an imaginative tradition, English pastoral has long been both nationally definitive and fraught with anxiety. At the heart of English pastoral lies the idea of the nation as garden idyll, where neither labor nor violence intrudes.[44] To stand as a self-contained national heritage landscape, English pastoral has depended on the screening out of colonial spaces and histories, much as the America wilderness ideal has entailed an amnesiac relationship toward the Indian wars of dispossession.[45]

But what happens when memories of colonial space intrude upon pastoralism, disturbing its pretensions to national self-definition and self-containment? The result is a kind of writing that I have called postcolonial pastoral, writing that refracts an idealized nature through memories of environmental and cultural degradation in the colonies.[46] Postcolonial pastoral can be loosely viewed as a kind of environmental double-consciousness.

We can see this process at work in Naipaul's autobiographical novel, *Enigma of Arrival*, which draws on his life on a manorial estate in Wiltshire—Thomas Hardy country, the heartland of English pastoral.[47] Naipaul self-consciously appends himself, in this novel, to the imaginative lineage of English pastoral by invoking William Constable, John Ruskin, Oliver Goldsmith, Thomas Gray, William Wordsworth, William Cobbett, Richard Jeffries, and Hardy. In the process, Naipaul engages the centuries-long English tradition of *hortus conclusus*, the enclosed garden.

However, Naipaul's perspective is that of an uprooted immigrant whose vision of England can never be fully self-enclosed. In other words, his experience of pastoral cannot be contained by the historical and spatial amnesias demanded by an all-English frame. Instead, through the double consciousness of postcolonial pastoral he experiences the *hortus conclusus* as indissociable from transnational, colonial environments and memories. The counterpoint to the manor garden that he inhabits in Wiltshire is the Trinidadian sugar plantation to which his grandparents were indentured from India. Thus Naipaul views his environment through the double prism of postcolonial pastoral: behind the wealth and tranquility of an English idyll he remembers the painful, dystopian shadow garden of the trans-Atlantic plantation that helped make that idyll possible.

Against this backdrop, we can approach Richard Drayton *Nature's Government* as, in part, a map of transnational shadow gardens. In his book—on the surface, a history of the Royal Botanical Gardens at Kew—Drayton examines, in his words, "how the natural sciences became included in an ideology of 'Improvement' which ordered enclosure at home and expansion abroad."[48] Kew, for Drayton, is not a self-enclosed English space, but part of an extraordinary network of imperial gardens (stretching from St. Vincent to South Africa, Ceylon, Australia, and beyond) that became implicated in entangled global developments of botanical knowledge, but also in economic power, political policy, and imperial administration.

If it is no longer viable to view environmentalism as a Western luxury, how are we best to integrate environmental issues into our approach to postcolonial literatures and vice versa? Jamaica Kincaid's work offers a rich place to tease out some of the possibilities such a rapprochement allows. Kincaid, a Caribbean-American postcolonial writer, was for many years the *New Yorker*'s resident gardening columnist—likely the only anticolonial gardening columnist the *New Yorker* will ever have. She was equally impassioned by lupines and by colonial history. At the heart of much of her nonfiction stands this blunt question: "What is the relationship between gardening and conquest?"[49]

Kincaid herself exemplifies that relationship, given that the British transported her violated ancestors to Antigua. But colonial ships also carried to Antigua the alien plants and animals that have since spread across the island. Kincaid's interest in Antigua's environmental viability thus becomes inseparable from her obsession with ancestral memories of displacement; from where she stands, the separation of botany from the history of slavery seems profoundly unnatural. That much becomes apparent in "The Flowers of Empire," an essay in which Kincaid recounts how, in a moment of botanical rapture, colonial history ambushed her:

> One day I was walking through the glasshouse area of Kew Gardens in London when I came upon the most beautiful hollyhock I had ever seen. Hollyhocks are among my favorite flowers, but I had never seen one quite like this. It had the characteristic large, flared petal, and it was a most beautiful yellow, a clear yellow, as if it—the color yellow—were just born, delicate, just at the beginning of its history as "yellow." It was on looking at the label on which was written its identification that my whole being was sent awhirl. It was not a hollyhock at all but gossypium, the common cotton. Cotton all by itself exists in perfection, with malice toward none. But it played a tormented, malevolent role in the bondage of my ancestors.[50]

Here, as in Naipaul's *Enigma of Arrival*, Kincaid's passion for nature is complicated by her postcolonial double consciousness.

One can read Kincaid's writings against John Elder's insistence that bioregionalism is a more responsible pedagogical model than cosmopolitanism. For Kincaid confounds such oppositions. *A Small Place*, her nonfictional polemic about Antigua and tourism, could be read as bioregional in approach: it takes as its starting point the natural boundaries of this tiny island. Yet the small place where Kincaid stands, the place where knowledge must begin, is inextricably local and transnational.[51] Place is displacement, for British colonists killed off the indigenous inhabitants and replaced them with transported slaves. In the process, the colonists turned what was once a well-wooded island into a desert, clearing the forests to grow slave crops—sugar and cotton.[52] As a result of this slave-era environmental degradation, the island has lost its ability to retain water and is, to this day, forced to import it.

This colonial-induced drought has deepened Antigua's economic reliance on tourism. So ironically, a place marked by a long history of coercive labor and violence has been reinvented as an Edenic retreat where Europeans and Americans can experience nature as pure—a paradise beyond reach of work and time. We can thus read *A Small Place* as Kincaid's effort to return this Eden to a transnational ethics of place. In this way, Kincaid allows us to see Antigua, like Naipaul's Trinidad, as a shadow island, a corrective to the spatial amnesia of a self-contained, regenerative England pastoral of the kind evident in, say, E. M. Forster's *Howard's End.*[53]

"Alien Soil," Kincaid's essay on English and colonial nature, captures her paradoxical position. In England, she is on alien soil; in Antigua, an island where none of the people and few of the plants are native, the soil constitutes the historic ground of her alienation. In Kincaid's words: "I come from a people with a wretched historical relationship to growing things."[54] However, despite that relationship, Kincaid retains a huge passion for botany and gardening—a passion that she recognizes as part of her English inheritance through conquest.[55] Yet she turns that inheritance against itself by insisting that her botanical enthusiasms be refracted through the prism of colonial history.

This is well illustrated by her response to an entry in the *Oxford Companion of Gardens* on George Clifford, the eighteenth-century Anglo-Dutch banker who built a gargantuan glasshouse, filled with plants collected from around the world. That glasshouse proved indispensable to Linnaeus when "Adam-like [he] invented modern plant nomenclature."[56] Kincaid observes how

> [t]he plants in [Clifford's] glasshouse could only have come to him through—and I quote from *Oxford Companion to Gardens*— "the influence of the world trade being developed by maritime powers such as the Netherlands and Great Britain." This being a way of expressing an extraordinary historical event—"trade being developed," leaving out the nature of the trade being developed: trade in people and the things that they possessed, plants, animals, and so on—never ceases to amaze me. I do not mind the glasshouse; I do not mind the botanical garden. This is not so grand a gesture on my part. It is mostly an admission of defeat— to mind would be completely futile; I cannot do anything about it anyway. I only mind the absence of this acknowledgment: that

perhaps every good thing that stands before us comes at a great cost to someone else.[57]

We can read Kincaid's pained reflections here as echoing, environmentally, Walter Benjamin's insistence that "there is no document of civilization which is not at the same time a document of barbarism."[58]

Given the cultural force of pastoral and wilderness mythologies, what kinds of aesthetic activism can reinsert the violence into the view? An especially powerful approach takes shape in the work of contemporary African-American painter Keith Washington. "Within Our Gates: Human Sacrifice in the American Landscape," Washington's series of mural-sized oil paintings, was partly prompted by responses to the 1995 Oklahoma bombing—by talk in the American media about "the arrival of domestic terrorism" on American soil.[59] Washington sought to devise an aesthetic response that could bear witness to a history of domestic terrorism—above all, against African Americans and native peoples—that long predated Timothy McVeigh. Each of the landscape paintings from "Within Our Gates" focuses on a different lynching site: these are lynching sites without ropes or mobs or dangling, mutilated men in them. The tree-lined rural and suburban scenes that Washington represents have no people in them, but beneath each bucolic painting, he has inscribed the name of the lynched man and the location. No date is given: the effect is of a violence that feels open ended, ongoing in its

Figure 4 James Sanders: Road Side Field, Bolton, MS. Oil painting by Keith Morris Washington, 2001. Reproduced by permission of the artist/photographer.

deep yet incomplete specificity. The paintings feel eerily becalmed: this is domestic terrorism domesticated by pastoral convention; by national amnesia; and by the overgrowths of time, vegetation, and rezoning. From these preternaturally ordinary trees hang amnesia's strange fruit.

Environmentalists sometimes refer to "ghost habitats," those ecological shadows of a once powerful presence in the landscape, traces from which one can reconstruct what might otherwise appear to have vanished entirely.[60] The term might well be adapted to Washington's paintings: rippling through his ghost habitats are the hauntings of a double violence—the original lynching and, superimposed on that, the quiet, gradual violence of forgetting, against which the work of art pushes back.

Washington marshals the naturalistic conventions of landscape painting, but does so with a twist. Some of his paintings have hazy distortions running through them, like exaggerated renditions of the reflected heat that rises up from a broiling summer road. In other paintings, overlapping rectangular boxes within the view unsettle the perspective. The effect is of a double consciousness—a tranquility simultaneously expressed and exploded through an ongoing history of the present that is violently, inextricably societal and natural. To observe these paintings after reading Naipaul and Kincaid is to feel the convergent impulses behind postcolonial pastoral's historical double take and an African-American pastoral that prompts us to see, behind some immediate bucolic calm, the domestic terrorism in the long view.[61]

Postcolonial Suspicion, Ecocritical Belatedness

I have outlined some of the primary conceptual divergences between postcolonial and environmental literary studies, but we need to understand their parallel development historically as well. That history is partly internal to the university and partly to do with broader conflicts over the meaning of environmentalism in American society and in the larger world. Of particular pertinence here is Ursula Heise's insight into why the environmental movement that burgeoned in the United States during the 1970s was slow to reshape literary studies.[62] Heise notes how the civil rights movement, feminism, the gay rights movement, and the Chicano/a movement all had a more immediate, powerful impact in recasting literary studies. The environmental movement, by contrast, seemed ill fitted to the emergent theoretical and pedagogical mood of the late 1970s and 1980s in which multicultural identity politics was transforming the literary field and in which, through poststructuralism's ascent, a suspicion of holistic thinking was becoming widespread. This is a crucial insight. However, in trying to grasp the long-standing mutual indifference between environmental and postcolonial studies, one should note that a large body of postcolonial or anti-imperial work—by figures as varied as Edward Said, Paul Gilroy, Hazel Carby, Anne McClintock, Mary Louise Pratt, Stuart Hall, Gauri Viswanathan, Ella Shohat, Benita Parry, Timothy Brennan, and Neil Lazarus—evidenced strong materialist commitments rather than distinctively poststructuralist ones. Yet apart from a rare aside, none of these influential thinkers engaged in any depth with a socially resurgent environmentalism.

To understand this schism more fully we need to step back from the university and consider more broadly the post–World War II power struggles within the American environmental movement—the contest over the movement's philosophical underpinnings and policy priorities, and the way those priorities made American environmentalism a cultural and commercial phenomenon while simultaneously rendering its dominant forms anomalous relative to environmental movements evolving elsewhere, in the global South and in much of the industrialized West. The most productive approach to these developments may be to read in tandem the work of Peter Sauer and Ramachandra Guha. In a series of essays for *Orion*, Sauer—the most trenchant contemporary American environmental essayist—gives historical dimension to his outrage at U.S. environmentalism's path not taken, specifically, the way "Earth Day ushered in a bio-based environmentalism, one that separated human from natural ecology."[63] The history of what Sauer sees as a betrayal of human ecology, however, stretches further back than that. In the wake of Hiroshima and Nagasaki, a sense of global urgency informed the 1946 meeting of the American Wilderness Society at which the members committed themselves to an expansive vision that sought to integrate America's environmental priorities into an agenda of world peace. To that end, the Wilderness Society created a Committee on Foreign Relations chaired by Aldo Leopold.[64]

This internationalist outlook was derailed by President Truman's announcement in 1949 that Russia possessed the bomb. American internationalism became starkly militarized and, under the shadow of the cold war, American environmentalism incrementally retreated from a vision of a global human ecology premised on the notion of a viable environment as a fundamental human right. The 1960s saw a resurgent concern with pollution and public health, largely catalyzed by *Silent Spring*, a concern that led to material legislative initiatives, like the creation of the Environmental Protection Agency, the Clear Air Act, and the Clean Water Act. Yet the permanent war footing of the United States repeatedly threatened those gains. As Sauer notes, at the 1972 International Conference on the Human Environment in Stockholm, after hundreds of worldwide meetings held over four years, the delegates committed to "environmental protection [as] an essential element of social and economic development."[65] In Western Europe and Australia in particular, public health policy became more integrally bound to environmental politics while, during that same period, the United States was traumatically focused on the divisive Vietnam War and the assassinations of Martin Luther King and Robert Kennedy. Neither the civil rights movement nor the antiwar movement was engaged, to any significant degree, by the precepts or goals of the American environmental movement.[66] During this period, the social justice concerns enunciated so powerfully by Carson began to hive off from the nation's environmental mainstream. The biocentric focus of the inaugural Earth Day in 1970 exacerbated this split, leaving American environmentalism isolated from trends elsewhere and reducing the nation's incipient environmental justice movement to (in both senses) a minority affair.[67]

Edward Said's *Orientalism*, the most decisive text in the rise of postcolonial studies, appeared in 1978, just two years before Ronald Reagan's election. President Reagan oversaw, domestically, a massive rollback of environmental regulation and, internationally, proliferating cold-war conflicts from Angola and Mozambique to Nicaragua, from the Horn of Africa to Laos and El Salvador.[68] Crucially, in terms of the postcolonial skepticism toward environmentalism that was cemented during the 1980s, few American environmentalists showed any interest in linking Reagan's transnational imperialism to socioenvironmental degradation in the global South. Instead, most American environmentalists became inwardly focused: on wilderness preservation, on wielding the Endangered Species Act against developers, and on saving old-growth forests. Given the domestic-cum-transcendental tenor of mainstream American environmentalism during the 1980s, a Wilderness

Society with a Committee on Foreign Relations would by then have been inconceivable. Indeed, in many instances American- and European-based international organizations, in the name of conservation, became complicit in paramilitary offensives against native peoples and their resources in the global South.

All this made it easy for the international Left, including many postcolonialists, to view environmentalism as either irrelevant or complicit in imperialism. It also made it easy to caricature the figure of the environmentalist as a whiter-than-white, hippy-dippy-tree-hugging-dopehead deep ecologist from an overprivileged background. Said, who in his final writings briefly gestured toward a green politics, for most of his career could not envisage mainstream environmentalism (as then configured) as an anti-imperial ally. More often—for the historical reasons outlined above—he was dismissive of environmental activism as complicit in structures of oppression and was unable to see environmentalists as playing a productive political role internationally.[69] Although Said never addressed the matter directly, if we consider the way many deep ecologists were concocting as their philosophical ally a mishmash of "Eastern" religious thought supposedly attuned to Mother Earth, that very appropriative gesture can be seen as profoundly Orientalizing—an extension into the environmental domain of the imperialist thinking Said had dissected and assailed.

I have argued throughout this book that the notion that environmental politics are a luxury indulgence available only to the world's wealthy—a boutique politics for the well-off—is utterly untenable. For as one of the first postcolonial literary critics to allude to ecological concerns, Gayatri Spivak, has noted, "the local in the South directly engages global greed."[70] Spivak made that observation two decades after *Orientalism* appeared: it is a perspective remote from the dominant version of environmentalism to which Said and other postcolonial scholars were exposed in the late 1970s and 1980s, namely, an in-turned environmentalism preoccupied with a wilderness ethic and largely indifferent to the international relationship between social inequities, environmental practices, and the cultures of nature espoused by the poor.

The most lapidary exposé of the drawbacks of a narrowly defined environmentalism appeared in Guha's brief, yet wide-ranging 1989 essay "Radical American Environmentalism and Wilderness Preservation: A Third World Critique."[71] Reflecting on how traditions of ecological practices and thought in India and Germany diverged from dominant American tendencies, Guha gave the idea of environmentalism a genealogical diversity that was historically, materially grounded. Guha was alive to the range of American environmental thinking, while spelling out the baleful consequences of the hegemonic rise of deep ecology's adherents and their scientific allies who anointed themselves custodians of tropical biodiversity. Together these wilderness crusaders assumed that the United States represented the environmental vanguard and that wilderness preservation—as philosophy and practice—needed to be universalized. In Roderick Nash's blunt formulation, hopefully "the less developed nations [will] eventually evolve economically and intellectually to the point where nature preservation is more than a business."[72] Here the purportedly selfless biocentrism that wilderness adherents advocated surfaces as imperially anthropocentric in its America-knows-best developmental ideology.

Most deep ecologists evinced a shallow grasp of the consequences of transferring wholesale an environmental ideology from a supremely rich, lightly populated, overconsuming, overmilitarized society like the United States to densely populated countries (India, Nigeria, Indonesia) where significant peasant communities subsisted off the land. For such communities, the idea of the wild could never be primarily a recreational counterpoint to an urban industrialized lifestyle, but was profoundly entangled with the kinds of threats I have outlined in this book: assaults from slow and direct violence on increasingly marginal ecosystems on which their livelihoods depended, ecosystems vulnerable to resource capture by transnational corporations; by third-world military, civilian, and corporate elites; and by international conservation organizations. In such peasant communities environmental sensibilities and practices existed, but they were often directly entangled with ongoing, quotidian struggles for survival.

Together Sauer, from within the American environmental movement, and Guha, from outside it, offer a profound account of deep ecology's disfiguring legacy. Their critiques help clarify why postcolonial and environmental studies have, at least in the literary domain, led such largely parallel lives. Guha's writings sharply impacted debates in environmental history, the environmental social sciences, and the biological sciences, but his ideas had very little resonance within ecocriticism, and then only belatedly. For ecocriticism only began to cohere as a field in the mid-1990s (with the appearance of Lawrence Buell's *The Environmental Imagination* in 1995 and Cheryl Glotfelty and Harold Fromm's *Ecocritical Reader* in 1996), years after Guha's essay had sparked controversy in other disciplines. Moreover, first-wave ecocriticism was skewed toward matters of genre and philosophy at the expense of environmental justice concerns, and showed scant interest in either the environmental social sciences or international environmental history. Only belatedly has environmental literary scholarship begun to broaden—and reconfigure conceptually—the parameters of the field in ways more accommodating of Sauer and Guha's forceful critiques.

Sea Changes and Tectonic Shifts

Any lingering postcolonial dismissal of environmentalism as marginal to "real" politics is belied by the proliferation of indigenous environmental movements across the global South. Saro-Wiwa was not some isolated epic hero: his actions were indicative of myriad environmental campaigns that have been locally motivated, locally led, and internationally inflected. Indeed, we have witnessed on the environmental front something similar to the mutation of feminism, which some thirty or forty years ago was often dismissed as white, privileged, and irrelevant to the needs of third-world women. Just as we have seen what counts as feminism change radically through the rise of social movements that have decentered and diversified the agendas of women's rights (in ethnic, geographic, religious, sexuality, and class terms), so too we have seen a related turn in environmentalism, opening up paths, inside the academy and beyond, to more diverse accommodations of what counts as environmental.[73] It is in this context that the environmental justice movement is beginning to achieve a more forceful presence within the greening of the humanities, a development that has immense consequences for our ability to engage, across multiple temporal and geographical scales, the politics of slow violence and the environmentalism of the poor.

"All human activity," William Beinart and Peter Coates have argued, "alters the composition of the natural world which in itself is never static. A critique which regards all change as decay begs the very legitimacy of human survival."[74] Non-Western environmental movements are typically alert to the interdependence of human survival and environmental change in situations where the illusion of a static purity cannot be sustained, much

less exalted. Such movements are also typically aware of how easily outside forces (including transnational corporations, the IMF, and the World
Bank) and internal authoritarian regimes, often in cahoots with each other,
can rend the delicate, always mutable mesh between cultural survival and a
viable environment.

In Ecuador, one such locally led campaign, Acción Ecológica, mobilized the nation's Confederation of Indigenous Nationalities against Texaco,
whose ransacking of the environment echoed the plunder, 10,000 miles
away, that generated Nigeria's Movement for the Survival of the Ogoni
People.[75] In India, the corporatizing of biodiversity proved a major rallying
point: 200,000 Indian farmers descended on Delhi in the so-called Seed Saty-
agraha to protest transnational efforts to wrest control over the reproduc-
tion and distribution of seeds from traditional farmers. Wangari Maathai
hailed "a new environmental awareness in Africa, [as] the African people
are responding to save the environment," an overly broad judgment perhaps, but indicative of some encouraging shifts.[76] In a voice that resonated
for many Africans suffering the fallout from kleptocracy, Kenyan student
leader Wycliffe Mwebi spoke of the "moral right to defend the environment
against a corrupt land grab."[77]

One productive (if insufficient) approach toward integrating these
shifts into the environmental humanities involves narrowing the divide
between the study of America's minority literatures—a recent growth area
of ecocriticism—and the study of postcolonial literatures from an environmental perspective. Lorraine Anderson et al.'s influential collection, *Literature and the Environment*, evidences the potential for and problems with
conjoining the two fields.[78] In one important regard, this is an encouraging
volume—the first environmental anthology to include a significant spread
of minority writers, many of them foregrounding issues the environmental justice movement has prioritized. By acknowledging what Langston
Hughes, bell hooks, Louis Owens, Clarissa Pinkola Estes, and Marilou Awi-
akta, among others add to environmental debate and testimony, the Anderson anthology marks a shift away from wilderness writing and the literature
of Jeffersonian agrarianism. Several of the essays address indigenous land
rights, community displacement, and toxicity, often in the context of urban
or poor rural experience. Encouragingly, these are some of the American
concerns that most readily connect with the environmental priorities that

predominate in postcolonial writing. One recognizes here rich possibilities for a deepening transnational rapprochement.

However, in helping redefine the field, *Literature and the Environment* (despite its expansive title) restricts itself to an almost all-American cast. Of the 104 contributions, only one is non-American: a maverick Wordsworth poem. So while applauding this diversification of environmental literature, we should be careful not to confuse American multiculturalism with international diversity or assume the latter flows automatically from the former. The Anderson volume leaves the need for a more global inclusiveness largely unaddressed.

The geographical distribution of interest in Lawrence Buell's groundbreaking study, *Writing for an Endangered World: Literature, Culture, and Environment in the U.S. and Beyond*, raises some similar issues.[79] Buell's earlier and justly influential study, *The Environmental Imagination*, centered on American nature writing and was written in the shadow of Thoreau. His sequel, however, takes a more generous and creative view of what counts as environmental literature, opening up questions of toxicity, biodegradation, urban experience, and engineered environments.[80] This enables Buell to engage, through detailed readings, a series of American minority writers: Gwendolyn Brooks, John Edgar Wideman, Richard Wright, and Linda Hogan among them.[81]

However, the expanded American diversity of Buell's later work is not matched by an attentiveness to diversity elsewhere. The limitations of trying to generate a transnational vision from an American-centered account of environmental writing becomes evident in Buell's solitary sustained reading of a postcolonial fiction, Mahasweta Devi's "Pterodactyl, Puran Sahay, and Pirtha," a Bengali novella translated into English by Spivak.[82] After praising "Pterodactyl" as a trenchant fiction of environmental justice, Buell remarks that the novella's "sometimes esoteric cultural particularism . . . may seem to make it an odd detour from the U.S.-focused texts I have mainly been discussing."[83] The image of a "detour" and the reference to "esoteric cultural particularism" foreground the intellectual challenge for ecocriticism of moving beyond a center-periphery model. The unsettling implication is that somehow American texts transcend "cultural particularism," are always already universalized in ways that postcolonial ones are not.[84]

What is required is more than simply diversifying the canon: we need to reimagine the prevailing paradigms. That much is evident from the enormous difficulty Saro-Wiwa had in gaining an audience in the United States and Europe. When he first appealed to Greenpeace representatives they said they didn't work in Africa, that it was off their environmental map.[85] Wherever he went, Saro-Wiwa was treated as an unfathomable anomaly. An African writer claiming to be an environmentalist? And claiming, moreover, that his people's human rights were being violated by environmental ethnocide? Part of Saro-Wiwa's problem in gaining a hearing for the Ogoni was not just economic and political—it was imaginative as well.

Saro-Wiwa campaigned for environmental justice. But he also campaigned, in effect, against a center-periphery paradigm. He had to contend not just with environmental racism but with prejudicial failures of geographical imagining. In American intellectual and media terms, a region like Ogoniland is almost completely unimaginable.[86] Yet the writings of Saro-Wiwa, Devi, and Roy allow us (in crucial ways that the self-perpetuating national lineage of Thoreau, Muir, Abbey, Berry, and Snyder does not) to engage environmental politics through conflicts between subnational micro-minorities, autocratic nation states, and transnational macroeconomic powers.[87]

In trying to diversify our thinking, we need to insure that we don't end up asking an environmental variant of Saul Bellow's dismissive question: "Where is the Zulu Tolstoy?" If we go scouting the equatorial forests for the Timorese Thoreau (or his Cameroonian cousin), we'll return alone. Nor can we content ourselves with a nominal international smattering—an Ishimure Michiko or Wordsworth text decorating the American eco-canon much as a Virginia Woolf or a Jane Austen once graced otherwise all-male courses and, later, a Toni Morrison or an Alice Walker were used to "diversify" white courses on women's writing.

To reject an add-on solution to the challenges of diversity is to refuse a vision of environmentalism as invented at the center and exported to (or imposed upon) the periphery.[88] Such center-periphery thinking has been, historically, both a source of postcolonialists' pervasive indifference to environmentalism and, conversely, a source of the debilitating strain of superpower parochialism that lingers even now among many American ecocritics and writers. Just as subaltern studies embarked on a project of provincializing the West, so too we need to persist in provincializing American environmentalism if we are to regenerate and diversify the field.

By the same measure, postcolonial studies could benefit from an infusion of the regenerative public urgency that a flexible, broadly imagined environmentalism can offer. Postcolonial studies has recently begun to stall for several reasons, four in particular. First, an involuted turn toward an abstruse prose accessible only to disciplinary initiates severed much postcolonial work from the public, communicative ambitions that, at its best, had provided much of the field's anti-imperial dynamism. Second, post–cold war and pre-9/11, issues of empire fell out of favor in the United States and, for many, became less pressing. As those issues resurfaced after the onset of the Iraq and Afghanistan wars, a new generation of younger scholars was— on account of that historical hiatus—unacquainted, in any textured way, with the anti-imperial work produced during the cold war. Third, especially since 9/11, in public policy debates and literary studies we have witnessed a paradigmatic shift toward globalization and world literature, respectively. As I've documented in this book, globalization's ascendancy, as process and paradigm, has led to some inspirational, if embattled transnational alliances among activists opposed to its neoliberal modes, not least among activists promulgating a grassroots transnationalism from below. My stance on the rise of world literary studies is ambivalent, as I intimated in my introduction. On the one hand, we have witnessed a heartening, necessary engagement by literary scholars with languages and literatures neglected by hidebound comparative literature departments; we have witnessed, too, some intriguing conceptual innovations. On the other hand, there is a powerful strain of world literary studies that, in its obsession with field definition, seems content with a campus-niche orientation: as such, it feels politically bloodless and, paradoxically, unworldly. Which brings us to the fourth, related reason for postcolonialism's relative retreat: together, the rise of world literary studies and the rise of the pro-globalization public intellectual have allowed many universities to phase out (or greatly reduce) their hiring and course offerings in postcolonial studies as a purportedly superannuated field. This would concern me less if I did not suspect this as being symptomatic of a broader scaling back within the humanities and the social sciences of the kind of radicalism that anti-imperial and postcolonial work often enabled.

A radically creative alliance between environmental and postcolonial studies can help push back against administrative and disciplinary efforts to corral for narrow ends what scholars alive to the power of word and story have to offer the wider world. What we can offer includes a belief in the value of multiple publics as we strive, among other things, to foster imaginative coalitions that may help redress environmental injustice.

Six years ago, in addressing the concerns laid out in this chapter, I wrote (as did Susie O'Brien and Graham Huggan) about the conceptual and political value of instilling in postcolonial studies a stronger environmental awareness.[89] I noted, for instance, the value of reconfiguring Black Atlantic studies in environmental terms beginning with Derek Walcott's aphoristic assertion: "the sea is history."[90] I also argued for more inventive transnational comparative work, by bringing into conversation, say, the rich literatures about nuclear colonialism and nuclear risk from the Pacific island nations, Australia, Britain, the United States, India, Pakistan, and those areas of the former Soviet Union still shadowed by the slow violence of the test zone. Crucially, I argued that we needed to rethink what it is we are looking for—what kinds of texts, what kinds of issues—when we engage transnational environmental literatures.

At the end of the twenty-first century's first decade, we are witnessing, across a range of intellectual fronts, some heartening initiatives that are starting to change hitherto dominant conceptions of what it might mean to green the humanities. We are witnessing the beginnings not just of an environmentally engaged Black Atlantic studies but also of Indian Ocean and Pacific Ocean studies animated by conjoined ecological and postcolonial concerns.[91] Comparative nuclear literary studies is generating high-caliber work, and we are seeing energetic new inquiry into the literatures of resource extraction across a range of geographies.[92] Caribbean environmental studies has emerged as a particularly fertile domain of interdisciplinary inquiry.[93] And as I write, the first anthology to bridge the African environmental humanities and social sciences is going to press, as are the first two anthologies of postcolonial environmental scholarship.[94] New books engaging, from an environmental stance, areas as diverse as Indian fiction, Australian and Pacific literatures, and the African novel are breaking new ground methodologically as well.[95]

This current of emergent work reminds us that there is no inherent incompatibility between postcolonial and environmental literary studies, despite their discrete institutional histories. However, one caveat is in order. It is tempting to return to influential anticolonial thinkers like Fanon,

Césaire, Kenyatta, and Said to unearth overlooked environmental concerns seaming through their work. While there is value in doing so, we should not forget the historical circumstances that, almost without exception, made such thinkers hostile or indifferent to environmentalists and vice versa. There is a risk of retrofitting flexible contemporary meanings of environmentalism anachronistically to earlier eras when anticolonial struggles over land rights and political independence clashed, again and again, with colonial legacies of conservation that were invariably racist and became emblematic of environmentalism in a decolonizing age. The prospects for postcolonial environmentalism today have been empowered by a spreading awareness among diverse international publics that ecological concerns are not only gaining urgency but are also less narrowly defined than even a decade ago—certainly less so than when *Orientalism* first made its mark or, sixteen years before that, *The Wretched of the Earth*. Crucially, the current, belated engagement between environmental and postcolonial literary studies does not result from a straightforward two-way conversation but is part of a broader series of dynamic exchanges, two of which warrant mentioning in particular. First, the transnational turn in American Studies, whether hemispheric or more broadly global, is achieving an unprecedented methodological and curricular authority. Such work, while of course not wholly new, is becoming a primary catalyst for energizing American studies, creating an intellectual climate in which questions of empire, globalization, and transnational structures of power and resistance are moving front and center.[96] This has clear environmental repercussions: it has the potential to shift the intellectual centers of gravity away from the in-turned, American exceptionalist tendencies of wilderness literature and Jeffersonian agrarianism and toward more diverse environmental approaches that are, crucially, more compatible with the impulses underpinning environmental justice movements around the world. Here Camille Dungy's 2009 anthology, *Black Nature. Four Centuries of African American Nature Poetry*, marks a breakthrough initiative, in its historical reach, its transnational resonances, its engagement with urban environmental literature, and its concern with the outer and inner landscapes of injustice.[97]

A second, related shift in the intellectual climate of the environmental humanities is emerging from within Native American studies. Native texts have, by now, a well-established history of ecocritical engagement. What is novel and striking, however, is the gathering interest among Native scholars in taking up postcolonial studies as a potentially productive interlocutor.[98] This turn becomes a second way of deterritorializing American studies by advancing comparative approaches to settler colonialism, land rights, environmental racism, resource conflicts, and the transnational circuits of toxicity while drawing on (and reconfiguring) postcolonial studies. Crucially, from an environmental perspective the emergent dialogue between Native studies and postcolonialism can help foreground the socioenvironmental relations between internal colonialisms and offshore imperialisms in all their historical and geographical variability. This postcolonial-Native turn thus helps further unsettle the dominant paradigms of American environmental literature and criticism while widening the potential avenues for comparative work around environmental justice on a global front.

Together these emerging tendencies in postcolonial, American, and Native studies can help deepen and diversify the dialogue I have sought to outline here, reframing oppositions between bioregionalism and cosmopolitanism, between transcendentalism and transnationalism, between an ethics of place and the experience of displacement. Through such a dialogue we can simultaneously think through nature-induced states of transport and the vast, brutal history of humans forcibly transported. In the process, we can aspire to a more historically answerable and geographically expansive sense of what constitutes our environment and which literary works we entrust to voice its parameters. Despite the recent advances toward that goal, ours remains an ongoing, ambitious, and crucial task—not least because for the foreseeable future, literature departments are likely to remain influential players in the greening of the humanities.

Epilogue

Scenes from the Seabed: The Future of Dissent

For God's sake, be economical with your lamps and candles! Not a gallon you burn, but at least one drop of man's blood was spilled for it.

—Herman Melville, *Moby-Dick*

The island of Atlantis, according to Plato, vanished into the ocean "in a single day and night of misfortune."[1] The engulfment threatening the Maldive Islands is nothing as unambiguously instantaneous as that. The Maldives face an incremental threat from rising, warming oceans, a threat difficult to dramatize and even harder to arrest—a form of slow violence that is rapid in geological terms but (unlike a tsunami) not fast enough to constitute breaking news. In an effort to infuse dramatic urgency into this incremental crisis, the president of the Maldives, Mohamed Nasheed, held an extraordinary underwater cabinet meeting in diving gear on October 17, 2009, shortly before the Copenhagen Climate Summit. President Nasheed and his wetsuit-clad ministers convened behind a conference table anchored to the seabed, a Maldive flag planted behind them. Oxygen mask in place, the president signed into law a national commitment to becoming carbon neutral within ten years.

President Nasheed's underwater convocation speaks directly to this book's concern with the environmentalism of the poor and the representational challenges posed by slow violence. The Maldive meeting was an explicit bid to turn the slow-motion urgency of a nation's fate into a newsworthy event and, beyond that, into a symbolic prompt to goad world leaders in Copenhagen to act against climate change. The subaqueous cabinet meeting put an apocalyptic spin on the global dithering of business as usual: this was drowning in paperwork with a vengeance. We can read the scene as an attempt to surmount two vexing dilemmas. First, how does a nation under climatic threat compensate for the drama deficit of climate change? Second, how does a minnow nation like the Maldives—which has contributed almost zero to global warming and has zero clout on the world stage—conjure enough agency to render visible the slow violence that poses an existential threat to it through inundation, through a terminal sea change?

This ghostly sea-bottom scene makes a statement—at once micronational and planetary—about environmental time. What we enter through photographs and video is a premonitory landscape prefiguring the consequences,

Figure 5 Maldives underwater cabinet meeting to highlight the threat of global warming, October 17, 2009. Reproduced by permission of the Maldives government media agency.

on a global scale, of wasted foreknowledge. The scene serves as a preview of the aftermath.

The Maldives are not wealthy: the nation, assembled from twenty-six coral atolls, had a per capita GDP in 2008 of $4,967. In terms of population and land mass, the archipelago constitutes Asia's most diminutive nation, a place of precarious postcolonial possibility doubly compromised by small-ness and by its status as the planet's lowest-lying nation-state. The Maldives boast a land mass of only 115 square miles (about 1.7 times the size of Wash-ington, DC) but possess a disproportionately long coastline that stretches for 400 miles. The capital, Male, also happens to be one of the planet's most densely populated cities. This confluence of factors—low altitude; high population density; a long, threatened coastline made more vulnerable by a dying protective barrier of coral reefs; and ironically, a tourist trade as a paradise untouched by time—have combined to turn the Maldives into the canary in the mine shaft of the climate crisis.

Through the compensatory realm of symbolic activism, President Nasheed sought to distill a narrative of planetary urgency from a crisis so attritional and so seemingly far-off that it might appear a causeless threat to an already invisible nation of no apparent consequence. But for Nasheed, like Saro-Wiwa before him, human rights are indissociable from environ-mental justice for a marginalized community that doubles as the bellwether of a broader crisis in transnational responsibility.

The Maldives is on the brink of becoming the first nation where the entire population would be climate refugees; even with a mere 400,000 citizens, the prospect of a climate-driven exodus on that scale constitutes a logistical nightmare and foreshadows an age of insurgent climate refugees on a far more threatening, chaotic scale.[2] Indeed, a 2003 Pentagon report warned of the security threat posed by millions of climate refugees, predicting that rich nations like the United States would have to respond by "building defensive fortresses around their countries."[3] This conventional neoliberal response—wall off the wealthy, raise the walls of denial—is classic short-termism, a security strategy built on the illusory, foundational assumption that address-ing the causes of slow violence can be infinitely deferred.

The Maldives may be at the forefront of the crisis, but it is not alone: at the 2010 Cancun climate talks 43 island nations announced that they face "the end of history" if the rich countries fail to act decisively and in concert against climate change.[4] Those 43 comprise the Alliance of Small Nation Island States—AOSIS, which sounds like a jumbled oasis, paradise thrown askew. The fate of the AOSIS nations foreshadows the looming, long-term threat to wealthier seaside cities everywhere, from Manhattan to China's coastal plains, from Venice and Rotterdam to New Orleans, and to the cities that hug Australia's shores—where 85 percent of the national population clings to the oceanic perimeter.

President Nasheed's underwater cabinet meeting offers an image of reverse inundation that speaks directly to the environmentalism of the poor. Here it's not brown immigrants threatening to "swamp" the neoliberal fortresses of the still predominantly white rich, but rather poor brown people confronting the threat of having their national territory swamped as a result of a 200-year experiment in hydrocarbon-fueled capitalism whose historic beneficiaries have been disproportionately rich and white. This image strikes at the heart of the debate over climate justice, at the inequities between those who have grown rich off hydrocarbon culture and the predominantly poor people—from the Maldives to Niger—who are low-level hydrocarbon consumers but at greatest initial risk from the climate crisis. Yet over time, that risk will be passed on, as today's imperiled islanders turn into climate refugees whose desperation will exacerbate the crisis in the richer, high-consumption nations whose profligacy triggered it in the first place.

Before the climate crisis, flag planting was associated more with mountain peaks than with ocean floors. (Flag planting, one suspects, was not a historically prominent activity in the Maldives, which boast a highest peak of seven feet and seven inches—one inch taller than Yao Ming). The Maldivian flag planted at the underwater cabinet meeting is a flag of involuntary conquest, a territorial marker not of national ascent but of national decline, as a nation-state subsides toward obliteration.

Without the compensatory agency that media images of the meeting bestowed on it, the Maldivian flag would have been left to flap invisibly underwater in the Indian Ocean currents. Yet I cannot observe this submerged flag of inverted conquest without thinking of a second submerged flag that might seem unrelated, yet speaks to the planetary feedback loop between the slow violence of the climate crisis and our transnational failure to begin to innovate and conserve our way beyond unsustainable levels of hydrocarbon dependency. In 2007, two years before the Maldivian cabinet assembled underwater, a Russian submarine descended to the sea-bed beneath the North Pole and planted a Russian flag. This flag planting marked a very different, less ironic oceanic land grab. Russian expedition leader Artur Chilingarov declared: "[T]he Arctic is Russian."[5] Denmark immediately disputed the Kremlin's claim to the Arctic continental shelf, as did Canada. Russia dispatched troop reinforcements to its Arctic edge, while Canada declared it would follow suit and was strengthening its claim by building a new Arctic port city. The United States, Norway, and the European Union (whose member states Sweden, Denmark, and Finland abut the Arctic) climbed into the controversy with claims of their own.[6]

Global warming was the trigger for this militant rhetoric and these troop movements. Melting circumpolar pack ice had opened the prospect of new sea-lanes and was exposing hitherto inaccessible mineral and energy deposits, especially gas and oil, the so-called Arctic hydrocarbon bonanza. On May 29, 2009, *Science* magazine made publicly accessible for the first time a comprehensive map of the projected circumpolar energy reserves, indicating that the region's oceans might harbor 30 percent of the world's unexploited gas deposits and 13 percent of its unexploited oil.[7] The oil majors and their political cheerleaders hailed the melting of the fragile circumpolar pack ice in a frontier idiom, capitalizing on the back-to-the-future mythic appeal of the Northwestern Passage.

And so we face the prospect of expanded suboceanic carbon reserves being extracted and burned courtesy of global warming, accelerating the very processes of slow violence that will drown the Maldives first but which, unchecked, will ultimately breach the walls that concretize our planetary delusion that we can segregate secure communities from insecure ones long term, and separate out orderly societies from those abandoned to destitution and climate chaos. From the perspective of climatic slow violence, the Arctic oil rush gives a whole new meaning to the race to the bottom.

The two flags in these far-flung underwater scenes may be geographically remote from each other yet serve, as it were, as carbon copies of a common crisis. Together they remind us that the climate crisis is both indivisible and unevenly felt, experienced—especially by some of the planet's most vulnerable peoples—as climate injustice. One seabed scene, beneath a disappearing ice pack, serves as a starting gun for the twenty-first-century scramble by global behemoths to grab even more of the earth's resources in another giant colonial carve-up. The other underwater scene, beneath a vanishing island nation, gives an oceanic environmental twist to the antico-lonial phrase "the development of underdevelopment."

Greenwashing and Big Oil Transcendentalism

We can read these two seabed scenes—the Arctic flag annexing new hydro-carbon claims, the tropical flag protesting a short-sighted hydrocarbon addiction—alongside a third, connected scene: the submerged slow violence triggered by the mile-deep blowout beneath the Deepwater Horizon rig. The idiom of new frontiers has long been integral to BP's public relations spin: in the corporation's insistence, for instance, that it is at the cutting edge of "the energy frontier," exhibit A "the deepest well ever drilled by the oil and gas industry." This exuberant frontier idiom is of a piece with BP's Big Oil transcendentalism, evident in the greenwashing slogan "Beyond Petro-leum" and in the clashing perceptual fields of Deepwater Horizon (down below stretches up ahead). Despite the airy transcendentalism of BP's slo-gan, according to the Atlas Economic Research Foundation BP spent less investing in solar, hydrogen, and wind energy over a six-year period than it did on a two-year advertising campaign to rebrand itself as "Beyond Petro-leum."[8] And so the post-carbon, transcendental vision thing is largely reduc-ible to a self-referential marketing metanarrative. BP did, however, find plenty of funds to help bankroll the Global Climate Coalition, a consortium of mainly Big Oil and Big Auto corporations that opposed U.S. ratification of the Kyoto Protocol to lower greenhouse emissions.[9]

BP has long sought to exploit the romance of the technological sub-lime—imagining the unimaginable, venturing into the unknown, confi-dent that some engineering breakthrough will save the day. The frisson of the technological frontier wins hands down against more prosaic, unnewsworthy stories of steady regulatory oversight. President Obama himself notoriously bought into this technological progress narrative when, three weeks before Deepwater Horizon went down in flames, he vindicated exposing formerly protected coastal areas to offshore drilling with the assurance that "oil rigs today generally don't cause spills. They are technologically very advanced."[10] In these terms, the bold advances are material but the unwise risks immaterial. Washington commentator Llewellyn King took the language of the technological sublime to its hubristic extreme when, in the explosion's aftermath, he could still express "wonder that we can build machines so remarkable that they can lift the lid off the underworld."[11]

That infernal, unlidded underworld let loose what the Keats epigraph to *Silent Spring* foreshadowed: "The sedge is wither'd from the lake, / And no birds sing." To read those words is to picture the Louisiana wetlands: the withered marsh grass and the oil-silenced pelicans, robbed of voice and flight, their slimed wings giving them the appearance of evolution sent into reverse, as if these were the very first birds struggling to extract themselves from the primordial ooze. And thus the pelicans, like the Exxon Valdez sea otters, became traumatic, charismatic stand-ins for a microbial and cellular catastrophe whose temporal and physical dimensions we are ill equipped to imagine and the science of which we do not adequately understand.

In the twenty-first century, we have crossed over into what Michael Klare calls the Age of Tough Oil.[12] As easily accessible reserves are exhausted, new finds entail heightened extractive costs and heightened environmental risks; ocean wells become ever deeper, and we become more dependent on horrendously polluting tar sand petroleum and fracking. Together, the costs exacted by Tough Oil and the Deepwater crisis ought to be incentives enough to encourage investment in cleaner alternatives to the hydrocarbon status quo, yet only a few farsighted nations—like Germany, Portugal, and Denmark—are making this switch on the necessary scale. Instead, within weeks of the Macondo wellhead being sealed, Greenland launched the next phase of the Arctic frontier oil rush by issuing new drilling licenses in far deeper, far colder waters than the Gulf, conditions under which oil would be even more resistant to dispersal.

In the Age of Tough Oil, the regulatory climate in the United States has grown more lax so that, as in the Gulf, we were left to watch 1970s shallow water cleanup technology being applied to a twenty-first-century deepwater catastrophe. We cannot reduce the conjoined crisis of environmental imagination and policy overhaul to something as simple as Republicans versus Democrats. The Obama administration is recapitulating the regulatory laxity that marked its Republican predecessors: critically, it was in 2009 that Obama's Interior Ministry granted BP a categorical exemption from a comprehensive environmental impact statement for Deepwater Horizon's Macondo wellhead.[13] And it was President Bill Clinton who, to appease the oil majors, rushed through the Deepwater Royalty Reduction Act of 1996, which accelerated deepwater drilling in the Gulf of Mexico by reducing fees on oil and gas production. A year later, the Clinton administration, "at the request of the industry," halved the frequency with which blowout preventers needed to be tested.[14] Clinton's rationale for such deregulation? Reducing dependence on foreign oil.

Thus we continue, decade after decade, to seesaw between two narrowly defined definitions of risk: the risk of relying on foreign oil and the risk of domestic drilling. What remains interminably deferred is the third option: increasing neither domestic nor foreign risk but investing, on a transformative scale, in post-hydrocarbon possibilities (what Beyond Petroleum gestures toward only in name). This should be the long-term focus of our risk management, an alternative option that holds out job-generating possibilities to boot.

Deepwater and the Lost Horizons of Slow Violence

Ours is an age of shape-shifting transnational corporations; of heightened corporate mobility; of megamergers; of disappearing problematic brand names like Union Carbide and Monsanto; and of acrostic subcontracting that can make it hard to nail down a corporate identity, let alone nail down blame. Against this bewildering backdrop, how does one ring-fence damage and culpability? President Obama initially tried to put the genie of neoliberal globalization back in the bottle of corporate nationalism through the populist ploy of calling BP, anachronistically, British Petroleum: the UK as historic oppressor turned rogue nation. Tony Hayward's British-accented, hyperdefensive, litigation-minded, tone-deaf performance created a ready way of focalizing the enemy—his ruddy face becoming a stand in for "foreign" business practices endangering American shores. Faced with the challenges of demarcating blame, the Republicans found themselves impaled on a symptomatic dilemma: was the enemy Big Government or Great Britain? Some in the Tea Party wing—like Rep. Joe Barton (R-Texas), who apologized to Tony Hayward for the $20 billion "shakedown"—accused the federal government of meddling in places government didn't belong; others relished the chance to flex their xenophobic instincts, revamping the iconography of tea-dumping anti-imperialism a la 1773.[15]

In the twenty-first century, drawing a line between domestic and foreign corporations is assuming an increasingly arcane complexity. BP is a London-based firm, but one that the Pentagon depends on for 37 percent of its oil. Americans hold 40 percent of BP shares. The feedback loop between government and the oil majors is intense: Gale Norton, for example, George W. Bush's Secretary for the Interior and point person for a massive wave of oil industry deregulation, is now a paid advisor to that most un-American sounding of the oil majors, Royal Dutch Shell.

How foreign is the foreign? This question bears directly on the way complex corporate complicities are outsourced and consumer complicities disowned. The question also impacts the way ostensibly foreign disasters get excised from a nationalized memory, the lessons they have to offer dissipated because they don't appear to jeopardize "our" environment or "our" national security. Disasters bracketed as foreign can be dismissed as irrelevant to policy overhaul or industry oversight.

The 1979 Ixtoc oil explosion off the Gulf of Mexico's coast is a classic instance of the problematically nationalized boundaries of disaster memory. Ixtoc remains the most pertinent precursor to Deepwater Horizon, far more so than any oil disaster within U.S. borders: Ixtoc occurred in the Gulf of Mexico, the same body of water as Deepwater Horizon; it was an uncapped spill that kept gushing for months; it occurred under warm water conditions; and unlike most oil disasters, it involved a deepwater well rather than emanating from a ruptured tanker or a land spill.[16] Yet if the 1969 Santa Barbara and 1989 Exxon Valdez spills are hazy enough in American memory, the Ixtoc blowout simply doesn't register.

The most striking parallel between Ixtoc and Deepwater is this: it took Pemex, the oil company responsible, 297 days of futile experimentation and clueless passivity before the Ixtoc spill ran its course, by which stage the company had managed to drill two relief wells. During those months of serial incompetence, 140 million gallons of crude spewed into the Gulf, destroying (among other things) a venerable fishing culture which, along with keystone species of marine life, has never fully recovered. Deepwater drilling today is much deeper than it was in the 1970s. But the crucial unlearned lesson remains: in pushing back the technological frontiers of oil extraction, the industry thirty years ago had, and still has, little motivation for making comparable advances in blowout prevention and cleanup technology. The standard operating procedure remains: it's cheaper for us to improvise when stuff happens—wetlands, deltas, marine life, tourist, and fishing industries be damned.

The unlearned lessons from Ixtoc call into question the line hewed by disaster optimists—engineers like Henry Petroski, David W. Fowler, and James R. Chiles—whose ideas have gained renewed prominence in Deepwater's aftermath. For Fowler, who teaches forensic engineering at the University of Texas, Austin, "the [oil] industry knows it can't have that happen again. It's going to make sure history doesn't repeat itself."[17] To the contrary, as Ixtoc suggests, one tenacious industry strategy is to wait (it doesn't take too long) for history, especially ostensibly foreign history, to go away.

Part of the problem is that disaster optimists are typically engineers who take a narrowly technological perspective, observing only how disaster can drive design. But unless the political climate under which innovative design operates is subject to an environmental justice overhaul, such innovations will have limited effect or indeed never be implemented. Without political pressure or quick profitability, what is there to motivate corporate will? And whenever (as with Deepwater Horizon) a corporation like Halliburton is involved, can what Naomi Klein has trenchantly called "disaster capitalism" be far behind?[18]

If the temporal horizons of the disaster zone are, on a number of fronts, difficult to keep in view, that difficulty was exacerbated in the Gulf of Mexico by BP's strategy of dousing the spill with the oil dispersant Corexit. Corexit sounds like a first cousin of Tippex, one brush stroke away from a simple whiteout, a fresh chance to rewrite past mistakes. But with a runaway gusher there is no simple corrective stroke and no exit. Corexit is so far from a problem solver that it is banned in the UK; the evidence suggests the product will operate less as a dispersant than (in Rachel Carson's term) a biocide. So in addressing the slow violence in the Gulf of Mexico we return to the vanishing acts performed by a name: Agent Orange as "herbicide" that continues to poison down the generations; "cluster bombs" that disperse their staggered casualties across the years; "Corexit" that through tide and wave action, ocean currents, and chemical diffusion, compounds a calamity it purports to redress.

In her investigative reporting on the Gulf oil catastrophe, Anne McClintock learned that BP and the Coast Guard were secretly deploying large numbers of military planes to carpet bomb the spill with Corexit by night.[19] The oil would disperse and sink, only later to reaccumulate. So the appearance and disappearance took on a certain rhythm: the mass spraying of Corexit occurred mostly under cover of night, effectively disappearing much of the surface oil, which did not vanish but merely dispersed and sank beneath the water to the sea bed or accumulated in underwater plumes. Thus the oil dispersant operated as an image dispersant: as McClintock observes, it was a way of "disappearing the story."[20] By dissipating the slicks without actually removing the oil from the ecosystems, BP was able to soften the imagery of disaster—as it had sought to do by Photoshopping oil slick images on its Web site and, as McClintock documents, by barring (with the Coast Guard's complicity) the media from accessing the worst-hit areas. With slow violence in general, I have suggested, the temporal projections of disaster are routinely foreshortened; in the Gulf of Mexico that foreshorten-ing was given a head start by the application of an image emollient

Hydrocarbon's Black Atlantic

The slow violence that underlies Deepwater Horizon long predates the out-of-control gusher. The temporal dimensions of the disaster zone must include a long history of successive administrations lavishing on Big Oil exemptions from regulation. The unseen violence of unregulated drill-ing has become institutionalized through a culture of encouraging the oil majors to oversee themselves, creating a direct connection between failed government oversight, corporate short-sightedness, and unseen violence-in-the-making. In tracking the temporal deep horizons of this scene we should include the attritional, exponential carbon-culture violence perpetrated by the oil majors in impoverished communities of the global South, a violence that, located offshore among the foreign poor, doesn't garner the media attention granted the Gulf of Mexico.

In questioning the environmental parameters of the "foreign," it is help-ful to consider, in transatlantic conjunction, two of Earth's greatest, most vulnerable delta wetlands—the Mississippi and the Niger. In Nigeria's south-eastern delta states –which satisfy 11 percent of American oil needs—546 million gallons of oil have spilled to date.[21] But those spills have occurred during five decades of drilling: Niger Delta communities have suffered the equivalent of an Exxon-Valdez sized spill annually for a half century.

This enduring, incremental disaster, however, has lacked a focal, fiery, news-grabbing explosion—and a spillcam. Superimposed on these representational disadvantages is the impediment of a racialized foreignness: the Nigerian spills, from an American or European perspective, are offshore-offshore—doubly removed from national consciousness. To grasp this discrepancy we need to recognize the racialized dimensions both to Ulrich Beck's observation that "pollution follows the poor" and to Fernando Coronil's account of "the international division of nature."[22]

On this score, we should widen our purview beyond Big Oil to include the comparative field of North-South disaster liability. To Bhopal, for example, where, as in the Gulf of Mexico, disaster resulted from regulatory laxity, a laissez-faire culture of corporate self-policing, corner cutting on equipment maintenance and elementary safety procedures and a corporate management that ignored or stonewalled warnings from employees and intrepid journalists that a catastrophe was in the making.[23]

Deep Horizon killed eleven people instantly, whereas Bhopal killed 3,500 instantly and thousands more in the months thereafter. According to Indian government records, the Union Carbide disaster adversely affected the health of 578,000 people. The U.S. Congress swiftly exacted from BP a pledge to ring-fence an initial $20 billion, with a projected compensation of $34 billion. Compensation could be claimed for, among other things, death, personal injury, environmental cleanup, public health concerns, property damage, lost jobs, and lost income. By contrast, in Bhopal the kind of damage subject to compensation was severely circumscribed: only death or personal injury counted. Moreover, after compensation the factory disaster site continues to inflict casualties: Dow (which bought out Union Carbide) still has not cleaned up 450 tons of hazardous waste that continues to leach into the city's aquifers and soil.

However inadequate the billions of compensation directed at the Gulf of Mexico, the U.S. administration could leverage its power against BP, whereas the Indian government found itself in a weak bargaining position in relation to a U.S.-based corporation. The Reagan administration—and subsequent administrations—made clear that future U.S. investment in India would be jeopardized if Union Carbide were penalized in the ways that the Bhopal Survivors' Movement and myriad Indians demanded. Successively cowed (and corrupt) Indian governments scaled back their demands, allowing the courts to go through the motions, decade after decade, without exacting material compensation. Union Carbide eventually paid out a trifling $470 million to the victims, who received an average $550 lifetime compensation—and then only after seventeen years of haggling.[24] Poor brown lives in the global South can be capped at a low dollar amount.

In June 2010, with the Macondo well still gushing, the Obama administration was in negotiations to provide nuclear technology for power stations in India. A new civil nuclear technology agreement between the United States and India would depend, they insisted, on capping damage liability. The United States, with one eye on the Bhopal disaster, demanded that the Indians agree in advance to a maximum $100 million liability in the event of a nuclear industrial accident.[25] So at the very moment that the Obama administration was retrospectively overriding the damage limits to which BP was contractually accountable, it was strong-arming the Indians into capping damage limits at 0.5 per cent of the initial amount ring-fenced for BP compensation. Thus does the precautionary principle operate on the unequal playing field of neoliberal liability between the global North and global South.

From Deepwater to *The Shallows*: The Future of Dissent

When a quarter century ago Edward Said urged intellectuals to master both long forms of writing and shorter, prompt interventions, he could not have anticipated either the hegemonic brevity or incessant promptness that would come to dominate contemporary communications. (Welcome to the world, the text, and the critic in 140 characters or less.) Nor could Rachel Carson, with her innovative metaphoric fondness for a planetary "web of life," have anticipated how future environmentalists would have at their fingertips a Worldwide Web seething with virtual ecologies of connection and distraction.

In an age that increasingly genuflects to the digital divinity of speed, how will environmental activists negotiate the representational challenges of slow violence—a violence that is by definition image weak and demanding on attention spans? How will writers, photographers, video artists, podcasters, and bloggers navigate the possibilities—and possible perils—opened up by a new media culture characterized both by extensive, instant connectivity and by impatient, distractive staccato rhythms? How will we distribute and maintain our attention over the *longue duree* as we seek to extend and sustain the pathways to environmental justice on a transnational scale?

Seven weeks after the Macondo wellhead blew, I found myself thinking about such matters in a state of symptomatic, oscillating simultaneity, my gaze flickering between the Deep Horizon spillcam and *The Shallows*, Nick Carr's thoughtful, fiercely debated analysis of neuroplasticity, depth of concentration, and community under the pressures of the digital age. Carr, marshaling an array of scientific evidence, expresses concern over the way the new media are altering our neural pathways, impeding our capacity for undivided attention and, while expanding access to data, simultaneously shrinking our power to consolidate memories. These neural changes have immense repercussions, he suggests, for selfhood and social amnesia.

I had just finished *The Shallows* when BP sealed the wellhead and there was supposedly nothing left to watch: the most visible phase of the disaster was over. At that point, the mainstream media scaled back decisively their reporting on the spill. I felt profoundly troubled by the image management involved. Yes, the spillcam had allowed us collectively to witness the irruptive trauma and mobilize around what we could see. But with the wellhead sealed I knew that attention spans—unanchored by visible evidence of catastrophe—would drift elsewhere. Meanwhile the incalculable, incremental damage spread through biomagnification of the toxins was only beginning. BP had not just capped the wellhead but, with the spillcam's assistance, had capped the disaster's perceived time frame as well. Powerful forces—including the Obama administration and the *New York Times*, which wanted to put the disaster behind them ahead of the midterms—were highly motivated to declare that the worst was over and move on.

It was in the context of Deep Horizon, then, that I found myself giving my reading of Nick Carr's *The Shallows* an environmental slant. Environmentalism is extraneous to Carr's concern with the changes to neural pathways, memory patterns, and identity induced by the digital age. Yet his approach is deeply and directly pertinent to the issues that have animated this book: how we perceive and inhabit environmental time; how we render visible, and act against, attritional slow violence that jeopardizes sustainable security, locally, nationally, and on a planetary scale. If, in the judgment of psychologist Christopher Chabris, the Web intensifies our tendency to "vastly overvalue what happens to us right now" how do we balance that restless drive for immediate novelty with activism that needs to remain focused on the long term?[26] How in an age characterized by chronic digital drift do we stay attentive to toxic drift that unfolds across a radically different time span? Crucially, what is the relationship between mobilizing dissent against the hydrocarbon status quo and the changing technological climate in which such activism must operate, a climate that is dramatically overturning how time is lived and perceived?

The challenges of sustaining urgency in a digital age are particularly acute in relation to climate change, given the temporal and geographical dimensions of the problem. Earth scientists may be alarmed by what they call the Great Acceleration—the speeded up, anthropogenically driven changes to Earth's biophysical systems since World War II—but most people, especially in our Age of Distraction, don't understand rapidity the way earth scientists do. The new media have expanded public access to climate change science; however, it remains uncertain what kind of impact the agile restlessness of the new media (and the brains they are reshaping) will have on an issue of this scale. Digitally coordinated civil disobedience certainly has a role to play in pressuring governments to enter into indispensable transnational accords: without such large-scale agreements, the damage inflicted by climate breakdown, from the Maldives to the Arctic, will be compounded.

The critical question remains the question of strategy—how, in our transnational quest for stronger alliances, to combine activist staying power with new media agility. No technological revolution has an innate politics: witness how WikiLeaks catalyzed Climategate on the one hand—by leaking University of East Anglia emails on climate change that were gleefully seized on by right-wing denialists—and, on the other, leaked the cables that enabled Ivory Coast environmental justice activists and their allies to achieve a settlement for damages from the British commodities giant, Trafigura, which for years had denied responsibility for dumping highly toxic oil slurry in landfills around Abidjan. The slurry killed fifteen people in the short term and sickened 108,000.[27] The activists' successful settlement in the Trafigura case was a digital-era warning shot against those who assume that the environmentally-afflicted poor are terminally invisible, disposable people.[28]

In volume and velocity, the new media have made available testimony on a previously unimaginable scale, testimony that can fortify the environmentalism of the poor and push back against the perpetrators of slow violence. When, for instance, the *New York Times*, along with American network and cable TV had largely baled on covering the Gulf oil disaster with any sustained, critical investigative edge, myriad new media sites kept skeptics and activists apprised. So, too, the underwater cabinet meeting staged in the Maldives was more than an isolated act of desperation by an imperiled micro-nation: the meeting achieved its global visibility not just randomly through YouTube but through the coordinated efforts of 350.com, a vast, creative transnational coalition to reduce carbon emissions, a coalition that links activists—in the ether and on the ground—across scores of countries.

Initiatives like 350.com are helping narrow the gap between new media landscapes and landscapes of slow violence, the former disproportionately available to the affluent, the latter disproportionately inhabited by the poor. Despite the digital divide, the exponential spread of cell phones has helped generate an activist connectivity even in regions without access to electricity. What we do not know—and warrants researching—is whether digital drift is more prevalent among the well-off than among the poor, whose online time is limited by cost and, moreover, whose communications may become more focally sustained when motivated by issues of ongoing, life-threatening urgency. If, for example, the answer to the Twitter slogan "What's happening right now?" is "Government goons have arrived and are beating up villagers and starting to cut down our forest," that "now" may remain front and center for some time. This is exactly what happened when in 2008 Peruvian *indigenistas* defeated a move by President Alan Garcia to pass legislation enabling corporations to undertake mining, oil, and timber extraction, without indigenous permission, in a 36,000 square mile tract of the Amazon. The scale of the protests, which brought together activists from 65 tribes as well as urban supporters, prompted the Peruvian congress to repeal the law, which had been slated as part of a neoliberal "free trade" deal with the United States. The *indigenistas* creatively mixed labor-intensive and digital dissidence, blocking roads with logs, occupying oil and electricity plants, and creating mobile protest units whose actions were coordinated via cell phone .[29]

As protests from Myanmar to Iran have evidenced, digital networks are a force, but a force that cannot guarantee an outcome.[30] They can be excellent for quickly disseminating damning or exhilarating evidence, but in the absence of political leadership and complementary, hierarchical forms of political organization, their socially transformative potential may run aground.[31] That said, if we are unlikely in any straightforward manner to tweet our way toward environmental justice, our age of Flickring connectivity has irreversibly changed the way future writer-activists will bear witness and agitate for change.

Addressing the vexed subject of literary commitment, Jean-Paul Sartre portrayed the writer as someone "who has chosen a certain method of secondary action which we may call action by disclosure."[32] The revolution in the technologies of disclosure—from WikiLeaks to my neighbor's blog— have altered the meaning of such secondary action unrecognizably. So, too, "writer" has become a more demotic designation: less grand, less glamorous, less distinctively vocational, and more likely to involve mongrel blends of word, image, and video. *Écriture engagée* will never again be a specialist calling à la Sartre—or even à la Ken Saro-Wiwa—now that we have entered what one might call the age of the writer-hacktivist.

Some writer-activists are fly-by-night operators, others are in for the long haul, as they strive to bring an attention-grabbing urgency to issues that might otherwise be marginalized by technological, neurobiological, and political forces of inattention. Whether our era of heightened connectivity and intensified distraction compounds or alleviates destructive environmental short-term thinking will be shaped, in large measure, by the politics of the commons. Will the vast, insurgent digital energies directed at defending the information commons help mount an equally spirited defense of the commons in its oceanic, atmospheric, and terrestrial forms?[33]

The new media offer no panacea, but deployed with inventive vigilance, they constitute a potential resource of hope within a broad coalition to advance environmental justice. Such a coalition must necessarily draw on the strategic energies—and, in turn, empower—more traditional activist constituencies: labor, native, and student groups, progressive scientists, and campaigners for human rights, women's rights, and civil liberties, as well as organized opponents of unchecked globalization. Within this coalition, that protean figure, the writer-activist, will continue to play a critical role by drawing to the surface—and infusing with emotional force—submerged stories of injustice and resource rebellions. For although the technological landscape may be changing at an exponential rate, some things remain more durable. Among them, the conviction, in Nadine Gordimer's words from a quarter century ago, that writers who believe in "the transformation of society are always seeking ways of doing so that their societies could never imagine, let alone demand."[34]

NOTES

ACKNOWLEDGMENTS

INDEX

Notes

Preface

1. Edward Said, "Worldly Humanism v. the Empire-Builders," *Counterpunch*, August 4, 2003, 5. I am grateful to Anthony Vital and Hans-Georg Erney for drawing my attention to this essay in their editorial "Postcolonial Studies and Ecocriticism," *Journal of Commonwealth and Postcolonial Studies* 13 (2007): 6. One can also detect hints of an incipient environmental awareness in Said's meditations on the politics of land in *Culture and Imperialism* (New York: Vintage, 1994), 75. For some insightful reflections on Said's potential relationship to environmental thought, see Elizabeth DeLoughrey and George Handley's introduction to their forthcoming volume, *Postcolonial Ecologies: Literatures of the Environment* (Oxford: Oxford University Press, 2010).

2. Said, "Secular Criticism," *The World, the Text, and the Critic* (Cambridge, Mass.: Harvard University Press, 1983), 3.

3. Said's relationship to postcolonial studies was an uneasy one, given that he viewed his work as more anti-imperial than postcolonial—particularly when the latter field became increasingly associated with poststructuralist methodologies. That said, Said is widely viewed as a foundational figure for postcolonial studies.

4. Ramachandra Guha, *How Much Should a Person Consume? Environmentalism in India and the United States* (Berkeley: University of California Press, 2006), 20.

5. Ibid., 1.

6. Ibid., 20.

7. Ramachandra Guha, "Radical American Environmentalism and Wilderness Preservation: A Third World Critique," *Environmental Ethics* 11 (1989): 71–83.

From their different vantage points, Murray Boochkin and Andrew Ross were also prescient figures in this dismantling.

8. Guha discusses the emergence of these terms in several places. See, for example, *How Much Should a Person Consume?* 214, 233; and Guha, *Environmentalism: A Global History* (New York: Longman, 2000), 98–124. A particularly decisive text for deepening and applying some of these core terms is Joan Martinez-Alier's *The Environmentalism of the Poor: A Study of the Ecological Conflicts and Valuation* (Cheltenham, UK: Edward Elgar Publishing, 2003).

9. Guha, *How Much Should a Person Consume?* 1.

10. Guha, *The Unquiet Woods: Ecological Change and Peasant Resistance in the Himalaya* (Delhi, India: Oxford University Press; Berkeley: University of California Press, 1989).

Introduction

1. Philip Arestis, "Furor on Memo at World Bank," *New York Times*, February 7, 1992. For insightful commentary on Summers' proposal, see also Upamanyu Pablo Mukherjee, *Postcolonial Environments: Nature, Culture and the Contemporary Indian Novel in English* (London: Palgrave Macmillan, 2010)

2. Kevin Bale, *Disposable People: New Slavery in the Global Economy* (Berkeley: University of California Press, 2004).

3. Andrew Ross, *Strange Weather: Culture, Science and Technology in the Age of Limits* (New York: Verso, 1991), 207–212.

4. The term "West" is inevitably shorthand. The environmentalism of the poor within North America and Europe, although not the focus of this book, helped goad affluent environmentalists in the global North to diversify their vision of what counts as environmentalism and to recognize—in the present and retrospectively—third-world-generated activism as a vital force and potential ally in the global resource wars. That said, as I indicate in my penultimate chapter on the ecological threats posed by so-called precision warfare, it is often very difficult to articulate as a single narrative of risk the threat slow violence poses to the health of troops conscripted from the rich-nation poor and the threat to the even more impoverished people who inhabit war zones long term, war zones that are overwhelmingly located in the global South. The very difficulty of integrating such conjoined (if unequal) threats is symptomatic of the layered invisibility that defines slow violence. The poor, of course, are hardly restricted to the global South, but they are dramatically, disproportionately concentrated there.

5. Ramachandra Guha and Joan Martinez-Alier, *Varieties of Environmentalism. Essays North and South* (London: Earthscan, 1997), 12.

6. Arundhati Roy has expressed some unease toward the very notion of the writer-activist. Yet her concerns—that the term makes activist writers sound exceptional, that it risks institutionalizing them as experts, and risks narrowing our perception of both writers and activists—need to be taken with a grain of salt, as an exercise in self-protectiveness and false modesty, given her ineluctably institutionalized role in the media as professional (albeit dissident professional) go-between. The fact is only a tiny minority of writers assume an overtly activist public role and that minority—especially when they shuttle between the novel or poetry on the one hand and engaged nonfiction on the other—are routinely skittish, insisting on their imaginative autonomy from ideological obligation while also declaring their political commitments. Such balancing acts between avowal and disavowal surface in the writings of Albert Camus, Jean-Paul Sartre, James Baldwin, Langston Hughes, Wole Soyinka, Derek Walcott, Gabriel Garcia Marquez, Carolyn Forche, Joseph Brodsky, Paul Muldoon, Mahmoud Darwish, and Nadine Gordimer to name but a few. For Roy's take on writer-activism, see *The Algebra of Infinite Justice* (London: HarperCollins, 2002), 186–187.

7. Edward Said, "The Public Role of Writers and Intellectuals," *The Nation*, September 17, 2001, 10.

8. Frantz Fanon, *The Wretched of the Earth*, trans. Constance Farrington (1963; repr., New York: Grove, 1968), 42.

9. Ibid., 36–37.

10. If historically Fanon was in no position to write about the slow violence of inequitably distributed environmental threats, he was, of course, alive to the psychological seepage of colonial values that could sustain neocolonialism. Furthermore, in "Colonial War and Mental Disorders" he is attuned to the slow violence that results from colonial "pacification," the psychological effects far outlasting specific acts of discernible violence. See ibid., 249–316.

11. Quoted in Stephanie Cooke, *In Mortal Hands: A Cautionary History of the Nuclear Age* (New York: Bloomsbury, 2009), 168.

12. Zohl de Ishtar, *Daughters of the Pacific* (Melbourne: Spinifex Press, 1994), 24. In the nuclear exceptionalism upheld by mainstream Japanese memory, amnesia persists about Micronesian and Polynesian casualties of what were, in terms of the environmental and epidemiological *longue durée*, effectively American and French nuclear attacks.

13. Edward W. Said, *Culture and Imperialism* (London: Chatto and Windus, 1992), 17; Michael J. Watts, *Struggles over Geography: Violence, Freedom, and Development at the Millennium* (Hettner Lectures no. 3, University of Heidelberg, Department of Geography, 2000), 8.

14. Faulkner's oft-misquoted remark appears in *Requiem for a Nun* (1951; repr., New York: Routledge, 1987), 17.

15. Anne McClintock, Aamir Mufti, and Ella Shohat, eds., *Dangerous Liaisons* (Minneapolis: University of Minnesota Press, 1997), 420–444.

16. For an astute examination of the impact of particulate residues on the timelines of environmental thinking—as well as on Victorian literary genres—see Jesse Oak Taylor's dissertation, "'A Sky of Our Manufacture': Literature, Modernity and the London Fog from Dickens to Conrad" (Ph.D. dissertation, University of Wisconsin-Madison, 2009).

17. Michael Crichton, *State of Fear* (New York: Avon, 2004), 626.

18. Rachel Carson, *Silent Spring* (1962; repr., Boston: Houghton Mifflin, 1992), 32.

19. Eric Sevareid, "An Explosive Book," *Washington D.C. Star*, October 9, 1962, 3.

20. Carson, *Silent Spring*, 238.

21. Johan Galtung, "Violence, Peace, and Peace Research," *Journal of Peace Research* 6 (1969): 167–191.

22. This is not the place for a full assessment of Galtung's prodigious writings about peace and violence. At a later point in his thinking, for instance, Galtung complicated his theory of structural violence by introducing the notion of cultural violence.

23. Wangari Maathai, *The Challenge for Africa* (New York: Pantheon, 2009), 83ff.

24. Jill S. Schneiderman, "Buddhist Living in the Anthropocene" (unpublished essay, 2010), 7. I am especially grateful to Schneiderman for a rich set of exchanges—including a comparison between Galtung's ideas and my own—in response to a talk I gave at Vassar College in 2008.

25. Ibid., 173.

26. In an indicative convergence of the tectonic shifts in geological thinking about speed and media technologies of speed, one notes that Crutzen first advanced his idea of the Anthropocene Age on his blog rather than going through the slower medium of a peer-reviewed academic journal ("The Anthropocene," http://www.mpch-mainz.mpg.de/~air/anthropocene/).

27. Will Steffen, Paul J. Crutzen, and John R. McNeill, "The Anthropocene: Are Humans Now Overwhelming the Great Forces of Nature?" *Ambio* 36 (2007): 618.

28. Libby Robin, "The Eco-humanities as Literature: A New Genre?" *Australian Literary Studies* 23 (2008): 290.

29. Cory Doctorow, "Writing in the Age of Distraction," *Locus Magazine*, January 7, 2009, http://www.locusmag.com/Features/2009/01/cory-doctorow-writing-in-age-of.html.

30. Quoted in Thomas Friedman, "The Age of Interruption," *New York Times*, July 5, 2006, A27.

31. "Vietnam in Retrospect," *New York Times*, March 23, 2003, A25.

32. Arnold Schecter et al., "Agent Orange and the Vietnamese: The Persistence of Elevated Dioxin Levels in Human Tissues," *American Journal of Public Health* 85 (1995): 516–522.

33. Janie Lorber, "Defoliant May Be Tied to New List of Illnesses," *New York Times*, July 25, 2009, A8.

34. George Perkins Marsh, *Man and Nature*, ed. David Lowenthal (1864; repr., Seattle: University of Washington Press, 2003), 15.

35. Leopold's address at the June 1934 dedication of the University of Wisconsin Arboretum, quoted in Scott Russell Sanders, "Speaking for the Land: Aldo Leopold as a Writer," author's personal Web site, http://www.scottrussellsanders .com/SRS%20entries/SRS_on_Leopold.htm. Leopold was inconsistent on this point, sometimes emphasizing an ethics of sensory immediacy grounded in local knowledge and sometimes emphasizing an intergenerational ethics less rooted in the moment or in a visible locale.

36. Mary Louise Pratt, *Imperial Eyes: Travel Writing and Transculturation* (New York: Routledge, 1992), 15–37.

37. See especially David Michaels, *Doubt is Their Product. How Industry's Assult on Science Threatens Your Health* (New York: Oxford University Press, 2008); Naomi Oreskes and Erik M. Conway, *Merchants of Doubt. How a Handful of Scientists obscured the Truth on Issues from Tobacco Smoke to Global Warming* (New York: Bloomsbury, 2010); and James Hoggan, *Climate Cover-Up. The Crusade to Deny Global Warming* (Vancouver: Greystone Books, 2009).

38. Here I am invoking John Brinckerhoff Jackson's distinction outlined in *Discovering the Vernacular Landscape* (New Haven, CT: Yale University Press, 1984). For a fine, nuanced interpretation of Jackson's insights in the context of American Indian literatures, see Joni Adamson, *American Indian Literature, Environmental Justice, and Ecocriticism: The Middle Place* (Tucson: University of Arizona Press, 2001), 90–92. The term "landscape" is of course a contentious one that has a vexed aesthetic and political history. It has been critiqued for implying an external stance toward the land rather than an immersion in place.

39. Annu Jalais, *Forest of Tigers: People, Politics and Environment in the Sundarban* (New Delhi: Routledge, 2010), 11.

40. John Berger, "Twelve Theses on the Economy of the Dead," in *Hold Everything Dear: Dispatches on Survival and Resistance* (New York: Pantheon, 2007), 4–5.

41. Although some of my conclusions about the viability of neoliberalism as an analytic tool are antithetical to hers, my thinking here was informed by a lecture by Karen Bakker, "The Limits of Neoliberal Nature" (Yi-Fu Tuan Lecture, University of Wisconsin, October 23, 2009).

42. Michael Pollan's *The Botany of Desire* (New York: Random House, 2001) mounts the argument that certain plants (species of apples, marijuana, and potatoes among them) have used humans to their advantage.

43. Robert Campbell, "Special Report: Deepwater Spills and Short Attention Spans," Reuters, June 14, 2010.

44. "Don Young: Gulf Oil Spill 'Not an Environmental Disaster,'" *Huffington Post*, June 6, 2010.

45. John Curry, quoted in Naomi Klein, "Gulf Oil Spill: A Hole in the World," *Guardian*, June 19, 2010, 7.

46. On the creation of dead zones, see congressional testimony by University of Georgia biogeochemist, Samantha Joye. http://www.nsf.gov/news/special_reports/science_nation/hiddenoilplumes.jsp

47. We should distinguish categorically between an attentiveness to deep time environmental changes and the hokiness of deep ecology, a movement permeated by misanthropy and at best indifferent, at worst hostile, to the environmentalism of the poor.

48. On resource omnivores, see especially Madhav Gadgil and Ramachandra Guha, *Ecology and Equity: The Use and Abuse of Nature in Contemporary India* (New York: Routledge, 1995), 177–178.

49. I completed my undergraduate degree—as a double major in English literature and African languages—without ever being required to read a single work of nonfiction, which was roundly disparaged as nonliterary. The days when professors viewed the novel and poetry as the imagination's soaring peaks and nonfiction as the valley of the shadow of death may be over, but nonfiction is still widely treated in literature departments as at best a subsidiary form.

50. I am aware that so-called biographical criticism has fallen out of favor. Yet it seems to me that biographical context often remains invaluable, especially (though not exclusively) when one is considering nonfiction.

51. Neither of Gordimer's immigrant parents went to university, and she herself never completed a degree.

52. Tambu is not given a last name in the novel.

53. Tsitsi Dangarembga, *Nervous Conditions* (London: Women's Press, 1988), 64.

54. Ibid., 58.

55. Jamaica Kincaid, *My Garden (Book)* (New York: Farrar, Straus and Giroux, 1999), 115.

56. Wai Chee Dimock remains the finest literary scholar on the subject of the unexpected imaginative connection that speaks across geographical and historical divides.

57. https://www.indymedia.ie/article/72983?author_name=T&condense_comments=false&userlanguage=ga&save_prefs=true. Irish activists also host an annual Ken Saro-Wiwa Memorial Seminar on resource struggles against the abuses of natural resources by corporate giants.

58. For a brilliant analysis of the way allegorical translation may inform environmental struggles cross-culturally, see Anna Lowenhaupt Tsing, *Friction: An Ethnography of Global Connection* (Princeton, NJ: Princeton University Press, 2005), 227–238.

59. On the integration of scientific theories into the environmental humanities and social sciences, see especially William M. Adams, "When Nature Won't Stay Still: Conservation, Equilibrium and Control," in *Decolonizing Nature: Strategies for Conservation in a Post-colonial Era*, ed. William M. Adams and Martin Mulligan (London: Earthscan, 2001), 220–246.

60. Within the general ecocritical indifference to social scientific scholarship, the most notable exception is the work on risk by the German sociologist, Ulrich Beck, which is receiving increasing attention. Among contemporary ecocritics, Pablo Mukherjee stands out as someone who has drawn creatively on disciplines that bridge the humanities and social sciences, most notably cultural geography and cultural anthropology.

61. Anne McClintock, *Imperial Leather* (New York: Routledge, 1995), 63. If ambivalence, irony, rupture, and hybridity are so pervasive, McClintock asks, how do the dominant powers become dominant in the first place; and how is power won and lost? What guarantees that some forms of power become dominant while others are subverted? Are the internal fissures in form and discourse just waiting to rupture from within, or is it the role of the critic (in an act of extreme professional self-regard) to facilitate such ruptures?

62. Ursula Heise, "Afterword," in *Postcolonial Green: Environmental Politics and World Narratives*, ed. Bonnie Roos and Alex Hunt (Athens: University of Georgia Press, forthcoming).

63. Wai Chee Dimock and Lawrence Buell, eds., *Shades of the Planet: American Literature as World Literature* (Princeton, NJ: Princeton University Press, 2007), 12. For an excellent example of such cross-border genre thinking, see Rachel Adams, "At the Borders of American Crime Fiction," in Dimock and Buell, *Shades of the Planet*, 249–273.

64. In the final chapter of this book, I elaborate on the implications of the belated engagement between postcolonial and ecocriticism, an engagement that has recently been energized from a variety of quarters.

65. Robert Vitalis, "Black Gold, White Crude: An Essay on American Exceptionalism, Hierarchy, and Hegemony in the Gulf," *Diplomatic History* 26 (Spring 2002): 187.

66. Greg Garrard, *Ecocriticism* (London: Routledge, 2004), 178.

67. Robert Vitalis, *America's Kingdom: Mythmaking on the Saudi Oil Frontier* (New York: Verso, 2008); Elizabeth DeLoughrey, "Heliotropes: Pacific Radiations and Wars of Light," in *Postcolonial Ecologies: Literatures of the Environment*, ed. Elizabeth DeLoughrey and George Handley (New York: Oxford University Press, 2010); and Susie O'Brien, "Survival Strategies for Global Times," *Interventions* 9 (2007): 83–98. DeLoughrey is particularly incisive on the transnational somatic, political, and imaginative fallout of American, British, and French

nuclear colonialism. For a rich engagement with transnational environmental literatures, see also *Postcolonial Ecologies*, ed. Elizabeth DeLoughrey and George Handley (New York: Oxford University Press, 2010).

68. Mike Davis, *Planet of the Slums* (New York: Verso, 2006), 72.

69. On grassroots globalization, see especially Al Gedicks, *Resource Rebels* (Boston: South End Press, 2001); Stuart Hall, "The Local and the Global: Globalization and Ethnicity," in *Culture, Globalization, and the World System*, ed. Anthony D. King (Minneapolis: University of Minnesota press, 1997), 1–21; and Arjun Appadurai, "Grassroots Globalization and the Research Imagination," in *Globalization*, ed. Arjun Appadurai (Durham, NC: Duke University Press, 2001), 1–29.

70. Anup Shah, "World Military Spending," Global Issues Web site, http://www.globalissues.org/article/75/world-militaryspendingInContextUSMilitarySpendingVersusRestoftheWorld.

71. George Lamming, *The Pleasures of Exile* (1960; repr., Ann Arbor: University of Michigan Press, 1991), 17.

72. Clearly, the problems of transnational answerability are not unique to the United States, but (until China's recent ascent) have assumed their most consequential form in relation to U.S. and Soviet military and economic foreign policy during the post–World War II era.

73. William Finnegan, "The Economics of Empire: Notes on the Washington Consensus," *Harper's*, May 1, 2003, 54.

74. Al Gedicks, *Resource Rebels* (Boston: South End Press, 2001). For a superb analysis of successful South-North alliances as well as the challenges they face, see Ashley Dawson, "Introduction: New Enclosures" (in a special issue he edited on Imperial Ecologies). *New Formations* 69 (2010), 8-22.

75. Anne McClintock, Ella Shohat, and Fernando Coronil, in particular, have put forward cogent arguments for the limitations of the term.

76. Wendell Berry, "Word and Flesh," in *What are People For?* (New York: North Point Press, 1990), 198.

77. For an economical, yet textured account of this alliance of doubt purveyors, see especially George Monbiot, *Heat. How to Stop the Planet From Burning* (Cambridge, Mass.: South End Press, 2007), 20-42.

78. Frank Luntz, "The Environment: A Cleaner, Safer, Healthier America" at http://reports.ewg.org/files/LuntzResearch_environment.pdf. Quoted Monbiot, *Heat*, 27.

79. This memo was put out by the tobacco company Brown and Williamson. As Monbiot documents, the tobacco industry and the oil majors have worked with the same public relations firm to generate similar strategies for disseminating doubt about the scientific consensus on, respectively, the health risks of smoking and the human causes of climate change. See anon, "Smoking and Health Proposal," Brown and Williamson document no. 680561778-1786 at http://legacy

.library.ucsf.edu/tid/nvs40foo/pdf;jsessionid=E0544FD253BBD9968FB57B01E6 3F9F6B.tobacco04. Quoted David Michaels, *Doubt is Their Product. How Industry's Assault on Science Threatens Your Health* (New York: Oxford University Press, 2008), p. 11.

80. Fanon, 38.

81. James Hoggan, *Climate Cover-Up. The Crusade to Deny Global Warming* (Vancouver: Greystone Books, 2009); Elizabeth Kolbert, *Field Notes from a Catastrophe: Man, Nature, and Climate Change* (New York: Bloomsbury, 2006); Naomi Oreskes and Erik M. Conway, *Merchants of Doubt. How a Handful of Scientists Obcured the Truth on Issues from Tobacco Smoke to Global Warming* (New York: Bloomsbury, 2010); Andrew Rowell, *Green Backlash. Global Subversion of the Environmental Movement* (London: Routledge, 1996); Tim Flannery, *The Weather Makers: How Man is Changing the Climate and What it Means for Life on Earth* (New York: Grove, 2001); Michaels, *Doubt is Their Product*; and Monbiot, *Heat*.

82. Matt Taibbi, "Taibbi's Takedown of 'Vampire Squid' Goldman Sachs," *Rolling Stone*, April 5, 2010, http://www.rollingstone.com/politics/story/28816321/inside _the_great_american_bubble_machine.

83. For a brilliant inquiry into the neglected field of public works in postcolonial literature, see Michael Rubenstein, *Public Works: Infrastructure, Irish Modernism, and the Postcolonial* (South Bend, IN: University of Notre Dame Press, 2010). Although his focus is Irish Modernism, Rubenstein's rich conceptual insights can be productively adapted to postcolonial literary studies at large.

84. Berger, "Undefeated Despair," 25.

85. Although the historical focus of Munif's novels *Cities of Salt* and *The Trench* stretches as far back as the 1930s, his perspective on the fallout from Saudi-U.S. petro-relations remains inflected by the geopolitics of the early to mid-1980s, when Munif was writing those two volumes of his oil quintet.

86. Sinha came to activism relatively late. He was (in his own words) an "accidental activist" whose commitments were triggered by two ad campaigns he devised for Amnesty International. Those campaigns raised funds for communities afflicted by two epochal acts of violence against the poor: Saddam Hussein's 1988 gas attacks on the Kurds and Union Carbide's 1984 gassing of Bhopal as a result of cost-cutting infrastructural neglect. Arguably, Sinha's professional training in the image world of advertising left him better equipped than most writer-activists of his generation to adapt his skills to the digital era.

1. Slow Violence, Neoliberalism, and the Environmental Picaresque

1. Raymond Williams, *Writing in Soci ety* (London: Verso, 1983), 238.

2. Quoted in Edward Soja, *Postmodern Geographies: Reassertions of Space in Critical Social Theory* (London: Verso, 1989), 22.

3. Raymond Williams, *Resources of Hope* (London: Verso, 1989), 115. Sinha has insisted that although *Animal's People* is fictional, every major event that happens in the novel occurred in Bhopal.

4. Like a number of picaresque novels, *Animal's People* simulates orality, in this case the technological orality of a series of tapes the narrator makes for a foreign "Jarnalis" in an effort to record (but retain command over) his story. Sinha also adapts another widespread feature of the picaresque, the readerly aside, addressed here to the anonymous "Eyes," suggestive of reader-as-voyeuristic-outsider. This strategy concentrates a core dilemma that the protagonist shares with Khaufpur's poor: a desire to be recognized by the world at large, to break free from invisibility, but a horror at the dehumanizing vertical dynamics of pity that such recognition typically entails.

5. In Don DeLillo's *White Noise* (New York: Penguin, 1998) we witness a shift toward a different mode of biological citizenship in the wake of an "airborne toxic event" (117). When Jack Gladney, a professor of Hitler studies, attempts to assess his survival prospects, a health technician responds with a battery of ambiguous computerized statistics: "It's what we call a massive data-base tally. Gladney, J. A. K. I punch in the name, the substance, the exposure time and then I tap into your computer history. Your genetics, your personals, your medicals, your psychologicals, your police-and-hospitals. It comes back pulsing stars. This doesn't mean anything is going to happen to you as such, at least not today or tomorrow. It just means you are the sum total of your data" (ibid., 141). Ironically, the toxic invasion of Gladney's body occasions a second invasion, of his privacy by the state. His sense of self is technologized—statistically expanded and humanly reduced—without him gaining, in exchange, any greater surety as to his survival prospects.

6. For the most detailed accounts of this widespread American argument, see T. R. Chouham, *Bhopal: The Inside Story* (New York: Apex, 1994); and Larry Everest, *Behind the Poison Cloud: Union Carbide's Bhopal Massacre* (Chicago: Banner, 1986).

7. Indra Sinha, "The Commonwealth Writers' Prize: A Dedication," http://www.indrasinha.com/blog?p=38.

8. William Finnegan, "The Economics of Empire: Notes on the Washington Consensus," *Harper's*, May 1, 2003, 41; Naomi Klein, *The Shock Doctrine: The Rise of Disaster Capitalism* (New York: Metropolitan, 2007), 163.

9. Adriana Petryna, *Life Exposed: Biological Citizens after Chernobyl* (Princeton, NJ: Princeton University Press, 2002), 1.

10. For a powerful, intimate account of the impact of the Chernobyl disaster on Belarus, see Hope Burwell, "Jeremiad for Belarus," in *The Future of Nature*, ed. Barry Lopez (Minneapolis: Milkweed, 2007), 78–90.

11. According to Petryna, by 2001, 50 percent of Ukraine's population was living below the poverty line (*Life Exposed*, 93).

12. Petryna notes that "present-day processes of recompense . . . were entangled with new patterns of inequality that themselves presented the most immediate issues of social injustice. The very framing of 'injury' now entailed the social and health costs associated with state and market transformations and emerging inequalities" (*Life Exposed*, 218).

13. Ibid., 78.

14. Ibid., 35.

15. Lorna Siggins, "Cúirt Takes Capitalism to Task on Climate Change," *Irish Times*, April 28, 2008, 12; Everest, *Behind the Poison Cloud*, 17.

16. Indra Sinha, *Animal's People* (London: Simon, 2007), 230. The forces playing for time include both Union Carbide leaders and certain high-ranking Indian government officials who are leery of alienating a prominent global corporation that they hope will continue to invest in India.

17. Eavan Boland, "Desolation Angel," *Village Voice*, February 6, 1996, SS11.

18. Anthony Lane, "Big Kills," *New Yorker*, June 30, 2000, 87.

19. Sinha had been struggling to find a satisfying voice and perspective for his novel "when a friend showed me some photographs from Bhopal. There was one of a young lad of about 19 who was on all fours because his back was so badly twisted, but he had a sort of cheeky look about him. And just seeing that, it was as if the character of Animal just leapt fully fledged into my head" ("The Accidental Activist," 11).

20. Sinha, *Animal's People*, 23.

21. Ibid., 78.

22. Petryna, *Life Exposed*, 30.

23. Ibid., 30.

24. Ibid., 3.

25. As Animal notes: "I was born a few days before that night, which no one wants to remember, but nobody can forget" (Sinha, *Animal's People*, 1). A preoccupation with making visible that which has been kept invisible and suppressed—not least the afflicted, forgotten poor themselves—recurs in the picaresque from the genre's beginnings.

26. The gold standard for literary discussions of toxic discourse remains the opening chapter of Lawrence Buell's *Writing for an Endangered World: Literature, Culture, and Environment in the U.S. and Beyond* (Cambridge, MA: Harvard University Press, 2001), 30–54.

27. Julia Kristeva, *Powers of Horror: An Essay on Abjection*, trans. L. S. Roudiez (New York: Columbia University Press, 1982), 5.

28. Ibid., 12.

29. For a fuller account of the economic context of the picaresque in the Span-ish Golden Age, see *The Picaresque: A Symposium on the Rogue's Tale*, ed. Car-men Benito-Vessels and Michael Zappala (Newark: University of Delaware Press, 1994); Giancarlo Maiorino, "Introduction: Renaissance Marginalities," in *The Picaresque: Tradition and Displacement*, ed. Giancarlo Maiorino (Minne-apolis: University of Minnesota Press, 1996), xi–xxviii; and Giancarlo Maiorino, "Picaresque Econopoetics: At the Watershed of Living Standards," in *The Picaresque*, 1–39.

30. Michel Serres, *The Parasite* (Baltimore, MD: Johns Hopkins University Press, 1982), 14.

31. In keeping with the picaresque fixation with sharp twists of fate, the novel achieves a comic resolution through marriage and sudden wealth, as Animal reveals that he has amassed enough secret savings to buy another member of the underclass, the prostitute Anjali, from her pimp and marry her.

32. *Animal's People* blends the picaresque with, among other genres, the zombie story, which is set in motion by the novel's opening words—"I was once human. So I'm told"—and culminating in Animal's drug-addled wanderings among hal-lucinations of the living dead. This calls to mind the Chernobyl worker who depicts himself as one of the "living dead": "Our memory is gone. You forget everything—we walk like corpses" (Sinha, *Animal's People*, 1, 3).

33. Maiorino, "Picaresque Econopoetics," xi.

34. Animal refuses, to the end, a surgical resolution to his penumbral, buckled sta-tus. He has his rationales. But by implication, at least, he has seen enough of humanity not to mistake an upright posture for a stance of moral rectitude. Sinha's strategy here is reminiscent of Günter Grass's in *The Tin Drum,* where his magic realist narrator of historical catastrophe, Oskar Matzerath, opts out of the "progress" narrative of childhood to adulthood and clings in protest to his diminutive stature. Both books somatize the antihumanist strains that per-meate them: Animal's and Oskar's bodies give physical testament to a convic-tion that, paradoxically, inhumanity ranks high among humanity's defining characteristics.

35. Sinha, *Animal's People*, 9.

36. Ibid., 185.

37. Ibid., 1, 214. Animal's Catholic adoptive mother (who after the disaster can only speak and comprehend French) also develops a tendency to babble apocalyptic portents that draw heavily on the Book of Revelation.

38. Ibid., 366.

39. Mike Davis, *Planet of the Slums* (New York: Verso, 2006), 206.

40. Michael Eric Dyson, *Come Hell or High Water: Hurricane Katrina and the Color of Disaster* (New York: Basic, 2006), 23.

41. Quoted in Jacob Weinberg, "An Imperfect Storm," *Slate*, September 7, 2005, 3. Here Dyson's argument is reminiscent of the case Mike Davis makes in *Late Victorian Holocausts: El Niño Famines and the Making of the Third World*. See also Naomi Klein's closely argued contention that "the idea of exploiting crisis and disaster has been the modus operandi of fundamentalist capitalism." *The Shock Doctrine: The Rise of Disaster Capitalism* (New York: Metropolitan, 2007), 9. "By the time Hurricane Katrina hit New Orleans, and the nexus of Republican politicians, think tanks and land developers started talking about 'clean sheets' and exciting opportunities, it was clear that this was now the preferred method of advancing corporate goals: using moments of collective trauma to engage in radical social and economic engineering" (ibid., 8).

42. See, for example, K. Gopalakrishnan, "Unskilled Worker Had Cleaned Tank," *Hindustan Times*, December 5, 1984, 1; and Archana Kumar, "Sirens Called Them to Death," *Hindustan Times*, December 5, 1984, 1.

43. Njabulo Ndebele, *Fine Lines from the Box: Further Thoughts about Our Country* (Roggebaai, South Africa: Umuzi, 2007), 137.

44. Environmental racism is alive and well in India, entangled as it is with discriminatory traditions of caste, class, gender, religion, and aboriginality. Arundhati Roy has been particularly vocal on this matter. See Roy in conversation with David Barsamian in *The Checkbook and the Cruise Missile: Conversations with Arundhati Roy* (Cambridge, MA: South End, 2004), 125–127.

45. See Ndebele, *Fine Lines*, 137. In contemporary South Africa this failure notoriously manifested itself in the Mbeki government's calamitous mixture of equivocation and denial regarding the causes of HIV/AIDS. One outraged commentator condemned the resultant mass deaths as "genocide by sloth."

46. Sinha, "The Accidental Activist," 11.

47. Sinha, *Animal's People*, 283.

48. Ibid., 92.

49. The character Shambhu is "a twice-victim of the Kampani. He had breathed the poisons of that night, plus the wells in his neighborhood were full of poisons leaked from the factory" (Sinha, *Animal's People*, 147). Sinha's account of this second, delayed hazard transmitted through well water recalls Rachel Carson's elegiac evocation of the poisoning of formerly pristine wells: "many man-made chemicals act in much the same way as radiation; they lie long in the soil, and enter into living organisms, passing from one to another. Or they may travel mysteriously by underground streams, emerging to combine, through the alchemy of air and sunlight, into new forms, which kill vegetation, sicken cattle, and work unknown harm on those who drink from once pure wells." Rachel Carson, *Silent Spring*, (1962; repr., Boston: Houghton Mifflin, 1992), 23–24.

50. Here I am adapting the term "ecosystem people" from Ramachandra Guha and Juan Martinez-Alier, *Varieties of Environmentalism* (London: Earthscan, 1997), 12–13.

51. Ulrich Beck, *Risk Society: Toward a New Modernity*, trans. Mark Ritter (London: Sage, 1992), 72.

52. Animal gives focus to these category leakages when he reflects on his beating at the hands of the police: "Neither Christian am I nor Hindu nor Muslim, not Brahmin nor Sufi nor saint, neither man am I nor beast. I don't know what is being beaten here. If they kill me what will die?" (Sinha, *Animal's People*, 313).

53. Key figures within the Indian government were complicit in this sleight of hand, as they were reluctant to alienate a global powerhouse like Dow and hoped it would continue to invest in India.

54. Sinha, *Animal's People*, 306.

55. Ibid., 185.

56. Carson, *Silent Spring*, 2–3.

57. Ibid., 8.

58. Sinha, *Animal's People*, 306.

59. Petryna, *Life Exposed*, 216.

60. Mike Davis, "Los Angeles after the Storm: The Dialectic of Ordinary Disaster," *Antipode* 27 (1995): 221–241.

61. Iain Boal et al., *Afflicted Powers: Capital and Spectacle in a New Age of War* (New York: Verso, 2005), 31.

62. The authenticity or realism of his animalized urchin voice is of no relevance here. Sinha's novel is such a patently hybrid mix of picaresque, magic realist, social realist, gothic, zombie, and apocalyptic narrative strategies that questions of authenticity evaporate. It is the subversive charisma and page-turning urgency of Animal's voice that matter, not whether real urchins speak like that in Bhopal (which, after all, is an inspiration for but hardly identical to Khaufpur).

63. Witness Nisha's tirade against the Kampani: "My father's precious justice is of no use, our government's of no use, appeals to humanity are no use, because these people are not human, they're animals" (Sinha, *Animal's People*, 332). On hearing this, Animal balks at Nisha's speciesism, which he reads as insulting to animals by debasing them to the level of humans.

64. Anon, *Lazarillo de Tormes*. Trans. Michael Alpert (Baltimore: Penguin, 1969), 23.

2. Fast-forward Fossil

1. For the title to this chapter, I am indebted to Ellen Driscoll's 2009 exhibit "Fast-ForwardFossil," a floor-sized environmental sculpture composed of recycled

plastic milk cartons that the artist harvested from dumps. Amalgamating features from three oil-drilling sites—the Niger Delta, the Alberta tar sands, and the North Sea—the exhibit creates a composite, subsiding landscape littered with abandoned oil derricks, sink holes, shattered trees, teetering houses, a gallows, and some empty cages. I read the salvaged plasticity of Driscoll's disposable landscape as the artist's way of giving imaginative shape to the slow violence of hydrocarbon time, past and future. The translucence of the recycled milk cartons—their material ghostliness—gives the sculpture an eerie, suspended quality that feels both elegiac and premonitory. http://www.youtube
.com/watch?v=q38bGDNWKQw

2. Although thinking about the resource curse began to take shape in the 1980s, Richard M. Auty's *Sustaining Development in Mineral Economies: The Resource Curse Thesis* (London: Routledge, 1993) proved decisive in giving the field a memorable catch phrase and a depth of analysis it had previously lacked. The literature on the resource curse is by now immense. For some useful overviews of the issues at stake, see *Escaping the Resource Curse*, ed. Macartan Humphreys, Jeffrey D. Sachs, and Joseph E. Stiglitz (New York: Columbia University Press, 2007); and Michael T. Klare, *Resource Wars: The New Landscape of Global Conflict* (New York: Metropolitan Books, 2001).

3. Antony Anghie, *Sovereignty, Imperialism and the Making of International Law* (Cambridge, UK: Cambridge University Press, 2007), 114–137. I am grateful to Adom Getachew for alerting me to Anghie's work and for encouraging me to clarify this point.

4. William Reno, *Warlord Politics and African States* (Boulder, CO: Lynne Rienner, 1999), 7.

5. Ryzsard Kapuscinski, *The Shah of Shahs*, trans. William R. Brand and Katarzyna Mroczkowska-Brand (New York: Vintage, 1985), 36.

6. Quoted in Fernando Coronil, *The Magical State: Nature, Money, and Modernity in Venezuela* (Chicago: University of Chicago Press, 1997), 1.

7. U.S. Census Bureau, *U.S. International Trade in Goods and Services, December 2009*, February 2010, http://www.census.gov/foreign-trade/Press-Release/2009 pr/12/.

8. Peter Maas, "The Ministry of Oil Defense," *Foreign Policy*, August 5, 2010, http://www.foreignpolicy.com/articles/2010/08/05/the_ministry_of_oil_defense.

9. Amitav Ghosh, "Petrofiction," *New Republic*, March 2, 1992, 29–34.

10. Despite some expansive excursions into the Russian Revolution and World War I, Sinclair's oil novel does not engage the international ties that have come to dominate the story of petroleum and, above all, the fraught bonds between the United States and the Middle East. The reasons for this silence are obvious: Sinclair published *Oil!* before any American petroleum corporation had signed a

concessionary agreement with a Gulf sheik and before the State of Israel existed. Arguably the most ambitious U.S. oil novel since Sinclair's is Linda Hogan's *Mean Spirit* (New York: Ivy Books, 1991). Set during the 1920s conflict over oil-rich Osage tribal lands in Oklahoma, *Mean Spirit* is informed by many of the "resource curse" concerns that animate the writings of both Munif and Saro-Wiwa.

11. Abdelrahman Munif's name sometimes also appears as Abd al-Rahman Munif. For consistency, I have deployed the former throughout, as it is the version of his name used in Peter Theroux's English translation.

12. For Leopold's land ethic, see his posthumously published *A Sand County Almanac* (1949; repr., New York: Oxford University Press, 2001), 59–73.

13. Aldo Leopold, "Game and Wild Life Conservation," *Condor* 34 (1932): 103.

14. Jacques Attali, *Millennium; Winners and Losers in the Coming Order* (New York: Three Rivers Press, 1992), 7. For a thoughtful essay on the indiscriminate use of the nomadic trope in contemporary theory, see Mokhtar Ghambou, "A Critique of Post/Colonial Nomadism," *Journal X* 6 (2001): 63–77.

15. Munif, quoted in David Gilmour, "Desert Ruritania," *New York Review of Books*, March 26, 1992, 19.

16. Bertolt Brecht, "An die Nachgeborenen (To posterity)," in *Selected Poems*, trans. H. R. Hays (New York: Grove Press, 1959), 177.

17. Sabry Hafez provides a fuller overview of Munif's life and works in his exemplary essay, "An Arabian Master," *New Left Review* 37 (January/February 2006): 39–67. See also Rasheed El-Enany, "*Cities of Salt*: A Literary View of the Theme of Oil and Change in the Gulf," in *Arabia and the Gulf: From Traditional Society to Modern States*, ed. Ian Richard Netton (London: Croom Helm, 1986), 213–222; and Ellen McLarney, "Empire of the Machine": Oil in the Arabic Novel," *Boundary 2* 2009 36 (2): 177–198.

18. Quoted in Hafez, "An Arabian Master," 43.

19. In Iskander Habash, "Unpublished Munif Interview: Crisis in the Arab World—Oil, Political Islam, and Dictatorship," *Al Jadid Magazine* 9 (2003): 3.

20. For Munif's belief in the instrumental role of literature as a form of resistance and a way of reclaiming the past, see especially Sonja Mejcher Atassi, "Writing—A Tool for Change: Abd Al-Rahman Munif," http://web.mit/edu/cis/www/mitejmes.

21. For Munif's reflections on his turn from organizational activism to (in his view) the more limited spheres of activism open to the public intellectual and writer, see Abdel Razzaq Takriti, "Writing—a Tool for Change," review of *Abdel Rahman Munif wal Iraq: Sira wa Dhikrayat*, ed. Maher Jarrar, *MIT Electronic Journal of Middle East Studies* 7 (Spring 2007), http://web.mit/edu/cis/www/mitejmes.

22. Interview in *Banipal*, October 1998, quoted in Hafez, "An Arabian Master," 47. The 1967 defeat reverberated for Munif, as for many Arabs, with the

humiliations suffered during the 1948 *nakbah*. A teenager at that time, Munif felt the shockwaves of the 1948 defeat closely as refugees poured into his hometown of Amman and transformed it. Munif testifies in the latter pages of his memoir how a young soldier, an Iraqi relative, made a lasting impression on him. The soldier passed through town twice: once as an exuberant young soldier en route to driving back the Zionists and then a second time as an angry, disillusioned member of the shambolic Arab retreat. Munif, *A Story of a City: A Childhood in Amman*, trans. Samira Kawar (London: Quartet, 1996), 275–307.

23. Habash, "Unpublished Interview," 3.

24. Although Munif's books would be banned in Saudi Arabia (and elsewhere in the region), the Saudis revoked his citizenship on political grounds some years before he turned to writing.

25. Many of his essays were infused with political polemic; others, however, addressed his great cultural passions, not least for the extensive traditions of Arab visual art, music, and architecture.

26. Habash, "Unpublished Munif Interview," 3.

27. Ibid., 4.

28. Amiri Baraka (formerly LeRoi Jones), "The Changing Same: (R&B and the New Black Music)," in *Black Music* (New York: W. Morrow, 1967), 11.

29. Indeed, the foreign oil-hunters try to camouflage their quest as a search for further water, but the locals are water-wise enough to suspect a ruse because the Americans are looking in the wrong places.

30. Abdelrahman Munif, *Cities of Salt*, trans. Peter Theroux (New York: Vintage, 1984), 86.

31. Retort, *Afflicted Powers: Capital and Spectacle in a New Age of War* (London: Verso, 2005), 75.

32. Fernando Coronil, *The Magical State: Nature, Money, and Modernity in Venezuela* (Chicago: University of Chicago Press, 1997), 7.

33. Ibid., 9.

34. Quoted Robert Vitalis, *America's Kingdom: Mythmaking on the Saudi Oil Frontier* (London: Verso, 2009), 31.

35. Wm. Roger Louis and Ronald Robinson, "The Imperialism of Decolonization," *Journal of Imperial and Commonwealth History* 22 (1994): 462–511.

36. Munif, *Cities of Salt*, 1.

37. Ibid., 86.

38. Ibid., 98.

39. Ibid., 106

40. Robert Vitalis provides the most detailed, incisive account of the Jim Crow practices of American oil corporations in Saudi Arabia. See *America's Kingdom*, 88–120.

41. Munif, *Cities of Salt*, 295.

42. Here I am in accord with Ghosh ("Petrofictions"), Hafez ("An Arabian Master"), and McLarney ("Empire of the Machine") who all remark upon Munif's overly romantic pursuit of a prior authenticity.

43. Shepard Krech III, *The Ecological Indian: Myth and History* (New York: Norton, 2000). For a particularly insightful response to this work, see Annette Kolodny, "Rethinking 'The Ecological Indian': A Penobscot Precursor," *Interdisciplinary Studies in Literature and the Environment* 14 (2007): 12–31. See also Greg Garrard's incisive reflections on assumed native environmental virtue in *Ecocriticism* (London: Routledge, 2004), 120–127.

44. See, for example, Munif's account of how "the people of this immense, harsh desert were born, lived and died in a grim natural cycle" (*Cities of Salt*, 161).

45. Ghosh is especially insightful on Munif's failure to give definition or interiority to the foreign workers, Asian and Middle Eastern, who are lured to Harran. See Ghosh, "Petrofictions," 34.

46. Michael Upchurch, "Abdelrahman Munif Interview: Mixing It Up with Oil, Politics, and Fiction," *Glimmer Train* 11 (1994): 69.

47. James Clifford, *Routes: Travel and Translation in the Late Twentieth Century* (Cambridge, MA: Harvard University Press, 1997).

48. Munif, *Cities of Salt*, 10.

49. John Updike, "Satan's Work and Silted Cisterns," in *Odd Jobs: Essays and Criticism* (New York: Knopf, 1991), 563–570.

50. In conversation, June 10, 2007.

51. Updike, "Satan's Work," 566. Munif is imaginatively seeking to enter into the mindsets of Bedouin characters who, for religious and imperial historical reasons, remain profoundly suspicious of the motives of foreigners. Munif himself has long been on record as an opponent of what he calls political Islam, whether embodied by the Ayatollah Khomeini or by the politicized Islamic movements that America frequently helped foment and fund during the cold war as a perceived counterweight to communism.

52. Ibid., 563.

53. Ibid., 563–564.

54. Ibid., 565.

55. John Updike, *Self-Consciousness* (New York: Fawcett, 1990), 37. Whatever Updike's strengths as a writer, he didn't possess any instinct for transnational imaginings, as evidenced by what is inarguably his most feeble novel, *The Terrorist*.

56. Munif, *Cities of Salt*, 367.

57. Munif's sense of how easily place and history can be irreparably fractured calls to mind sentiments that Czeslow Milosz voices in *The Captive Mind*. As a Pole, through historical hardship, Milosz learned that what he calls the "natural" social and environmental order can be irreversibly undone at high speed.

On arriving in the United States, he was startled by the widespread American assumption that the world they inhabited would "naturally" continue more or less the same. Milosz read this assumption as an imaginative shortcoming born of historical amnesia and geographical isolation. See Milosz, *The Captive Mind*, trans. Jane Zielonko (New York: Penguin, 1980), 25–30.

58. I am grateful to Samer Alatout for elucidating this meaning of 'al-Tih in conversation, June 6, 2009.

59. Vitalis, "Crossing Exceptionalism's Frontier," 12.

60. William E. Mulligan Papers, quoted in Vitalis, "Black Gold," 205.

61. Patrick Flynn, "What It Means to Work for ARAMCO," manuscript from 1984, box 11, folder 32, William E. Mulligan Papers, Special Collections Division, Lauinger Library, Georgetown University, Washington, DC. Quoted in Vitalis, *America's Kingdom*, xi. Wallace Stegner, more ambiguous about his role as cheerleader for American corporate expansionism, nonetheless buys into a glossy magazine Orientalism: "This was Arabia as a romantic imagination might have created it; nights so mellow that they lay out under the scatter of dry bright stars, and heard the silence beyond their fire as if the whole desert hung listening. Physically, it might have been Arizona or New Mexico, with its flat crestlines, its dry clarity of air its silence. But it felt more mysterious than that; and the faces of soldiers and guide and interpreter, dark, bearded, gleaming in teeth and eye as they spoke or laughed, corroborated Hamilton's sense that this was authentic Arabia, hardly touched by the West." Wallace Stegner, *Discovery! The Search for Arabian Oil* (1971; repr., Portola St. Vista, CA: Selwa Press, 2007), 15.

62. Quoted in Aaron David Miller, *Search for Security: Saudi Arabian Oil and American Foreign Policy, 1939–1949* (Chapel Hill: University of North Carolina Press, 1980), 200.

63. Updike, "Satan's Work," 565.

64. Jennifer Wenzel, "Petro-magic-realism: Toward a Political Ecology of Nigerian Literature," *Postcolonial Studies* 9 (2006): 449–464. Genres are of course never pure or absolute, but in terms of the mingled strands in Munif's quintet, historical epic and satire are more prominent than magic realism.

65. Munif, *Cities of Salt*, 140–141.

66. Of course, the predominantly oral Bedouin community will have encountered writing before. However, what distinguishes the Americans is the way they write and how their writing is ritually enfolded into the customary shape of their strange days.

67. Munif, *Cities of Salt*, 45.

68. John Brinckerhoff Jackson, *Discovering the Vernacular Landscape* (New Haven, CT: Yale University Press, 1984).

69. Munif, *Cities of Salt*, 545.

70. Abdelrahman Munif, *The Trench*, trans. Paul Theroux (New York: Vintage, 1993), 479.

71. John Berger, "Stones," in *Hold Everything Dear: Dispatches on Survival and Resistance* (New York: Pantheon, 2007), 69.

72. Tim Flannery, *The Future Eaters: An Ecological History of the Australasian Lands and Peoples* (New York: Grove Press, 2002).

73. Upton Sinclair, *Oil!* (1927; repr., New York: Penguin, 2007), 527. Despite their many differences, Munif, like Sinclair, was a great observer of the technologies of power—and of crowd power and worker insurrections.

74. Human Development Index compiled by United Nations Development Program. http://lib.stat.cmu.edu/datasets/humandevel.

75. Michael J. Watts, "Violent Geographies: Speaking the Unspeakable and the Politics of Space," *City and Society* 8 (2001): 88.

76. Abdelrahman Munif, "Other Voices—Saudi Bomb Attack an Act of Despair," trans. Peter Theroux, *Jinn Magazine* (Pacific News Service) 2 (June 30–July 2, 1996): 7.

77. Quoted in Tariq Ali, "Farewell to Munif: A Patriarch of Arab Literature," *Counterpunch*, January 31/February 1, 2004, http://www.counterpunch.org/ali0131 2004.html.

78. Munif, "Other Voices," 7.

79. Ibid.

80. Ibid.

81. Hafez, "An Arabian Master," 58.

82. Stegner, *Discovery*. The fifteen-year delay between Stegner's submission of the book and its publication is attributable to concerns within Aramaco that it might upset relations with the House of Saud. That said, *Discovery* is, for the most part, hell-bent on defending both the idea of American exceptionalism and the honorable role the American oil corporation played in Saudi uplift.

83. Ibid., xvi.

84. Ibid., xxix, xxx, xxvi.

85. Ibid., xvii.

86. Abdelrahman Munif, *Ul-Khalij*, November 21, 1984, 10. Quoted in Rasheed El-Enany, "Cities of Salt: A Literary View of the Theme of Oil and Change in the Gulf," in *Arabia and the Gulf: From Traditional Society to Modern States*, ed. Ian Richard Netton (London: Croom Helm, 1986), 220.

87. Quoted in Tariq Ali, "Farewell to Munif."

88. Munif also laments the absence of fundamental rights in Saudi Arabia and, above all, the third-class status of Saudi women that he argues has profound repercussions for Saudi dignity and belonging.

3. Pipedreams

1. Ken Saro-Wiwa, *A Month and a Day: A Detention Diary* (London: Penguin, 1995).

2. Quoted in Richard Synge, "Ken Saro-Wiwa: An Obituary," *Independent (London)*, November 11, 1995, 20.

3. Ken Saro-Wiwa, "Prison Letter," *Mail and Guardian (Johannesburg)*, November 11, 1995, 1.

4. William Boyd, "Death of a Writer," *New Yorker*, November 27, 1995, 53.

5. Ken Saro-Wiwa, *Genocide in Nigeria: The Ogoni Tragedy* (Port Harcourt, Nigeria: Saros, 1992), 9.

6. Saro-Wiwa repeatedly uses the terms "recolonization" and "indigenous colonialism" to describe relations between Nigerian regimes that have favored the three major ethnic groups and violently suppressed the rights and claims of extreme minorities like the Ogoni. See, for example, *Genocide in Nigeria*, 20; and *Nigeria: The Brink of Disaster* (Port Harcourt, Nigeria: Saros, 1991), 71.

7. Saro-Wiwa, *A Month and a Day*, 131.

8. Quoted in Saro-Wiwa, *Genocide in Nigeria*, 19. On the problems bequeathed by the colonial invention of Nigeria, see also *Nigeria: The Brink of Disaster*, 45–46.

9. For a fuller description of the beginnings of the Nigerian petroleum industry, see Michael Watts, "Sweet and Sour," in *Curse of the Black Gold: Fifty Years of Oil in the Niger Delta,* ed. Michael Watts (New York: Powerhouse, 2008), 36.

10. Watts, "Sweet and Sour," 43.

11. This clause referred to revenue generated by both mineral sales and mining rents. See Saro-Wiwa, *Genocide in Nigeria*, 21.

12. Even that figure exaggerates the amount they have received, for most of the 1.5 percent has been unilaterally "borrowed" by the powerful states where the Yoruba, the Igbo, and the Hausa-Fulani are in the majority.

13. David Wheeler, "Blood on British Business Hands," *New Statesman and Society*, November 17, 1995, 14.

14. Robert Vitalis, "Black Gold, White Crude: An Essay on American Exceptionalism, Hierarchy, and Hegemony in the Gulf," *Diplomatic History* 16 (Spring 2002): 186.

15. Al Gedicks, *Resource Rebels* (Boston: South End Press, 2001), 49.

16. Quoted by Claude Ake, in an interview with Andrew Rowell, *Green Backlash: Global Subversion of the Environmental Movement* (London: Routledge, 1996), 27.

17. For the most authoritative account of the events leading up to these killings, see Human Rights Watch/Africa, *Nigeria: The Ogoni Crisis—A Case-Study of Military Repression in Southeastern Nigeria, Human Rights Watch/Africa* 7, no. 5 (1995), esp. 7–25. See also Andy Rowell, "Trouble Flares in the Delta of Death," *Guardian*, November 8, 1995, 10; and Rowell, "Shell Shocked," *Village Voice*, November 21, 1995, 21.

18. Sam Bakilo Bako, quoted in Saro-Wiwa, *Genocide in Nigeria*, 58.

19. Panedom Badom, quoted ibid., 66.

20. Oamen Enaholo, quoted ibid., 79.

21. David Wheeler, "Blood on British Business Hands," *New Statesman and Society*, November 17, 1995, 14.

22. Saro-Wiwa argues that the African writer ought to be *l'homme engage* in *A Month and a Day*, 81.

23. Ken Saro-Wiwa, *Sozaboy: A Novel Written in Rotten English* (Port Harcourt, Nigeria: Saros, 1985). For a discussion of Saro-Wiwa's use of dialect, see Chantal Zabus, "Mending the Schizo-Text: Pidgin in the Nigerian Novel," *Kunapipi* 14 (1992): 119–127; and Willfried F. Feuser, "The Voice from Dukana: Ken Saro-Wiwa," *Matatu* 1 (1987): 49–57.

24. For Saro-Wiwa's own reflections on this experience, see Ken Saro-Wiwa, "A Television Drama in Nigeria: A Personal Experience" (paper presented at the African Literature Association Conference in Pittsburgh, April 1988).

25. Saro-Wiwa, *Nigeria: The Brink of Disaster*, 118.

26. This is not, of course, to suggest that all Saro-Wiwa's multigeneric output was overtly instrumental, just that a considerable body of his writing, particularly his nonfiction, was expressly so. See, for example, his insistence that "literature in a critical situation such as Nigeria's cannot be divorced from politics. Indeed, literature must serve society by steeping itself in politics, by intervention. . . . [Writers] must play an interventionist role . . . The writer must be *l'homme engage*: the intellectual man of action." Quoted in Charles R. Larson, ed., *Under African Skies* (New York: Farrar, Straus and Giroux, 1997), 210.

27. The traditions of socialism were never as prominent in Anglophone West Africa as they were in Southern and East Africa, not least because West Africa was more shallowly colonized than Kenya, South Africa, Zimbabwe, Namibia, Mozambique, and Angola. West Africa was thus spared the ravaging anticolonial wars in which the goals of decolonization and socialism typically converged.

28. Ngugi wa Thiong'o, *Barrel of a Pen: Resistance to Repression in Neo-colonial Kenya* (Trenton, NJ: Africa World Press, 1983); Mafika Gwala, "Writing as a Cultural Weapon," in *Momentum: On Recent South African Writing*, ed. M. J. Daymond, J. U. Jacobs and Margaret Lenta (Pietermaritzburg, South Africa: Natal University Press, 1984), 37–44.

29. Cited in Aaron Sachs, "Eco Justice: Linking Human Rights and the Environment," (Washington, DC: Worldwatch Paper 127, 1995), 53.

30. David C. Korten, *When Corporations Rule the World* (London: Earthscan, 1995), 124.

31. Saro-Wiwa, *Genocide in Nigeria*, 7.

32. Saro-Wiwa, *A Month and a Day*, 88.

33. Ibid., 88.

34. Ken Saro-Wiwa, interviewed on *Without Walls: The Hanged Man—Nigeria's Shame*, Channel 4 (UK), November 15, 1995.

35. Saro-Wiwa, *A Month and a Day*, 79.

36. Ibid., 94.

37. Ibid., 183.

38. Ibid., 73.

39. The phrase "judicial murder" was coined by then British prime minister John Major. See Michael Homan, "Commonwealth Challenge," *Financial Times*, November 13, 1995, 18.

40. *A Month and a Day*, 165.

41. Bob Herbert, "Unholy Alliance in Nigeria," *New York Times*, January 26, 1996, A27.

42. For Saro-Wiwa's insistence that corporate racism and Nigerian domestic colonialism are equally at fault, see *Without Walls*. He also makes this case in both *Genocide in Nigeria* (8, 82) and *A Month and a Day* (18, 73, 186–188).

43. Greenpeace International, *Shell Shocked: The Environmental and Social Costs of Living with Shell in Nigeria* (Amsterdam: Greenpeace International, 1994), 9. See also Rob Nixon, "The Oil Weapon," *New York Times*, November 17, 1995, A31.

44. Saro-Wiwa, *A Month and a Day*, 170.

45. On the flaring, see Nick Aston-Jones, in Rowell, *Green Backlash*, 291; Ike Okonta and Oronto Douglas, *Where Vultures Feast: Shell, Human Rights, and Oil* (London: Verso, 2003); and Michael Watts, "Black Gold, White Heat: State Violence, Local Resistance and the National Question in Nigeria," in *Geographies of Resistance*, ed. Steve Pile and Michael Keith (London: Routledge, 1997), 53.

46. Robert J. C. Young, "Dangerous and Wrong: Shell, Intervention and the Politics of Transnational Companies," *Interventions* 1 (1999): 457.

47. Saro-Wiwa, *Genocide in Nigeria*, 82.

48. Rowell, "Trouble Flares in the Delta of Death," 11.

49. The Igbo dream of creating an independent secessionist nation called Biafra would not have been viable without the sea of oil beneath the Niger Delta, which they included in their projected Biafra. The prospect of losing that oil wealth intensified the ferocity of the Hausa-Yoruba response to the secessionists.

50. Saro-Wiwa, *A Month and a Day*, 187.

51. Ken Saro-Wiwa, *On a Darkling Plain: An Account of the Nigerian Civil War* (Lagos, Nigeria: Saros, 1989), 29. See also Saro-Wiwa, *Genocide in Nigeria*, 87–88.

52. Saro-Wiwa, *Genocide in Nigeria*, 7. The neocolonial rapport between the Nigerian leadership and the oil companies may be illustrated by the case of Philip Asiodu, a Nigerian director of Chevron. Asiodu has reassured investors, "Given the small size and population of the oil-producing areas, it is not cynical to

observe that even if the resentments of oil producing states continue, they cannot threaten the stability of the country nor affect its continued economic development" (quoted in Saro-Wiwa, *Genocide in Nigeria*, 87). Before becoming a director of Chevron, Asiodu had held a prominent post in Nigeria's Federal Ministry of Mines and Power. Nor is he the only such crossover figure: the Abacha regime and the transnationals held the delta micro-minorities in similar contempt, treating them principally as impediments to personal fortune.

53. Jonathan Freedland, "American Blacks on Nigeria," *Guardian*, March 26, 1996, 5.

54. Saro-Wiwa, *A Month and a Day*, 188.

55. See, for example, his interview on *Without Walls* in which he called for economic sanctions and Nigeria's expulsion from the United Nations. He argued that "[t]he military governments of Nigeria have sat on other Nigerians in a way that is just as evil as what was done in South Africa."

56. General Sani Abacha and his military regime annulled the democratic elections of November 1993 and imprisoned president-elect Mashood Abiola and other internal opposition leaders on trumped up charges of treason. In July 1995, former president Olusegun Obasanjo and forty other opponents of the regime were convicted and sentenced to death. After an international outcry, these sentences were commuted to life in July 1995. Four months later, another of Abacha's kangaroo courts condemned Saro-Wiwa and the Ogoni Eight to hang.

57. Mandela's stance echoed that of his first deputy, Thabo Mbeki, who had visited Nigeria in July 1995, and failing to dissuade Abacha from his hardline course had nonetheless concluded that "[w]e need a more equal relationship. Western countries must accept the capacity of African countries to set an African agenda." Quoted in "Too Gentle Giant," *Economist*, November 18, 1995, 42.

58. "Pretoria Blunders as Nigeria Burns," *Mail and Guardian (Johannesburg)*, November 11, 1995, 3

59. Rahana Rossouw, "You Can't Blame Mandela," *Mail and Guardian (Johannesburg)*, November 17, 1995, 17.

60. Robert Block, "When Mandela Went Missing," *Independent*, November 21, 1995, 17.

61. Quoted in Steve Crawshaw and James Robers, "Pressure Mounts for Nigeria Oil Ban," *Independent*, November 13, 1995, 1.

62. "Where Oppression Has No Tribe," *New Statesman and Society*, November 17, 1991, 15.

63. Peter Vale, quoted in Robert Block, "When Mandela Went Missing," *Independent*, November 21, 1995, 17.

64. Piqued by South African condemnations of Nigeria after Saro-Wiwa and the Ogoni Eight were executed, Abacha barred the national soccer team (and African champions at the time), the Eagles, from participating in the African Cup

of Nations in South Africa. The symbolic import of this competition, contested by fifty-two African nations, can scarcely be overestimated: throughout Africa it is the premier event on the sporting calendar. The Eagles' inability to defend their title (and South Africa's ensuing victory) became a deep source of national mourning in Nigeria and the surest mark of the country's growing isolation.

65. This ad was placed by the Philippine government in *Fortune* in 1975. Quoted in Korten, *When Corporations Rule the World*, 159.

66. See Eyal Press, "Freeport-McMoran at Home and Abroad," *The Nation*, July 31, 1995, 125; Warren St. John, "Last Resort," *Lingua Franca*, November/December, 1993: 15–17; Aidan Rankin, "Primitive? Then What Are We?" *Independent (London)*, January 17, 1996, 16.

67. Quoted in Rankin, "Primitive," 16.

68. Ibid.

69. For two powerful accounts of the battle over the Oriente, see Judith Kimerling, *Amazon Crude* (San Francisco: National Resources Defense Council, 1991); and Joe Kane, *Savages* (New York: Alfred Knopf, 1995).

70. Rick Bass, quoted in Kimerling, *Amazon Crude*, iv.

71. Quoted in Robert D. Kaplan, *The Ends of the Earth: A Journey at the Dawn of the 21st Century* (New York: Random House, 1996), 63.

72. David Orr, "Shell Wins Over Village with Cash and Liquor," *Independent (London)*, December 1, 1995, 18.

73. Joseph Conrad, *Heart of Darkness* (1899; repr., New York: Signet, 1978), 99.

74. Saro-Wiwa, *Genocide in Nigeria*, 91.

75. James Ferguson, "Seeing Like an Oil Company: Space, Security, and Global Capital in Neoliberal Africa," *American Anthropologist*, 107 (September 2005): 380.

76. Quoted in Cameron Duozu, "Cry the Beloved Country," *Observer*, November 12, 1995, 24.

77. Quoted John Berger, *Hold Everything Dear*, 66.

78. Donatella Lorch, "Is Kenya Sliding Back Toward Repression?" *New York Times*, October 29, 1995, 3.

79. Ian Black, "Nigeria Defies World With Writer's Judicial Murder," *Guardian (London)*, November, 11, 1995, 1.

80. Ibid.

81. Watts, "Sweet and Sour," 37.

82. Ken Wiwa, *In the Shadow of a Saint: A Son's Journey to Understand His Father's Legacy* (South Royalton, VT: Steerforth Press, 2001), 251.

83. Ibid., 148.

84. Ibid., 180.

85. Jad Mouawad, "Shell Agrees to Settle Abuse Case," *New York Times*, June 9, 2009, B1, B5; "Spilling Over," *Economist*, June 11, 2009, 23.

86. Ken Saro-Wiwa, *Genocide in Nigeria*, 91.

87. Mouawad, "Shell Agrees to Settle Abuse Case," B5.

88. Okonta and Douglas, *Where Vultures Feast*, 204.

89. Ibid., 163.

90. Watts, *Curse of the Black Gold*, 197.

91. Mouawad, "Shell Agrees to Settle Abuse Case," B5.

92. Okonta and Douglas, *Where Vultures Feast,* 112.

93. Quoted in Watts, *Curse of the Black Gold*, 217.

94. Ibid., 44.

95. Xan Rice, "Oil Find Sparks New Hope for Uganda's People," *Guardian (London)*, August 25, 2009, 11.

4. Slow Violence, Gender, and the Environmentalism of the Poor

1. Anna Lappe and Frances Moore Lappe, "The Genius of Wangari Maathai," *International Herald Tribune*, October 15, 2004, 1–2.

2. Wangari Maathai, *Unbowed: A Memoir* (New York: Knopf, 2006), 175.

3. Lester R. Brown, "The Price of Salvation," *Guardian*, April 25, 2007, 1.

4. Hendrik Hertzberg, "The War in Iraq," *New Yorker*, March 27, 2003, 15.

5. Ibid.

6. The insistence that shock and awe was the beginning of a war unprecedented in its humanitarian precision was heard across the political spectrum. Donald Rumsfeld, most memorably, insisted that the futuristic weaponry the United States deployed in the war exhibited "a degree of precision that no one dreamt of in a prior conflict," resulting in bombings that were morally exemplary: "The care that goes into it, the humanity that goes into it, to see that military targets are destroyed, to be sure, but that it's done in a way, and in a manner, and in a direction and with a weapon that is appropriate to that very particularized target. . . . I think that will be the case when ground truth is achieved" (United States Department of Defense, "DoD News Briefing—Secretary Rumsfeld and Gen. Myers," March 21, 2003).

7. Wangari Maathai, *The Green Belt Movement: Sharing the Approach and the Experience* (New York: Lantern Books, 2003), 38.

8. See especially Vandana Shiva, *Earth Democracy: Justice, Sustainability, and Peace* (Boston: South End Press, 2005); and *Soil Not Oil: Environmental Justice in an Age of Climate Crisis* (Boston: South End Press, 2008).

9. Wes Jackson, "The Agrarian Mind: Mere Nostalgia or a Practical Necessity?" in *The Essential Agrarian Reader*, ed. Norman Wirzba (Washington, DC: Shoemaker and Hoard, 2003), 141.

10. Maathai, *Unbowed*, 281.

11. Ngugi wa Thiong'o, *Petals of Blood* (1977; repr., London: Penguin, 2002).

12. Laura Wright, *Wilderness Into Civilized Shapes: Reading the Postcolonial Environment* (Athens: University of Georgia Press, 2010), 33–35.

13. For a related and insightful discussion of what she calls "articulated categories," see Anne McClintock, *Imperial Leather: Race, Gender and Sexuality in the Colonial Contest* (New York: Routledge, 1995), 4ff.

14. Ato Quayson, *Calibrations* (Minneapolis: University of Minnesota Press, 2003), 73.

15. Meera Selva, "Wangari Maathai: Queen of the Greens," *Guardian*, October 9, 2004, 9.

16. William Finnegan, "The Economics of Empire: the Washington Consensus," *Harper's*, May 2003, 48.

17. Bertolt Brecht, "An die Nachgeborenen" (To posterity), in *Selected Poems*, trans. H. R. Hays (New York: Grove Press, 1959), 173.

18. The time frame here is crucial. With the help of international donors, Maathai put in place a system whereby each woman was paid a modest amount not for planting a tree, but for keeping it alive for six months. If it were still growing at that point, she would be remunerated. Thus the focus of the group's activities was not the single act of planting but maintaining growth over time. The literature on desertification is complex and conflicted, largely around questions of the scale and source of the problem as well as the quality of the research. Given the fraught debates over the implications of desertification, I have avoided the term, preferring simply to reference the slow violence of soil erosion and deforestation. For two useful accounts of the spread of positions on this issue, see Jeremy Swift, "Desertification: Narratives, Winners and Losers," in *The Lie of the Land: Challenging Received Wisdom on the African Environment*, ed. Melissa Leach and Robin Mearns (Oxford: James Currey, 1996); and William M. Adams, "When Nature Won't Stay Still: Conservation, Equilibrium and Control," in *Decolonizing Nature: Strategies for Conservation in a Post-Colonial Era*, ed. William M. Adams and Martin Mulligan (London: Earthscan, 2003).

19. Michela Wong, *It's Our Turn to Eat: The Story of a Kenyan Whistle-Blower* (New York: Harper 2009), 37.

20. Maathai, *Unbowed*, 262.

21. Michael Pollan, *Second Nature: A Gardener's Education* (New York: Dell, 1991), 194.

22. Ramachandra Guha, *Environmentalism: A Global History* (New York: Longman, 2000), 115–124.

23. A major precursor to the conflict over Karura had occurred in 1989. The regime had been steadily appropriating and privatizing parts of Nairobi's Uhuru Park, which Maathai has likened to New York's Central Park and London's Hyde Park as a vital green space, a space for leisure and for political gatherings. When

Maathai learned that the ruling party was to erect a sixty-story skyscraper for new party headquarters and a media center in Uhuru Park, battle was joined. Green Belt activists spearheaded a successful movement to turn back the regime's efforts to privatize public land under the deceptively spectacular iconography of national development. The regime would not forgive Maathai for humiliating them in this manner.

24. Amitabh Pal, "Maathai Interview," *Progressive*, May 2005, 5.

25. I've adapted the phrase from Al Gedicks' book, *Resource Rebels: Native Challenges to Mining and Oil Corporations* (Cambridge, MA: South End Press, 2001).

26. For the history of the forest fighters, see Caroline Elkins, *Imperial Reckoning: The Untold Story of Britain's Gulag in Kenya* (New York: Holt, 2005); Wunyabari O. Maloba, *Mau Mau and Kenya: An Analysis of a Peasant Revolt* (Bloomington: Indiana University Press, 1998); and especially David Anderson, *Histories of the Hanged: The Dirty War in Kenya and the End of Empire* (New York: Norton, 2005), 230–288.

27. For the most comprehensive discussion of this literature, see David Maughan-Brown, *Land, Freedom and Fiction: History and Ideology in Kenya* (London: Zed Press, 1985).

28. The Mau Mau uprising was far from being an undivided revolt: numerous fault lines opened up at times, not least between educated nationalist leaders and the predominantly peasant forest fighters.

29. Byron Caminero-Santangelo, "Different Shades of Green: Ecocriticism and African Literature," in *African Literature: An Anthology of Criticism and Theory*, ed. Tejumola Olaniyan and Ato Quayson (Oxford: Blackwell, 2007), 702.

30. In many Kenyan novels about the Mau Mau period, the forest fighters are depicted with a cloying if understandable romanticism. On the complex and varied legacies of colonial cultures of nature, one notes Maathai's admiration for the Men of the Trees, an organization founded in Kenya in the 1920s that brought together British and Kikuyu leaders to promote tree planting (Maathai, *Unbowed*, 131).

31. Although the initial resistance came from the Green Belt Movement, the resistance spread to the streets of Nairobi, where it was taken up by a broad swath of the population, particularly students, both female and male.

32. Maathai, *Unbowed*, 120.

33. See William Beinart and Peter Coates, *Environmental History: The Taming of Nature in the U.S.A. and South Africa* (London: Routledge, 1995); Jane Carruthers, *The Kruger National Park: A Social and Political History* (Pietermaritzburg, South Africa: Allen, 1995); and A. Fiona D. Mackenzie, "Contested Ground: Colonial Narratives and the Kenyan Environment, 1920–1945," *Journal of Southern African Studies* 26 (2000): 697–718.

34. James C. Scott, *Seeing Like a State: How Certain Schemes to Improve the Human Condition Have Failed* (New Haven, CT: Yale University Press, 1998), 264.

35. Fiona Mackenzie, "Contested Ground," 27. Mackenzie, like Beinart, stresses that there were among colonial officialdom some dissident voices who recognized the value and applicability of local agricultural and environmental knowledge.

36. Stuart Jeffries, "Kenya's Tree Woman," *Mail and Guardian*, February 28, 2007, 7.

37. Maathai, *Unbowed*, 179.

38. For an ambitious experiment in adaptively blending a singular self, a social movement, and a polemical agenda, see W. E. B. Du Bois, *Dusk of Dawn: An Essay Toward an Autobiography of a Race Concept* (1940; repr., New York: Transaction Publishers, 1983).

39. An important distinction should be made between the routes that Carson and Maathai took to their writing and their activism. Carson was a lifelong writer who remade herself as an activist late in life, after she traded her lyrical voice (which she'd honed as a celebrant of marine life) for the voice of elegy and apocalypse in *Silent Spring*. Maathai's trajectory was in the opposite direction: an activist all her adult life, she became a writer of testimony only in her later years.

40. Linda Lear, *Rachel Carson: Witness for Nature* (New York: Holt, 1997), 254.

41. Quoted in Lear, *Rachel Carson*, 429.

42. "Pesticides: The Price of Progress," *Time*, September 28, 1962, 45. Quoted in Lear, *Rachel Carson*, 461. Additionally, a review by Carl Hodge was entitled "*Silent Spring* Makes Protest Too Hysterical," *Arizona Star*, October 14, 1962, 7.

43. Quoted in Lear, *Rachel Carson*, 417.

44. Quoted ibid., 409.

45. Quoted in "The Silent Spring of Rachel Carson," transcript, *CBS Reports*, April 3, 1963.

46. Anon, "Controversial Book by Rachel Carson Lives Up to Advance Warnings," *Aerosol Age*, October 1962, 81. I'm grateful to Lindsay Woodbridge for first drawing my attention to this review in her fine unpublished senior thesis, "The Fallout of Silent Spring" (University of Wisconsin-Madison, Women's Studies, 2007).

47. This misogyny, together with the regime's authoritarian intolerance of dissent, had profound professional and financial repercussions for Maathai. In 1982, after teaching at the University of Nairobi for sixteen years, she decided to run for parliament. To do so, she was told she had to resign from her job at the university. She was then promptly informed by the electoral committee that she was disqualified (on a trumped up technicality) from running for parliament. So, twelve hours after resigning as chair of the university's Department of Veterinary Anatomy, Maathai asked for her job back. Under pressure from the regime, the university refused to reemploy her and, moreover, denied her

all pension and health benefits. Maathai, a forty-one-year-old single mother with no safety net, was thrown out onto the streets. One notes that, in 2005, shortly after Maathai was awarded the Nobel Prize, the very university that had treated her so appallingly tried to cash in on her international fame by awarding her an honorary doctorate in science.

48. Meera Selva, "Wangari Maathai: Queen of the Greens," *Guardian*, October 9, 2004, 8.

49. Quoted in Jim Motavelli, "Movement Built on Power of Trees," *E: The Environmental Magazine*, July–August 2002, 11.

50. Maathai, *Unbowed*, 110.

51. Ibid., 111. For a more elaborate account of the burden of traditionalism placed on women in the context of a Janus-faced modernity, see Anne McClintock, *Imperial Leather: Race, Gender and Sexuality in the Colonial Contest* (New York: Routledge, 1995), 294–300.

52. Maathai, *Unbowed*, 115, 196. There are echoes between the nativist arguments mounted against Maathai by President Moi and the arguments of her ex-husband, Mwangi, who testified in court that he was divorcing her because she was ungovernable: "[T]oo educated, too strong, too successful, too stubborn, and too hard to control" (quoted in *Unbowed*, 146).

53. Kwame Anthony Appiah, *In My Father's House* (New York: Oxford University Press, 1992), 55.

54. Maathai, *Unbowed*, 44-46.

55. Maathai, *Unbowed*, 4.

56. Quoted in Patrick E. Tyler, "In Wartime, Critics Question Peace Prize for Environmentalism," *New York Times*, October 10, 2004, A5. Morten Hoeglund, a member of Norway's Progress Party, concurred with Hagen, arguing that "the committee should have focused on more important matters, such as weapons of mass destruction" (quoted in Selva, "Wangari Maathai," 9).

57. Quoted in Patrick E. Tyler, "Peace Prize Goes to Environmentalism in Kenya," *New York Times*, October 9, 2004, A5. See, for example, Maathai's insistence that through a focus on reforestation and environmental resource management, "we might preempt many conflicts over the access and control of resources" (*Unbowed*, xvi).

58. In Kenya, which boasts some forty ethnicities, the sources of ethnic tension are complex, but have often been especially explosive along the fault lines between pastoralists and farmers where resources are overstressed. Divisive politicians have manipulated these tensions to their advantage, for instance, during the violence that beset the Rift Valley, Nyanza, and Western provinces in the early 1990s and, more broadly, during the aftermath of the disputed national elections of 2007. The slow violence of resource depletion, a mistrust of government, and

political leaders who play the ethnic card can easily kindle an atmosphere of terror that fuels social unrest.

59. Wai Chee Dimock, "World History According to Katrina," in *States of Emergency*,
ed. Russ Castronovo and Susan Gillman (Chapel Hill: University of North Carolina Press, 2009), 148. I have elaborated elsewhere on the environmental, class,
and gender dimensions to the violent conflicts that swept through Kenya in the
aftermath of the December 2007 elections. The widespread, reductive media por-
traits of the violence as simply an eruption of "atavistic tribal hatreds" ignores the
profound socioenvironmental inequalities that were masked by the official portrait of Kenya as a nation, under Moi's successor, President Mwai Kibaki, of ascendant growth. See Rob Nixon, "Slow Violence, Gender, and the Environmentalism
of the Poor," *Journal of Commonwealth and Postcolonial Studies* 13 (2008): 29-31.

60. Quoted in Ofeibea Quist-Arcton, "Maathai: Change Kenya to Benefit People,"
http://www.greenbeltmovement.org.

5. Unimagined Communities

1. See especially Lawrine Platzky and Cheryl Walker, *The Surplus People: Forced
Removals in South Africa* (Johannesburg: Ravan, 1998).

2. Quoted in Jacques Leslie, *Deep Water: The Epic Struggle over Dams, Displaced People, and the Environment* (New York: Farrar, Straus and Giroux, 2005), 156.

3. On the basis of a country report by the World Commission on Dams, Arundhati Roy puts the figure for India's dam-displaced at 56 million, while Patrick
McCully argues that—prior to the Three Gorges project—Chinese dams alone
may have displaced 60 million. See David Barsamian and Arundhati Roy, *The
Checkbook and the Cruise Missile* (Cambridge, MA: South End Press, 2004), 25.

4. David Le Page, "World Bank Defends its Dam Policies," *Mail and Guardian*, May
2, 2001, 7.

5. Rebecca Solnit, *Savage Dreams: A Journey into the Landscape Wars of the American
West* (Berkeley: University of California Press, 2000).

6. In *Savage Dreams*, Solnit commits herself to repopulating those places of cultural
and imaginative evacuation. Her restorative ambitions are both temporal and
spatial: she gives back to these deserts an environmental and cultural memory as well as connecting them globally, by tracing the cold-war links between
Nevada and Kazakhstan. These links include new forms of imaginative awareness generated by a transnational protest movement.

7. Solnit, *Savage Dreams*, 154.

8. Across the world, the people who are reconstituted as uninhabitants seldom
belong to large or powerful ethnic groups. This is true of all the desert nuclear
test sites internationally: in the Nevada Test Site; in the deserts of Kazhakstan,

Pakistan, and India; in the Central Desert in Australia; the French test sites in preindependence Algeria; in western China; and in Southern Africa's Kalahari Desert. In all these areas, the people who are strategically recast as virtual uninhabitants are micro-minorities from marginalized ethnic groups. They are also very often nomads, people who traditionally have had to learn to live, through movement, within the limits of the land.

9. Quoted in Patrick McCully, *Silenced Rivers: The Ecology and Politics of Large Dams: Enlarged and Updated Edition* (London: Zed, 2001), 75.

10. Ibid., 74–76.

11. Quoted in John McPhee, *Encounters with the Archdruid* (New York: Farrar, Straus and Giroux, 1971), 200.

12. Ibid., 240.

13. Quoted in Susan Zakin, *Coyotes and Town Dogs: Earth First! and the Environmental Movement* (New York: Viking, 1993), 166

14. Arundhati Roy, "The Greater Common Good," *The Cost of Living* (New York: Modern Library, 1999), 63.

15. Edward Abbey, *Desert Solitaire* (New York: McGraw-Hill, 1968), 165.

16. Roy, *Cost of Living*, 93.

17. Ibid., 106.

18. Wallace Stegner, *Where the Bluebird Sings to the Lemonade Springs: Living and Writing in the West* (New York: Random House), 75.

19. Roy, *Cost of Living*, ix. The Narmada Valley project has since been surpassed— both in the scale of its engineering and the scale of environmental calamity—by the Three Gorges Dam.

20. If the advent of the nuclear age has inspired a long tradition of activist polemic— from John Hersey, Jonathan Schell, Rebecca Solnit, and Rachel Carson to Kobo Abe, E. P. Thompson, and Martin Amis—the rise of the megadam has prompted a much more modest literature, largely associated (as I've suggested) with the wilderness ethic of the American West and, more recently, the Three Gorges Dam in China.

21. Roy, "The End of Imagination," 125.

22. William Finnegan, "The Economics of Empire: Notes on the Washington Consensus," *Harper's*, May 1, 2003, 53.

23. Arundhati Roy, *The God of Small Things* (New York: Random House, 1997), 14.

24. John Berger, "Ten Dispatches about Place," in *Hold Everything Dear: Dispatches on Survival and Resistance* (New York: Pantheon, 2007), 122–123.

25. Quoted in Roy, *Cost of Living*, 13.

26. C. V. J. Sharma, ed., *Modern Temples of India: Selected Speeches of Jawaharlal Nehru at Irrigation and Power Projects* (New Delhi: Central Board of Irrigation and Power, 1989), 40.

27. McCully estimates that 40 percent of oustees are Adivasis.

28. Quoted in Leslie, *Deep Water*, 54.

29. Regarding the rationalizing of irrational rivers, Maxim Gorky observed that Soviet dam builders sought to make "mad rivers sane" (quoted in McCully, *Silenced Rivers*, 17). The discourse of insanity is an insistent one, attached by megadam proponents to "wild" rivers and by opponents to the impact of damming on floodplains, deltas, and rates of flow and silting that result in longer and more catastrophic floods. Janet Abramovitz, for example, depicts the predictable 1993 floods of the Mississippi and Missouri rivers as a direct result of overdamming, providing "a dramatic and costly lesson on the effects of treating the natural flow of rivers as a pathological condition." Abramovitz, *Imperiled Waters, Impoverished Future: The Decline of Freshwater Ecosystems*. (Washington, DC: Worldwatch Institute, 1996), 27

30. Marq de Villiers, *Water: The Fate of Our Most Precious Resource* (Boston: Mariner Books, 2001), 121.

31. Zeyev Volfson, writing in the 1970s under the pseudonym Boris Komarov, proclaimed that "there is far more important information about the history of hydro-electric construction in the USSR in Alexander Solzhenitsyn's *Gulag Archipelago* than in all the textbooks on hydraulic engineering." See Volfson, *The Destruction of Nature in the Soviet Union*, trans. Michel Vale and Joe Hollander (London: Pluto, 1980), 29.

32. See especially McCully, *Silenced Rivers*, 239ff.

33. John Waterbury, *Hydropolitics of the Nile Valley* (New York: Syracuse University Press, 1979), 116. I am indebted to Patrick McCully for drawing my attention to this book.

34. On the impact of the Hoover Dam in unleashing a flood of international emulators, see especially de Villiers, *Water: The Fate of Our Most Precious Resource*, 120–128. Joan Didion, in the complex tones of the apocalyptic sublime, invoked the affective power of the Hoover Dam in her 1970 essay "At the Dam." *The White Album* (New York: Farrar, Straus and Giroux, 1979), 198–201. For a stinging attack on "water-project boondoggles" in the American West, including megadams that fail to realize their promise, see Wallace Stegner's fine essay "Striking the Rock," in *Where the Bluebird Sings* (New York: Penguin, 1992), 76–98.

35. Decades later Hoover still had the power to terrorize the Soviets into playing catch-up.

36. Leslie, *Deep Water*, 117.

37. Quoted in Sharma, ed., *Modern Temples of India*, 52–56.

38. Arundhati Roy, *Power Politics* (Cambridge, MA: South End Press), 43.

39. See, for example, her critique of "a corporate globalization [that] has increased the distance between the people who take decisions and the people who have

to suffer those decisions" (Barsamian and Roy, *The Checkbook and the Cruise Missile*, 73).

40. Roy, *Power Politics*, 32

41. Ibid, 32.

42. See Leslie, *Deep Water*, 20; and Ramachandra Guha, "The Arun Shourine of the Left," *The Hindu*, December 10, 2000. Even before her nonfictional turn, Roy was no stranger to controversy. The intercaste relationship in *The God of Small Things* resulted in Roy being charged with obscenity, and Kerala's Communist Party railed against her fictional depiction of local Marxist history. She was taken to court for "corrupting public morality." Aijaz Ahmed, though admiring of the novel's style and ambition, takes Roy to task for her depiction of Left history and for the novel's reliance on an erotic plotting of the political. See Ahmed, "Reading Arundhati Roy Politically," *Frontline* 14 (August 8, 1997): 103–111.

43. George Perkins Marsh, *Man and Nature: Physical Geography as Modified By Human Action* (1864; rpt. Ann Arbor: University of Michigan Library, 2001), 27.

44. McCully, *Silenced Rivers*, 174. In *The Cost of Living*, Roy acknowledges McCully's incomparable book as "the rock on which this work stands."

45. Roy, *Cost of Living*, 123.

46. Vandana Shiva, *Water Wars: Privatization, Pollution, Profit* (Boston: South End Press, 2002), 15.

47. "Frontline: The World of Water," BBC2, March 28, 2009.

48. Al Gedicks, *Resource Rebels. Native Challenges to Mining and Oil Corporations* (Boston: South End Press, 20010), 8-10.

6. Stranger in the Eco-village

1. My use of the term postapartheid in this chapter comes with all the familiar caveats. The nation's democratic turn on April 27, 1994 was a critical marker in South African history. But "surely," Njabulo Ndebele correctly insists, "the death of apartheid is a social process not an event." (*Fine Lines from the Box: Further Thoughts About Our Country* (Roggebaai, South Africa: Umuzi, 2007), 93). That process is uneven and ongoing. This chapter is, in part, an attempt to explore from the angle of environmental justice the limits and pacing of that systemic transformation.

2. Njabulo S. Ndebele, "Game Lodges and Leisure Colonialists," in *Blank: Architecture After Apartheid*, ed. Hilton Judin and Ivan Vladislavic (Cape Town: David Phillips, 1998), 12.

3. Taxidermy is located at the complex crossroads of Enlightenment science, colonial trophy hunting, and hypermasculine interior design. Taxidermal time is, in multiple senses, suspended time: the mounted corpses are frozen in animated

positions, usually (for predators) with fangs exposed. The period reference is anachronistic as is the craft itself, which projects a musty, neo-Victorian aura of white male risk-management.

4. African culture, of whatever ethnicity, was present only in the interior atmospherics: the reed baskets and masks that afforded the game lodge lobby a decorative indigeneity.

5. The Eastern Cape is primarily a Xhosa region. It has very few Zulu inhabitants. But Kleinhans understood that Zulu had greater international recognition value, in the push for African authenticity, than Xhosa. Besides, Zulu was easier for foreigners to pronounce.

6. Donna Haraway, "Teddy Bear Patriarchy: Taxidermy in the Garden of Eden, New York City, 1908–1936," *Social Text* 11 (1984): 20–64.

7. The cultural histories of game lodges dedicated to game viewing, private reserves where hunting is part of the experience, and national parks are all differently inflected. Although a full accounting of those differences is beyond the scope of this chapter, performances of the eco-archaic and racialized ecologies of looking remain, I believe, a constitutive element in all those varied spaces.

8. Ndebele, "Game Lodges and Leisure Colonialists," 12.

9. Anne McClintock, *Imperial Leather: Race, Gender and Sexuality in the Colonial Contest* (New York: Routledge, 1995), 244–245.

10. For an insightful examination of the spatial politics of Ndebele's essay, see Rita Barnard, *Apartheid and Beyond: South African Writers and the Politics of Place* (Oxford: Oxford University Press, 2007), 171–172.

11. One of the most notorious of these forced removals in the name of conservation involved the Makuleke when the Kruger National Park was extended northward. Another controversial case involved the Tonga, who were moved twice: in 1924 to make way for the Ndumo Game Reserve, then again in the 1990s to create a corridor that would give elephants greater freedom of movement and access to water which, accordingly, became more difficult for the Tonga to access. Martha Honey, *Ecotourism and Sustainable Development: Who Owns Paradise?* (Washington, DC: Island Press, 1999), 367. For a broader, international perspective on conservation refugees, see especially Ramachandra Guha, *Environmentalism: A Global History* (New York: Longman, 2000); and Mark Dowie, *Conservation Refugees* (Boston: MIT Press, 2009).

12. Ndebele, "Game Lodges and Leisure Colonialists," 11.

13. Fritz Fanon, *Black Skin, White Masks*, trans. Charles Lam Markmann (London: Pluto, 1991), 90, 92.

14. Ndebele, "Game Lodges and Leisure Colonialists," 13.

15. Njabulo S. Ndebele, *Rediscovery of the Ordinary: Essays on South African Literature and Culture* (Johannesburg: COSAW, 1991), 67.

16. Ndebele, "Game Lodges and Leisure Colonialists," 10. On her flight back from her Bahamas vacation, Jordan is likewise "burning up," on the verge of what she calls "a West Indian fit." "Report from the Bahamas," in *A Stranger in the Village: Two Centuries of African-American Travel Writing*, ed. Farah J. Griffin and Cheryl J. Fish (Boston: Beacon Press, 1998), 326.

17. On the role of effaced labor in landscape aesthetics, Raymond Williams's *The Country and the City* (Oxford: Oxford University Press, 1975) and J. M. Coetzee's *White Writing* (1988; repr., New Haven, CT: Yale University Press, 1990) remain invaluable. William Cronon's related work in an American context remains foundational, while Robert Marzec's analyses of effaced labor, landscape, and enclosures in British and postcolonial environments are incisive. See Robert Marzec, *An Ecological and Postcolonial Study of Literature: From Daniel Defoe to Salman Rushdie* (London: Palgrave Macmillan, 2007).

18. Jordan, "Report from the Bahamas," 327.

19. Kincaid, *In a Small Place* (New York: Plume, 1988), 55.

20. Ndebele, "Game Lodges and Leisure Colonialists," 12.

21. The environmentalist literature on the construction of Caribbean Edens is rich and increasingly vast. See especially *Caribbean Literature and the Environment: Between Nature and Culture*, ed. Elizabeth DeLoughrey et al. (Charlottesville: University of Virginia Press, 2007); George B. Handley, *New World Poetics: Nature and the Adamic Imagination of Whitman, Neruda, and Walcott* (Athens: University of Georgia Press, 2007); and Sarah Phillips Casteel, *Second Arrivals: Landscape and Belonging in Contemporary Writing of the Americas* (Charlottesville: University of Virginia Press, 2007).

22. *South African Eden*, James Stevenson-Hamilton's influential memoir on his Kruger Park years appeared in 1937, the same year as Karen Blixen's *Out of Africa*. Both books invoked an elegiac, Edenic rhetoric to help mobilize a megafauna-centered conservationist movement whose legacy continues to shape the contemporary economic and cultural landscapes of South African and Kenya. Stevenson-Hamilton, a Scottish immigrant (and the Kruger Park's first warden), was arguably as pivotal a figure, through his actions and writings, in the shaping of South African conservation as that other Scottish immigrant conservationist, John Muir, was in the United States.

23. See especially Elaine Freedgood, *Victorian Writing about Risk* (Cambridge, England: Cambridge University Press, 2000).

24. James Baldwin, "Stranger in the Village," in *Notes of a Native Son* (1953; rpt. Boston: Beacon Press, 1984), 159.

25. Ibid.

26. Ibid., 164.

27. Baldwin's position here bears comparison with Jordan's reflections on "The Native Show on the Patio" performed at the Sheraton British Colonial. Her

racial and gender identification with the Bahamian women who perform in the "Native Show," who serve her, or hawk trinkets on the street is compromised by the structures of the tourist industry: "We are not particularly women anymore; we are parties to a transaction designed to set us against each other" (Jordan, "Report from the Bahamas," 321).

28. This is not to suggest that the relationship between local white ideologies and foreign ones always dovetail. Ndebele mentions, for instance, an American family who remark on the oddity of cross-dressing as "leisure colonialists." Ndebele, "Game Lodges and Leisure Colonialists," 12.

29. Amitava Kumar, *Bombay-London-New York* (New York: Routledge, 2002), 64.

30. Baldwin, "Stranger in the Village," 169.

31. Ibid., 173.

32. Clearly, the postapartheid redistribution of political, economic, and cultural power remains profoundly uneven.

33. Ibid., 175.

34. The routine comparison of Kruger with Israel reaffirms the park's status, particularly in Afrikaner cultures of nature, as a place of spiritual pilgrimage, a chosen people's chosen land. Kruger Park was officially established under the 1926 National Parks Act, although it was then much smaller than its current size.

35. The status of the Kruger Park as an overdetermined buffer zone was intensified by the ascent to power of Marxist guerillas in 1975, an event that marked the end of Portuguese colonial control of Mozambique and served, in addition, as a partial revolutionary inspiration for the Soweto uprising the following year. During the ensuing Mozambican civil war, the apartheid regime deemed Mozambique (which served as a base for ANC guerillas) a terrorist state. The South African regime, with strong backing from the Reagan administration, funded, trained, harbored, and armed forces opposing the Mozambican government. By the late 1980s, the civil war had displaced 2 million of Mozambique's 14 million people and killed 100,000 of them.

36. Gordimer's compelling essay on the Kruger Park-Mozambique border zone, "The Ingot and the Stick," seems to have passed under the critical radar. It goes unmentioned both in Stephen Clingman's extensive critical work on Gordimer and in Ronald Roberts's 750-page biography of her.

37. Jane Carruthers, *The Kruger National Park: A Social and Political History* (Pietermaritzburg, South Africa: University of Natal Press, 1995), 17.

38. Ibid., 31.

39. After the discovery of gold in 1877, white immigration to the Transvaal surged. The resultant rapid ascent of industrialization and urbanization in turn fed the rise of commercial agriculture. White mining magnates and white farmers were thrust into competition with each other for scarce black labor. Waves

of legislation were passed intent of making rural survival more precarious for black subsistence communities, thereby forcing increasing numbers into capitalist wage-labor on the mines and farms. The 1913 Land Act was particularly devastating, barring blacks from buying or leasing land from whites except in the designated native reserves. From a white ruling-class perspective, this land squeeze had the double advantage of forcing blacks into wage labor and removing a source of agricultural competition. For a more textured history of these developments, see William Beinart, *The Rise of Conservation in South Africa: Settlers, Livestock, and the Environment 1770–1950* (New York: Oxford University Press, 2008). Although it is beyond the scope of this chapter, a fuller accounting of the rise of game reserves in relation to colonial cultures of labor and leisure would engage J. M. Coetzee's reflections on idleness in *White Writing* (1988; rpt. New Haven: Yale University Press, 1990) and Syed Hussein Alata's *The Myth of the Lazy Native* (New York: Routledge, 1977).

40. This poacher-conservationist dyad helps explain an erratic policy toward human habitation inside the Kruger National Park. After initially barring Africans from the park in the early twentieth century, the white authorities allowed about 3,000 Africans to reside there, but charged them rent (Carruthers, *Kruger National Park*, 81).This rent provided a revenue stream and ensured that those residents would be forced to sell their labor for menial amounts. Black bodies—of African renters and, later, prison gangs—were dragooned into erecting fences, building roads and camps, and catching poachers. The invention and maintenance of a wild, Edenic purity is, after all, a labor-intensive business.

41. Relevant here is Johannes Fabian's account of the two primary colonial responses to the bodily contest over land: forced removal (whether through genocide or deportation) or manipulating "the other variable—Time. With the help of various devices of sequencing and distancing one assigns to the conquered populations a different Time." Fabian, *Time and the Other: How Anthropology Makes its Object* (New York: Columbia University Press, 1983), 29–30.

42. Carruthers, *Kruger National Park*, 86.

43. Labuschagne, 26–27; 63–64. Quoted in Carruthers, *Kruger National Park*, 83.

44. For a suggestive history of the way the Grand Canyon was marketed to American tourists as a destination associated with the religious archaic, the sublime, and patriotic spiritual elevation, see Stephen J. Pyne, *How the Canyon Became Grand* (New York: Viking, 1998).

45. Gordimer's essay "The Ingot and the Stick" is a companion piece to a BBC2 television documentary she presented as part of a series on frontiers. Gordimer, "The Ingot and the Stick, The Ingot and the Gun: Mozambique-South Africa," in *Frontiers*, ed. George Carey (London: BBC Books, 1990), 50–77.

46. "The principle of the agreements has never changed. Gold and other mining interests in South Africa are granted large-scale labour recruiting of Mozambican men in return for a portion of the men's wages to be paid in gold, to Portugal during colonial times, later to independent Mozambique." Ibid., 56.

47. Ibid., 61.

48. Gordimer, "The Ultimate Safari," in *Telling Tales*, ed. Nadine Gordimer (New York: Farrar, Straus and Giroux, 2004), 272.

49. Ibid., 273.

50. Ibid., 271, 277.

51. Ibid., 281.

52. Gloria Alzaldua, *Borderlands/La Frontera: The New Mestiza* (San Francisco: Aunt Lute, 1987), 3.

53. In a broader theoretical context, Liisa Malkki's work on the pathologizing of refugees as "unnatural" has a particular resonance here. See her *Purity and Exile: Violence, Memory, and National Cosmology among Hutu Refugees in Tanzania* (Chicago: University of Chicago Press, 1995).

54. The girl's ethnicity goes unmentioned, but the story contains plenty of geographical and linguistic indications that she is Shangaan. (The Shangaan's ethnic self-designation has varied historically and geographically. Shangaan are frequently called Tsonga in South Africa.)

55. Gordimer, "The Ultimate Safari," 280.

56. Before Zimbabwe's descent into chaos shrank the ambitions of the project, a three-nation transfrontier park was in the works, joining Kruger to national parks in Mozambique and Zimbabwe and thereby affording the prospect of greater freedom of movement for humans (exclusive subspecies, tourist) and other mammalian herds. The project has been dogged by controversy, not least because it would entail further involuntary removals (notably in Mozambique) and the economic benefits to local inhabitants have been at best hazily sketched out. The status of this transfrontier park, dubbed an African "super park," remains uncertain, although the corridor linking Mozambique and Kruger appears to be going ahead.

57. From the Kruger Park's colonial beginnings, the "gate guards" were historically Shangaan. As David Bunn notes, these uniformed guards "dramatize[d] two orders of time and racial identity—one that of the 'improved' native and the other that of the customary, ethnic collective—that [could not] easily coexist outside the boundaries of the reserve." Bunn, "Relocations: Landscape Theory, South African Landscape Practice, and the Transmission of Political Value," *Pretexts* 4 (1993): 53.

58. For a thoughtful contrastive analysis of the treatment of white tourists and African immigrants, see Kathryn Mathers and Loren B. Landau, "Tourists

or 'Makwerekwere': Good Versus Bad Visitors and the Possibilities of Ethical Tourism in South Africa" (paper presented to the International Sociological Association Congress Durban, South Africa, July 2006, Forced Migration Working Paper Series #27, Forced Migration Studies Programme, University of Witwatersrand), 1–16.

59. Hector Magome and James Murombedzi, "Sharing South African National Parks: Community Land and Conservation in a Democratic South Africa," in *Decolonizing Nature: Strategies for Conservation in a Post-Colonial Era*, ed. William M. Adams and Martin Mulligan (London: Earthscan, 2003), 131.

60. For instance, the range of endemics in the vast Kruger National Park cannot compare with that of a seldom-visited, much smaller reserve on the Namaqualand coast that is biodiversity rich but megafauna poor. One notes also how, in a creative attempt to legitimate and market its expansion, the Greater Addo National Park has pitched itself as the only park in the world to boast the Big Seven (adding the southern right whale and the great white shark to the conventional lion, elephant, rhino, buffalo, and leopard) while also boasting that it has the greatest variety of biomes of any South African national park.

61. Tsing, *Friction*, 1.

62. Ndebele, "Game Lodges and Leisure Colonialists," 14.

7. Ecologies of the Aftermath

1. Paul Virilio, interviewed in James DerDerian, *Virtuous War: Mapping the Military-Industrial-Media-Entertainment Network* (Boulder: Westview Press, 2001), 64–65.

2. Ibid.

3. By (among others) Robert Hughes on the back cover of *Martyr's Day*.

4. Mike Kelly, *Martyr's Day: Chronicle of a Small War* (1993; repr., New York: Random House, 2001), 229.

5. Ibid.

6. Carol Picou, "Living with Gulf War Syndrome," in *Metal of Dishonor*, ed. John Catalinotto and Sara Flounders (New York: International Action Center, 1997), 44–45.

7. Akira Tashiro, *Discounted Casualties: The Human Cost of Depleted Uranium*, trans. Transnet (Hiroshima: Chugoku Shimbun, 2001), 94–95.

8. Ibid.

9. Picou, *Metal of Dishonor*, 46.

10. The best account of the role the Gulf War played in exorcising Vietnam syndrome is to be found in Andrew J. Bacevich, *The New American Militarism: How Americans are Seduced by War* (New York: Oxford University Press, 2005).

11. Kelly, *Martyr's Day*, 362.

12. Mike Kelly, *Martyr's Day: Chronicle of a Small War,* 2nd ed. (New York: Vintage Books, 2001), xiii. In the foreword to the 2001 edition of *Martyr's Day,* Kelly qualifies his surgical metaphor, but only by arguing, like many hawks, for a spurious connection between Saddam Hussein and the 9/11 attacks. Desert Storm, Kelly now insists, was a war of mistaken brevity, as the United States' failure to topple Saddam had opened the way for the attacks on the World Trade Center and the Pentagon.

13. For Kelly there are two levels of surgery in the "theatre" of the war: the local, surgical strikes—the small, precise incisions—within the larger clinical performance of the surgical war itself.

14. See also, for example, Fred Smoler on the Iraq War of 2003: "Why were civilian casualties so low? In part because of the self-restraint—with a few exceptions—shown by Coalition troops and in part due to a technological revolution, the use of precision-guided munitions, particularly GPS-guided munitions, in unprecedented quantities." Smoler, "Cakewalk: Getting It Wrong—U.S. Military Might and Myths," *Dissent* 47 (Summer 2003): 39.

15. Tashiro, *Discounted Casualties.*

16. Military usages of surgical metaphors are not unique to the Gulf War, of course. Consider, for instance, the American general who during the 2003 Iraq War declared that "we need to make a decision on when the cancer of Fallujah needs to be cut out." Quoted in Eliot Weinberger, *What I Heard About Iraq* (London: Verso, 2005), 9. However, what is particularly acute in Kelly's book is his representation of the entire war as surgical in its efficient, healing, and ethical brevity.

17. Rachel Carson, *Silent Spring* (1962; repr., Boston: Houghton Mifflin, 1992), 127.

18. Showalter argues that "hysteria not only survives in the 1990s, it is more contagious than in the past. Infectious epidemics of hysteria spread by stories circulated through self-help books, articles in newspapers and magazines, TV talk shows and series, films, the Internet, even literary criticism." *Hystories: Hysterical Epidemics and Modern Media* (New York: Columbia University Press, 1998), 5.

19. Ibid., 6.

20. As one anonymous commentator notes on Amazon.com: "had Showalter's book been written at the turn of the [nineteenth] century, she would have included multiple sclerosis (once known as 'faker's disease') among her list of 'hysterias.'"

21. Showalter, *Hystories,* 4.

22. Steven Reinberg, "Toxic Chemical Blamed for Gulf War Illness," *U.S. News & World Report,* November 17, 2008, 5.

23. Ibid.

24. Duncan Graham-Rowe, "Depleted Uranium Casts Shadow Over Peace in Iraq," *New Scientist*, April 15, 2003, 2.

25. Thomas Whiteside's *The Withering Rain: America's Herbicidal Folly* (New York: Dutton, 1971); and John Lewallen, *Ecolcgy of Devastation* (New York: Puffin, 1971).

26. Harvey Wasserman and Norman Solomon, *Killing Our Own: The Disaster of America's Experience with Atomic Radiation* (New York: Delacorte, 1982).

27. See Robert Fisk, "The Evidence Lies Dying in Basra," *Independent*, January 25, 2000, 11; and Patsy McGary, "Iraqi Child Cancers Link to Gulf War Weapons," *Irish Times*, November 30, 1999, 2.

28. Quoted in Dan Fahey, "The Use of Depleted Uranium in the 2003 Iraq War: An Initial Assessment of Information and Policies," www.wise-uranium.org.

29. Ibid. See also U.S. General Accounting Office, *Hazardous Waste: Information on Potential Superfund Sites*, GAO/RCED-99-22 (Washington, DC: Government Printing Office, 1998), 170; Michael Orey, "Uranium Waste Site Has a Historic New England Town Up in Arms," *Wall Street Journal*, March 1, 2001, B1; Jesse D. Edmands et al., "Uptake and Mobility of Uranium in Black Oaks: Implications for Biomonitoring Depleted Uranium-Contaminated Groundwater," *Chemosphere* (2001) 44: 789–795.

30. For an incomparably astute analysis of language as an instrument of warfare, see Mary Louise Pratt, "Harm's Way: Language and the Contemporary Arts of War," *PMLA* 124 (2009), 1515-1531.

31. Quoted in Tashiro, *Discounted Casualties*, 56–57.

32. Ibid.

33. Doug Rokke, interview by Rob Nixon, July 7, 2005.

34. Quoted in Hillary Johnson, "Is the Pentagon Giving Our Soldiers Cancer?" *Rolling Stone*, October 2, 2003, 83.

35. Ibid.

36. Quoted in David Rose, "Weapons of Self-Destruction," *Vanity Fair*, December 2004, 217.

37. Quoted in Johnson, "Is the Pentagon Giving Our Soldiers Cancer?" 87. Naughton's reference here to tungsten is pointed: the German military had banned depleted uranium from its arsenal on account of the radioactive and chemical risks it posed, replacing DU with tungsten, a high-density (and more expensive) metal that proved effective both as a penetrator and in the armoring of tanks.

38. Doug Rokke, interview by Rob Nixon, July 7, 2005. If four years after the war Rokke had 432 micrograms of uranium per liter of urine, after eight years that figure had dropped to 42 micrograms. But as Rokke pointed out, that drop didn't mean his body had eliminated the rest but rather that, over time, much of that uranium had become sequestered in his soft organs and bones.

39. Ibid.

40. Leonard Dietz, "DU Spread and Contamination of Gulf War Veterans and Others," in *Metal of Dishonor*, ed. John Catalinotto and Sara Flounders (New York: International Action Center, 1997; rev. ed. 1999), 134.

41. Avril McDonald, ed., *The International Legal Regulation of the Use of Depleted Uranium Weapons* (Den Haag, 2005), especially the essay "Environmental and Health Consequences of DU Munitions," 173–192.

42. See Duncan Graham-Rowe, "Depleted Uranium Casts Shadow Over Peace in Iraq," *New Scientist*, April 15, 2003, 2–6. See also, "Special Report: Waging a New Kind of War," *Scientific American*, June 2000, 2–17.

43. Sara Flounders, "Iraqi Cities 'Hot' with Depleted Uranium," http://www.coastal post.com/03/09/11.htm. For the full story, see Scott Peterson, "Remains of Toxic Bullets Litter Iraq," *Christian Science Monitor*, May 15, 2003, 3.

44. Ibid.

45. Quoted in Dan Fahey, "Science or Science Fiction? Facts, Myths and Propaganda in the Debate Over Depleted Uranium Weapons," 31.

46. Quoted in Rose, "Weapons of Self-Destruction," 219.

47. Bonham et al., *Human Cost of the War in Iraq*, 22.

48. Quoted in Johnson, "Is the Pentagon giving Our Soldiers Cancer?" 93.

49. Ibid.

50. Rabadrinath Tagore, "Persia, April 13, 1934," in *Rabadrinath Tagore: An Anthology*, ed. Krishna Dutta and Andrew Robinson (New York: St. Martin's Press, 1997), 127.

51. Walt Whitman, "Drum-Taps," in *Whitman, The Complete Poems*, ed. Francis Murphy (New York: Penguin, 2005), 305.

52. Quoted in Weinberger, *What I Heard About Iraq*, 3.

53. The other most vocal defendant of cluster bombs has been Russia during the war in Chechnya.

54. Quoted in *Clearing the Fields: Solutions to the Global Landmines Crisis*, ed. Kevin M. Cahill (New York: New Press, 1996), 3.

55. Quoted Richard Norton-Taylor, "Rights Groups Warn of Danger of Unexploded Cluster Bombs," *Guardian*, August 18, 2006, 7.

56. Woodford Agee Heflin, *United States Air Force Dictionary*, http://www.knovel .com.

57. "Personnel," http://www.websters-online-dictionary.org.

58. Bonnie Docherty, *Human Rights Watch* 14, no. 7 (2002): 44.

59. Robert Fisk, "Wailing Children, the Wounded, the Dead: Victims of the Day Cluster Bombs Rained on Baghdad," *Independent*, April 13, 2003, 5.

60. Lydia Monin and Andrew Gallimore, *The Devil's Garden: A History of Landmines* (London: Random House, 2002).

61. Eric Prokosch, *The Technology of Killing: A Military and Political History of Antipersonnel Weapons* (New York: Zed, 1995), 173.

62. Henry Michaels, *US Uses Cluster Bombs to Spread Death and Destruction in Iraq*, World Socialist Web Site, http://www.wsws.org.

63. Quoted in Cahill, ed., *Clearing the Fields*, 192.

64. Human Rights Watch, *Off Target: The Conduct of the War and Civilian Casualties in Iraq* (New York: Human Rights Watch, 2003), 73.

65. Human Rights Watch, *Off Target*, 17. See also Kenneth Rutherford, "The Evolving Arm Control Agenda: The Implications of the Role of NGOs in Banning Anti-Personnel Landmines," *World Politics* 53 (October 2000): 74–114.

66. Human Rights Watch, *New U.S. Landmine Policy: Questions and Answers* (New York: Human Rights Watch, 2004), 13.

8. Environmentalism, Postcolonialism, and American Studies

1. One thinks here of innovative works like Richard Grove, *Green Imperialism: Colonial Expansion, Tropical Island Edens, and the Origins of Environmentalism, 1600–1860* (Cambridge, England: Cambridge University Press, 1995); Tom Griffiths and Libby Robin, eds., *Ecology and Empire: Environmental History of Settler Societies* (Seattle: University of Washington Press, 1997); David Arnold and Ramachandra Guha, eds., *Nature, Culture, Imperialism: Essays of the Environmental History of South Asia* (Delhi, India: Oxford University Press, 1995); William Beinart and Peter Coates, *Environment and History: The Taming of Nature in the USA and South Africa* (London: Routledge, 1995); and Susan M. Darlington et al., *Nature in the Global South* (Durham, NC: Duke University Press, 2003). For an excellent recent examination of the possibilities that debates in cultural geography might open up for a postcolonial ecocriticism, see Upamanyu Pablo Mukherjee, *Postcolonial Environments: Nature, Culture and the Contemporary Indian Novel in English* (London: Palgrave Macmillan, 2010).

2. Jay Parini, "The Greening of the Humanities," *New York Times Magazine*, October 23, 1995, 52–53.

3. Rob Nixon, "The Oil Weapon," *New York Times*, November 17, 1995, A24. See also my essay, "Pipedreams: Ken Saro-Wiwa, Environmental Justice, and Micro-Minority Rights" *London Review of Books*, April 7, 1996, 11.

4. Lawrence Buell, *The Environmental Imagination: Thoreau, Nature Writing, and the Formation of American Culture* (Cambridge, MA: Harvard University Press, 1996); Cheryll Glotfelty and Harold Fromm, eds., *The Ecocritical Reader: Landmarks in Literary Ecology* (Athens: University of Georgia Press, 1996); Max Oelschlaeger, *The Idea of Wilderness* (New Haven, CT: Yale University Press, 1991); Daniel Payne, *Voices in the Wilderness: American Nature Writing and Environmental*

Politics (Hanover, NH: University Press of New England, 1996); Scott Slovic, *Seeking Awareness in American Nature Writing* (Salt Lake City: University of Utah Press, 1992).

. No book illustrates the limitations of this approach more lucidly than *The Idea of Wilderness*, in which Oelschlaeger argues for the timeless, primal, universal value of wilderness. He roots his argument in ruminations on Paleolithic, Neolithic, and ancient Mediterranean notions of nature, then seeks to secure his case by analyzing an exclusively American canon of writers (Thoreau, Muir, Leopold, Jeffers, and Snyder prominent among them).

5. Ken Saro-Wiwa, *Nigeria: The Brink of Disaster* (Port Harcourt, Nigeria: Saros International Publishers, 1991), 71.

6. Ken Saro-Wiwa, *A Month and A Day: A Detention Diary* (London: Penguin, 1995), 7.

7. Ibid., 80.

8. Ibid., 79.

9. For a prescient postcolonial challenge to the American wilderness obsession, see Ramachandra Guha, "Radical American Environmentalism and Wilderness Preservation: A Third World Critique," *Environmental Ethics* 11 (Spring 1989): 71–83.

10. For an invaluable critique of the wilderness tradition of "purity," see William Cronon, "The Trouble with Wilderness; or, Getting Back to the Wrong Nature," in *Uncommon Ground: Rethinking the Human Place in Nature*, ed. William Cronon (New York: Norton,1996), 69–90. Since Cronon's pathbreaking essay, other ecocritics and environmental writers have recognized how a fixation with wilderness is imaginatively distorting and politically costly. However, the legacy of the wilderness obsession remains a continued source of suspicion for writers and communities who in the past have felt alienated by that emphasis.

11. For an insightful essay on the possibility of reconciling cosmopolitanism with a located patriotism, see Kwame Anthony Appiah, "Cosmopolitan Patriots," *Critical Inquiry* 97 (1997): 129–144.

12. J. M. Coetzee, *White Writing* (New Haven, CT: Yale University Press, 1990), 62.

13. Donald E. Pease, "National Identities, Postmodern Artifacts, and Postnational Narratives," in *National Identities and Post-Americanist Narratives*, (Durham, NC: Duke University Press, 1994), 4.

14. For an excellent discussion of the dangers of an excessive preoccupation with displacement, see Amitava Kumar, *Passport Photos* (Berkeley: University of California Press, 2000), 13–14. See also Ian Buruma, "The Romance of Exile," *New Republic*, February 12, 2001, 23–30.

15. Parini, "The Greening of the Humanities," 53.

16. Ibid., 53.

17. Ibid.

18. On Abbey's anti-immigrant environmentalism, which became more prominent in his later years, see Rick Scarce, *Eco-Warriors: Understanding the Radical Environmental Movement* (Chicago: University of Chicago Press, 1990), 92. For Austin's anti-Semitism, see Tom Athanasiou, *Divided Planet: The Ecology of Rich and Poor* (Boston: Little, Brown, 1996), 297. At the crossroads where environmentalism and immigration politics meet, we continue to encounter what Betsy Hartmann has called "the greening of hate." To commemorate the fortieth anniversary of Earth Day in April 2010, the Federation for American Immigration Reform (FAIR), a driving force behind Arizona's notorious Senate Bill 1070, issued a fifty-three-page report, "The Environmentalist's Guide to a Sensible Immigration Policy." As Andrew Ross recounts, FAIR—and allied groups like the Center for Immigration Studies—have actively sought to build a green anti-immigrant constituency, dividing the environmental movement. FAIR spin blames undocumented immigrants for everything from biodiversity loss and wilderness desecration to accelerating climate change and increased greenhouse emissions. A Center for Immigration Studies press release, urging more draconian enforcement in southern Arizona's national forests deploys the standard coupling of immigration and impurity: "How long will these beautiful lands remain unspoiled if the border is not secured?" Andrew Ross, "Greenwashing Nativism, *The Nation*, August 16, 2010, 6.

19. Richard Rodriguez, *Days of Obligation: An Argument with My Mexican Father* (New York: Penguin, 1992), 5.

20. Quoted in Kirkpatrick Sale, "The Forest for the Trees: Can Today's Environmentalists Tell the Difference," *Mother Jones* 11, no. 8 (1986): 36.

21. D. H. Lawrence, *Selected Poems* (London: Penguin, 1972), 93.

22. Rick Bass, "A Landscape of Possibility," *Outside* (December 1995): 100–101.

23. Gayatri Chakravorty Spivak, *The Post-Colonial Critic: Interviews, Strategies, Dialogues* (New York: Routledge, 1990), 72.

24. Aldo Leopold, "Game and Wildlife Conservation," in *Game Management* (1933; repr., Madison: University of Wisconsin Press, 1986), 23.

25. Jennifer Oladipo, "Global Warming is Colorblind," *Orion*, November/December 2007: 5.

26. For two brilliant accounts of this process, see Rebecca Solnit, *Savage Dreams: A Journey into the Landscape Wars of the American West* (New York: 1994), 215–385; and Mark Dowie, *Conservation Refugees* (Cambridge, MA: MIT Press, 2009), 1–22.

27. Richard Rodriguez, "True West," in *The Anchor Essay Annual: The Best of 1997*, ed. Phillip Lopate, (New York, 1998), 331.

28. Melvin Dixon, *Ride Out the Wilderness: Geography and Identity in Afro-American Literature* (Urbana-Champaign: University of Illinois Press, 1987).

29. Camille T. Dungy, "Writing Home," in Camille T. Dungy, ed., Black Nature. : Four Centuries of African American Nature (Athens: University of Georgia Press, 2009), 285.

30. University of California, Berkeley, "Black Nature: A Symposium on the First Anthology of Nature Writing by African-American Poets" (video of panel discussion, March 5, 2010), YouTube.com, http://www.youtube.com/watch?v=bkBs81CUcpg (accessed April 29, 2010). I'm grateful to Jalylah Burrell for alerting me to this panel discussion of the Black Nature anthology.

31. Richard Mabey, Landlocked: In Pursuit of the Wild (London: Sinclair Stevenson, 1994), 71.

32. Raymond Williams, Toward 2000 (London: Chatto and Windus, 1983), 195. For a related perspective on community and place, see Williams, "Homespun Philosophy," New Statesman and Society, June 19, 1992, 8–9.

33. Williams, Toward 2000, 195.

34. Ibid., 195.

35. Paul Gilroy, There Ain't No Black in the Union Jack (London: Hutchinson, 1987), 49–50. Stuart Hall questions Williams' prioritizing of rooted settlements in similar terms. See Hall, "Our Mongrel Selves," New Statesman and Society, June 19, 1992, 6–7.

36. An early, important resource on environmental writing beyond the United States is Patrick Murphy's Literature of Nature: An International Sourcebook (Chicago: Fitzroy Dearborn, 1998). Scott Slovic has sought to counter the complaint that "environmental literature is an exclusively Americanist preserve" by pointing, among other things, to the rise in international submissions to the premier journal in the field, ISLE: Interdisciplinary Studies in Literature and Environment. This is, indeed, a promising development, but the subjects and authors of environmental literary criticism remain overwhelmingly American. The internationalizing of ecocriticism, moreover, should not simply involve additive diversification in a center-periphery fashion. As I've argued above, we need to address the way ecocriticism's dominant models and intellectual priorities remain skewed by their American genesis. See Slovic, "Forum on Literatures of the Environment," PMLA 114 (Oct. 1999), 1102.

37. Scott Russell Sanders, "Staying Put," in The Future of Nature: Writing on a Human Ecology, ed. Barry Lopez (Minneapolis: Milkweed, 2007), 353–367. This essay has been adapted from Sanders' book-length polemic on this subject, Staying Put. Making a Home in a Restless World (Boston: Beacon Press, 1993).

38. Ibid., 357.

39. I am (to use a loaded word) a "naturalized" U.S. citizen who has lived in the Midwest for thirteen of my twenty-six American years. As such, I am sympathetic to some of Sanders' regional prickliness: bicoastal and transatlantic condescension toward (and ignorance of) the Midwest remains tenacious.

40. One exception to the dearth of minority writers and public intellectuals domiciled in rural England has been V. S. Naipaul, for whom Wiltshire has served primarily as a launching pad for his international travels and as a hermitic place to write. Certainly, to judge from *The Enigma of Arrival* and Patrick French's biography of him, Naipaul never entered into the kind of community-minded engagements that Sanders associates with staying put. Moreover, Naipaul has been a renter, not a rural landowner of the kind that Sanders, Leopold, and Berry extol.

41. Sanders, "Staying Put," 356.

42. Ibid., 362.

43. Ibid., 365.

44. Raymond Williams' *The Country and the City* (New York: Oxford University Press, 1973) remains the most wide-ranging account of the English pastoral tradition.

45. For an eloquent and economical account of the relationship between wilderness thinking and Indian dispossession in the United States, see Cronon, "The Trouble with Wilderness," 95–96.

46. Rob Nixon, *London Calling: V. S. Naipaul, Postcolonial Mandarin* (New York: Oxford University Press, 1992), 161. For a luminous analysis of postcolonial pastoral in a Caribbean context, see Sarah Phillips Casteel, *Second Arrivals: Landscape and Belonging in Contemporary Writing of the Americas* (Charlottesville: University of Virginia Press, 2007). Graham Huggan and Helen Tiffin have also productively carried forward this line of thinking in *Postcolonial Ecocriticism: Literature, Animals, Environment* (London: Routledge, 2010).

47. V. S. Naipaul, *The Enigma of Arrival* (New York: Knopf, 1987).

48. Richard Drayton, *Nature's Government: Science, Imperial Britain, and the "Improvement" of the World* (New Haven, CT: Yale University Press, 2000), xvi.

49. Jamaica Kincaid, *My Garden* (New York: Farrar, Straus and Giroux, 2001), 132.

50. Ibid, 139.

51. Jamaica Kincaid, *A Small Place* (New York: Farrar, Straus and Giroux, 1988).

52. Ibid., 16.

53. E. M. Forster, *Howard's End* (1910; repr., New York, 1975). This is an illuminating novel to read alongside the Naipaul and the Kincaid. Although imperial spaces trouble the edges of *Howard's End*, Forster anxiously seeks to screen out their implications by advancing a pastorally contained vision of English regeneration. In a key scene, the narrator stands on a Dorset hilltop gazing down at what he defines as a quintessential English vista. His angle of vision is akin to what Mary Louise Pratt, in an imperial context, calls the monarch-of-all-I-survey. In keeping with this tradition, Forster's method is panoramic: he creates a verbal painting that allows him to symbolically consume all of England at a glance in

the surrogate, pastoral form of the Isle of Wight. Gazing steadfastly at the Isle of Wight "the imagination swells, spreads, and deepens, until it becomes geographical and encircles England" (102). This scene's visual geometry, one might say, is one of panoramic bioregionalism.

In this passage, the Isle of Wight, with its grassy downs and chalky cliffs, becomes England's epitome and the guardian "till the end of time" of the nation's "purity." This act of synecdoche shrinks England to a nonhybrid nation of hyperpastoral. Forster thus performs here a kind of political and spatial amnesia, using a visual act of geographical circumscription to generate a highly selective notion of nationhood. By having the Isle of Wight stand in for England, Forster excludes the working classes and the polluted cities of the nation's industrial north, as well as London, with its expansive cosmopolitan matrices. Crucially, for my larger argument about postcolonial pastoral, Forster's vision excises colonial space from the idea of England: Cyprus and Nigeria, flickering on the edges of the novel, have no visible relation to the Isle of Wight. In this manner, Forster deploys geographical synecdoche and panoramic pastoral to foreclose from the idea of England, people, places, and histories that unsettle the book's project of selective national regeneration and redefinition.

54. Kincaid, *My Garden*, 142.

55. For some fine insights into the relationship between botany and colonialism in Kincaid's work, see Rachel Azima, "'Not-the-Native': Self-Transplantation, Ecocriticism, and Postcolonialism in Jamaica Kincaid's *My Garden (Book)*," *Journal of Commonwealth and Postcolonial Studies* 14 (2006): 101–119; and Jill Didur, "'Gardenworthy': Rerouting Colonial Botany in Jamaica Kincaid's *Among Flowers: A Walk in the Himalaya*," *Public* 41 (2010): 172–185.

56. Ibid., 143.

57. Ibid., 137.

58. Walter Benjamin, "Theses On the Philosophy of History," in *Illuminations*, trans. Harry Zohn (New York, 1969), 256.

59. Keith Morris Washington in video interview with *Basic Black*, YouTube.com, http://www.youtube.com/watch?v=rtGQt1woe-Y.

60. See, for example, Richard Mabey, "Ghost Habitats," in *A Brush With Nature* (London: BBC Books, 2010), 208–210.

61. The double consciousness of African-American pastoral surfaces repeatedly in Camille Dungy's superb, pathbreaking anthology, *Black Nature: Four Centuries of African American Nature* (Athens: University of Georgia Press, 2009).

62. Ursula Heise, "Ecocriticism and the Transnational Turn in American Studies," *American Literary History* 20, no. 1–2 (2008): 383–84. A crucial moment in the rise of environmental literary studies in the United States was the founding in 1992 of the Association for the Study of Literature and the Environment (ASLE).

63. Peter Sauer, "Reinhabiting Environmentalism: Picking Up Where Leopold and Carson Left Off," in *The Future of Nature: Writings on a Human Ecology from Orion Magazine*, ed. Barry Lopez (Minneapolis: Milkweed, 2007), 8.

64. Peter Sauer, "Global Ethics: An American Perspective," *Orion* (Winter 2002): 3.

65. Sauer, "Global Ethics," 5.

66. It was the African-American civil rights leader, Dr. Benjmin Chavis, who coined the term "environmental racism." But he did so in 1981, long after the civil rights movement had crested.

67. Two critical texts that boosted the academic credibility of the environmental justice concerns of American minorities were Benjamin Chavis, *Toxic Wastes and Race in the United States of America* (Washington D.C.: Commission for Racial Justice, 1987) and Robert D. Bullard, *Dumping in Dixie: Race, Class, and Environmental Quality* (1990; rpt. Boulder: Westview Press, 2000). However, the influence of these texts in American universities was centered in the social sciences and had at best a very limited impact on the conceptual or imaginative priorities of environmental literary studies in the United States.

68. Said himself was leery of the term "postcolonial." However, the rise of anti-imperial and postcolonial literary studies were both largely catalyzed by *Orientalism* and, in any event, were often intimately entangled.

69. Said described environmentalism, for instance, as "the indulgence of spoiled tree huggers who lack a proper cause" (personal communiqué with author, June 7, 1994).

70. Gayatri Chakravorty Spivak, "Attention: Postcolonialism!" *Journal of Caribbean Studies* 12 (1997/98): 166. Guha's work on ecological change and peasant resistance in the Himalaya and Vandana Shiva's work on gender, environmental violence, and biodiversity are just two instances of the turn toward deepening our historical understanding of the links between ecological, colonial, and postcolonial concerns.

71. Ramachandra Guha, "Radical American Environmentalism and Wilderness Preservation: A Third World Critique," reprinted in *The Great New Wilderness Debate*, ed. J. Baird Callicott and Michael P. Nelson (Athens: University of Georgia Press, 1998), 231–245.

72. Roderick Nash, *Wilderness and the American Mind*, 3rd ed. (New Haven, CT: Yale University Press, 1982). Quoted in Guha, "Radical American Environmentalism," 239–240.

73. The South African refugee writer Bessie Head is a classic example of this historical turn. Head was a self-declared antifeminist who in the 1970s saw no resonance in Western feminism for the kinds of issues faced by the village women whom she lived with in Botswana. Yet Head's fictional explorations of gender dynamics and women's communal resistance have since turned her into a

widely taught writer in women's studies courses. On Head's politics, see Rob Nixon, *Homelands, Harlem and Hollywood* (New York: Routledge, 1994), 176–192.

74. Beinart and Coates, *Environment and History*, 3. This book offers a fine comparative history of national parks in the United States and South Africa.

75. See Joe Kane, *Savages* (New York: Knopf, 1995); Suzana Sawyer, "The Politics of Petroleum: Indigenous Contestation of Multinational Oil Development in the Ecuadorian Amazon" (MacArthur Consortium Occasional Papers Series, MacArthur Program, University of Minnesota, 1997); and Melina Selverston, "The 1990 Indigenous Uprising in Ecuador: Politicized Ethnicity as Social Movement" (Papers on Latin America, no. 32, Columbia University Institute of Latin American and Iberian Studies, New York, 1993).

76. See "Kenya Students Confront Moi in Battle of the Forest," *Independent on Sunday*, February 7, 1999, 18.

77. Ibid.

78. Lorraine Anderson, Scott Slovic, and John P. O'Grady, eds., *Literature and the Environment: A Reader on Nature and Culture* (New York: Longman, 1999). Of the 104 essays and poems included by Anderson et al., 26 are by African-American, American Indian, Latina/o, or Asian-American writers. This marks a significant advance over the more typical spectrum of Cheryll Glotfelty and Harold Fromm's influential *Ecocriticism Reader*, which found room for only two minority essays out of twenty-six.

79. Lawrence Buell, *Writing for an Endangered World: Literature, Culture, and Environment in the U.S. and Beyond* (Cambridge, MA: Harvard University Press, 2001).

80. Buell, *Writing for an Endangered World*, 24.

81. The broader scheme of the second book also encourages Buell to discuss some urban European writers, notably Dickens, Woolf, and Joyce.

82. Mahasweta Devi, "Pterodactyl, Puran Sahay, and Pirtha," in *Imaginary Maps*, trans. Gayatri Chakravorty Spivak (New York: Routledge, 1995), 95–96.

83. Buell, *Writing for an Endangered World*, 230.

84. Drawing on Gayatri Spivak's interview with Devi, Buell alludes briefly to Devi's overarching concern for the plight of first peoples globally, including Native Americans. However, he doesn't explore the implications of this for an American-centered environmentalism (ibid., 230).

85. See Saro-Wiwa, *A Month and a Day*, 88.

86. Ogoniland belongs to the tropical belt that runs through the Amazon, West and Central Africa, Indonesia, and Papua and New Guinea, a zone that possesses the world's most diverse, ethnically fractured populations (400 ethnicities in Nigeria, several thousand in New Guinea) as well as unusually rich natural resources (oil, precious minerals, and timber). It is in this strip that American, European, Japanese, and Chinese extraction industry multinationals,

frequently supported by authoritarian regimes, operate with maximum violence and impunity.

87. Pedagogically, an excellent place to start would be to read Saro-Wiwa's prison diary, *A Month and a Day*, alongside both Wole Soyinka's prefigurative early play *The Swamp Dwellers* and recent work by Nigerian environmental philosopher Kaoawole Owolabi. For a resonant comparison one could turn to Joe Kane's account in *Savages* of another contest between an equatorial micro-minority (Ecuador's Huaorani Indians) and a petroleum multinational (Texaco).

88. For an excellent theoretical account of the conceptual limitations that result from a center-periphery model, see Timothy Mitchell, "The Stage of Modernity," in Timothy Mitchell, ed., *Questions of Modernity* (Minneapolis: University of Minnesota Press, 2000), 1-34. Mitchell's critique focuses on Western-centered genealogies of modernity; however, many of his insights can be applied adaptively to ecocriticism.

89. Rob Nixon, "Postcolonialism and Environmentalism," in *Postcolonialism and Beyond*, ed. Ania Loomba et al. (Durham, NC: Duke University Press, 2005), 233–251; Susie O'Brien, "Articulating a World of Difference: Ecocriticism, Postcolonialism and Globalization," *Canadian Literature* 170/171 (2001): 140–158; Graham Huggan, "Greening Postcolonialism: Ecocritical Perspectives," *Modern Fiction Studies* 50 (2004): 701–733.

90. http://www.poetryconnection.net/poets/Derek_Walcott/7728

91. New Zealand, Indian, South African, Australian, Californian, and Hawaiian scholars have been at the forefront of this new oceanic scholarship.

92. See especially Elizabeth DeLoughrey, "Pacific Heliotropes: Ecology and the Wars of Light," in *Postcolonial Ecologies*, ed. Elizabeth DeLoughrey and George Handley (New York: Oxford University Press, 2010); and Jennifer Wenzel, "Petro-magic-realism: Toward a Political Ecology of Nigerian Literature," *Postcolonial Studies* 9 (2006): 449–464.

93. Prominent ecocritical work that engages the Caribbean includes Casteel, *Second Arrivals*; Elizabeth DeLoughrey, *Roots and Routes: Navigating Caribbean and Pacific Island Literatures* (Honolulu: University of Hawaii Press, 2007); Elizabeth DeLoughrey, Renee Gosson, and George Handley, eds., *Caribbean Literature and the Environment* (Charlottesville: University of Virginia Press, 2005); George Handley, *New World Poetics: Nature and the Adamic Imagination in Whitman, Neruda, and Walcott* (Athens: University Of Georgia Press, 2007); and Lizabeth Paravisini-Gebert's work in progress, *Endangered Species: Ecology and the Discourses of the Caribbean Nation.*

94. Byron Caminero-Santangelo and Garth Myers, eds., *Environment at the Margins* (Athens: Ohio University Press, 2011); DeLoughrey and Handley, eds., *Postcolonial Ecologies*; Alex Hunt and Bonnie Roos, eds., *Postcolonial Green* (Charlottesville:

University of Virginia Press, 2010). Also directly pertinent in its transnational ambitions is Stephanie Lemeneger and Teresa Shewry, eds., *Environmental Criticism for the Twenty-First Century* (New York: Routledge, 2011).

95. Graham Huggan and Helen Tiffin, *Postcolonial Ecocriticism: Literature, Animals, Environment* (London: Routledge, 2010); Upamanyu Pablo Mukherjee, *Postcolonial Environments: Nature, Culture and the Contemporary Indian Novel* (London: Palgrave Macmillan, 2010); and Laura Wright, *Wilderness into Civilized Shapes: Reading the Postcolonial Environment* (Athens: University of Georgia Press, 2010). Although Murphy doesn't address postcolonial studies directly, there is also much of pertinence to transnational environmentalism in Patrick D. Murphy, *Ecocritical Explorations in Literary and Cultural Studies* (Lanham, MD: Lexington Books, 2009).

96. The contemporary transnational turn in American studies is too vast to address here comprehensively. Key texts include Russ Castronovo and Susan Gillman, eds., *States of Emergency: The Object of American Studies* (Chapel Hill: University of North Carolina Press, 2009); Wai Chee Dimock, *Through Other Continents: American Literature Across Deep Time* (Princeton, NJ: Princeton University Press, 2006); Wai Chee Dimock and Lawrence Buell, eds., *Shades of the Planet: American Literature as World Literature* (Princeton, NJ: Princeton University Press, 2007); Inderpal Grewal et al., ed., *Transnational America* (Durham, NC: Duke University Press, 2005); Heise, "Ecocriticism and the Transnational Turn in American Studies"; J. Michael Dash, *The Other America: Caribbean Literature in a New World Context* (Charlottesville: University Press of Virginia, 1998); Donald E. Pease and Robyn Wiegman, eds., *The Futures of American Studies* (Durham: Duke University Press, 2002); John Carlos Rowe, ed., *Post-Nationalist American Studies* (Berkeley: University of California Press, 2000); and Janice Radway, "What's in a Name? Presidential Address to the American Studies Association, 20 November 1998," *American Quarterly* 51, no. 1 (1999): 1–32.

97. Dungy, *Black Nature*. Another exemplary recent anthology is Laird Christensen, Mark C. Long, and Fred Waage, eds., *Teaching North American Environmental Literature*, (Washington DC: Modern Language Association of America, 2008) which contains a powerful, diverse set of engagements with environmental justice literatures and methodologies from a variety of transnational perspectives.

98. The increasingly prolific engagements between native and postcolonial studies include: Sean Kicummah Teuton, *Red Land, Red Power: Grounding Knowledge in the American Indian Novel* (Durham, NC: Duke UP, 2008); Janice Acoote et al, *Reasoning Together: The Native Critics Collective* (Tulsa, OK: University of Oklahoma Press, 2008); Linda Tuhiwai Smith, *Decolonizing Methodologies: Research and Indigenous Peoples* (London: Zed, 1999); Eric Cheyfitz, "The (Post)Colonial Predicament of Native American Studies," *Interventions* 4 (2002): 405-427;

Karen M. Morin, "Postcolonialism and Native American Geographies," *Cultural Geographies* 9 (2002): 158–180; James Mackay, "Review Essay: Native American Literary Theory," *Journal of American Studies*, 41(2007): 675–680; Ann Laura Stoler, "Tense and Tender Ties: The Politics of Comparison in North American History and (Post) Colonial Studies," *The Journal of American History* (88) 2001: 1-41; and Arnold Krupat, "Postcolonialism, Ideology, and Native American Literature," in Amritjit Singh and Peter Schmidt, eds., *Postcolonial Theory and the United States: Race, Ethnicity, and Literature* (Oxford, Mississippi: University Press of Mississippi, 2000), 73-94.

Epilogue

1. Plato, *Timaeus*, trans. R. G. Bury (New York: Loeb Classical Library, 1929), 24e.
2. For a sober assessment of the scale of climate flight—underway and projected—see the report by the United Nations Refugee Agency (UNHCR), http://www.unhcr.org/pages/49e4a5096.html.
3. Naomi Klein, "Climate Rage," *Rolling Stone*, November 11, 2009, 18.
4. John Vidal, "Don't Consign us to History, Plead Island States at Cancun," *Guardian*, December 1, 2010, 9.
5. Toni Johnson, "Thawing Arctic's Resource Race," Council on Foreign Relations, http://www.cfr.org/publication/13978/thawing_arctics_resource_race.html.
6. Denmark's claim was mounted through its colonial relationship to Greenland, which has since gained independence.
7. Alok Jha, "New Survey of Africa Mineral Riches," *Guardian*, May 29, 2009.
8. http://thinkprogress.org/2010/04/30/bp-greenwashing-drill/
9. Other prominent members of the Global Climate Coalition included: DaimlerChrysler, Exxon/Esso, Ford Motor Company, General Motors Company, Shell Oil USA, Texaco, and the American Highway Users Alliance.
10. Barack Obama, "Remarks by the President in a Discussion on Jobs and the Economy in Charlotte, North Carolina" (Celgard, LLC, Charlotte, North Carolina, April 2, 2010) http://www.whitehouse.gov/the-press-office/remarks-president-a-discussion-jobs-and-economy-charlotte-north-carolina.
11. Quoted in Naomi Klein, "Gulf Oil Spill," June 19, 2010, 15.
12. "Michael Klare: Grappling With the Age of 'Tough Oil,'" NPR, June 30, 2010, http://www.npr.org/templates/story/story.php?storyId=128212150. See also, Elizabeth Kolbert, "Oil Shocks," *New Yorker*, May 31, 2010, 13.
13. John McQuaid, "The Gulf of Mexico Oil Spill: An Accident Waiting to Happen," *Environment* 360, May 10, 2010, http://e360.yale.edu/content/feature.msp?id=2272.
14. Ibid.

15. Matt DeLong, "Joe Barton's BP 'Shakedown' Comments Are Nothing New," *Washington Post*, June 17, 2010, http://voices.washingtonpost.com/44/2010/06/joe-bartons-bp-shakedown-comme.html.

16. Ixtoc was a 150-foot-deep well, a fraction of the depth at which deepwater drilling routinely occurs today. But for the late 1970s that constituted innovative deepwater drilling, with all the technological challenges that entailed.

17. Quoted in William J. Broad, "Taking Lessons From What Went Wrong," *New York Times*, July 20, 2010, D1. On this score, see also Henry Petroski, *Success Through Failure: The Paradox of Design* (Princeton, NJ: Princeton University Press, 2006).

18. Naomi Klein, *The Shock Doctrine: Disaster Capitalism* (New York: Metropolitan Books, 2007).

19. Anne McClintock, "Slow Violence and the BP Coverups," *Counterpunch*, August 23/24, 2010, http://www.counterpunch.org/mcclintock08232010.html.

20. Ibid.

21. Adam Nossiter, "Far From Gulf, a Spill Scourge Five Decades Old," *New York Times*, June 16, 2010, A1.

22. Ulrich Beck, *World Risk Society* (Oxford: Blackwell, 1999), 5; Fernando Coronil, *The Magical State: Nature, Money, and Modernity in Venezuela* (Chicago: University of Chicago Press, 1997), 11.

23. In 1981, three years before the disaster struck, a Bhopal-based reporter, Raajkumar Keswani, predicted that the Union Carbide factory was a disaster waiting to happen.

24. In June 2010, twenty-six years after the Bhopal Disaster, an Indian court finally convicted of negligence seven former executives of Union Carbide's Indian subsidiary. The men received two-year jail sentences and were fined the equivalent of $2,100 each. No Americans were prosecuted. Lydia Polgreen and Hari Kumar, "Indian Court Convicts Seven in Bhopal Disaster," *New York Times*, June 7, 2010, 9.

25. Ibid.

26. Christopher F. Chabris, "You Have Too Much Mail," *Wall Street Journal*, December 15, 2008, 7.

27. The hacked emails of climate scientists at the University of East Anglia were seized on by the right as evidence that climate change was a conspiratorial hoax. However, in the immediate aftermath of climategate, five independent investigations concluded that the science remained entirely sound. http://www.huffingtonpost.com/2010/07/12/climategate-debunking-get_n_642980.html

28. In the Trafigura case, the claimants' out of court settlement (for 30 million pound sterling plus costs) following the WikiLeaks revelations was particularly significant for two reasons. First, the case successfully combined rich-nation

digital civil disobedience with more traditional grass roots activism mounted by the afflicted poor. Second, the settlement broke a double silence: the silencing of slow violence and the silencing of the British media who, in an extraordinary measure, had been hit with a "super-injunction" that barred them from covering the parliamentary debate over the suppressed scientific Minton report warning of the toxic implications of the Trafigura contamination. The settlement was a classic instance of new media strategy, old media credibility, scientific testimony, legal resources, and grassroots activism among the poor combining to counter an assault on both the environmental and the information commons. http://www .guardian.co.uk/world/2009/oct/16/carter-ruck-abandon-minton-injunction

29. http://another-green-world.blogspot.com/2008/08/lucha-indigena-defeat-alan-garcias.html

30. For two detailed accounts of the limits—in scale and efficacy—of the so-called Twitter revolution, see Annabelle Sreberny and Gholam Khiabany, *Blogistan: The Internet and Politics in Iran* (London: I.B. Tauris, 2010) and Evgeny Morozov, *The Net Delusion: The Dark Side of Internet Freedom* (London: Allen Lane, 2010). James Harkin has rightly charged the technophile Andrew Sullivan with strategic naivete and "irrational exuberance" for proclaiming that Twitter was "the critical tool for organizing the resistance in Iran" and that "the Revolution will be twittered." Harkin, "Cyber-Con," *London Review of Books*, December 2, 2010, 20.

31. Malcolm Gladwell has famously accused wiki-activism of being hampered by low-risk "weak ties" and "horizontal associations," in contrast to the civil rights movement, which transformed American society through high-risk, deeply committed, and vertically organized activism. Gladwell criticizes "the digerati" for "refusing to accept the fact there is a class of social problems for which there is no technological solution." But, one might ask, do we always know in advance what class of social problems those are? While Gladwell's dismissal of the unalloyed technophilia embodied by Clay Shirky and Andrew Sullivan is spot on, my own position is somewhat less skeptical than his. I believe that some fusion between old-style, high-risk, vertically organized strategies and wiki-activism can generate significant social change, even though such successful fusions, over the long term, can be challenging to sustain. See Gladwell, "Small Change," http://www.newyorker.com/reporting/2010/10/04/101004fa_fact_gladwell

32. Jean-Paul Sartre, *What is Literature?*; trans. Bernard Frechtman (1948; rpt. London: Methuen, 1970), 37.

33. For a lively, imaginative website that seeks to integrate activism pertaining to the environmental and the information commons, see http://www.onthe commons.org/

34. Nadine Gordimer, "The Essential Gesture" (1985). In Gordimer, *Telling Times: Writing and Living, 1954-2008* (New York: Norton, 2008), 422.

Acknowledgments

Special thanks go to the many friends and scholars from around the world who have afforded me opportunities to test run my ideas and, in addition, to the editors who have given me invaluable feedback along the way: Matthew Abraham, Rita Barnard, Betty Bayer, Anna Bernard, Byron Caminero-Santangelo, Hazel Carby, Jane Carruthers, Christine Catanzarite, William Cronon, Ashley Dawson, Manthia Diawara, Elizabeth DeLoughrey, Mario DiGangi, Emory Elliott, Jed Esty, Ziad Elmarsafy, Susan Friedman, Tom Griffiths, George Handley, Clifford Hill, Jean Howard, Suvir Kaul, Amitava Kumar, Ania Loomba, Jorge Marcone, Sharon Marcus, Robert Marzec, Craig McLuckie, Toby Miller, Gregg Mitman, Garth Myers, Libby Robin, Margaret Ronsheim, Andrew Rubin, Jill Schneiderman, David Simpson, Jean Tamarin, Marianna Torgovnick, Gauri Viswanathan, Anthony Vital, Molly Wallace, Tim Watson, and Paige West.

For their encouragement, provocation, and stimulation, I wish to thank audiences at Australian National University, Columbia University, Duke University, Georgetown University, Hobart and William Smith College, New York University, Pennsylvania State University, Queens University (Ontario), Rutgers University (New Brunswick), University of California-Davis, University of California-Riverside, University of Chicago, University of Illinois at Urbana-Champaign, University of Kansas, University of Louisiana at Lafayette, University of Miami, University of Wisconsin-Madison, University of Wisconsin-Oshkosh, Vassar College, Yale University, and University of York.

My gratitude goes to the University of Wisconsin-Madison on a number of fronts, not least for creating an unsurpassed arena for interdisciplinary work in the environmental humanities. Particular thanks go to the Center for Culture,

History, and Environment, to its recent directors, William Cronon and Gregg Mitman, and to my lively, generous colleagues in the English Department. In addition, I extend my deep appreciation to the fellows and staff at the Institute for Research in the Humanities and to its director, Susan Friedman, for fostering an atmosphere supportive of interdisciplinary initiatives. Further thanks go to the University of Wisconsin Graduate School for summer research funding and to the African Studies Program.

I gratefully acknowledge permission to reprint revised or excerpted versions of the following essays: "Stranger in the Eco-village: Race, Tourism, and Environmental Time," in *Postcolonial Ecologies*, ed. Elizabeth DeLoughrey and George Handley (Oxford University Press: 2010); "Unimagined Communities: Developmental Refugees, Megadams and Monumental Modernity," *New Formations* 69 (2010): 62-80; "Neoliberalism and the Environmental Picaresque," *Modern Fiction Studies* 55 (2009): 443–67; "Slow Violence, Gender, and the Environmentalism of the Poor," *Journal of Commonwealth and Postcolonial Studies* 13 (2008): 14–37; "Of Land Mines and Cluster Bombs." *Cultural Critique* 67 (2007): 160–74; "Environmentalism and Postcolonialism," in *Postcolonialism and Beyond*, ed. Ania Loomba and Suvir Kaul (Duke University Press, 2005), 233–251; and "Pipedreams," *London Review of Books*, April 4, 1996.

For their research assistance, I am grateful to Davis Aitchison, David Callenberger, Thom Dancer, Jesse Oak Taylor, and especially Stillman Wagstaff. In addition, I have been privileged to work with some fine graduate and former graduate students whose dissertations have addressed environmental issues: Rachel Azima, Pete Boger, Sarah Phillips Casteel, Robert Emmett, Lucienne Loh, Andrew Mahlstedt, Monica Seger, Jesse Oak Taylor, and Stillman Wagstaff.

A profound thank you to Hazel Carby for inviting me to present a draft of this book at her Yale graduate seminar "Transnational Imaginaries" and to the seminar members for their rich, timely interventions.

My enduring gratitude goes to Clifford Hill. For an immigrant, first-generation college student like myself, his professional example and support over the years have been lifesavers in a sea of improvisation.

I am grateful, too, to all my family members—Andy, Carol, Kay, both Marions, Megan, Sheelagh, Ruth, and Tessa for their support—particularly in their passion for the environment and their bone-deep understanding of displacement. The writing of this book would have been impossible without some remarkable friends, too many to mention. But I would like to thank, in particular, Samer Alatout, Leslie Bow, Hazel Carby, Russ Castronovo, Neville Choonoo, Ashley Dawson, Elizabeth DeLoughrey, Michael Denning, Colleen Dunlavy, Clifford and Kathleen Hill, Amitava Kumar, Staci Lowe, Michael McColly, Tejumola Olaniyan, Ron Radano, Andrew Ross, Ella Shohat, Robert Stam, and Gauri Viswanathan.

Special thanks to Harriet Barlow, Ben Strader, and everyone at the incomparable Blue Mountain Center—sanctuary and inspiration.

My appreciation goes to the three anonymous reviewers of this book who provided me with encouragement and trenchant suggestions. I am especially indebted to everyone at Harvard University Press who provided critical support along the way, particularly Lindsay Waters, Susan Wallace Boehmer, Michael Higgins, Tim Jones, and Hannah Wong. Thanks, too, to Marianna Vertullo and the editorial staff at IBT Global for their meticulous editing.

Finally, this one is for Anne. Thank you beyond measure for your sustaining love, your intellectual and personal radiance, and your passions (for words, politics, justice, travel, and the environment). Your many worlds inspire me.

Index

Gramley Library
Salem Academy and College
Winston-Salem, N.C. 27108